International Criminal Law and Sexual Violence against Women

This book explores the prosecution of wartime sexual violence in international criminal law and asks what the juridicalisation of gender-based violence signifies for women. The book explores the portrayal of the various gendered identities that surface in armed conflict and it asks whether the law is capable of reflecting these in subsequent judgements.

Focusing on the International Criminal Tribunal for the Former Yugoslavia and the International Criminal Tribunal for Rwanda as well as subsequent developments in the International Criminal Court, the book shows how the tribunals have delivered landmark jurisprudence in the area of sexual violence against women and provided a legacy for how gender justice is incorporated into international law. However, Daniela Nadj argues that in the relevant cases there is a tendency to depict women in monolithic fashion with little agency or sense of identity beyond their ethnicity. By bringing to the surface the complexity and multi-faceted gendered identities in wartime, the book calls for a reconceptualisation of notions of femininity in armed conflict.

Daniela Nadj is a Lecturer in Public Law at Queen Mary University of London, UK.

Routledge Research in International Law

Available

The Rule of Unwritten International Law
Customary Law, General Principles, and World Order
Peter G. Staubach

State Interest and the Sources of International Law
Doctrine, Morality, and Non-Treaty Law
Markus P. Beham

Demilitarisation and International Law in Context
The Åland Islands
Sia Spiliopoulou Åkermark and Saila Heinikoski

International Criminal Law and Sexual Violence against Women
The Interpretation of Gender in the Contemporary International Criminal Trial
Daniela Nadj

Unilateral Acts
A History of a Legal Doctrine
Betina Appel Kuzmarov

Regional Developmentalism Through Law
The Use of Law to Support the Effective Establishment of an African Economic Community
Jonathan Bashi Rudahindwa

China's One Belt One Road Initiative and Private International Law
Poomintr Sooksripaisarnkit and Sai Ramani Garimella

For more information about this series, please visit: www.routledge.com/Routledge-Research-in-International-Law/book-series/INTNLLAW

International Criminal Law and Sexual Violence against Women

The Interpretation of Gender in the Contemporary International Criminal Trial

Daniela Nadj

Routledge
Taylor & Francis Group
LONDON AND NEW YORK

First published 2018
by Routledge

2 Park Square, Milton Park, Abingdon, Oxfordshire OX14 4RN
52 Vanderbilt Avenue, New York, NY 10017

Routledge is an imprint of the Taylor & Francis Group, an informa business

First issued in paperback 2020

British Library Cataloguing-in-Publication Data
A catalogue record for this book is available from the British Library

Library of Congress Cataloging-in-Publication Data
A catalog record for this book has been requested

ISBN: 978-1-138-65254-5 (hbk)
ISBN: 978-0-367-59041-3 (pbk)

Typeset in Galliard
by Apex CoVantage, LLC

Contents

Cases

Yugoslavia

International Criminal Tribunal for the former Yugoslavia (ICTY)

The Prosecutor v. Tadic (Decision on the Defense Motion for Interlocutory Appeal on Jurisdiction) (IT-94–1-AR72) (2 October 1995)

The Prosecutor v. Tadic (Trial Chamber) (IT-94–1-T) (7 May 1997) (Judgement)

The Prosecutor v. Tadic (Appeals Chamber) (IT-96–21-A) (15 July 1999) (Judgement)

The Prosecutor v. Nikolic (IT-94–2) (4 November 1992) (First Amendment Indictment)

The Prosecutor v. Nikolic (IT-94–2) (18 December 2003) (Trial Chamber Judgement)

The Prosecutor v. Mejakic et al. (IT-95–4) (13 February 1995) (Initial Indictment)

The Prosecutor v. Anto Furundžija (IT-95–17/1) (2 November 1995) (Initial Indictment)

The Prosecutor v. Anto Furundžija (IT-95–17/1-PT) (2 June 1998) (Amended Indictment)

The Prosecutor v. Furundžija (IT-95–17/1) (10 December 1998) (Trial Chamber Judgement)

The Prosecutor v. Aleksovski (IT-14/1-T) (25 June 1999) (Trial Chamber Judgement)

The Prosecutor v. Furundžija (Appeals Chamber) (IT-95–17/I-T) (21 July 2000) (Trial Chamber Judgement)

The Prosecutor v. Kupreškic et al. (IT-95–16), 'Lašva Valley' (14 January 2000) (Trial Chamber Judgement)

The Prosecutor v. Blaškic (IT-95–14) (3 March, 2000) (Trial Chamber Judgement)

The Prosecutor v. Todorovic (IT-95–9/1), 'Bosanski Šamac' (31 July 2000) (Trial Chamber Sentencing Judgement)

The Prosecutor v. Došen, Kolundžija and Sikirica (IT-95–8), 'Keraterm Camp' (13 November 2001) (Trial Chamber Sentencing Judgement)

Prosecutor v. Kovac, Kunarac and Vukovic (IT-96–23-T/1-T) (22 February 2001) (Trial Chamber Judgement)
The Prosecutor v. Kunarac (IT-96–23-T/1-A) (12 June 2002) (Appeals Chamber Judgement)
The Prosecutor v. Kvocka (IT-98–30/1-T) (2 November 2001) (Trial Chamber Judgement)
The Prosecutor v. Kvocka, Case No IT-98–30/1-A (25 February 2005) (Appeals Chamber Judgement)
The Prosecutor v. Cerkez and Kordic (IT-95–14/2) (26 February 2001) (Trial Chamber Judgement)
The Prosecutor v. Kos, Kvocka, Prcac, Radic and Žigic (IT-98–30/1), 'Omarska, Keraterm, Trnopolje Camps' (2 November 2001) (Trial Chamber Judgement)
The Prosecutor v. Bralo (IT-95–17), 'Lašva Valley' (7 December 2001) (Sentencing Judgement)
The Prosecutor v. Krnojelac (IT-97–25), 'Foca' (15 March 2002) (Trial Chamber Judgement)
The Prosecutor v. Milan Simic (IT-95/9/2), 'Bosanski Šamac' (17 October 2002) (Trial Chamber Sentencing Judgement)
The Prosecutor v. Vasiljevic (IT-98–32), 'Višegrad' (IT-98–32) (29 November 2002) (Trial Chamber Judgement)
The Prosecutor v. Stakic (IT-97–24) (31 July 2003) (Trial Chamber Judgement)
The Prosecutor v. Plavšic (IT-00–39 &40/1) (27 September 2003) (Sentencing Judgement)
The Prosecutor v. Blagoje Simic (IT-95–9/9-T), 'Bosanski Šamac' (17 October 2003) (Trial Chamber Sentencing Judgement)
The Prosecutor v. Banovic (IT-02–65/1), 'Omarska and Keraterm Camps' (28 October 2003) (Trial Chamber Sentencing Judgement)
The Prosecutor v. Cesic (IT-95–10/1) (11 March 2004) (Trial Chamber Sentencing Judgement)
The Prosecutor v. Krstic (IT-98–33), 'Srebrenica-Drina Corps' (19 April 2004) (Trial Chamber Judgement)
The Prosecutor v. Brdanin (IT-99–36), 'Krajina' (1 September 2004) (Trial Chamber Judgement)
The Prosecutor v. Halilovic (IT-01–48), 'Grabovica-Uzdol' (16 November 2005) (Trial Chamber Judgement)
The Prosecutor v. Rajic (IT-95–12), 'Stupni Do' (8 May 2006) (Trial Chamber Sentencing Judgement)
The Prosecutor v. Krajišnik (IT-00–39) (27 September 2006) (Trial Chamber Judgement)
The Prosecutor v. Boškoski & Tarculoski (IT-04–82) (10 July 2008) (Trial Chamber Judgement)
The Prosecutor v. Rasim Delic (IT-04–83) (15 September 2008) (Trial Chamber Judgement)
The Prosecutor v. Milutinovic et al. (IT-05–87) (26 February 2009) (Trial Chamber Judgement)

The Prosecutor v. Vlastimir Dordevic (IT-05/87/1-PT) (9 July 2008) (Fourth Amended Indictment)
The Prosecutor v. Ratko Mladic (IT-09–92) (24 July 1995) (Initial Indictment)
The Prosecutor v. Ratko Mladic (IT-09–92) (1 June 2011) (Prosecution's Second Amended Indictment)

Rwanda

The Prosecutor v. Akayesu (ICTR-96–4-T) (2 September 1998) (Trial Chamber Judgement)
The Prosecutor v. Musema (ICTR-98–39-A) (6 April 2000) (Trial Chamber Judgement)
The Prosecutor v. Gacumbitsi (ICTR-2001–64-A) (7 July 2006) (Appeals Chamber Judgement)
The Prosecutor v. Pauline Nyiramasuhuko & Arsénes Ntahobali (ICTR-97–21-I) Joint Case (ICTR-98–42-T) (18 September 2007) (Trial Chamber II Judgement)

Table of human rights reports, legislation and international instruments

United Nations documents

International Labour Organization Constitution (adopted by the Peace Conference in Versailles in April 1919), entered into force on 28 June 1919 and the Declaration concerning the Aims and Purposes of the International Labour Organization (ILO) (adopted at Philadelphia on 10 May 1944). Available at: www.ilo.org/ilolex/english/constq.htm.
Charter of the United Nations, San Francisco (adopted by the United Nations on 26 June 1945), entered into force on 24 October 24 1945, UKTS
The Universal Declaration of Human Rights (UDHR) (adopted by General Assembly Resolution 217 A (III) (10 December 1948)
International Covenant on Civil and Political Rights, adopted and opened for signature, ratification and accession by General Assembly Resolution 2200A (XXI) of 16 December 1966
UN Human Rights Committee, 'General Comment 28', UN Doc. CCPR/C/21/Rev. 1/Add.10 (29 March 2000)
UN Committee on the Elimination of Racial Discrimination (CERD), General Recommendation XXV, Gender-Related Dimensions of Racial Discrimination (2000), UN Doc A/55/18, annex V at 152 (2000), para. 1
Convention on the Elimination of all Forms of Violence against Women (CEDAW), 1249 U.N.T.S. 13, 19 ILM 33 (1980), adopted and opened for signature, ratification and accession by General Assembly Resolution 180 (XXXIV) of 18 December 1979, entered into force: 3 September 1981

Convention against Torture and Other Cruel, Inhuman and Degrading Treatment or Punishment (CAT), adopted and opened for signature, ratification and accession by General Assembly Resolution 39/46 of December 1984; entered into force: 26 June 1987

United Nations Committee on the Elimination of all Forms of Discrimination against Women (CEDAW Committee) General Recommendation No. 12, U.N. Doc. A/44/38 (Eighth session, 1989)

United Nations Committee on the Elimination of all Forms of Discrimination against Women CEDAW General Recommendation No. 19, U.N. Doc A/47/38 (Eleventh session, 1992)

United Nations Economic and Social Council (ECOSOC) Agreed Conclusions, 1992 Inter-American Convention on the Prevention, Punishment and Eradication of Violence against Women, adopted by the General Assembly of the OAS (9 June 1994), Doc. OEA/Ser.P AG/doc. 3115/94 rev. 2 (commonly referred to either as the Convention of Belém do Para, or the Inter-American Convention against Violence)

United Nations Development Fund for Women (UNIFEM) 'Facts and Figures on Violence against Women-Gender Issues: Violence Against Women', 1997; www.unifem.org/attachments/gender_issues/violence_against_women/facts_figures_ violenceagainst_women_2007.pdf.

United Nations Office of the High Commissioner of Human Rights, Fact Sheet No.23 'Harmful Traditional Practices Affecting the Health of Women and Children'; 1995; www.unhchr.ch/html/menu6/2/fs.23.htm.

Third World Conference on Human Rights, Vienna Declaration and Programme of Action, adopted at the World Conference on Human Rights in Vienna, U.N. Doc. A/CONF. 157/23 (12 July 1993).

Fourth World Conference on Women, Beijing Declaration and Platform for Action, adopted at the World Conference on Human Rights in Beijing, U.N. Doc. A/CONF.177/20 (1995) and A/CONF.177/20/Add.1 (1995) (15 Sept 1995)

Report of the Economic and Social Council for 1997, U.N. GAOR, 52nd Sess., Supp. No.3, at 24, U.N. Doc. A/52/3 Rev.1 (1997).

Provisional Summary Record of the 20th Meeting, U.N. ESCOR, 1997 Substantive Sess., U.N. Doc. A/52/3/Rev. 1 (1997).

United Nations Human Rights Committee, 'General Comment 28' UN Doc.CCPR/C/21/Rev. 1/Add.10, 29 March 2000.

'Women, Peace and Security: CEDAW and Security Council Resolution 1325: A Quick Guide'. Available at: www.unrol.org/files/CEDAWand UNSCR1325_eng.pdf.

UN Commission on Human Rights, Towards an Effective Implementation of International Norms to End Violence against Women (2004), Report of the Special Rapporteur on Violence against Women, its Causes and Consequences, Yakin Ertürk, E/CN.4/2004/66, 26 December 2003

UN Commission on Human Rights, Intersections of Violence against Women and HIV/AIDS (2005), Report of the Special Rapporteur on

Violence Against Women, its Causes and Consequences, Yakin Ertürk, E/CN.4/2005/72, 17 January, 2005.

The United Nations Special Rapporteur on Violence against Women, its Causes and Consequences', '15 Years of the United Nations Special Rapporteur on Violence Against Women (1994–2009) – A Critical Review'; www2.ohchr.org/english/issues/women/rapporteur/docs/15YearReviewofVAWMandate.pdf

UN Commission on Human Rights, Towards an Effective Implementation of International Norms to End Violence against Women (6 June 2011), Report of the Special Rapporteur on Violence against Women, Its Causes and Consequences: Mission to the United States, Ms. Rashida Manjoo, A/HRC/17/26/Add.5. Available at: http://daccess-ddsny.un.org/doc/UNDOC/GEN/G11/138/26/PDF/G1113826.pdf?OpenElement.

Report of the United Nations Special Rapporteur on violence against women, its causes and consequences, Rashida Manjoo, A/HRC/20/16, Human Rights Council, 23 May 2012.

Declaration adopted at the United Nations World Conference Against Racism, Xenophobia and Related Intolerance, A/CONF. 189/12, adopted on 8 September, 2001 in Durban, South Africa. Available at: www.un.org/en/ga/durbanmeeting2011/pdf/DDPA_full_text.pdf

Resolution adopted by the General Assembly (on the report of the Third Committee (A/57/806), at its fifty-seventh session, UN Doc. A/Res/57/228 B Khmer Rouge Trials (22 May 2003). Available on the United Nations Assistance to Khmer Rouge Trials (UNAKRT) website at: http://unakrt-online.org/04_documents.htm

International Criminal Court (ICC) The Rome Statute of the International Criminal Court (PrepCom), adopted by the United Nations Diplomatic Conference of Plenipotentiaries on the Establishment of an International Criminal Court on 17 July 1998, U.N. Doc. A/CONF. 183/9 (1998), entered into force on July 1, 2002

International Criminal Court, Rules of Procedure and Evidence, Rules 70,72 ICC-ASP 1/3, adopted on September 9, 2002 United Nations Security Council Final Report of the Commission of Experts (Yugoslavia), Established Pursuant to Security Council Resolution 780 (1992), U.N. Doc. S/1994/674, 27 May 1994, also known as the 'Bassiouni Report'

First Mazowiecki Report, Commission Resolution 1992/S-1/1 27 October 1992, UN Doc. E/CN./1992/S-1/9

Second Mazowiecki Report I, 17 November 1992, UN Doc A/47/666 and S/24809

Third Mazowiecki Report II, 10 February 1993, UN Doc.E/CN.4/1994/8

Fourth Mazowiecki Report II, 6 September 1993 UN Doc.E/CN.4/1994/8

Fifth Mazowiecki Report II, 17 November 1993, UN Doc. E/CN.4/1994/47

Sixth Mazowiecki Report II, 21 February 1994, UN Doc. E/CN.4/1994/110

International Criminal Tribunal for the former Yugoslavia, Security Council Resolution 827, U.N. SCOR, adopted at its 48th Sess., 3217th meeting, at 29, U.N. Doc. S/827/1993

United Nations Security Council Resolution 808 on the International Criminal Tribunal for the former Yugoslavia (1993), U.N. SCOR, adopted at its 48th Session, U.N. Doc S/25706 (1993)

International Criminal Tribunal for Rwanda, United Nations Security Council Resolution 955 U.N. SCOR, adopted at its 49th Sess., 3453rd meeting of 8 November, 1994 at 15, U.N. Doc. S/955/1993, Annex (1994)

The Special Court for Sierra Leone, United Nations Security Council Resolution 1315 (2000) U.N. SCOR, adopted at its 4168th meeting of 14, August 2000, U.N. Doc S/RES/1315/2000

United Nations Security Council Resolution 1325 (S/Res/1325) on Women, Peace and Security, adopted by the Security Council at its 4213th meeting (31 October 2000) S/Res/1325 (2000).

United Nations Transitional Administration in East Timor (UNTAET) UNTAET/REG/2001/25, Regulation on the Amendment of UNTAET Regulation No. 2000/11 on the Organization of Courts in East Timor and UNTAET Regulation No. 2000/30 on the Transitional Rules of Criminal Procedure 14 September 2001

United Nations Security Council Resolution 1664 (SC/8677) (2006) requesting the Establishment of International Tribunal for Killing of Former Lebanese Prime Minister Hariri, adopted unanimously at its 5401st meeting (29 March, 2006).

United Nations Security Council Resolution 1820 (S/Res/1820) on Women and Peace and Security, adopted by the Security Council at its 5916th meeting (June 19 2008) (S/Res/1820)

United Nations Security Council Resolution 1888 (S/Res/1888) on Peacekeeping Missions to Protect Women, Girls from Sexual Violence in Armed Conflict (SC/9753), adopted by the Security Council at its 6195th meeting (30 September 2009)

United Nations Security Council Resolution 2106 (S/Res/2106), adopted by the Security Council at its 6984th meeting (24 June 2013) (S/Res/2106)

United Nations Security Council Resolution 2122 (S/Res/2122), adopted by the Security Council at its 7044th meeting (18 October 2013) (S/Res/2122)

United Nations Security Council Resolution 2242 (S/Res/2242), adopted by the Security Council at its 7533rd meeting (13 October 2015) (S/Res/2242).

Regional human rights reports and legislation European Commission on Human Rights

EC Investigative Mission into the Treatment of Muslim Women in the former Yugoslavia (The Warburton Mission II) (1993); www.womenaid.org/press/info/humanrights/warburtonfull.htm

Inter-American Convention on the Prevention, Punishment and Eradication of Violence against Women, adopted by the General Assembly of the OAS

(9 June 1994), Doc. OEA/ Ser.P AG/doc. 3115/94 rev. 2 International Court of Justice (ICJ)

Legal Consequences of the Construction of a Wall in the Occupied Palestinian Territories, International Court of Justice, Advisory Opinion of 9 July 2004; www.icj-cij.org/docket/files/131/1671.pdf.

Table of international humanitarian law treaties and conventions

Law of the Hague

1899 Hague Convention (Hague II) with Respect to the Laws and Customs of War and its annex: regulations concerning the Laws and Customs of War on Land, The Hague, 29 July 1899, 32 Stat. 1803; 26 Martens Nouveau Recueil (ser. 2) 949, 187, entered into force Sept., 4, 1900

1907 Hague Convention Concerning the Laws and Customs of War on Land, Oct. 18, 1907, 36 Stat. 2277, 3 Martens Nouveau Recueil (ser. 3) 461, entered into force Jan. 26, 1910

Law of Geneva

Geneva Convention (I) for the Amelioration of the Condition of the Wounded and Sick in Armed Forces in the Field, 6 U.S.T. 3114, 75 U.N.T.S. (First Geneva Convention)

Geneva Convention (II) for the Amelioration of Wounded, Sick and Shipwrecked Members of the Armed Forces at Sea, 6 U.S.T. 3217, 75 U.N.T.S. (Second Geneva Convention)

Geneva Convention (III) Relative to the Treatment of Prisoners of War, 6 U.S.T. 3316, 75 U.N.T.S. 135 (Third Geneva Convention) Geneva Convention (IV) Relative to the Protection of Civilians in Time of War, 6 U.S.T. 3516, 75 U.N.T.S. 287 (Fourth Geneva Convention)

Protocol Additional to the Geneva Conventions of 12 August 1949, and Relating to the Protection of Victims of International Armed Conflicts (Protocol I), June 8, 1977, 1125 U.N.T.S. 3, 16 I.L.M. (entered into force Dec. 1978) (First Additional Protocol to the Geneva Conventions)

Protocol Additional to the Geneva Conventions of 12 August 1949, and Relating to the Protection of Victims of Non-International Armed Conflicts (Protocol II), June 8, 1977, 1125 U.N.T.S. 3, 16 I.L.M. (entered into force Dec. 1978) (Second Additional Protocol to the Geneva Conventions)

Control Council Law No. 10, Dec. 20, 1945, Control Council for Germany, Official Gazette, Jan. 31, 1946 at 50, reprinted in 6 Trials of War Criminals Before the Nuremberg Military Tribunals Under Control Council Law No. 10 at xviii. Art. II (1) (c) (1952)

Introduction

This book is about the prosecution of wartime sexual violence in international criminal tribunals. It explores what this development means for gender justice and equality in an era where feminism seemingly has made significant strides in international law. It addresses what the juridicalisation of gender-based violence represents for women in the contemporary context by adopting a critical legal feminist position. Its key argument is that modern-day international criminal tribunals have constructed women in wartime as either helpless women, mothers or wives of soldiers. Tribunals have often foreclosed the possibility that women could exercise resistance, or even be perpetrators of war crimes. By focusing on cases that show women's agency during war, the book suggests that to gain greater legitimacy, international criminal tribunals should encompass a broader understanding of female identity in armed conflict.

The volume explores the portrayal of the various female identities that surface in armed conflict by asking whether international law is capable of reflecting multiple gendered subjectivities in subsequent judgements. Two major legal developments underpin this book; the first is the creation of the ad hoc International Criminal Tribunal for the former Yugoslavia (ICTY) in 1992 by United Nations Security Council Resolution 827, established to prosecute individuals for the most serious violations of international humanitarian law committed during the Yugoslav conflict from 1991 to 1995. The second is the establishment of the ad hoc International Criminal Tribunal for Rwanda (ICTR) through U.N. Security Council Resolution 955 in 1994 to prosecute individuals for the most serious violations of international humanitarian law committed during the genocide that took place from April to July 1994. Both tribunals have been instrumental in placing wartime sexual violence on the map by prosecuting and convicting perpetrators of gender-based crimes. In the case of the Rwandan prosecutions, the judges redefined rape as an instrument of genocide, whereas in the case of the Yugoslav tribunal, rape was conceptualised as a crime against humanity. These redefinitions allowed the prosecution to focus on sexual violence as a deliberate wartime strategy.

ICTY wartime sexual violence jurisprudence, moreover, has been particularly substantive in defining, delineating and developing new crimes. The tribunal has rendered decisions concerning the nature of modern-day armed conflict, such as on the application and scope of Common Article 3 of the 1949 Geneva Conventions, while also 'breathing life' into the grave breaches regime by being the first institution to systematically apply it to sexual violence offences.[1]

The ICTY has added significant definitional value to the Geneva Conventions by identifying comprised acts, such as rape and other sexual violence crimes, as well as distinguishing these acts from those enumerated in the 1984 United Nations Convention against Torture. In substantially redefining gender-based crimes as serious human rights violations, both tribunals have, moreover, drawn attention to the widespread use of rape as a weapon of war and have made the connection between gendered and sexualised harm by linking it to the definition of war crimes in international law. The courts have also been pivotal in incorporating a definition of 'gender' into the Rome Statute underpinning the International Criminal Court and in criminalising a host of gender-based crimes, ranging from enslavement as a crime against humanity to an incorporation of rape as a form of torture and a crime against humanity.

While these legal successes have been extensively analysed in feminist legal scholarship and in international scholarly publications, less space has been dedicated to other crucial perspectives. The voices of feminist legal scholars who view these developments with trepidation have been largely sidelined from the dominant discourse on gender-based violence in international law. The book argues that they are just as central to the debate surrounding wartime sexual violence against women. It critically reflects on dominant feminist discourses surrounding wartime sexual violence by challenging the idea that a critique of the 'women-friendly' successes achieved by international criminal tribunals necessarily signifies the destabilisation of the female subject. Liberal feminist scholars, in particular, have voiced their concern that the legal results accomplished through the concerted efforts of feminist advocacy over the past two decades could be undermined in this way. What is most interesting is that there has been a palpable absence of gendered identities that slightly depart from the stereotypical roles associated with women in war. Unorthodox roles occupied by women have been scarcely reflected in the judgements of the tribunals. Only rarely are instances of female agency apparent in the decisions, with very few examples of female resistance emerging in the portrayal of female identities.

The special concern of this project is to examine how constructions of female identity have been informed by two key trends, namely the conception of women through either the victimhood or the motherhood lens. The central argument is that rather than dismantling patriarchal notions of female identity in wartime, the tribunals have often contributed to a framing of women as either helpless victims of war, or as wives and mothers of soldiers. What is lost in the legal narrative constructed is the possibility of women exercising agency and resistance even in circumstances which seem inherently coercive. The stories of female shopkeepers, small business owners, teachers, police officers, politicians or even perpetrators have not emerged in the case files, but are just as important in understanding gendered identities in wartime.

The second objective is to bring to the surface the multiple gendered subjectivities that materialise in wartime by deconstructing the dichotomised understanding currently adopted in international law. Rather than regarding the law as operating in a vacuum, it has to be conceived of as a broader discipline intersecting with politics, sociology, philosophy and anthropology. Law is neither neutral, nor separate from the very process by which 'crime' and 'order' are constituted. Another claim developed is that the responsibility for promoting gender justice and gender equality falls not solely to international criminal tribunals, but now includes a much wider spectrum of politicians, NGOs and other civil society actors who need to establish formal and informal networks to provide long-lasting support services for women impacted by armed conflict. Rather than trying to invest complete faith in the instrument of the criminal trial as a way of achieving redress, this is a call on feminists to step back and conceive of alternative ways by which to bring about gender justice.

The book echoes the call of Wendy Brown, who, in her work on tolerance, has made room for the possibility of imagining a feminist critique that can be perceptive, without necessarily destabilising the female subject.[2] The successes achieved, thanks in large part to feminist advocacy over the past two decades, should be accorded the recognition they deserve, but without losing sight of the critical lens with which to reflect on these crucial moments in legal history. The key questions to be addressed are:

- How are wartime identities represented in international wartime sexual violence jurisprudence?
- What does the increasing juridicalisation of gender-based violence mean for women?
- Are current feminist investments in the law the way forward in advancing the twin normative aims of gender justice and gender equality?

Methodology

The core chapters discuss how women are portrayed in key international legal decisions. These cases have, variously, been hailed as landmark moments in feminist legal discourses and have shaped the trajectory of wartime sexual violence jurisprudence. They discuss the legal tactics by which female identity is constructed, by adopting an intersectional feminist frame to address the extent to which ethnicity, frequently, is used as identity marker constitutive of female identity in the courtroom. The landmark cases to be analysed include cases such as *The Prosecutor v. Kunarac* (IT-96–23&23/1),[3] *The Prosecutor v. Furundzija* (IT-95–17/1),[4] *The Prosecutor v Nikolic* (IT-94–2),[5] The *Prosecutor v. Bralo* (IT-95–17-S)[6] and the celebrated *Celebici Camp* (IT-96–21)[7] case. In the context of the Rwandan tribunal, the book examines landmark cases, such as the *Akayesu* case (ICTR-96–4-T),[8] the *Gacumbitsi* case (ICTR-2001–64-A),[9] the *Kajelijeli* case (ICTR-98–44A-I),[10] the *Muhimana* case (ICTR-95–1B-1)[11] and the *The Prosecutor v. Pauline Nyiramasuhuko & Arsénes Ntahobali* case (ICTR-97–21-I).[12] Arguments advanced by both the prosecution and the defence are examined in detail to suggest that there is a tendency to depict women in monolithic fashion with little sense of identity beyond their ethnicity. These chapters, moreover, analyse how the boundaries between ethnicity, nationality, female identity, religion and culture are continually blurred to construe a narrative of war with a clear aggressor and a defined victim. This is important from a feminist legal perspective, as the judgements imply a direct correlation between gender, ethnicity, culture and victimhood, therefore making intersectionality an appropriate framework for analysis. Notions of women as the 'mothers of the nation' are, in this way, frequently invoked in the judgements of the tribunals, in particular in relation to Bosnian Muslim women.[13] This is problematic in so far as such evocations conjure up stereotypical and patriarchal ideas of female identity, which are not conducive to conceptualising the possibility of female agency in wartime.

The central argument weaving itself through the chapters is that the self-contained nature of the criminal trial, with its emphasis on punitive measures rather than on healing, and the law as its vehicle of expression are insufficiently flexible in capturing the multi-dimensional nature of female identity in wartime. The language of international criminal law can only begin to fully reflect women's multiple wartime identities if it recaptures female agency, rather than if it assumes women in wartime to inevitably be victims.

Counterpoint and intersectionality

The book is underpinned by a critical method, which has been formulated by Wendy Brown as follows:

> What kind of subject, produced by what kind of politics is led to seek what kind of rights, in the context of what kind of legal, cultural and state discourses with what kind of effects?[14]

Counterpoint is predominantly concerned with the effects and implications of debating wartime sexual violence issues within a contemporary liberal, universalist international legal framework. It does not purport to produce a comprehensive doctrinal analysis of recent developments in international criminal jurisprudence. Rather, it uses the legal materials as a springboard to consider wider issues of gender, ethnicity, culture and violence as they are manifested in the contemporary violence against women debate.

Intersectionality is another important methodological framework, as it showcases the multiple dimensions by which women are discriminated against across all areas of public life. It has been defined as signifying 'the complex, irreducible, varied and variable effects, which ensue when multiple axis of differentiation – economic, political, cultural, psychic, subjective and experiential – intersect in historically specific contexts'.[15] From a methodological perspective, it has raised awareness of the intersection between power relations, cultural practices and gender roles, drawing attention to their intertwined nature. It is primarily concerned with subjectivity referring to a particular paradigm based on individual categories,[16] as well as with the interplay of different power relations and/or systems of oppression in society. Furthermore, it has made a significant impact beyond feminism, notably in the international human rights arena. This book traces the origins of intersectionality, its international success and its relevance to a critical legal feminist perspective on an issue such as wartime sexual violence against women, while also examining its drawbacks.

Notes

1 K. Roberts, 'The Contribution of the ICTY to the Grave Breaches Regime', 7 *Journal of International Criminal Justice* (2009), at 743. Article 3(3) of the ICTR Statute also provides that rape, enforced prostitution and any kind of indecent assault can constitute a grave breach of the Geneva Conventions 1949.
2 W. Brown, *Regulating Aversion: Tolerance in the Age of Identity and Empire* (Princeton, NJ: Princeton University Press, 2008).
3 *The Prosecutor v. Kunarac* (IT-96–23&23/1), Trial Chamber Judgement, 22 February 2001.
4 *The Prosecutor v. Furundzija* (IT-95–17/1), Trial Chamber Judgement, 10 December 1998.
5 *The Prosecutor v Nikolic* (IT-94–2), First Amended Indictment (IT-94–2), 4 November 1992.
6 *The Prosecutor v. Bralo* (IT-95–17-S), Amended Indictment (IT-95–17), 18 July 2005.
7 *The Prosecutor v. Mucic et al.* (IT-96–21-A), '*Celebici* Judgement', Appeals Chamber Judgement, 2003.
8 *The Prosecutor v. Akayesu* (ICTR-96–4-T), Judgement, September 1998.
9 *The Prosecutor v. Gacumbitsi* (ICTR-2001–64-A), Judgement, 7 July 2006.
10 *The Prosecutor v. Kajelijeli* (ICTR-98–44A-I), Trial Chamber Judgement, 23 May 2005.
11 *The Prosecutor v. Muhimana* (ICTR-95–1B-1).
12 *The Prosecutor v. Pauline Nyiramasuhuko & Arsénes Ntahobali Case* (ICTR-97–21-I).
13 In D. Zarkov, *The Body of War: Media, Ethnicity, Gender in the Breakup of Yugoslavia* (Durham, NC: Duke University Press, 2007).
14 W. Brown, 'Revealing Critique: A Response to Kenneth Baynes', 28 *Political Theory* (2000), at 469, 477.
15 A. Brah & A. Phoenix, 'Ain't I a Woman? Revisiting Intersectionality', 5 *Journal of International Women's Studies* (2004), at 75–76.
16 Ibid at 1771 (emphasis added).

1 Wartime sexual violence as a feminist topic of analysis

> In times of extreme crisis, identities may become vague or else, perhaps more often, they are starkly defined.
>
> —Maria Todorova, *Imagining the Balkans*

Introduction

Wartime sexual violence against women is one of the central preoccupations animating international feminist scholarship today, primarily because it is an obviously feminist issue, but also because armed conflict, in particular 'inter-ethnic' conflict, has proliferated over the past two decades generating very modern typologies of war that have resulted in increasing casualties amongst civilians.[1] Crucial legal successes have been achieved in international law with respect to the advancement of the twin feminist normative aims of gender equality and gender justice. In particular the acknowledgment by international human rights law, whose principal aims are the promotion of equality and non-discrimination in all areas of public life, that women's rights are human rights has been a landmark development.

Another undisputed milestone for women's human rights has been achieved by way of the prosecution of wartime sexual violence cases in international criminal tribunals. International human rights law has been of vital importance to this development, having turned its gaze to armed conflict in an effort to extend rights protections to civilians.[2] The turn of human rights to a focus on armed conflict is at the same time emblematic of the contemporary liberal moment, which has focused strongly on the suffering of civilians during armed conflict,[3] resulting in a 'hypervisible'[4] degree of attention paid to the levels of sexual violence committed against women in wartime in contemporary international legal scholarship. This type of attention has not necessarily been an unequivocal success for women, or for the feminist movement.

The prosecution of wartime sexual violence against women has undoubtedly provoked some strong regulatory responses and achieved significant legal victories, but it has also caused controversy and debate in feminist quarters about how to respond to such acts, raising questions about whether feminism has been removed from its original politics. These responses have not always been helpful for the advancement of the twin normative feminist aims of gender justice and equality. The book traces, on the one hand, how international criminal law currently absorbs wartime sexual violence and, on the other hand, analyses how feminist scholars and activists have responded to these developments.

As Anne Orford points out in the context of what she terms 'feminist complicity' in the 'imperialist project' of international law, the production or reproduction of knowledge about the 'real world' of women is one of the ways in which some feminist international legal texts continue to be part of a tradition of imperialism. In this way, the appropriate disciplinary role of feminist theory is to render the 'Third World' woman the object of knowledge of 'First World' international lawyers. Feminists can take their place as part of a set of human sciences by establishing the 'native as the self-consolidating other'.[5] It is therefore entirely conceivable that rather than always offering solutions, an overzealous feminist focus on gender-based violence could occlude attention being paid to more structural forms of violence, such as pay discrimination and food poverty, which are gendered phenomena.

The chapter provides a preliminary sense of the importance of wartime sexual violence for a feminist legal analysis, while revealing some of its concerns with the parameters in which the debate is conducted. Particular concern is raised in relation to the visibility of the violated body in current wartime sexual violence literature. The chapter opens up the debate on what such visibility might imply for women in the contemporary political and legal moment. Subsequently, it assesses counterpoint as a methodological tool for interrogating feminist approaches towards wartime sexual violence. It then analyses the underlying salient discourses that inform this area of the law and reviews their centrality to a discussion as significant as wartime sexual violence in feminist legal scholarship.

i) The violated body of the woman as a subject of analysis

Rape has received particular prominence in the feminist and non-feminist literature surrounding the armed conflict in the former Yugoslavia due to the widespread reporting of such incidents. Both the Yugoslav and Rwandan conflicts have given feminism new epistemic purchase in the debate around the regulation of wartime sexual violence in international law by reiterating the sense that rape most vividly encapsulates the symbolism of sexuality during wartime. By catapulting the violated body of the woman onto the front pages, debates around victimisation, nationality and female suffering in wartime have been reawakened and feminist insights have suddenly become *en vogue*. From that moment onwards, rape has been a constant concern of legal feminist scholarship. Yet the focus on rape has wittingly or unwittingly created problematic consequences for feminism, as it has intertwined female identity with notions of victimhood. One of the central questions to answer, therefore, is whether, paradoxically, feminists have contributed to the sense that women civilians, when caught up in armed conflict, will inevitably be subjected to some form of sexual violence and are inescapable victims of war, as well as victims of their cultural identity.[6] That victimisation is a problematic conceptualisation of female identity has been persuasively demonstrated by legal feminist historian Joanna Bourke, who has analysed the historical trajectory characterising the shifting meanings of rape and female identity.[7] As she has put it:

> If Man becomes an amorphous threat, free-floating, signifying danger then Woman is (always) scared. Before His body, she quakes. In this analysis, the female body is portrayed as already and always violated. Further, by virtue of being female, the woman is already the victim, the wounded, suffering, gendered subject. She is defined in relation to 'it' – the penis. In this sense, the words fear and rape have become 'intimately connected'.[8]

History, however, suggests that this has not always been the case. Thanks in large part to the advent of psychoanalysis in the early twentieth century with its understandings of the relationship between the mind and body, sexual violence came to be regarded as an attack upon a woman's sexual identity creating a 'psychic wound', or a violation of the self. As sex became increasingly linked to psychological events shifting away from genitals and reproduction, the 'wrong' of acts such as date rape or marital rape acquired much greater significance. These attacks became construed not only as attacks on the body but on the very integrity of the self. Whereas rape in nineteenth century Britain and America, for example, was seen as an attempt to undermine women's class position, their earning power and respectability, by the twentieth century, the consequences of rape were no longer seen as 'a question of debauchery' but were rather seen as a shattering of identity, an incurable wound to which the victim seems doomed.[9] As Bourke has noted:

> This intense focus on the body as marker of identity and as locus of truth is a profoundly modern conception.[10]

The rapist endangered the nineteenth-century woman by attempting to undermine her class position, earning power and respectability. Sexual attack then was less a matter of offence to sexual identity than an affront to a woman's ability to support herself. As a consequence, women placed emphasis on physical injury and the threat of pregnancy. The accuser was 'spoiling' or 'ruining' a female victim's gendered social position.

While during the nineteenth-century rape was typically conceptualised less as a matter of identity, or 'inner trauma' but more as an external harm, by the twentieth century, rape was considered to be an affront against identity, a rupture against the very self.

According to Bourke:

> The historically inflected balance between social ('external') and psychological ('internal') trauma resulting from sexual violation has had a major impact upon feminist strategy. Earlier generations of feminists were keen to portray women as resilient in the face of sexual violence. The threat to sexual violence was to be fought through comprehensive intervention in social structures.[11]

By the 1970s and 1980s, a specific temporal juncture that saw a strong reinvigoration of liberal ideas, one influential strand moved 'decisively towards a trauma model and the notion of women's pervasive victimisation entirely abandoning the idea of earlier female resilience when confronted with sexual assault'.[12]

So-called 'second-wave' Western feminists insisted on emphasising emotion and insight into feelings, which were deemed to be sources of 'unique truth'. While on the one hand still compassionately committed to building up women's power and resisting oppressive male institutions, these feminists shifted their emphasis onto female emotional and psychic fragility in the face of injurious social structures. More specifically, femininity became defined as 'victimhood', while the related sense of unhappiness was tied to subjugation. The concept of the victim as the 'revelatory voice' of experience naturalised the experience of sexual violence by individualising it.[13] The narratives surrounding female victimisation have therefore undergone a notable development to the extent that they have become disengaged from earlier assertions of collective female agency.

According to Bourke:

> Against the persistence of male violence and its destructive effects, many women retain the subject position of victimhood, but in a context where the supportive community has largely fragmented. Feminist camaraderie vanished. Rape certainly did not.[14]

The recent turn in international feminist legal scholarship to 'governance feminism' can therefore perhaps be understood as a way of bringing back the sense of lost camaraderie or solidarity Bourke refers to. At the same time this renewed form of female solidarity with the plight of the rape victims of the Yugoslav war might not have been uniformly positive, as it came at the expense of women who were deemed to be on the 'wrong' side of the war and were left out of the legal narratives and resulting 'victories' celebrated in international criminal tribunals.

Violence against women is a widespread and endemic offence against female autonomy affecting the lives of millions of women around the world.[15] Given the scale of the problem, the book revisits the feminist discourses that have informed the debate around wartime sexual violence produced as a result of the Yugoslav and Rwandan wars in order to understand how gender justice for the victims could be best delivered. There is a strong concern around the 'depoliticisation' of wartime sexual violence in contemporary feminist scholarship and the renaissance of identity politics. Specifically, a disproportionate amount of attention has been placed on culture as a lens for understanding armed conflict.[16] It has been argued, for example, that the specific character of Yugoslavia, and of the Balkans, stemming from patterns of patriarchal, pastoral and communal life[17] with its own mythical views of heroism and a specific code of shame[18] is to blame for the high incidence of sexual violence against women – a perspective that has in many instances been embraced by leading feminist scholars. This tendency has reified Yugoslav women as a cultural species quite apart from similarly constructed Western women. In this way, dominant feminist discourses have failed to ask pressing and urgent questions regarding the impact of women's material status during wartime. They have never fully explored the extent to which underlying socio-economic conditions contributed to the outbreak of armed conflict, as well as seldom distinguishing between differently situated groups of women, according to education, occupation and other criteria, as the case law analysis reveals. Moreover, cultural framings of conflict have not been able to account for the absence of sexual violence in certain modern armed conflicts.[19]

ii) Counterpoint as a method of feminist inquiry

This book is a critical feminist analysis of wartime sexual violence as it is constructed in international criminal jurisprudence and the surrounding debate. It asks: what is the adjudication of wartime sexual violence in international criminal tribunals, more specifically in ad hoc tribunals, considered to represent for women in the current historical and political moment? In essence, this question is a variation of a critical method that has been formulated by Wendy Brown as follows:

> What kind of subject, produced by what kind of politics is led to seek what kind of rights, in the context of what kind of legal, cultural and state discourses with what kind of effects?[20]

This book is predominantly concerned with the effects and implications of debating wartime sexual violence issues within a contemporary liberal, universalist international legal framework. It does not produce a comprehensive doctrinal legal analysis of all recent developments in international criminal jurisprudence. Rather, it uses the legal materials as a springboard to consider wider issues of gender, ethnicity, culture and violence as they are manifested in the contemporary violence against women debate. It aims to contribute to the wider feminist literature that engages with these discourses. The term 'critical feminist' analysis implies engagement with the very parameters of the debate, rather than an advocating for straightforward legal change. This is not to minimise the merit of other feminist as well as non-feminist contributions which might pursue such a course. Rather, the method adopted can be described as guided by the idea of counterpoint.

This has been described as:

> A deliberate practice of multiplicity that exceeds simple opposition and does not carry the mythological or methodological valence of dialectics or contradiction. At once open-ended and tactical, counterpoint emanates from and promotes an anti-hegemonic sensibility and requires a modest and carefully styled embrace of multiplicity in which contrasting elements, featured simultaneously, do not simply war, harmonise, blend or compete, but rather bring out the complexity that cannot emerge through a monolithic or single melody. This complexity does not add up to a whole but, rather, sets off a theme by providing an elsewhere to it indeed; it can even highlight and thus contest dominance through its work of juxtaposition.[21]

In essence, counterpoint provides a technique for a critical analysis which does not insist on the correctness of its approach. Rather, it presents a set of observations in counterpoint to other arguments advanced on the subject. It offers a perspective, rather than objectivity or comprehensiveness. It chooses to explore certain angles and advance arguments and perspectives in opposition to currently prevailing positions. This does not necessarily imply disagreement with those; rather it complicates them by providing an alternative vision.

Original contribution

Three key contributions to original knowledge can be specifically listed. First, the book assesses whether contemporary feminist investments in international criminal law are desirable for women in the current political and legal moment. It contributes to the growing literature on ICTY wartime sexual violence jurisprudence by focusing closely on the case law arising from the conflict in Bosnia-Herzegovina, with its attendant phenomena such as the mass sexual violence perpetrated inside the detention camps, from a critical feminist perspective. But unlike many contemporary feminist texts, it aims to provide a platform for further reflection and analysis on the existing debate, rather than a prescription of how wartime sexual violence ought to be legally regulated.

Secondly, an analysis of how wartime identities materialise in key ICTY decisions and how identity categories such as gender and ethnicity intersect is offered. The book draws attention to the legal modalities by which female agency has been erased from international criminal jurisprudence through the deployment of gendered stereotypes that construe women as either mothers, wives or victims of war. It builds on the existing critical legal scholarship pursued by, for example Doris Buss, Karen Engle and Janet Halley, while adopting a more critical angle that links the turn to identity politics in feminist debates around the Yugoslav war to the 'ethnicisation' of the conflict in popular discourse. Here, the book ties in the representation of wartime identity in international criminal tribunals with the 'depoliticisation' strategy identified by Wendy Brown in the context of tolerance discourses surfacing in a post–September 11th world. By examining 'governance feminism' – a variation of structural or radical feminism – as the paradigmatic manifestation of the consensual approach currently adopted by feminists in the wartime sexual violence debate, it moreover questions whether, at this moment, feminism is transmitting a new tradition for which it may be the sovereign authority itself.[22]

Thirdly, it reinstates critique as an important methodological tool for current feminist legal scholarship by examining in detail the current feminist anxiety about critique, which is also ubiquitous in contemporary political and legal culture. The concern is built around the idea that the destabilisation of female subjectivity might rob feminism of elements of theory and practice that are indispensable to its goals. This is particularly so in light of feminism's close association with activism and practice over the past two decades, which is explored in detail. An important alternative perspective to the debate is offered by arguing that the distancing from critique often blocks intellectual and practical developments within feminist theory, which might be neither intellectually justifiable, nor politically desirable. In sum, the book contributes insight into what has been 'lost or unseen when ethnicity becomes unquestionably the explanatory framework'[23] through which wartime identities are represented in feminist and non-feminist discourses.

iii) The structure of the book

The book pursues a straightforward structure. The opening two chapters, including the present one, provide a discussion and analysis of the salient developments concerning gender-based violence and wartime sexual violence. The middle stage is constituted by chapter 4, which serves as the transitional stage from the overview of the salient legal developments to their critical feminist analysis, which is fully carried out in chapters 5 and 6.

Chapter 2 examines the genealogy of gender-based violence in international human rights law and revisits the recognition of women's rights as human rights as significant junctures in feminist scholarship and activism, which ultimately have propelled wartime sexual violence to the top of the international legal agenda. It explains why gender-based violence is significant from a feminist legal perspective and it reflects on the visibility of the Violence against Women movement (VAW) within contemporary human rights discourses. Moreover, it provides the background for the ensuing critical analysis pursued in later chapters by showing how the definitional and legal evolution of gender-based violence paved the way for the later incorporation of wartime sexual violence into international criminal law. It also offers a critique of specific institutional policies such as a 'gender mainstreaming', which have become prevalent across international legal institutions exploring what these developments signify for women in the current political and legal moment.

This provides the stepping stone for chapter 3, which focuses in detail on the key developments in contemporary wartime sexual violence jurisprudence achieved by the ad hoc tribunals for Yugoslavia and Rwanda. It provides a historical and legal overview of wartime sexual violence against women in armed conflict in order to illuminate some of the traditional reasons for its marginalisation in the annals of history and in international criminal law until the 1990s. It maps out the evolution of wartime sexual violence in international criminal law by reflecting on some of the salient legal achievements such as the definition of rape in international criminal law and the recognition of rape as a form of torture produced by the tribunals. In this way, it sketches out the critical legal approach adopted in this text, while at the same time making room for a stronger critique to emerge in the remaining chapters.

Chapter 4 acts as the first pillar in the methodological transition from the discussion of wartime sexual violence developments to their actual analysis pursued in chapters 5, 6 and 7. Various feminist approaches to human rights, gender, ethnicity culture and armed conflict are mapped out in order to crystallise the actual 'critical feminist' method that subsequent chapters employ. This chapter overviews these approaches in order to highlight their advantages and disadvantages from the point of view of engaging with an issue such as wartime sexual violence against women. The types of approaches overviewed are first, liberal/universalist; second, radical and 'governance' feminist; third, poststructuralist feminist and fourth, postcolonial and intersectionality feminism. The book suggests an alternative perspective that focuses on the impact of economic globalisation, military intervention and structural violence as a more desirable option to the feminist approaches currently in play. Although each of the approaches reviewed is not without merit, new studies drawing away from identity politics might offer a more refreshing and alternative insight into the complex power relations that characterise modern-day armed conflict.

Chapter 5 provides a critical overview of the most significant recent legal developments in ICTY wartime sexual violence jurisprudence. Its aim is not to cover all developments, but to provide an insight into the legal and semantic modalities deployed by the tribunal in interpreting the Yugoslav conflict, which in turn provides ground for the critical feminist approach pursued in chapter 6. The chapter briefly documents the historical trajectory of the conflict in Yugoslavia, and it crystallises the methodological approach adopted in the selection of case law. The cases selected are deemed landmark decisions in the area of wartime sexual violence jurisprudence and they feature specific gendered phenomena, such as the mass rape in detention camps that has become closely associated with the Yugoslav conflict in the popular imagination. Moreover, they illustrate how gender and ethnicity intersect in the legal decisions in a manner that depoliticises, or removes the significance of the Yugoslav conflict as a political event from the historical powers that shaped it. This chapter, alongside chapter 3, constitutes a methodological bridge between the discussion of wartime sexual violence developments provided in chapters 2 and 3 and their critical analysis pursued in chapters 4, 5 and 6.

Chapter 6 is where the critical feminist analysis of wartime sexual violence is actually crystallised. The chapter purports to assert the value of critique as itself a worthwhile transformative academic and political strategy in contrast with some feminist preoccupations with legal reform. It argues that the absence of a unified subject need not block certain feminist pursuits by highlighting two salient trends in ICTY wartime sexual violence jurisprudence: the reading of gendered identity through an ethnic lens, and the portrayal of women as either mothers or victims that form the feminist core of the debate on wartime sexual violence jurisprudence. These legal tactics have produced a problematic narrative of gendered identity in wartime. The chapter suggests that there are limitations to viewing women in this way and it proposes adding another layer to the analysis by conceptualising wartime agency in different terms. It argues that women's subordination and gendered inequality might not be solved by feminism alone and that an alternative framework, which is not necessarily inspired by feminist thinking or reliant on the increased criminalisation of sexual violence, might be the way forward in conceptualising female identity in wartime differently.

Part IV

Some underlying 'depoliticising' discourses

The book pursues a critical feminist analysis of ICTY wartime sexual violence jurisprudence and the surrounding debate. In order to facilitate this task, it is necessary to provide an account of some background discourses and tendencies, cutting across much of contemporary feminist and identity politics, as well as their underlying political and legal formations. Wendy Brown regards these discourses and tendencies as manifestations of the late modern phenomenon of depoliticisation.[24] This entails an array of contemporary depoliticising discourses, such as liberalism, individualism, human rights and culture. All of these are complicit in each other's operation. In broad strokes, Brown defines depoliticisation as 'removing a political phenomenon from comprehension of its historical emergence and from recognition of the powers that produce and contour it'.[25] The construction and representation of the subject in such discourses inevitably reinforces certain 'ontological naturalness or essentialism' in our understanding of the 'sources of deep political and social problems'.[26]

Brown argues that tolerance tends to cast group conflict as '[r]ooted in ontologically natural hostility toward essentialised religious, ethnic, and cultural difference'. In this way, 'tolerance discourse reduces conflict to an inherent friction among identities and makes religious, ethnic and cultural difference itself an inherent site of conflict, one that calls for and is attenuated by the practice of tolerance'.[27]

i) 'Naturalisation/culturalisation'/personalisation

The first strand of depoliticisation is 'naturalisation/culturalisation', the deployment of which serves to characterise 'instances of inequality and social injury' as 'matters of individual or group prejudice'.[28] The second strand, personalisation, refers to the substitution of 'emotional and personal vocabularies for formulating solutions to political problems'.[29] Historical injustice so often underlying the outbreak of conflict is reduced to the phenomenon of difference rendering identity itself, comprising of certain 'practices and beliefs', the problem that needs to be tolerated and managed. Power and history are equally overlooked and ignored in the quest to find the formulation of solutions to these problems. The consequence of substituting justice or equality in favour of tolerance results in historically induced suffering being reduced to 'difference', or a problem of personal feeling. The field in which the 'political battle' and 'political transformation' ought to take place gets replaced with an agenda of emotional practices.[30]

ii) Liberalism/individualism

Brown terms liberalism as the most profound achievement of 'depoliticisation'. She attributes the excessive emphasis on the individual and tropes such as self-making, agency and a 'relentless responsibility for itself' as contributing factors in the personalisation of politically contoured conflicts and inequalities. The result of these tendencies is the elimination from view of various norms and social relations, especially those relating to capital, race, gender and sexuality that construct and position subjects in liberal democracies.[31] The reduction of freedom to rights and of equality to equal standing before the law often eliminates from view many sources of subordination, marginalisation and inequality that organise liberal democratic societies and fashion their subjects.[32]

Individualism is another depoliticising discourse, inextricably tied to liberalism. Rooted in the American cultural emphasis on the importance of individual belief and behaviour and of individual heroism and failure, it is at the same time relentlessly depoliticising. In a similar vein, Costas Douzinas has argued that human rights have been 'triumphant' in modernity because nature has ceased to be the standard of right, meaning that all individual desires could be turned into rights.[33] Hence, rights in postmodernity have become the legal recognition of individual will. People acquire their humanity and subjectivity by having rights, and a general agreement that a desire or interest is constitutive of humanity is sufficient for the creation of a new legal right. In this way,

> [i]s and ought are collapsed, rights are reduced to facts and agreements expressed in legislation, or, in a more critical vein, to the disciplinary priorities of power and domination.[34]

The individual has become the 'triumphant' centre of our postmodern world, which is evident in the relentlessly recurring turn to identity and identity-related politics, which intersect with a return of morality to politics and a return of humanism to law in the proceedings of the ICTY.[35] With its firm focus on the prosecution of the individual and the attribution of responsibility for gross human rights violations on individual actors, it could be argued that the ICTY strategy behind the individualisation of international criminal law is to create the perception that deep social problems are fully redressable through individual litigation. As Martti Koskenniemi has argued in his discussion of the Miloševic trial:

> Focusing on the individual abstracts the political context, that is to say, describes it in terms of the actions and intentions of particular, well-situated individuals.[36]

The author agrees with this view, as the intentions and actions of individuals can best be grasped by placing attention on structural causes, such as economic or functional necessities, or institutional frameworks that in the first place allow certain individuals to create potent social effects through their actions.[37] From a feminist perspective, the emphasis on rights might create the illusion that deep social problems are fully redressable through individual legal litigation, as they are, in essence, matters of 'remarks, attitudes, and speech'.[38] The invocation of the individual in human rights law has often also been critiqued for its construction of a masculinist worldview which occludes women from the picture.[39] Moreover, it can be contended that the prosecution of certain key individuals, but sometimes marginal figures, too,[40] has not brought about a basis for political peace and reconciliation in post-conflict situations.

iii) Human rights

Human rights is a particularly prominent late modern liberal depoliticising discourse. According to Douzinas, human rights are 'both creations and creators of modernity, the greatest political and legal invention of modern political philosophy and jurisprudence'.[41] On his view, their essential characteristics in the modern turn can be described as follows:

> First, they mark a profound turn in political thought from duty to right, from civitas and communitas to civilization and humanity. Secondly, they reverse the traditional priority between the individual and society. While classical and medieval natural law expressed the right order of the cosmos and of human communities within it, an order that gave the citizen his place, time and dignity, modernity emancipates the human person, turns him from citizen to individual and establishes him at the centre of social and political organization and activity.[42]

Human rights with its emphasis on reason as a chief virtue is supposed to transcend geographical and historical differences, its narrative looking to *teloi*, and ends as the way forward on the path to human emancipation. As Douzinas sees it, human rights have won the ideological battle of modernity, and yet if the twentieth century is the epoch of human rights, their triumph is something of a paradox, given that the modern age has witnessed more violations of their principles than any of the previous and less 'enlightened' epochs.[43] There is thus a huge discrepancy between theory and practice of human rights, which is not helped by the fact that official thinking and action on human rights has been entrusted in the hands of triumphalist columnist writers, bored diplomats and rich international lawyers in New York and Geneva, people whose experience of human rights violations is confined to being served a bad bottle of red wine. In the process, human rights have mutated from a discourse of rebellion and dissent into that of state legitimacy.[44]

The recent repercussions of this historic depoliticising move are therefore contradictory: on the one hand, universal rights operate on the assumption of the autonomous, rational 'relentlessly self-interested subject of liberalism', which discursively erases differences and the disadvantage hinging on them. On the other, rights, refashioned for and by the particular subject as pertaining to a specific identity (be it women, blacks or gays, or even Bosnian Muslim women), further entrench what 'Brown calls the 'identity's constitutive injury', as well as the discourses that frame it. In this way, human rights become inextricably linked with the markedly anti-emancipatory function of identity, which she conceptualises drawing on the theorisation of Friedrich Nietzsche's slave mentality and his view of 'ressentiment' as the impulse driving those who see themselves as disenfranchised from the system.[45]

Human rights and international law as depoliticising discourses, informed by identity politics, are of tremendous relevance to the critical feminist analysis of the wartime sexual violence debate, which this book pursues. This is because the discourse of human rights provides the primary framework through which sexual violence in times of armed conflict is articulated in the international legal system.

It is now widely accepted that human rights have become the quintessence of the project of modernity, alongside other institutionalised discourses such as secularism, market freedom and democracy.[46] As former ICTY President Antonio Cassese has observed, human rights have today assumed the status of a 'quasi secular religion'.[47] They have become the global expression of the Western liberal tradition, having minimised other previously useful vocabularies such as socialism, the labour movement and even Christianity.[48] Moreover, from a feminist liberal perspective, human rights have been central in seeking redress for gender-based violence. This is because the human rights idea is one of the few moral visions ascribed to internationally, striking 'deep chords of response among many'.[49] Importantly, human rights have been seen as the vehicle that allowed the specific experiences of women to be made visible in international law.

The contemporary ascendancy of human rights also involves a certain conflation between local and international discourses of human rights. Domestic rights frameworks increasingly embrace 'international standards' not just through classic incorporation, but also through a range of innovative ways such as judges using international human rights law as 'persuasive' authority. On the other hand, it has become common for international tribunals to refer to the practice of other international bodies and/or domestic courts. These tendencies turn international law into a process both of 'particularisation of the universal' and 'universalisation of the particular'.[50] The result is that a rigid distinction between 'domestic' and 'international' jurisdictions becomes somewhat artificial in the discussion of human rights, entailing significant repercussions for the feminist movement. Indeed, it has been observed that 'the domestic legal feminist enterprise increasingly seems incomplete where it lacks an international aspect'.[51] International law has therefore firmly become 'the official language of human rights, quite distinct from customary or even constitutional rights regimes'.[52] Its language, moreover, has been seen as the 'only, sole legitimate discourse of resistance recognised by law'.[53] But as this book argues, the production and reproduction of knowledge about the 'real world' of women is one of the ways in which some feminist international legal texts continue to be part of traditional imperialism that perpetuates problematic gender stereotypes.[54] In this version of the appropriate disciplinary role for feminist theory, the suffering of the 'Third World Woman' becomes the object of knowledge of 'First World International Lawyers'.[55]

iv) The culturalisation of politics

As to the other depoliticising discourses, Wendy Brown highlights the recent phenomenon of the culturalisation of politics, which helps to illustrate how tolerance can be utilised '[i]n a manner that equates or conflates non-commensurable subjects and practices', with ethnicity, race, religion and culture being especially interchangeable.[56] This overdetermination is profoundly asymmetrical and to a large degree patronising, as it is marked by a division between those who 'have culture' and those whom 'culture has': the late modern versus the pre-modern non-West. Culture is not only the driving force of political conflict or the dividing line between the civilised and the uncivilised, but also the problem for which liberalism itself is proffered as a solution.[57] A poignant example of the turn to liberalism as the solution for those 'whom culture has' is offered in Hagan's account of the political motivations driving the Yugoslav Tribunal, as the transformation of then U.S. President Bill Clinton's initially firm stance on sending troops to Bosnia shows. Based on this version of events, it was Clinton's reading of the book *Balkan Ghosts*[58] that convinced him that the region was 'chronically violent', persuading him to distance himself from the Vance-Owen Plan, which had proposed to divide Bosnia into 'ethnic cantons' and had cautioned against using air strikes against Bosnian Serbs.[59] The decision to launch a significant military intervention was allegedly taken based on essentialised assumptions about a region and its people as cultural entities that had to be rescued from themselves and ultimately 'civilised' at the hands of the benign West.

The international community

International community norms are widely considered to be a major feature of modernity and liberalism. According to Gerry Simpson, the public pronouncements of key officials are careful to invoke the international community 'at every turn'.[60] The 'great powers' do not purport to act in the name of narrow self-interest, but on behalf of community interests, or humanity itself, lending credence to their mission through the invocation of 'common values'. A necessary corollary to this rhetorical and legal tradition is the presence of states and groups operating outside of the universal community acting in the cause of inhumanity. Wars are not fought between adversaries but between the international community and international outlaws, or between the 'universal and the particular', so human rights, for instance, are posited against Islamic terrorism. But such discourses do not necessarily lead to a questioning of the underlying, structural inequalities that contribute to such events, nor to a questioning of the broader international legal commitment to trade and financial liberalisation, nor to challenges of the international community's support of certain kinds of militarism, while outlawing the conduct of 'terrorists' or 'rogue states'.[61]

In the context of the run-up to the Yugoslav war, Susan Woodward has, for example, shown that rather than acting as a benign influence, the international community strengthened the causes of violence: it contributed to the weakness of the federal government and its state capacity; it legitimised the people and ideas that would eventually win and it failed to understand the hard work that was needed to make peace when it accepted the peacemakers' role.[62] An example of such an initiative was the EC-sponsored Badinter Commission, designed to address legal questions around international statehood and to encourage negotiations with the presidents of the then Yugoslav republics. But rather than leading to stability in the region, its findings arguably accelerated the war.[63] Significantly and not by accident, the creation of the ICTY was set against the backdrop of expansionist terminology that accompanied the redefinition of the 'international community' away from a sovereign state-centric notion of international law to a cosmopolitan ideal understood as a form of international public law that binds sovereign nations.[64] But often the same international community has served as a 'self-congratulatory' and elusive mechanism, allowing trials to be conducted by foreign prosecutors and before foreign judges. As such, it can be argued that no moral community has been affirmed, as no judgement has been sufficient to restore the dignity of the victims and no symbolism persuasive enough to justify drawing a thick line between past and future.[65] The only 'community' that has stood to benefit from such processes is the symbolic 'international community', whose official stamp of approval has largely served to legitimise its own moral authority.[66] Moreover, the international community paradigm has contributed to the sense that 'ancient ethnic rivalries' informed by notions of 'barbarism and primitivism' accounted for the violence witnessed during the Yugoslav conflict. In this way, the international community has posited its own superior sense of morality against the perceived barbarism of the uncivilised natives.[67] This has reinstated the clash between the 'civilised' West against less exalted civilisations driven by cultural values and ways of life, which stultify both their political and economic development and from which they cannot escape. The depoliticising discourses of liberalism, individualism, human rights and the culturalisation of politics and international community provide the background analysis against which the book should be read.

Notes

1 The rise of one-sided violence and the indiscriminate use of violence against civilians has been a very particular form of modern-day armed conflict. Relatively low-scale but constant one-sided violence appears to be the overriding pattern in most areas of conflict. One-sided violence is defined in a recent report on modern-day trends in armed conflict as 'the intentional use of armed force against civilians by a government or formally organised group that results in at least 25 deaths in a calendar year'. Further, it directly and intentionally targets civilians who cannot defend themselves with arms. It is also distinct from battle-related violence that incidentally harms civilians, who for example, are caught up in the crossfire between combatants. According to the report, 99 percent of fatalities from one-sided violence occur in countries affected by armed conflict. Interestingly, there has been a relative decline in states' direct involvement in one-sided violence and a growing reliance on 'government-aligned' actors, such as clan militias or breakaway rebel factions; these actors may be attached to government forces, or be relatively autonomous and motivated by their own socio-political interests or clan divisions. This could be deemed a form of 'outsourcing' of one-sided violence and other tasks to loosely affiliated and less accountable actors, who often prove to be particularly brutal in their treatment of civilians. In E. Stepanova, 'Trends in Armed Conflicts: One-Sided Violence against Civilians', in *Stockholm Peace Research Institute Yearbook 2009: Armaments, Disarmament and International Security* (Oxford: Oxford University Press, 2009), 39.

2 The International Court of Justice in its Advisory Opinion on the Legal Consequences of the Construction of a Wall in the Occupied Palestinian Territory held that international human rights was applicable and intersected with international humanitarian law in times of armed conflict to the extent that Israel was bound to comply with its obligations under both regimes to respect the right of the Palestinian people to self-determination. It was, thus, under an obligation of international law to put an end to the violations of its international obligations flowing from the construction of the wall in the Occupied Palestinian territory and to allow access to the 'Holy Places' that came under its control following the 1967 War. International Court of Justice, Advisory Opinion of 9 July 2004, Legal Consequences of the Construction of a Wall in the Occupied Palestinian Territories, paras 149, 150. Available at: www.icj-cij.org/docket/files/131/1671.pdf (last accessed in May 2011).

3 Civilians play an increasingly complex role as both victims and perpetrators in modern-day armed conflict. There has, however, undoubtedly been a rise in civilian casualties in armed conflicts – casualties not resulting from direct military engagement, as figures obtained by the International Red Cross from the armed conflict in the Democratic Republic of Congo (DRC) attest. In the DRC, it is estimated that there were 2.5 million deaths between 1998 and 2001, yet only 350,000 of those were killed in actual battle. For an overview, see: A. Wenger & S.J.A. Mason, 'The Civilianization of Armed Conflict: Trends and Implications', 827 *International Review of the Red Cross* (December 2008), at 835–836. Available at: www.icrc.org/eng/assets/files/other/irrc-872-wenger-mason.pdf (last accessed in May 2011).

4 I borrow the term 'hypervisible' from Doris Buss, who argues that rape has almost taken on a 'hypervisible' quality in the international wartime sexual violence jurisprudence with problematic consequences for an understanding of the more nuanced forms of gender-based violence perpetrated during armed conflict. In D. Buss, 'The Curious Visibility of Wartime Rape: Gender and Ethnicity in International Criminal Law', 25 *Windsor Journal of Access to Justice* (2007), at 3–22. In a similar vein, Alice Miller has argued that until the 1980s it was exceedingly difficult to get the human rights world to pay either attention to women as rights claimants or to sexual harm as a form of harm. However, once 'sex' became accepted as an area of concern, a 'hyper attention' to sex ironically operated to exclude attention to other types of harm. In A. Miller, 'Sexuality, Violence against Women, and Human Rights: Women Make Demands and Ladies Get Protection', 7 *Health and Human Rights* (2) (2004), at 16, 18–19.

5 In A. Orford, *Reading Humanitarian Intervention* (Cambridge: Cambridge University Press, 2003), at 59.

6 In the context of the war in Bosnia-Herzegovina, the term 'mass rape' has assumed increasing valence within feminist discourses, the argument being that there are specific patterns of war crimes against women, which not only destroy the physical and psychological existence of the women concerned but also inflict harm on the culture and the collective identity of the whole group, ethnicity or nation under attack. Feminists of this persuasion would argue that war crimes against women have symbolic meaning and must be analysed within the symbolic contexts of the nation and gender system. See for example R. Seifert, 'The Second Front: The Logics of Sexual Violence in Wars', 19 *Women's Studies International Forum* (1996), at 35–43; J. Barkan, 'As Old as War Itself: Rape in Foca', *Dissent* (2002), 1–7; A. Stiglmayer, 'The Rapes in Bosnia-Herzegovina', in *Mass Rape: The War against Women in Bosnia-Herzegovina* (Lincoln, NA: University of Nebraska Press, 1994), 82–164; C. MacKinnon, 'Rape, Genocide, and Women's Human Rights', in A. Stiglmayer (ed.), *Mass Rape: The War against Women in Bosnia-Herzegovina* (Lincoln, NA: University of Nebraska

Press, 1994), at 183–195; C. MacKinnon, 'Rape, Genocide, and Women's Human Rights', 17 *Harvard Women's Law Journal* (1994), at 5; B. Allen, *Rape, Warfare: The Hidden Genocide in Bosnia-Herzegovina and Croatia* (Minneapolis: University of Minnesota Press, 1996).

7 J. Bourke, *Rape: Sex, Violence and History* (Berkeley, CA: Shoemaker and Hoard, 2007), at 421.

8 Ibid at 421.

9 Ibid at 425.

10 Ibid at 426.

11 Ibid.

12 Ibid at 428.

13 As Bourke suggests, while the deployment of the 'victim' label to refer to women served as an effective strategy from which to confront patriarchal institutions and customs, paradoxically, however, the very success of second-wave feminists created difficulties for the next generation of feminists, who used their newfound partial freedoms to forge even more individualistic paths to power and self-fulfilment. Ibid at 428–429.

14 Ibid at 429.

15 A 2007 UNIFEM-sponsored report asserts that some 70 percent of the casualties in recent conflicts have been non-combatants, most of whom have been women and children. With respect to gender-based violence committed in conflicts that have catapulted the phenomenon onto the front pages, it is estimated that in Rwanda up to half a million women were raped during the 1994 genocide, and around 60,000 during the Yugoslav war. Moreover, in Sierra Leone, the number of incidents of war-related sexual violence among internally displaced women from 1991 to 2001 was as high as 64,000. UNIFEM, 'Facts and Figures on Violence against Women-Gender Issues: Violence against Women'. Available at: www.unifem.org/attachments/gender_issues/violence_against_women/facts_figures_violenceagainst_women_2007.pdf. The number of victims from the Yugoslav conflict is highly contested and the precise figures are unknown – for a discussion see, C. Niarchos, 'Women, War and Rape', 17 *Human Rights Quarterly* (4) (1995), at 649. The commonly accepted estimate of victims is 20,000 first given in the EC Investigative Mission into the Treatment of Muslim Women in the former Yugoslavia (The Warburton Mission II) (1993), at para 14. As the Mission states, direct evidence from the women is extremely difficult to obtain, as women are 'understandably reluctant' to recall details of the atrocities done to them. Nonetheless, the Mission estimates that it is possible to speak of many thousands of victims with estimates varying widely and ranging from 10,000 to as many as 60,000. The most 'reasoned' estimates, as the Mission puts it, are of 20,000 victims of sexual violence. Available at: www.womenaid.org/press/info/humanrights/warburtonfull.htm This figure is confirmed by Cherif Bassiouni in Sexual Violence: An Invisible Weapon of War in the Former Yugoslavia (Occasional Paper No.1 International Human Rights Law Institute, De Paul University College of Law, 1996). It is interesting to note that the EC decided to commission an investigative mission into the treatment of Muslim women during the conflict, but failed to do the same for Croat or Serbian women. As Susan Brownmiller previously pointed out in her discussion of the mass rape in Bangladesh, mass rape in war is not unique. The number of rapes per capita during the nine-month occupation of Bangladesh, for example, was not greater than the incidence of rape during one month of occupation in the city of Nanking in 1937 (estimated at up to 400,000), than per capita incidence of rape in Belgium and France as the German army marched unchecked during the first three months of World War I, nor greater than the violation of women in 'every village' in Soviet Russia in World

War I. In S. Brownmiller, 'War', in *Against Our Will: Men, Women and Rape* (London: Penguin Books, 1975), at 86.

16 On the emergence of Serbian nationalism, for example, Spyros Sofos has argued that this was promoted by mobilising elements of popular and folk culture, including historically conditioned fears and anxieties. Slobodan Milošević, then a still relatively young leader, placed himself at the heart of the emerging nationalist movement after his 1987 visit to Kosovo Polje, where he pledged to protect the members of the Serbian and Montenegrin minority in the province from 'persecution by the Albanian majority'. By adopting a nationalist rhetoric, allying himself with the Serbian Orthodox church and reinforcing the moral panic regarding the 'Albanisation' of Kosovo by mobilising aspects of folk and popular culture, Milošević was then able to capture the leadership. For a more in-depth discussion, see S. Sofos, 'Inter-Ethnic Violence and Gendered Constructions of Ethnicity in the Former Yugoslavia', 2 *Social Identities* (1) (1996), at 73, 79.

17 In relation to the phenomenon of sexual violence, Sofos has argued that the objectification and marginalisation of women can be explained by anthropological research on the pastoralist cultures of the rural and mountainous areas of Bosnia-Herzegovina, Montenegro and Serbia, from which most of the Serb, Croat and Muslim irregulars and the majority of their leadership originated. These were also the areas, where most of the conflict took place. Thus, according to Sofos' anthropological readings of the marginalisation of women in kinship groups and in the cultural life of the community, it is Balkan pastoralist culture, where women are not deemed significant components of the nation, that is to blame for the high incidence of rape. It is this pastoralist culture that perceives rape as an act of 'fertilization' of women, an acceptable way of rectifying historical injustice, the loss of contested lands, and the sacrifices of each of the warring communities.

18 Ibid at 87.

19 Political theorist Elizabeth Jane Wood has produced interesting research into the variations of the use of sexual violence during war arguing that whereas in some conflicts sexual violence is widespread, such as in Rwanda or Yugoslavia, in others – including ethnic conflicts – such as Sri Lanka, or Israel/Palestine it is relatively limited. The assertion that sexual violence against women necessarily accompanies war strategies is thus placed in doubt, and it contradicts the more dominant discourses on violence against women, which locate it across the spectrum of modern-day armed conflict affecting women on a widespread scale. In E. Wood, 'Variation in Sexual Violence during War', 34 *Politics & Society* (2006), at 307–341; see also: E.J. Wood, 'Armed Groups and Sexual Violence: When is Wartime Rape Rare?', 37 *Politics & Society* (2009), 131.

20 W. Brown, 'Revealing Critique: A Response to Kenneth Baynes', 28 *Political Theory* (2000), at 469, 477.

21 W. Brown, 'Gender in Counterpoint', 4 *Feminist Theory* (2003), at 365, 367.

22 D. Otto, 'Lost in Translation: Re-Scripting the Sexed Subjects of International Human Rights Law', in Anne Orford (ed.), *International Law and Its Others* (Cambridge: Cambridge University Press, 2007), at 320.

23 In Buss (2007), at 6.

24 In Brown (2006), at 15.

25 Ibid at 15.

26 Brown's understanding of 'politicisation' is far broader than the classical liberal understanding, which is largely limited to the democratic legislative process. In Brown (2000), at 475.

27 Brown (2006), at 15.

28 Brown's understanding of 'politicisation' is far broader than the classical liberal understanding, which is largely limited to the democratic legislative process. In Brown (2000), at 475.

29 Ibid at 15.

30 As Brown points out, 'Substituting a tolerant attitude or ethos of political redress of inequality or violent exclusions not only reifies politically produced differences, but reduces political action and justice projects to sensitivity training.' In short, a justice project is replaced with a therapeutic, or behavioural one. Ibid.
31 The reduction of freedom to rights and of equality to equal standing before the law often eliminates from view many sources of subordination, marginalisation and inequality that organise liberal democratic societies and fashion their subjects. Ibid.
32 Ibid at 17.
33 C. Douzinas, *The End of Human Rights* (Oxford: Oxford University Press, 2000), at 11.
34 Ibid at 11.
35 The return to humanism in the law is particularly well illustrated in Gary Bass' in-depth account of the inside machinations underlying the ICTY. Describing the rather chaotic first few years of the ICTY's life he argues that the act of establishing the Yugoslav Tribunal was an 'act of tokenism' by the world community, which despite being largely unwilling to sacrifice its own soldiers and military through military intervention of Yugoslavia did not mind creating an institution that would give the 'appearance' of moral concern. These considerations thus point to the infusion of morality into the law as a means of addressing serious violations of international humanitarian law. In G. Bass, *Stay the Hand of Vengeance: The Politics of War Crimes Tribunals* (Princeton, NJ: Princeton University Press, 2000), at 207.
36 M. Koskenniemi, 'Between Impunity and Show Trials', 6 *Max Planck Yearbook of United Nations Law* (2002), at 13.
37 Koskenniemi cites Hannah Arendt's critique of the Eichmann trial for its inability to provide an understanding of the way the Shoah came about not as a series of actions by deviant individuals with a criminal mind but through 'Schreibtisch' acts by obedient servants of a criminal state.
38 W. Brown, 'Symptoms: Moralism as Anti-Politics', in W. Brown (ed.), *Politics out of History*, (Princeton, NJ: Princeton University Press, 2001), at 18, 40.
39 See for example D. Otto, 'Rethinking Universals: Opening Transformative Possibilities in International Human Rights Law', 18 *Australian Yearbook of International Law* (1997), at 1, 12.
40 Duško Tadic, for example, would be considered a relatively marginal figure within the Yugoslav conflict because of his low-ranking status within the Bosnian-Serb paramilitary hierarchy. Gary Bass best invokes the sense that Tadic was only of marginal significance by describing the appearance of Tadic in the courtroom in the following way: 'He is not a man of great importance. He is neither a president, nor a general, nor, by all accounts, a person with great political aspirations, or indeed any particular ambition.' Bass describes the physical stature of Tadic as 'short, with small eyes, visibly nervous and subdued.' In Bass (2000), 206. Tadic, in fact, merely served as a low-level civilian traffic officer. Prosecutor v. Tadic, (IT94–1-T), Opinion and Judgement, (IT-94–1-T) (7 May 1997) at paras 526,533. For an insightful account of the Tadic judgement, see also: M. Scharf, 'The First Defendant: The Tale of Dusko Tadic', in *Balkan Justice* (Durham, NC: Carolina Academic Press, 1997), 93.
41 Douzinas (2006), 19.
42 Ibid at 19–20.
43 Ibid at 2.
44 Ibid at 7.
45 Brown argues that contemporary identity politics (including feminism) is traceable to Nietzschean slave morality, in which the subject (of feminism/identity politics) feels morally right and politically righteous because she is disadvantaged. According to Nietzsche, ressentiment channels the subject's otherwise unendurable

suffering into a 'negative form of action', deploring the nature's 'true reaction', as well as denouncing power and action as themselves morally wrong. Brown sees in identity politics the enactment of the moralising revenge of the powerless, 'the triumph of the weak as the weak', which is as likely to seek generalised political paralysis . . . as it is to seek its own or collective liberation through empowerment'. W. Brown, 'Postmodern Exposures, Feminist Hesitations', in *States of Injury: Power and Freedom in Late Modernity* (Princeton, NJ: Princeton University Press, 1995), at 43–45.

46 D. Kennedy, 'The International Human Rights Movement: Part of the Problem?', 15 *Harvard Human Rights Journal* (2002), at 101, 114.

47 A. Cassese, *International Criminal Law* (Oxford: Oxford University Press, 2003), at 335.

48 But as Dianne Otto argues in her poignant critique of human rights standards, 'Far from being "universal", the dominant paradigm of human rights erases or compromises human traditions and experience that are not commensurate with Europe's androcentric standards of human dignity. Further, the way in which international human rights normativity is currently understood depends on the foundational belief that absolute, value-free universal knowledge is possible.' European knowledge 'masquerades' as universal knowledge in the form of human rights law, erasing context and specificity, while privileging heterosexual European male likeness in a world of 'enormous diversity'. In Otto (1997), at 15.

49 C. Bunch, 'Women's Rights as Human Rights: Toward a Re-Vision of Human Rights', 12 *Human Rights Quarterly* (1990), at 486.

50 R. Teitel, 'The Universal and the Particular in International Criminal Justice', 30 *Columbia Human Rights Law Review* (1989–1990), at 285.

51 T. Murphy, 'Feminism Here and Feminism There: Law, Theory and Choice' in D. Buss & A. Manji (eds.), *International Law: Modern Feminist Approaches* (Oxford: Hart Publishing, 2005), at 67, 75.

52 Rajagopal (2007), at 275.

53 There is a broad feminist agreement on the importance of the international language of human rights. See for example C. Bunch, or D. Sullivan, or R. Eisler. D. Otto, 'Holding Up Half the Sky, but for Whose Benefit? A Critical Feminist Analysis of the Fourth World Conference on Women', 6 *Australian Feminist Law Journal* (1996), 7.

54 As well as producing knowledge about 'Third World Women', international law has authorised feminists to design rules that contribute to the protecting or saving of other women within the human rights and international criminal legal order. In Orford (2003), at 59.

55 For a critical analysis of the role played by international lawyers in today's globalised context see: P. Alston, 'The Myopia of Handmaidens: International Lawyers and Globalization', 3 *European Journal of International Law* (1997), 43.

56 Brown (2006), at 19.

57 In Brown (2000), at 20–21. On civilisational discourse see Brown (2006), chapters 6 and 7.

58 See: R. Kaplan, *Balkan Ghosts: A Journey Through History* (New York, NY: Vintage Books: Random House, 1994).

59 In Bass (2000), at 214.

60 G. Simpson, *Great Powers and Outlaw States: Unequal Sovereigns in the International Legal Order* (Cambridge: Cambridge University Press, 2004), x. As Dianne Otto points out in her subaltern analysis of international law, the driving force behind the dominant discourse of the international community is the European production of the desire for democracy, the norms of self-determination and sovereign equality. She sees these norms as having been narrowly and unevenly applied to date to a community theorised as a society of nation-states to which European

standards apply universally in practice. D. Otto, 'Subalternity and International Law: The Problems of Global Community and the Incommensurability of Difference', 5 *Social & Legal Studies* (3) (1996), at 337, 356.

61 Byers, M. & G. Nolte (eds.), *United States Hegemony and the Foundations of International Law* (Cambridge: Cambridge University Press, 2003), at 60.

62 S. L. Woodward, 'Violence-Prone Area or International Transition?', in V. Das & A. Kleinman (eds.), *Violence and Subjectivity* (Berkeley, CA: University of California Press, 2000), at 32.

63 The Badinter Commission was composed of the heads of the constitutional courts of France, Germany, Italy, Spain and Belgium and was chaired by Judge Robert Badinter of France. On 16 December 1991, the foreign ministers of the European Community (EC) issued a document entitled 'Guidelines on the Recognition of New States in Eastern Europe and in the Soviet Union along with a Declaration on Yugoslavia'. The heads of states adopted a common position on the process of recognition of new states, including respect for the provision of the Charter of the United Nations and the commitments subscribed to in the Final Act of the Helsinki Charter and in the Charter of Paris concerning the rule of law, democracy and human rights. The EC also demanded that the states guarantee the rights of ethnic minorities and national groups, that they respect the inviolability of all frontiers to be only changed by peaceful means and by common agreement. The states also had to settle by agreement all questions concerning states succession and regional disputes. In a second statement in 1992, the EC agreed to recognise the independence of all the Yugoslav republics fulfilling these conditions. Thereupon, Slovenia, Croatia, Bosnia and Macedonia sent their applications for recognition to the EC, which passed them first to the Badinter Commission. In January 1992, the Commission issued opinions on each of the four claimants' applications, deciding to approve those of Slovenia and Croatia. Thereafter, on 17 September 1992 Macedonia declared its independence, and on 14 October Bosnia-Herzegovina followed suit. As a response to the latter's declaration of independence, Serb-dominated parts of Bosnia held a referendum for a 'common Yugoslav state'. On 25 September 1992 the U.N. Security Council, citing that the U.N. Charter principle that 'territorial gains could not be brought about by force', imposed an arms embargo on all of Yugoslavia. In J. Dunoff, S. Ratner & D. Wippman (eds.), *International Law Norms, Actors, Processes: A Problem Oriented Approach* (New York, NY: Aspen Law & Business, 2002), at 108–109.

64 72 According to Benhabib, cosmopolitan norms of justice, whatever the conditions of their legal orientation, accrue to individuals as moral and legal persons in worldwide civil society. Their unique feature is that they endow individuals, rather than states and their agents with certain rights and claims. In S. Benhabib, *Another Cosmopolitanism* (Oxford: Oxford University Press, 2006), at 16.

65 These discourses are likely to be revived in the context of the capture and arrest of the until then most wanted and high-profile ICTY fugitive, General-Colonel and former Commander of the Main Staff of the army of the Serbian Republic of Bosnia Herzegovina/Republika Srpska, Ratko Mladic on 26 May 2011 in the village of Lazarovac, 50 kilometres north of the Serbian capital Belgrade. Mladic had been indicted by the Tribunal on 25 July 1995 and was a fugitive for almost 16 years. The Statement of the Office of the Prosecutor, Serge Brammertz on the arrest of Ratko Mladic is available at: www.icty.org/sid/10670. Charges against Mladic include genocide; persecution on political, racial and religious grounds; extermination; murder; deportation and inhumane acts (crimes against humanity) and acts of terror and unlawful attacks against civilians and taking of hostages (war crimes). For an overview of the full indictment, see: ICTY Case Information Sheet Ratko Mladic (IT-09–92). Available at: www.icty.org/x/cases/mladic/cis/en/cis_mladic_en.pdf.

66 Koskenniemi (2002), at 11. Mladic stands accused, amongst other serious violations of international humanitarian law, of serious command responsibility for the 1995 Srebrenica massacre.

67 As Bass points out in his description of the U.S. administration's reaction to the start of the conflict in Bosnia-Herzegovina, Warren Christopher, Clinton's Secretary of State, following his tour of European capitals to sound out America's allies on a policy of lifting the arms embargo on Bosnia and launching air strikes against the Bosnian Serbs, at a congressional hearing on 18 May, proclaimed Bosnia a 'problem from hell', born of 'ancient and therefore presumably unmanageable ethnic hatreds'. In Bass (2000), at 214.

2 The evolution of gender-based violence in international law

Part I

Introduction

Violence against women, in particular sexual violence, has been a greatly topical issue in recent years in both feminist and non-feminist legal scholarship and in the popular imagination. There have been important legal developments within international law, which have provoked much academic and, in particular, legal commentary. On one level, the book contributes to this commentary. At the same time, its aim is to add to a broader feminist theory, which engages with questions of human rights, identity, gender, armed conflict, culture and violence.

The chapter provides a sense of the status of women's human rights in international law by revisiting the incorporation of gender-based violence into the human rights framework as a significant moment for feminist activism and scholarship. It aims is to show the symbiotic relationship between the evolution of gender-based violence in international human rights law and the legal recognition of acts of wartime sexual violence. By charting the most crucial human rights developments from a feminist perspective, it provides a sense of the importance of sexual violence in feminist discourses, while at the same tightening its analytical grip by interrogating the effects produced by the criminalisation of gender-based violence in international law. It questions whether in spite of the incorporation of gender-specific harms against women, or the adoption of gender mainstreaming policies, feminist inclusion strategies might have, nonetheless, reproduced unequal relations of power in their efforts to make women's gender-specific human rights violations legally identifiable.

Part II provides a brief definitional background of how gender replaced the term 'women' in the international legal vocabulary and it explains why it has become the preferred strategic trope for feminist legal scholars. It outlines why gender-based violence is a topic of constant interest to feminist legal scholarship and it looks at the conceptual and definitional hurdles of incorporating the term 'gender' into the Rome Statute.

Part III gives some essential background in respect of the institutionalisation and incorporation of gender-based violence into international law by charting the key stages in the recognition in international law of women's rights as human rights. In this way, it prepares the ground for the ensuing analysis, which turns increasingly critical in later chapters. Part IV addresses the policy of gender mainstreaming, which has been described as having become the 'mantra'[1] in international institutions, and is a technique used for responding to the inequalities between men and women that is prevalent across the majority of United Nations institutions. Gender mainstreaming strategies have increasingly been deployed in U.N. Security Council Resolutions as a means of visibilising gender-based violence against women during armed conflict, while at the same time seeking to increase female participation in peace processes and truth and reconciliation mechanisms. The segment also overviews the salient feminist criticism made in relation to these strategies, adding critical perspective to the debate by querying the potential of international humanitarian law to achieve substantive gender equality. Part V provides the conclusion.

Part II

The emergence of 'gender' in contemporary human rights discourses

The use of the term 'gender' is ubiquitous in international human rights discourses today. It has to a significant extent replaced 'the woman' from international legal texts.[2] According to feminist historian Joan Wallach Scott, gender denotes the social organisation of the relationship between the two sexes.[3] In its simplest usage, gender is a synonym for women. But rather than using the politically charged term 'women', American feminists in particular began to make usage of this trope to evoke the fundamental sense of social inequality based on distinctions around sex. Gender, therefore, carries an implicit rejection of the biological determinism inherent in the use of terms such as 'sex' or 'sexual difference'. Moreover, gender stresses the relational aspect of normative definitions of femininity, a key advantage from a feminist perspective.[4] As a substitute term for women, it also carries the suggestion that information about women is necessarily information about men, that one implies the study of the other. As Scott has put it, 'This usage insists that the world of women is part of the world of men, created in and by it.'[5]

Given its focus on social relations between the sexes and its explicit rejection of biological explanations, such as those that locate diverse forms of female subordination in women's ability to give birth and men's greater muscular strength, gender is understood as a cultural construct, a system of relationships that may include sex, but is not entirely determined by sex or sexuality.[6] From the author's point of view, the most significant development in relation to the deployment of gender in contemporary human rights discourses is its disassociation from the politics of feminism. As Scott has put it:

> Gender does not carry with it a necessary statement about inequality or power, nor does it name the aggrieved and (hitherto invisible) party.[7]

This, for instance, renders it distinctly different from the term 'women's history', which proclaims its politics by asserting that women are valid and historical subjects. Gender includes but does not name women and therefore seems to pose no critical threat to the official language of international law.[8]

i) The Rome Diplomatic Conference

By the time of the 1998 Rome Diplomatic Conference,[9] which had seen unprecedented and sustained feminist lobbying and advocacy take place, gender no longer seemed a controversial term, but an acceptable part of the international legal vocabulary with a majority of states having expressed support for the integration of gender-specific provisions. The Rome Diplomatic Conference served as the precursor to the establishment of the International Criminal Court, the world's first permanent international criminal court.[10] In 1998, the term 'gender' was used and defined for the first time in a legally binding international treaty, the Rome Statute of the International Criminal Court. While gender was not specifically incorporated into the statutes of the previous two ad hoc tribunals, feminist advocates made sure that it would be defined this time. The incorporation of gender as a separate identity category in Article 7(3) of the Rome Statute was the result of highly contentious negotiations and discussions over its meaning serving as a lightening road for conservatives who held strong concerns over its perceived sexual connotations. Article 7(3) reads as follows:

> For the purposes of this Statute, it is understood that the term 'gender' refers to the two sexes, male and female, within the context of society. The term 'gender' does not indicate any meaning different from the above.[11]

The adoption of this term mirrored the increasingly common use of the term in international human rights law over past decades. Naming crimes committed in armed conflict as gender crimes was, moreover, seen as raising increased global awareness of the sexually targeted nature of the crimes,[12] which historically had been accepted as inevitable bi-products or 'spoils of war' and were at the time consistent with women's status in international law. The incorporation of gender within the Rome Statute, moreover, highlighted the strong, organised women's movement represented by the Women's Caucus for Gender Justice (WCGJ), whose objective was to ensure that a gender perspective would be integrated throughout the Statute.[13] Women's Caucus members were active in lobbying in their countries and capitals before participating in the PrepComs and the Rome Diplomatic Conference.[14] But unlike with other identity markers such as race and ethnicity, the definition and incorporation of gender drew far louder protest. From the very beginning, and especially during the negotiations, the Women's Caucus had to deal with fierce opposition from an alliance between anti-choice groups and delegations representing states where discriminatory treatment is justified through religion.[15] The Women's Caucus pushed for the term 'gender' as opposed to sex because of the latter's reference to the biological differences between men and women, whereas gender typically denotes the socially constructed roles of men and women.[16] It similarly regarded the term 'gender crimes' preferable to sexual violence because of its inclusion of crimes which target men or women because of their gender roles regardless of any sexual element.[17]

Given the tensions underlying the negotiations, some feminist commentators viewed the outcome as a victory for women's rights because the narrower terms 'sex' and 'sexual violence' had been eschewed in favour of the term 'gender crime' to denote the sociological differences between men and women.[18] But other observers disagreed, pointing out that the definition was 'oddly worded', 'circular' and reflective of the 'constructive ambiguity' underlying the negotiations.[19] This reflected the tension within feminist legal discourse between those who hailed the definition as a spectacular victory for women's human rights, and others who decried the conflation of gender and sex, the limitations of the reference to the 'context of society', the potential for the exclusion of sexual orientation, and the sidelining of other gender issues.[20]

The next segment charts the social, political and moral difficulties encountered by advocates, who waged notable battles in order to gain acknowledgment of gender-based violence as a serious human rights violation, mirroring the conceptual struggles described earlier at Rome.

ii) The strategy of promoting women's specificities in the new era of universality

GENDER-BASED VIOLENCE AS SUBJECT OF ANALYSIS

Gender-based violence is an obviously feminist issue, as it is a violation that affects predominantly women.[21] It is also an issue that has long preoccupied feminist and human rights advocates. The Committee charged with enforcing the Convention on the Elimination of All Forms of Violence against Women (the CEDAW Committee) in General Recommendation No. 19 (also known as the 1992 Declaration on Elimination of Violence Against Women) defines gender-based violence as:

> [a] form of discrimination which seriously inhibits women's ability to enjoy rights and freedoms on a basis of equality with men. It includes acts that inflict physical, mental or sexual harm or suffering, threats of such acts, coercion and any other deprivations of liberty.[22]

In international law gender-based violence is now the most broadly accepted term used to denote differential acts of violence committed against women given that its broad remit encompasses harms of a non-sexual nature. It has therefore largely been embraced by feminist scholars. Kelly Dawn Askin, for example, has defined gender-based violence as violence that '[t]argets or affects women exclusively or disproportionately primarily because of their gender'.[23]

The first U.N. Special Rapporteur on Violence against Women, Radhika Coomaraswamy, has described it as a major impediment to women's fulfilment and enjoyment of human rights around the world, such as their participation in social and public life, which prevents the exercise of their democratic rights.[24] The definition also includes violence perpetuated along socially constructed or stereotyped gender roles and it has been understood to refer to violence directed against women because they are women. The previous U.N. Special Rapporteur on Violence against Women, Rashida Manjoo, has argued that gender-based violence has to be situated within a neo-liberal context. According to Manjoo it is a reflection of the fact that women do not share equal social and economic rights with men or have equal access to productive resources. Moreover, capital markets exacerbate women's social and political inequality in a way that impacts their health rights; food and water security; education and housing; livelihoods and labour markets; migration; and conflict, peace and nation-building.[25]

While gender-based violence denotes wide-ranging acts of harm against women such as economic deprivation, sexual violence is a more specific form of gendered violence which has been seen as a direct attack on female honour. Traditional definitions of sexual violence against women often referred to gender-specific acts carried out against distinctly female traits, such as their reproductive capacity.

iii) The public/private dichotomy and the hidden nature of gender-based violence

The path towards full international legal recognition has not been a smooth one as Sally Engle Merry, a leading anthropologist concerned with the interplay of culture and gender, has shown. The location of gender-based violence within the private realm of the family and personal relationships has insulated this form of violence from state scrutiny for a long time, while at the same time naturalising the practice as something inevitable.[26]Similarly, Christine Chinkin has argued that the binary division in international law between the public and the private world and the conceptualisation of the former as superior to the latter has marginalised women from public life.[27] It is therefore unsurprising that gender-based violence has remained hidden from view, as the family is often the site where the most severe forms of violations against women's physical and mental integrity take place. In some contexts, the state has perpetuated this *status quo* by exercising power over family or privacy rights with detrimental consequences for women, pushing certain groups even further onto the margins of society.[28]

Due to its confinement in the private sphere, the recognition of gender-based violence in international human rights law has been slow. Crimes such as domestic violence, which disproportionately affect women, for instance, have been entirely silenced by international law. The public/private dichotomy has ensured that only the more sensationalist forms of violence, of which intimate violence is not a part, get visibilised in international legal texts.[29] Given the more systemic and structural nature of domestic violence, which often takes place in secret, such offences have not been made subjects of international law. To date, there is still not a binding international convention criminalising gender-based violence against women. According to Rhonda Copelon, this is also a direct result of the patriarchal structure ingrained in the social fabric, which serves to perpetuate male superiority and female inferiority not only in international law but in everyday life.[30] This stands in stark contrast to the way in which torture is approached in international law. Although widely practised, torture is universally condemned as one of the most heinous forms of violence, while domestic violence, consisting of equivalent elements, is omitted from the narrative.[31]

Part III

The genealogy of women's human rights in international law

In order to appreciate how gender-based violence became, first, a cause for feminist activism, and, second, a violation of international human rights law it is necessary to resort to feminist activism of the late 1970s and early 1980s when feminist scholars first began to articulate radical strategies. Constructions of sexuality began to be seen as crucial to women's oppression, and feminists argued that discrimination against women was not a side effect of patriarchy, but rather that it was central to the construction of the world along male lines.[32] The key strategies of the feminist movement of the 1990s sought to dismantle the binary division between male/female roles, to protect women's reproductive autonomy, and to incorporate violence against women into the international agenda.[33] More specifically, the aim of the movement was to create an international consensus about the eradication of violence against women in all societies.[34] The liberalist environment of the 1990s was especially conducive to such concerns, allowing feminists to embrace the 'women's rights as human rights strategy', seeking explicit recognition of gender-specific rights abuses as human rights violations.[35] The very public nature of gender-based violence committed during the conflicts in the former Yugoslavia and Rwanda, which propelled the issue to the very top of feminist advocacy in the early 1990s in many ways collided with a feminist liberal renaissance in international law. This visibility of women's human rights issues later also allowed feminists to refocus their attentions onto other types of female empowerment, such as the 'mainstreaming' of women's human rights, as a paradigmatic institutional strategy seeking to promote gender justice in international law.[36] These feminist strategies and achievements proved decisive in the later evolution of wartime sexual violence in international criminal jurisprudence.

Feminist calls for a reconceptualisation of gender-based violence as a human rights violation reflected the mind-set of a majority of Western feminist activists, who in the 1990s had gained a high-profile platform for their ideas. This has, for example, been illustrated by the Violence against Women (VAW) campaign, which has sought to bring to the world's attention the multiple ways in which women face discrimination, as well as drawing attention to the physical and emotional abuse they endure in all areas of life.[37] The VAW movement has been overwhelmingly successful in translating very specific violations experienced by individual women into a more general human rights discourse, having incorporated gender-specific concerns into the fabric of international criminal law through the deployment of legal modalities that create particular subjectivities. According to Ratna Kapur, the VAW campaign has succeeded partly because of its 'appeal to the victim subject', which has quickly morphed into a shared location from which women from different cultural and social contexts can speak. The victim status in particular provided women with a subject that repudiated the 'atomized, decontextualized, and ahistorical' subject of liberal rights discourses, while offering to women a unitary subject enabling them to continue to make claims based on their commonality of experience.[38]

In spite of these apparent successes, many of the current feminist debates around the representation of wartime sexual violence reveal a profound feminist anxiety at destabilising the female subject and rupturing the perceived successes achieved to date in international law. Those that have sought to question current representations of wartime identity in international law and have proposed critical introspection have often been sidelined from the dominant debate and from activism for fear that their concerns would lead to a renewed denial of feminist subjectivity. The book therefore seeks to present the voices of feminists whose views have been largely drowned out in the current era of feminist triumphalism, which witnessed the incorporation of women's human rights into mainstream international legal frameworks.

i) *The paternalistic approach to women in early international human rights treaties*

For as long as masculine subjects have been constituted by international law, so too have women been produced as the necessary 'Other' against which the masculinity of the regime's normative actors could be projected.[39] Right from the outset advocates for women's rights did not start 'with a clean slate', for women had already been constituted as a subjugated category, more often implicitly than explicitly, by international legal instruments that defined what was 'possible in the post-war moment'.[40] In one of the earliest manifestations of international law's production of women as objects of masculine and legal protection, the 1919 Constitution of the International Labour Organization (ILO)[41] described its goals as:

> [t]he protection of the workers against sickness, disease and injury arising out of his employment; and the protection of children, young persons and women.[42]

Subsequent protective instruments included banning women from night work, from exposure to lead, while also mandating 'maternity leave for six weeks following the birth of the child'.[43] The preoccupation of these instruments was 'patently' with the rights of men; women were brought into being only as objects of international law, rather than as its full subjects. But this did not mean that women were entirely absent from international law; rather it was suggestive of the fact that they were implicit in every representation as masculinity's 'Other'.

The early treaties in particular took a paternalistic approach to women, reconstituting the traditional gender hierarchies as 'natural' and thereby misrepresenting the constructed nature of human experience and removing it from discursive contestation.[44] By the time of the adoption of the U.N. Charter in 1945, however, a new space was opened for feminist engagement with international law, primarily through the recognition of the 'equal rights of men and women', 'and the international community's emphasis on the principle of non-discrimination, which sought to ensure universal respect for fundamental human rights without distinction as to race, sex, language, or religion'.[45]

The U.N. Charter directly propagated the idea of universality as an opening that had the potential to jettison the earlier exclusionary gender tropes and constitute a fully inclusive subject in the new era of human rights law. But as Dianne Otto has argued in her critical analysis of the then newly established Commission on Human Rights (CHR), this promise was not fulfilled,[46] as is demonstrated through a review of the work of the Commission on the Status of Women (CSW), which had been established under the guise of the CHR in 1946. One of the central goals of the CSW was the promotion of women's equality, as its members had rejected the idea that sex was an entirely natural category. Their strategy revolved around ensuring that explicit reference was made to rights that were specific to women's experiences, but within the framework of women's equality with men, rather than as protective measures.[47] The members understood their project primarily in the context of the tensions between protectionism and equality, but this perspective ran contrary to more classical liberal ideas, illustrated by the formal approach to equality and the distinction between public and private spheres ultimately adopted.[48] The CSW's views most notably clashed with those of the majority of the CHR, including former U.S. First Lady and President of the Commission Eleanor Roosevelt, who felt that the general prohibition of discrimination based on sex (Article 2) was sufficient to ensure women's equal enjoyment of universal human rights, and that explicit references to women would weaken their position by undermining the meaning of 'everyone', and by introducing rights that were not universal in nature.[49] But as Otto has noted, the majority failed to understand that the imagined universal subject was already gendered and that the 'abstract bearer of human rights' already possessed masculine characteristics, which were reflected in legal standards of equality and non-discrimination. The CSW tried to solve this problem by having women's specific human rights recognised as universal.[50] In line with its equality approach, it sought to explicitly include women as bearers of all human rights, which would make it more difficult to relegate such rights to special categories requiring protective measures. But the inclusion of gendered language was only partial, as the masculine pronoun remained in 14 of the UDHR's 30 articles. The only successful provision was Article 16 on family rights, which recognised the equal rights of men and women 'to marriage, during marriage, and its dissolution' in a hitherto unprecedented development in international law.[51] Article 16 has been considered a significant achievement, given that it moved against the grain of the major traditions that had informed the drafting of the UDHR, while challenging entrenched gender hierarchies. But one of the problems with this declaration, as with other international human rights instruments, is that the trope of the wife and mother in need of protection survived in the text.[52] This is significant for the critical feminist perspective adopted in this book, as the 'reinvigoration' of all three of the marginalised female subjectivities – the figure of the wife and mother, who needs 'protection' during times of both war and peace; the woman, who is formally equal with men, at least in the realm of public life; and thirdly, the victim subject, who is produced by colonial narratives of gender, as well as by notions of women's sexual vulnerability produced by earlier international instruments survived in the refashioned international legal texts, despite the CSW's best efforts not to replicate these stereotypes.

The CSW's acceptance of these provisions is suggestive of the continuing ambivalence in the feminist imagination about protective conceptions of women, especially notions revolving around motherhood. It is also reminiscent of the cultural feminist 'ethics of care' argument, which holds on to the existence of a female core based on women's natural characteristics of caring and nurturing, which are seen as diametrically opposed to the traits of rationality, objectivity and abstractness as the central characteristics defining male subjectivity.[53] Despite some important changes including the opening up of the private sphere to human rights scrutiny and formal equality replacing protectionism as the dominant approach, the main subject of international law remained 'tenaciously masculine', leading Otto to wonder whether the persistence of marginalising representations of women suggests that the discourse of human rights is itself built on histories and structures of domination, and therefore, ironically, 'reliant' for its existence on the reproduction of hierarchical gender subjectivities.[54]

Given that the CSW was unable to effectively promote the rights associated with women's physical integrity and sexual autonomy it meant that the UDHR remained silent in relation to gendered violence and reproductive rights. As Otto has summarised it, the CSW delegates were left with the 'impossible task of conceptualizing women's different experiences in a framework of equality; pressing against the established discourses of protection, salvation and formal equality'.[55] But while their efforts resulted in several important references to equality in the UDHR's substantive provisions,[56] they did not achieve the CSW's goals of including rights that could reflect women's specific gendered experiences. The gendered subjects produced by the UDHR in 1948 were, on the one hand, rendered formally equal, while women's specific gendered experiences were left in the realm of protection.[57]

ii) CEDAW

At the outset and despite decade-long feminist activism in the areas of gender-based violence, the 1979 Convention on the Elimination of all Forms of Discrimination against Women (CEDAW) did not mention violence against women.[58] Nonetheless, it has been central to the incorporation of women into the human rights framework and has therefore occupied centre stage in feminist discourses on international law. Constituting an amalgam of ideas about women's status developed during the 1950s, 1960s and 1970s, and situated in the 'hopeful context'[59] of the U.N.'s International Decade for Women (1976–85) CEDAW has been described as an international bill for women's rights.[60] In calling for universal gender equality, the treaty requires the elimination of laws and institutional practices that violate the core human rights principles of equal rights and respect for human dignity. From a feminist perspective, CEDAW's achievement lies in its articulation of gender equality and state responsibility principles, as well as in its application of these principles to the countries under scrutiny.[61] Moreover, its drafters challenged the conceptual boundaries of human rights law by explicitly reconstituting the universal subject as a woman,[62] while strongly endorsing affirmative action principles through promoting goals based on notions of substantive equality.[63] Another virtue of CEDAW is its distinction of affirmative action principles from protectionist ideas, which is reflected in its advocacy 'against the maintenance of unequal or separate standards'.[64] CEDAW has also been emphatic in the prohibition of discrimination against women in the private sphere, rejecting the boundaries between the public and private space that have often served to perpetuate protective ideas about women. The public/private dichotomy in international law in particular has often served to obscure the extent of gender-based violence perpetrated in the private sphere, such as domestic violence, through failing to regulate violence in the home by, for example, imposing sanctions against the perpetrators.[65] As Rebecca Cook has pointed out, the Women's Convention stands out from other human rights treaties for its eschewal of sexually neutral norms 'usually measured by how men are treated', in favour of a recognition of the distinctive characteristics of women and their specific vulnerabilities to discrimination.[66] Despite the absence of state responsibility for private acts of sexual discrimination, it requires states to take responsibility in accordance with their international obligations under customary or treaty law for substantive breaches originating in the private sphere committed by individuals acting in a non-official capacity. It follows that the state is bound to undertake means to eliminate or mitigate the incidence of private discrimination, despite not being formally bound in international law.[67] CEDAW has in this way effectively contributed towards the visibilisation of women in the public sphere, by reinterpreting human rights in order to reconstitute its subject as a woman.[68] In relation to the right to education, for instance, it has ensured that gender-specific issues affecting women's equal enjoyment such as the elimination of stereotypical representations from educational materials were abolished, or that school retention strategies directed specifically at women and girls were implemented.[69] It has also dispensed – in some instantiations – with the model of comparison with men, such as when it addresses issues around pregnancy and motherhood.[70] Given these significant developments, CEDAW has naturally provided a fertile ground for discussion in feminist legal circles, not all of which have celebrated its achievements.

CEDAW's omissions are therefore just as significant a topic for this analysis as are its successes. Its initial failure to address gender-based violence, such as domestic sexual violence or rape, was a particularly glaring shortcoming.[71] Moreover, rights regarding consensual sex were not included in Article 16 (1), which asks state parties to ensure equal rights between men and women with regards to the 'ownership of property, choice of spouse and choice of occupation'.[72] In addition, and despite its innovative and detailed elaboration of substantive equality, its understanding of sex equality largely continues to evolve around women's functions as mothers and wives. It fails to, for example, include abortion among the guaranteed rights, instead deferring to protective domestic legislation, which possibly impairs women's employment rights on this matter.[73]

Protective representations of women also survive in Article 6 of CEDAW, which requires the 'suppress[ion] . . . of the exploitation of prostitution of women'.[74] As such, it does not recognise the rights of women, either as the victims of forced prostitution or as workers in the sex industry. Instead, it casts all prostitution as 'exploitation' and all prostitutes as always needing protection resurrecting the victim subject evoked by Kapur, while at the same time oversimplifying the complexity of women's economic decision-making, which denies women's agency and reflects gendered anxieties about women's sexuality.[75] Most significantly from a critical feminist perspective is the sense that CEDAW retains all three marginalised subjectivities alluded to earlier on. As Otto points out:

> The 'victim' subject of the discourse of (neo) colonialism is also evident in CEDAW. She overlaps, to some extent, with the protected figure of the prostitute in that the problem driving the adoption of Article 6 in 1979 was no longer the 'white' slave trade but the movement of women from developing countries to the West.[76]

Postcolonial feminist scholars in particular have widely argued that such images have kept alive a distinction between Western women and those 'native' others, who still need the West to speak for them. Such imagery, moreover, has ensured the continued marginalisation of women from the universal frame of human rights,[77] despite the adoption of a treaty specifically to promote women's equality and the innovative efforts of the CEDAW Committee to promote the understanding of equality in substantive terms. CEDAW's failure to promote substantive equality at the outset possibly explains why it took the CEDAW Committee until 1989 to develop an initial recommendation, General Recommendation 12, which finally urged states to consider gender-based violence as a serious issue affecting women around the world.[78] Amongst its key objectives was the requirement placed on states to produce statistics on gender-based violence. This led to a broader recommendation in 1992 that defined gender-based violence as a form of discrimination.

iii) The Declaration on Elimination of Violence Against Women (DEVAW) and the Vienna Conference

The 1992 Declaration placed violence against women firmly within the rubric of human rights and fundamental freedoms and made clear that states were obliged to eliminate violence perpetrated by public authorities and by private persons.[79] Although lacking in binding force, it has been described as a comprehensive document that defines violence against women broadly to encompass physical, sexual and psychological harm or threats of harm in public or private life.[80] Significantly, the Declaration names gender-based violence as a violation of human rights and an instance of sex discrimination and inequality, while attributing the roots of gender violence to historically unequal power relations between men and women based on socially constructed realities rather than on 'natural' or biological attributes, which have prevented the full advancement of women in society.[81] Moreover, it affirms that wartime violence against women violates international human rights and international humanitarian law:

> Violations of the human rights of women in situations of armed conflict are violations of the fundamental principles of international human rights and humanitarian law. All violations of this kind, including in particular murder, systematic rape, sexual slavery, and forced pregnancy, require a particularly effective response.[82]

The Declaration provides a definition of gender-based violence, and it highlights the ways in which violence against women is of relevance to each of the articles of CEDAW by identifying that traditional attitudes around the globe contribute to women's subordinate status, most typically perpetuated through certain stereotypes about women, which allow gender-based violence to be maintained as a legitimate form of women's suppression.[83] Violence against women is one of the crucial social mechanisms which forces women into a subordinate position to men. Further, the Declaration enumerates the rights and freedoms infringed through gendered violence, such as the right to equality in the family and the right to equal protection under the law. As a result, CEDAW now prohibits discrimination and disparaging treatment, including violence against women on the basis of gender. The DEVAW has also proved inspirational to other treaties, such as the Inter-American Convention on Violence, which urges protection against all forms of violence against women, including sexual violence, whether committed in peacetime or in wartime, in the public sphere or in the private sphere.[84] This has prompted Radhika Coomaraswamy to declare the Declaration as the most important international legal effort in the prevention of violence against women. It has been especially singled out for not allowing states the discretion to invoke considerations of custom, tradition or religion as a way of justification for non-compliance with treaty obligations. It certainly symbolises the joint effort of the international community in seeking to combat gender-based violence on a universal scale.[85]

Given the significance of the Declaration, 1994 was the year that saw the universal condemnation of gender-based violence by the U.N. Commission on Human Rights, which culminated in the appointment of the Special Rapporteur on Violence against Women, whose mandate includes the collection of information relating to violence against women and the issuing of recommendations and measures to states to remedy the situation on the ground.[86] Overwhelmingly regarded as positive developments in international law, both the DEVAW and the post of the Special Rapporteur were instituted within six months of the joint appeal of governments and feminist advocates present at the 1993 Vienna Conference. It was the latter forum with its promulgation of the 1993 Vienna Declaration and Programme of Action that proved to be the pivotal moment for women's human rights.[87] The Vienna Conference demonstrated how women could organise successfully at the regional and global levels to advocate on behalf of women's rights. It also provided a forum for women's advocates to express their condemnation of gender-based violence in situations of armed conflict by calling on governments to integrate women's rights into the mainstream of the U.N. system.[88]

Part IV

Gender mainstreaming

i) The 1995 Beijing Platform for Action

The 1995 Fourth World Conference on Human Rights held in Beijing built on the women's human rights momentum earlier created at Vienna and, most significantly, it gave expression to and prioritised the term 'gender mainstreaming' as the mechanism to achieve gender equality.[89] Gender mainstreaming has been defined by the U.N. Economic and Social Council as follows:

> Mainstreaming of gender perspective is the process of assessing the implications for women and men of any planned action, including legislation, policies or programmes, in all areas and at all levels. It is a strategy for making women's as well as men's concerns and experiences an integral dimension of the design, implementation, monitoring and evaluation of policies and programmes in all political, economic, societal spheres so that women and men benefit equally and inequality is not perpetuated. The ultimate goal is to achieve gender equality.[90]

Gender mainstreaming was, moreover, identified as one of the most important mechanisms whereby to achieve the ambitious goal of formal equality for women across all United Nations agencies and non-governmental organisations. It encompassed specifically the adoption of the terminology of gender equality; it stipulated that a gender mainstreaming policy be put into place and that gender mainstreaming be uniformly implemented.[91] By the time of the Beijing Conference, it was evident that the concept of 'gender mainstreaming' had achieved great popularity.[92] It appeared throughout the lengthy Beijing Platform for Action in twelve critical area of concern, including education,[93] health,[94] as victims of violence,[95] armed conflict,[96] the economy,[97] decision-making[98] and human rights.[99] The Platform for Action also asked governments to promote an active and visible policy of mainstreaming a gender perspective in all its policies and programmes, so that before decisions were taken, an analysis of their impact on both women and men was made. According to observers, although a non-binding legal instrument, the Beijing Platform represented a global agenda for change used by women's rights activist to advocate for reform in their respective countries.[100] Given these ambitions, the Beijing Platform commitment to gender mainstreaming was taken up by other U.N. bodies, such as the U.N. Commission on the Status of Women,[101] the U.N. Secretary-General, and then by the U.N. Economic and Social Council (ECOSOC), which organised a high-level panel discussion on gender mainstreaming in 1997.[102] Moreover, the U.N. General Assembly has since been continuously encouraged to incorporate mainstreaming into all areas of its work, in particular on 'macroeconomic questions, operational activities for development, poverty eradication, human rights, humanitarian assistance, budgeting, disarmament, peace and security, and legal and political matters'.[103] As a policy, gender mainstreaming is omnipresent today in the international arena with almost all U.N. bodies and agencies having formally endorsed it.[104] This suggests that this policy is to become standard practice across all of its programmes.[105]

While it is evident that gender mainstreaming has become an integral part of the fabric of U.N. institutions, the same has not necessarily been the case across the U.N. system for the protection of human rights.[106] One reason for the rather muted response of U.N. human rights bodies to gender mainstreaming is the low representation of women in the system, which has contributed to the minimal impact of the policy in the human rights sphere.[107] While it might not have been difficult to encourage the adoption of the vocabulary of gender mainstreaming, there is little evidence of monitoring and follow-up. A consistent problem for all U.N. organisations that have adopted gender mainstreaming policies, moreover, is translating the verbal commitment into action. This is frequently caused by fatigue within the U.N. generated in turn by a lack of adequate support and training.[108] But the problem with gender mainstreaming has not only been one of institutional invisibility. Rather, the way in which this concept has been deployed by U.N. agencies and treaty bodies carries problematic connotations, as the next segment points out.

ii) U.N. Security Council Resolution 1325

Today, eight U.N. Security Council Resolutions dedicated to women, peace and security explicitly call on states to recognise the importance of integrating women closely into peace negotiations and into conflict dispute resolution mechanisms. Despite the feminist critique of gender mainstreaming strategies, U.N. Security Council Resolution 1325, the first-ever resolution to addresses the impact of war on women and promote their contribution to conflict resolution and sustainable peace, has pursued this strategy.[109] The Resolution builds on the commitments of the Beijing Declaration and Platform for Action in calling for the inclusion of women at all decision-making levels, but especially so in conflict resolution mechanisms. This is in light of its concern, as stated in the Preamble, that civilians, made up predominantly of women and children, account for the vast majority of casualties during armed conflict.[110] Acknowledging the absence of a female perspective in peace and reconciliation processes, Resolution 1325 identifies the need to increase female participation at all decision-making levels during the peace process, to expand the role and contribution of women in U.N. field-based operations, and to incorporate a gender perspective into peacekeeping operations.[111] It therefore conceptualises a gender mainstreaming perspective in relation to conflict prevention, peace negotiations, peacekeeping operations, humanitarian assistance, post-conflict reconstruction and disarmament, demobilisation and reintegration initiatives.[112] It also reaffirms the need to fully implement international humanitarian law and human rights law to protect women and girls from human rights abuses, including gender-based violence.[113]

Resolution 1325 is further significant because it marked the first time that the U.N. Security Council turned its full attention to the subject of women and armed conflict, acknowledging the role of women as active agents in the negotiation and maintenance of peace agreements, thus providing a clear legal basis for addressing the issue.[114] On a symbolic level, it marked the impact of war on women and provided high-level recognition that the exclusion of women from conflict resolution is a threat to peace, while on a practical level, it triggered the immediate and ongoing attention of the U.N. to women, peace and security, by providing for ongoing U.N. Secretary-General reporting on its implementation.[115] Peace negotiations and agreements have become a focus of feminist intervention because they respond to the post–Cold War proliferation of peace agreements and the use of negotiated settlements as the key mechanism by which to bring violent social conflict to an end. They therefore correspond to the new liberal impulse earlier discussed in relation to human rights.[116] Given that peace agreements serve to document agreement between warring parties in an attempt to end the conflict and establish politics as an alternative to military violence, the inclusion of women into such negotiations is an important starting point in achieving broader political, legal and social gains for women. The scale of the practice, today, is rather overwhelming, with around as many states having peace processes and agreements as those that do not.[117]

The gender mainstreaming perspective of Resolution 1325 is enshrined in paragraph 8, which talks of the need to adopt a 'gender perspective'. Bell and O'Rourke have remarked that this concept goes well beyond whether the terms 'gender' or 'women' have entered an agreement to include, for instance, how civilians/combatant distinctions are dealt with, how provisions for socio-economic rights are made, what role customary law assumes, to assessing conceptualisations of equality underpinning any new constitutional order.[118] Specific references to women, moreover, are a key indicator of whether a broader gender perspective has been used, or whether the agreement is constructed in terms of gender equality.[119] The most startling finding produced by the study is the finding that out of a total number of 585 agreements, only 92 agreements, or 16 percent mentioned women.[120] However, post–Resolution 1325, quantitatively, references to women have increased, with the rise being more marked where the U.N. had a third-party role. In spite of the modest increase in specific references to women in peace agreements touching on the issues raised by Resolution 1325, this is a rather unsystematic pattern, which indicates that the impact of the Resolution on substantive equality for women has been modest. Despite the lofty ambitions underlying gender-mainstreaming policies, it is far from certain that these normative standards have made a difference, whether they could make a difference in future, or what the negative trade-offs for women might be.

iii) Post–U.N. Resolution 1325

Eight years later, due to a series of normative gaps in Resolution 1325, the U.N. Security Council reiterated its dedication to the eradication of wartime sexual violence in Resolution 1820 (2008), stressing that sexual violence is a tactic of war used to deliberately target civilians 'as part of a widespread or systematic attack against civilian populations', which can significantly exacerbate situations of armed conflict and impede the restoration of maintenance and peace.[121] It called on the parties to armed conflict to cease all acts of sexual violence against civilians and demanded, amongst other stipulations, that armies take appropriate disciplinary measures and uphold the principle of command responsibility, therefore mandating that troops on the ground be trained on the categorical prohibition of all forms of sexual violence against women including the debunking of myths that fuel sexual violence. Further, the Resolution notes that rape and other forms of sexual violence could constitute war crimes, crimes against humanity, or could be a constitutive act of genocide, in a nod to the important legal precedents emerging out of the wartime sexual violence jurisprudence produced by the ad hoc tribunals.[122] In September 2009 the Security Council extended these provisions in Resolution 1888 (2009), which calls for the specific protection of women and girls from sexual violence in armed conflict at the hands of peacekeeping missions. It also calls on already existing measures for the protection of women and children to be enhanced through the identification of women's protection advisers in human rights protection units.[123] Its main focus is on the implementation measures dealing with sexual violence, as its Preamble notes 'the underrepresentation of women in formal peace processes, the lack of mediators and ceasefire monitors with proper training in dealing with sexual violence, and the lack of women as chief or lead peace mediators in United Nations-sponsored peace talks' as impediments to long-lasting peace.[124] Resolution 1888 was immediately followed by U.N. Security Council Resolution 1889 (2009), aimed at increasing awareness and achieving implementation of Resolution 1325 while affirming earlier key peace process provisions. The fourth specific recognition of the gendered dimension underpinning conflict, U.N. Resolution 1889, calls for further strengthening of women's participation in peace processes, recognising women as active players in post-conflict contexts in even greater detail.[125] It calls for the development of indicators to measure the progress of Resolution 1325. This involves in particular the establishment of action plans requiring states to adopt a coherent blueprint for how to tackle gender-based violence across all spheres, both in private and in all other areas of public life, such as in government-related sectors. Moreover, Resolution 1889 recognises sexual violence as a war crime and a crime against humanity. It goes as far as to name sexual violence as a 'tactic of war' deployed against women on account of their uniquely gendered status and their vulnerability to sexual violence, which is frequently exacerbated by the vicissitudes of war.

U.N. Resolution 1960, the U.N. Security Council's fifth resolution on the theme of women, war and peace sets out the United Nations' commitment to a full implementation of Resolution 1325, acknowledging the fact that states have frequently failed to abide by their commitments in this sphere. It also puts forward the rather innovative idea that former participants in war should be actively included in the peace effort.[126] Most significantly, it introduces a 'naming and shaming' procedure whereby states are encouraged to adopt accountability mechanisms to address endemic wartime sexual violence against women perpetrated by non-state actors in particular. In this way, it asks states to develop global indicators showcasing trends in how to most effectively deal with sexual violence. This includes calls for parties to conflicts to develop specific commitments to combat sexual violence and to continue strengthening the policy of zero tolerance on sexual exploitation and abuse by U.N. peacekeeping and humanitarian personnel. It also urges the Secretary-General to engage in continued monitoring and reporting of the actions of state parties, armed groups and U.N. actors in line with earlier resolutions. The Resolution, moreover, notes that sexual violence incidents during wartime continue to be hampered by the notion of impunity and by a lack of prosecution of those most responsible for the commission of such crimes. Resolution 1820, therefore, tries to close the 'accountability gap' earlier identified by Resolution 1325. The Resolution is also targeted at peacekeepers, noting that they are increasingly involved in the perpetration and commission of grave forms of sexual abuse against women. But its shortcoming is that it emphasises women as victims and dismisses difference amongst and between women. In this way, it manifests a form of class and race essentialism in contemporary approaches to women, peace and security.

In 2001, U.N. Resolution 2106, inaugurated in the immediate aftermath of a G8 meeting of ministers, came into place.[127] It calls on those involved in peace negotiations not only to prosecute those most responsible for the commission of crimes, but to analyse the underlying socio-economic causes underpinning armed conflict. The Resolution adds an intersectional dimension to the U.N.'s efforts to tackle wartime sexual violence, acknowledging the multiple layers of discrimination women face in everyday society as a key factor accounting for the rise of sexual violence–related crimes during conflict. It calls on actors to address the long-term consequences of armed conflict and it urges states to fully implement Resolution 1325 in all its forms. The Resolution, once more, notes the vulnerability of women and girls to sexual violence and the gendered nature of this type of harm, acknowledging that economic realities in conflict zones contribute to women's vulnerability to sexual violence.

U.N. Resolution 2122, adopted in October 2013, reiterates the principles set out in the Beijing Platform for Action. It calls on state parties to reaffirm their obligation under the Convention on the Elimination of all Forms of Discrimination against Women (CEDAW) by urging states who have not yet acceded or ratified the treaty to do so.[128] A mid-term analysis, it notes that sexual violence in wartime still remains a persistent, deep-seated phenomenon, which in many conflict situations around the world has gone unaddressed. On a positive note, it remarks that there has been a level of good practice incorporated into the operation of the Secretary-General's efforts to address wartime sexual violence. Moreover, it highlights the need for women's economic empowerment in all areas of life, addressing the contextual and often intersecting dimensions of armed conflict. There is an explicit acknowledgment that the level of vulnerability women experience is often a product of wage inequality and economic exploitation across all sectors.

More recently, Resolution 2242, passed in 2015, signalled the U.N.'s continued commitment to combatting wartime sexual violence.[129] The Resolution reiterates that conflict-resolution and counter-terrorism strategies can no longer be decoupled from efforts to protect and empower women and girls. It stresses the need to integrate a gender analysis on the drivers and impacts of violent extremism, urging more consultation with women's organisations affected by conflict-related violence. It also encourages ambitious new targets, for example, increasing the numbers of female peacekeepers through the use of incentives for troop-contributing countries to be set. It acknowledges that there is a need for more senior women leaders at all levels of decision-making in relation to peace and security. Resolution 2242 also notes the need to train mediators on the impact of including more women in decision-making functions, taking seriously research findings which have shown that women's participation leads to more sustainable peace agreements.

It is difficult to gauge the impact of these instruments on substantive gender equality in wartime, but as the previous discussion has shown, the feminist arguments overviewed need to form a critical part of the debate, as they show that while women may have achieved a sense of formal equality in international law, this has not necessarily guaranteed substantive equality or gender justice.

Part V

Conclusion

The chapter has argued that gender-based violence is today conceptualised as a universal violation of human rights law. In particular as a result of sustained feminist lobbying in the 1990s it has turned into one of the most visible human rights causes animating feminist activists and scholars of varying persuasions and backgrounds. This has been evident, for example, in the contentious negotiations between feminist activists and state representatives around the deployment of a gender terminology in the Rome Statute, as seen in the cultural relativist approach adopted by states to deny the entrenched discrimination of women in everyday life. The reluctance to incorporate gender into the Rome Statute is not only a reflection of the paternalist attitudes adopted by states, but is also a product of international law, itself rooted in patriarchal notions which have ensured a rigid public/private divide between officially sanctioned 'male harms' and violence in the private sphere, such as domestic violence, which predominantly affect women.

Paradoxically, had it not been for the reports of mass rapes in Yugoslavia and Rwanda, which prompted international law to consider different forms of violence against women and to advance related definitions, the law might have remained silent on women's human rights and it might have failed to recognise gender-based violence as a serious human rights violation. The recognition of gender-based violence as a standalone issue of international law has, therefore, contributed to the broadening of traditional definitions of sexual violence against women based on women's reproductive capacities and their specific female traits to take into account different forms of gendered violence, such as female poverty. The realisation that sexual violence is a pervasive phenomenon of armed conflict has, moreover, shifted the perception that such acts occur solely in the private realm, prompting international law to acknowledge the public dimensions of gendered violence.[130] Moreover, the increased focus of the United Nations on women, peace and security – through both a protection and a participation lens – has provided ample opportunities to reinforce normative obligations and commitments undertaken by states in relation to strengthening women's rights during wartime. In addition, as the more recent Resolutions showcase, structural factors that serve as a barrier to effective protection and participation in peace and security negotiations have finally been addressed.[131]

Nonetheless, the chapter has suggested that the enormity of these legal successes came at a cost to the feminist movement. Rather paradoxically, these normative developments have led to much feminist anxiety about any critique that could potentially destabilise female subjectivity, or jeopardise future rights claims for broader global recognition of women's human rights. In short, feminists fear losing their new sense of power. But, as Kapur has argued, the exclusive reliance on the victim subject to make rights claims and slogans based on women's empowerment has some serious limitations, chief among them that the victim subject is based on gender essentialism, or overgeneralised claims about women. These generalisations in particular efface the problems, perspectives and political concerns of women who are marginalised because of their class, race, religion, ethnicity, sexual orientation and/or socio-economic status in society and may therefore be counterproductive to the feminist cause.[132] The chapter has shown that feminist ideas today permeate the institutions of international law. However, while these developments in principle ought to be welcome, questions around the turn of Western feminism to human rights and international criminal law as its preferred mode of deploying power in policy and law-making need to be sustained.

Notes

1 H. Charlesworth, 'Not Waving but Drowning: Gender Mainstreaming and Human Rights in the United Nations', 18 *Harvard Human Rights Journal* (2005), at 1.

2 D. Nadj, 'A Subject without Name-the Inclusion of Gender and the Erasure of the Woman in International Human Rights Law', 2 *Westminster Law Review* (1) (April 2013).

3 J. Scott, 'Gender: A Useful Category of Historical Analysis', 91 *American Historical Review* (1986), 1053.

4 Jane Flax has, for example, has argued that the term 'gender relations' captures gender as a complex set of social processes. Gender as an analytical category and social process is thus seen as relational, while gender relations are complex and unstable processes . . . constituted by and though interrelated parts.' J. Flax, 'Postmodernism and Gender Relations', in L. Nicholson (ed.), *Feminism/Postmodernism* (New York, NY: Routledge, 1990), 44.

5 Scott (1986), at 1056.

6 Ibid at 1056–1057.

7 Ibid at 1056.

8 The term gender was, for example, only included in the 1995 Beijing Declaration and Platform for Action after states agreed that it was to be interpreted according to its 'ordinary, generally accepted usage', and that no new connotation differing from its original usage would be deployed in the Beijing Platform for Action. For a discussion, see: B. Bedont & K. Hall Martinez, 'Ending Impunity for Gender Crimes under the International Criminal Court', 6 *The Brown Journal of World Affairs* (1999), at 66–67; V. Oosterveldt (2005), at 55–56.

9 The Preparatory Commission and Assembly of State Parties (hereinafter Prepcom) conducted the drafting and promulgation of the ICC Rules of Procedure and Evidence and the ICC Elements of Crime. For an extensive critical feminist overview of this process, see: Halley (2008–2009), at 18.

10 The treaty to establish the ICC was adopted in Rome on 17 July 1998 with the affirmative vote of 120 countries at the 'Rome Conference'. See: The Rome Statute of the International Criminal Court, adopted by the United Nations Diplomatic Conference of Plenipotentiaries on the Establishment of an International Criminal Court on 17 July 1998, U.N. Doc. A/CONF. 183/9 (1998), entered into force on 1 July 2002 (hereinafter the Rome Statute). The key provisions of the Rome Statute regarding women's rights are contained in the definitional sections of the statute. The definitional sections in Part II of the statute define the crimes that will come within the jurisdiction of the Court.

11 Art. 7(3) Rome Statute.

12 For a discussion, see: Bedont & Hall Martinez (1999), at 66; Oosterveldt (2005), at 55–56.

13 This was an alliance of feminist legal activists and scholars mostly composed of Canadian and U.S. representatives. They were part of a larger, yet loosely knit global campaign for women's human rights, which identified the 1993 Vienna World Conference on Human Rights as a target for grassroots organising on behalf of women's human rights. Counting about 200 affiliates at the time the Conference began, its overarching aim was to transform existing human rights discourses through the integration of women's rights. It therefore adopted a consolidated and coherent platform for reform and lobbied hard in the Rome Statute negotiations. For a discussion see: Bedont &Hall-Martinez (1999), at 66. As Janet Halley has argued, although a large number of NGOs were involved in the Prep Com I, the WCGJ, as the only nominally women's or feminist organisation, successfully became their coalition leader. As Halley points out, this alone is evidence that it mastered the 'behavioral codes' that gave some NGOs legitimacy. For a critical discussion of its activities, see Halley (2008–2009), at 22–23.

14 Bedont & Hall-Martinez (1999), at 66.

15 These delegations included the Vatican and a core group of Islamic states, who were hostile to the idea of adopting the concept of gender when addressing gender crimes. Ibid at 67; see also: V. Oosterveldt, 'Sexual Slavery and the International Criminal Court: Advancing International Law', 25 *Michigan Journal of International Law* (2003), at 605.
16 Oosterveldt (2005), at 55–56.
17 But some Arab states, for example, objected to the term 'gender', claiming that it may be understood to include sexual orientation. Such positions also served to justify obstructions on many provisions throughout the statute which promoted women's rights. The dispute regarding terminology thus threatened the inclusion of certain gender crimes, of a non-discrimination clause, and of special protective measures under the procedural provisions. In Bedont & Hall- Martinez (1999), at 67.
18 Bedont & Hall-Martinez (1999), at 65–85. For a discussion on the conceptual differences between 'gender' and 'sex crimes', moreover, see: I. Skjelsbaek, 'Sexual Violence and War: Mapping out a Complex Relationship', 7 *European Journal of International Relations* (2001), at 212.
19 Oosterveldt (2005), at 71.
20 Charlesworth and Chinkin, for example, argue that the phrase presents gender as an issue of biology rather than social construction, and that the definition therefore has limited transformative edge. They fault the definition's lack of attention to aspects of social relations that are culturally contingent and without a foundation in biological necessity, as use of the term 'gender' should do. In H. Charlesworth; C. Chinkin, *The Boundaries of International Law* (Manchester: Manchester University Press, 2000), at 335.
21 As Elena Loizidou states, 'Sex and gender are always at the centre of feminist debates'. In E. Loizidou, 'The Trouble with Rape: Gender Matters and Legal "Transformations"', 7 *Feminist Legal Studies* (1999), at 279.
22 United Nations Committee on the Elimination of all Forms of Discrimination against Women, General Recommendation No. 19, U.N. Doc A/47/38 (Eleventh session, 1992). (Hereinafter General Recommendation No. 19), at para 1.
23 K. Askin & D. Koenig, *Women and International Human Rights Law* (New York, NY: Transnational Publishers, 1999), at 42.
24 R. Coomaraswamy & L. Kois, 'Women and International Human Rights Law', in K. Askin & D. Koenig (eds.), *Women and International Human Rights Law* (Ardsley, NY: Transnational Publishers, 1999), at 178.
25 Report of the Special Rapporteur on violence against Women, its Causes and Consequences, Rashida Manjoo, A/HRC/20/16, Human Rights Council, 23 May 2012.
26 In S. Engle Merry, *Human Rights & Gender Violence* (Chicago: University of Chicago Press, 2006), at 25.
27 C. Chinkin, 'A Critique of the Public/Private Dimension', 10 *European Journal of International Law* (1999), 387.
28 The disproportionately negative impact of the private/public binary in international law has also been theorised by Donna Sullivan in the United States context. She has argued that state intervention into private life only seems to have occurred only in relation to disempowered communities, such as black women upon whom the state had sought to impose coercive reproductive health policies in the past. Thus, race, class, ethnicity and sexual orientation have all shaped definitions of what constitutes a family life entitled to protection against state intervention. In D. Sullivan, 'Women's Human Rights and the 1993 World Conference on Human Rights', 88 *American Journal of International Law* (January 1994), at 126–127.

29 R. Copelon, 'Intimate Terror: Understanding Domestic Violence as Torture', in R. Cook (ed.), *Human Rights of Women: National and International Perspectives* (Philadelphia: University of Pennsylvania Press, 1994), at 116.

30 Ibid at 120.

31 As Copelon describes it, 'Like torture, domestic violence commonly involves some form of usually escalating physical brutality. The methods of intimate violence resemble the common methods of torture, and include beating with hands or objects, spitting, punching, kicking, slashing, stabbing, strangling, burning and attempted drowning. The consequences include physical and mental pain and suffering, disfigurement, temporary and permanent disabilities, miscarriage, maiming and death.' Ibid at 122.

32 See for example R. Coomaraswamy & L. Kois, 'Women and International Human Rights Law', in K. Askin and D. Koenig (eds.), *Women and International Human Rights Law* (New York, NY: Transnational Publishers, 1999), at 180.

33 One of the central preoccupations of feminist legal scholarship, as Hillary Charlesworth points out is to silence of women. This sense of inferiority has been reinforced in international law through the exclusive focus on the public sphere at the expense of the private sphere, the latter having traditionally served as the site of oppression for women. Charlesworth, thus, contrasts the male sphere of the workplace, law, economics, politics, intellectual and cultural life with the 'home, heart and family' preserve of female identity, arguing that the public/private distinction operates to obscure and justify men's domination over women. In H. Charlesworth et al., 'Feminist Approaches to International Law', 93 *American Journal of International Law* (1991), at 616. The public/private distinction in international law has extensively been critiqued elsewhere, and in the early and mid-1990s dominated international feminist scholarship. See: H. Charlesworth, 'Human Rights as Men's Rights', in Wolper Peters (eds.), *Women's Rights: Human Rights* (London: Routledge, 1995), 103–114; K. Engle, 'After the Collapse of the Public/Private Distinction: Strategizing Women's Rights', in D. Dallmeyer (ed.), *Reconceiving Reality: Women and International Law*, at 143–157; F. Olsen, 'International Law: Feminist Critiques of the Public/Private Distinctions', in *Reconceiving Reality: Women and International Law*, 157–171; C. Romany, 'State Responsibility Goes Private: A Feminist Critique of the Public/Private Distinction in International Human Rights Law', in R. Cook (ed.), *Human Rights of Women* (Philadelphia: University of Pennsylvania Press, 1994), at 85–116.

34 See Coomaraswamy (1999), at 180.

35 C. Bunch, 'Women's Human Rights as Human Rights: Toward a Re-Vision of Human Rights', 12 *Human Rights Quarterly* (1990); for a critique see D. Otto, 'Holding Up Half the Sky but for Whose Benefit? A Critical Analysis of the Fourth World Conference on Women', 6 *Australian Feminist Law Journal* (1996), 7.

36 The Beijing Declaration and Platform for Action, adopted at the Fourth World Conference on Women in Beijing in 1995 established gender mainstreaming as 'the global strategy for promoting gender equality'. See Gender Mainstreaming: An Overview (DAW/OSAGI, New York, 2001) and Gender Mainstreaming: Strategy for Gender Equality (New York, OSAGI, 2001). At the United Nations, gender mainstreaming was created through the adoption of the Economic and Social Council's (ECOSOC) Agreed Conclusions on gender mainstreaming in 1997 and through the Secretary-General's communication to management the same year. The ECOSOC Agreed Conclusions gave the U.N. women-centred institutions – the intergovernmental Commission on the

Status of Women and the Secretariat institutions, the Division for the Advancement of Women and the Office of the Special Adviser on Women's Advancement and Gender Issues – the mandate to develop, initiate and promote U.N. ge der mainstreaming. The ECOSOC Agreed Conclusions also stressed that gender mainstreaming is a system-wide and broad-based strategy. In short, equality between the sexes should no longer be addressed as a separate women's issue, but the promotion of equality should be part of all U.N. activities. See ECOSOC Agreed Conclusions 1992.

37 See for example: C. Bunch, 'Transforming Human Rights from a Feminist Perspective', in J. Peters & A. Wolper (eds.), *Women's Rights, Human Rights: International Feminist Perspectives* (New York, NY: Routledge, 1995), at 11; R. Cook, 'International Human Rights and Women's Reproductive Health', in Peters and Wolper (eds.), (1995), at 256; I. Gunning, 'Arrogant Perception, World-Travelling and Multicultural Feminism: The Case of Female Genital Surgeries', 23 *Columbia Human Rights Law Review* (1991–92), at 189; R. Copelon, 'Recognising the Egregious in the Everyday: Domestic Violence as Torture, 25 *Columbia Human Rights Law Review* (1994), at 291; D. Otto, 'Violence Against Women: Something Other than a Human Rights Violation?', 1 *Australian Feminist Law Journal* (1993), 159. For an excellent critique of the VAW discourse: see: R. Kapur, 'The Tragedy of Victimization Rhetoric: Resurrecting the "Native Subject" in International/Post-Colonial Feminist Legal Politics', 15 *Harvard Human Rights Journal* (2002), at 1. Also see: V. Nesiah, 'Toward a Feminist Internationality: A Critique of U.S. Feminist Legal Scholarship', 16 *Harvard Women's Law Journal* (1) (1995), at 32.

38 In Kapur (2002), at 1.

39 For an in-depth discussion, see: D. Otto, ' Lost in Translation: Re-Scripting the Sexed Subjects of International Human Rights Law', in A. Orford (ed.), *International Law and Its Others* (Cambridge: Cambridge University Press, 2006), at 318, 321.

40 The UDHR was passed by General Assembly Resolution 217 A (III) (10 December, 1948). For a discussion see also Otto (2006), Ibid.

41 International Labour Organization Constitution (adopted by the Peace Conference in Versailles in April 1919), entered into force on 28 June 1919 and the Declaration concerning the Aims and Purposes of the International Labour Organization (ILO), adopted at Philadelphia on 10 May 1944. Available at: www.ilo.org/ilolex/english/constq.htm. (last accessed in July 2011).

42 Preamble to the Constitution of the International Labour Organization, as contained in the Treaty of Versailles; cited in Otto (2006), at 323 (original emphasis).

43 Ibid at 321–322.

44 Ibid at 322.

45 U.N. Charter, San Francisco, 26 June 1945, entered into force on 24 October 1945, UKTS (1946), at 67, see: Preamble.

46 As Otto documents, the CHR was tasked with drafting the UDHR in 1946. Moreover, the members of the Commission on the Status of Women (CSW), also established in 1946, were active in the drafting sessions, making recommendations aimed at the inclusion of women. The active participation of women together with Eleanor Roosevelt's involvement as Chair of the CHR also made the drafting process unusual in that in formulating their recommendations the CSW members worked closely with women's NGOs, drawing directly on their own experience and feminist efforts during the preceding years of the League of Nations and indirectly on at least five centuries of women's struggles for emancipation. For a critical appraisal of the work of the CSW, see Otto (2006), at 329–337.

47 Ibid at 330. For further discussion, see also: H. Charlesworth, 'The Mid-Life Crisis of the Universal Declaration of Human Rights', 55 *Washington and Lee Law Review* (1998), at 781.

48 The public/private dichotomy in international law has been extensively theorised by leading feminist legal scholars. Thus, Hillary Charlesworth has argued that international human rights law is built on a 'partial and androcentric' foundations that have privileged the 'masculine' worldview. Given that the very structures of the law have been built on the silence of women they have been rendered powerless in both the public and in the private world. The argument is that international law has reinforced this sense of inferiority through its exclusive focus on the public at the expense of the private sphere as the primary site for women's oppression. For a more extensive discussion, see the foundational text: H. Charlesworth, 'What are "Women's International Human Rights"?', in R. Cook (ed.), *Human Rights of Women* (Philadelphia: University of Pennsylvania Press, 1994), at 58–64. Elsewhere, Charlesworth, Chinkin and Wright have argued that the public/private dichotomy operates to obscure women's realities and justify male domination, as its absence of focus on the private dimensions of women's lives contributes to the maintenance of the status quo, which ensures that a 'distinctive women's experience' gets factored out of the international legal process, thus preventing the latter from assuming universal validity. See: H. Charlesworth, C. Chinkin & S. Wright, 'Feminist Approaches to International Law', 93 *American Journal of International Law* (1991), at 616. For another critique underlying the binary model in international law, see: C. Chinkin, 'A Critique of the Public/Private Dimension', 10 *European Journal of International Law* (1999), at 387.

49 Otto (2006), at 330–331.

50 Ibid at 331.

51 The Third Committee of the General Assembly was responsible for the ultimate formulation, which survived by a very close vote despite the resistance from Christian groups to the reference to divorce. Ibid at 332.

52 This is evident from the description of the family as 'the natural and fundamental group unit of society', a provision that reintroduces the suspect language of nature, masking the political character of the family and suggesting that it is still exempt from human rights scrutiny. Article 25, for example, which recognises the right of everyone to an adequate standard of living for 'himself and his family', evidently conflicts with the Article 16 guarantee of equal marriage rights, implicitly giving renewed life to the protected female subject and the masculine figure of the household, the head and breadwinner, who still needs a family wage in the era of universal human rights. Ibid at 333.

53 The 'ethics of care' theory was developed by clinical psychologist Carol Gilligan in her seminal work: C. Gilligan, *In a Different Voice: Psychological Theory and Women's Development* (Cambridge, MA: Harvard University Press, 1982).

54 Ibid at 321.

55 Otto (2006), at 334.

56 Otto cites Arts. 21 (3), 23 92) and 26 (1) as examples. Ibid.

57 Similarly, imperialist constructions of women in international law survived in the UDHR. Ibid at 334.

58 See Convention on the Elimination of all Forms of Violence against Women (CEDAW), 1249 U.N.T.S. 13, 19 ILM 33 (1980), adopted by GA. Res. 180 (XXXIV) (18 Dec. 1979), entered into force: 3. Sept. 1981.

59 Otto (2006), at 338.

60 CEDAW is one of six U.N. Conventions that have been widely ratified and are monitored regularly by the CEDAW Committee. As one of six conventions

forming the core of the human rights system, it has been firmly dedicated to the principle of universalism, or the idea of 'minimal' standards of human dignity that must be protected in all societies. For an extensive overview see Engle Merry (2006), at 73.

61 Furthermore, the process of ratification, preparing reports, and presenting and discussing reports, for example, has been seen as fostering new cultural understandings of gender and violence, given that countries all over the world endeavour to present themselves as human rights–compliant and co-operative with the international regime of treaty laws. For a discussion see: Engle Merry, (2006).

62 As Otto describes, this was done through the expansion of the definition of discrimination against women, which ensured that both direct and indirect forms of discrimination were included and that substantive goals such as those directed towards 'women's enjoyment' and their 'exercise of human rights and fundamental freedoms' were encompassed. Otto cites as an example Article 1 of the Convention, but also points to Article 2 (a) ('the practical realization' of equality between women and men') as another example. In Otto (2006), at 339.

63 Article 4(1) declares 'temporary special measures aimed at accelerating de facto equality between men and women', not to be discriminatory under the Convention, so long as they do not entail the 'maintenance of unequal and separate standards'. Reprinted in: Otto (2006), at 339.

64 Article 4(1).

65 See: Charlesworth, Chinkin & Wright (1991), at 616.

66 R. Cook, 'State Accountability under the Women's Convention', in Cook (ed.), *Human Rights of Women: National and International Perspectives* (Philadelphia: University of Pennsylvania Press, 1994), at 235.

67 As Cook points out, state responsibility arises when a state fails to act appropriately under municipal law in terms of failing to punish offenders or failing to provide compensation for violations of international human rights law. A state also bears liability when it has failed to act to prevent anticipated violation of human rights. Ibid at 237.

68 For example in the sphere of work, unfair dismissal has been redefined to include dismissal on the grounds of pregnancy, maternity leave and marital status. As Otto points, out Article 1 of CEDAW does not limit its prohibition of discrimination to the public sphere. Otto (2006), at 339.

69 Arts. 10 (c) and Art. 10 (f), cited in: Ibid at 340.

70 As Otto points out, it makes available maternity leave with pay or comparable benefits, without the attendant loss of 'employment, seniority, or social allowance', and women's health-related rights have been drafted to include autonomous access to appropriate reproductive health care services, not conditioned on equality with men. Ibid.

71 For a critique, see, for example: S. Zearfoss, 'The Convention for the Elimination of All Forms of Discrimination against Women: Radical, Reasonable or Reactionary?', 12 *Michigan Journal of International Law* (1997), at 912.

72 Ibid at 913.

73 Article 12 (1) of CEDAW requires state parties to ensure 'access to health care services, including those related to family planning', but it only specifies services in connection with childbirth, such as 'adequate nutrition during pregnancy and lactation'. CEDAW, Art. 12(1).

74 CEDAW, at Art. 6.

75 See: Otto (2006), at 341.

76 Ibid at 342.

77 This links in with the fact that CEDAW is one of the most heavily reserved international human rights conventions. As Otto has argued, this indirectly keeps

alive the protective approaches of CEDAW, as the sweeping reservations entered into against CEDAW limit substantially limit state obligations under the treaty. She cites as examples of reservations those entered into by Egypt and Libya, which condition their compliance on CEDAW's consistency with Shariah law. Ibid at 342.

78 United Nations Committee on the Elimination of all Forms of Discrimination against Women (CEDAW Committee) General Recommendation No. 12, U.N. Doc. A/44/38 (Eighth session, 1989).

79 United Nations Committee on the Elimination of all Forms of Discrimination against Women, General Recommendation No. 19, U.N. Doc A/47/38 (Eleventh session, 1992). (Hereinafter General Recommendation, No. 19).

80 Merry Engle (2006), at 23.

81 General Recommendation No.19, Preamble. According to Engle Merry, this statement '[p]laced violence against women squarely within the rubric of human rights and fundamental freedoms' and it made clear that states would be obliged to eliminate violence perpetrated by public officials or authorities, as well as private actors. See: Engle Merry (2006), at 21. On Otto's view, moreover, the CEDAW framework has by way of these General Recommendations strengthened the substantive equality framework that advances the project of 're-imagination' of women's rights by further releasing CEDAW's subject from comparison with men. A further example Otto provides is of General Recommendation 16, which urges state parties to recognise and value women's unpaid contributions and makes it clear that the Committee considers unpaid work in family enterprises to be a form of exploitation of women contrary to CEDAW. See: Otto (2006), at 340.

82 Vienna Declaration and Programme of Action, part. II, para 38.

83 General Recommendation 19 defines gender-based violence as a form of discrimination that 'seriously inhibits women's ability to enjoy rights and freedoms on a basis of equality with men'. Gender-based violence is violence directed against a woman 'because she is a woman or that affects women disproportionately. It includes acts that inflict physical, mental or sexual harm or suffering, threats of such acts, coercion and any other deprivations of liberty.' General Recommendation, No.19, at para 1.

84 Inter-American Convention on the Prevention, Punishment and Eradication of Violence against Women, adopted by the General Assembly of the OAS (9 June 1994), Doc. OEA/Ser.P AG/doc. 3115/94 rev. 2 (commonly referred to either as the Convention of Belém do Para, or the Inter-American Convention against Violence).

85 As she has put it, 'The recognition that violence against women is a social creation allows the freedom to challenge its use and suggest alternative plans and programs for its elimination. It grants opportunities to create a new history in which violence against women would be condemned and not recognized as an inevitable and unchangeable consequence of gender relations.' See Coomaraswamy (1999) at 177.

86 The Special Rapporteur forms part of the special procedures under the newly established Human Rights Council. For a recent overview of the work of the Special Rapporteur on Violence against Women, its Causes and Consequences, see: '15 Years of the United Nations Special Rapporteur on Violence Against Women (1994–2009) – A Critical Review'. Available at: www2.ohchr.org/english/issues/women/rapporteur/docs/15YearReviewofVAWMandate.pdf; (last accessed in April 2011). For a discussion of the key roles inherent in the post, see: H. Charlesworth & C. Chinkin, *The Boundaries of International Law* (Manchester: Manchester University Press, 2000), at 149–150.

87 The concluding document formally recognises the human rights of women as 'an inalienable integral and indivisible part of human rights'. General Assembly A/CONF. 157/23 World Conference on Human Rights, Vienna Declaration and Programme of Action, adopted at the World Conference on Human Rights in Vienna, U.N. Doc. A/CONF. 157/23 (12 July 1993), at para 18. Available at: www.unhchr.ch/huridocda/huridoca.nsf/(symbol)/A.CONF.157.23. En?OpenDocument (last accessed in May 2011).

88 Beijing Declaration and Platform for Action, Fourth World Conference on Women, A/CONF.177/20 (1995) and A/CONF.177/20/Add.1 (1995) (15 September 1995).

89 For an in-depth discussion of the 1995 Beijing Platform for Action, see: C. Moser & A. Moser, 'Gender Mainstreaming since Beijing: A Review of Success and Limitations in International Institutions', 13 *Gender and Development* (2) (July, 2005), at 11.

90 United Nations (1997) 'Report of the Economic and Social Council for 1997', A/52/3, 18 September, 1997.

91 Moser & Moser (2005), at 11.

92 In Charlesworth, (2005), at 1, 3.

93 See *Beijing Declaration and Platform for Action*, 1 Report of the Fourth World Conference on Women, Beijing 4–15 September 1995, U.N. Doc A/CONF.177/REV.1, U.N. Sales No. 96 IV.13 (1996), at para 79.

94 At para 105.

95 Ibid at para 123.

96 Ibid at para 141.

97 Ibid at para 164.

98 Ibid at para 189.

99 Ibid at para 229.

100 Oosterveldt (2005), at 82.

101 Foreign & Commonwealth Office (U.K.), Inclusive Government: Mainstreaming Gender into Foreign Policy (2004), cited in Charlesworth (2005), at 3.

102 Provisional Summary Record of the 20th Meeting, U.N. ESCOR, 1997 Substantive Sess., U.N. Doc. A/52/3/Rev. 1 (1997). 181 Report of the Economic and Social Council for the Year 1997, U.N. GAOR, 52nd Sess., Supp. No.3, at 24, U.N. Doc. A/52/3 Rev. 1 (1997).

103 Report of the Economic and Social Council for the Year 1997, U.N. GAOR, 52nd Sess., Supp. No.3, at 24, U.N. Doc. A/52/3 Rev. 1 (1997).

104 The gender policy of the World Health Organisation (WHO), for instance states that the 'WHO, will as a matter of policy and good public health practice, integrate gender considerations in all facets of its work.' See: WHO Gender Policy: Integrating Gender Perspectives in the Work of WHO 1 (2002). Cited in Charlesworth (2005), at 5.

105 This has been similarly reiterated across various U.N. mission statements, such as the U.N. Development Programme (UNDP); U.N. Educational, Scientific and Cultural Organization (UNESCO); the Food and Agricultural Organization (FAO); the World Bank; and the International Labour Organization (ILO). Moreover, gender mainstreaming is also firmly entrenched inside the European Union and the Organization for Security and Cooperation in Europe and the Commonwealth. Ibid at 6.

106 For details of the response of human rights treaty bodies between 1995 and 1997, see A. Gallagher, 'Ending the Marginalization: Strategies for Incorporating Women into the United Nations Human Rights System', 19 *Human Rights Quarterly* (1997), at 283. For a survey of the six treaty bodies' work in this area, see: S. Kouvo, 'The United Nations and Gender Mainstreaming: Limits and

Possibilities', in D. Buss & A. Manji (eds.), *International Law: Modern Feminist Approaches* (Oxford and Portland, ON: Hart, 2006), at 237.

107 For example in 2004, women made up approximately 40 percent of the overall membership of the human rights treaty bodies, but most women (74 percent) were concentrated in two committees: the Committee on the Elimination of Discrimination against Women and the Committee on the Rights of the Child, whereas the overall proportion of women in other committees was 15 percent. In Charlesworth (2005), at 7.

108 Ibid at 11.

109 United Nations Security Council Resolution 1325 (S/Res/1325) on Women, Peace and Security, adopted by the Security Council at its 4213th meeting, 31 October 2000. S/Res/1325 (2000) (hereinafter U.N. Resolution 1325).

110 The Preamble also expresses concern for refugees and internally displaced persons, as they are increasingly targeted by combatants and armed elements. See: S.C. Resolution 1325, Preamble.

111 Ibid at paras 1–5.

112 Resolution 1325 has been described as a 'thematic' resolution best understood as a Chapter VI U.N. Charter non-binding resolution. Its legal authority was enhanced by the fact that it was passed unanimously, and that the resolution uses the language of obligation. For the status and nature of the Resolution, see: C. Bell & C. O'Rourke, 'Peace Agreements or Pieces of Paper? The Impact of UNSC Resolution 1325 on Peace Processes and Their Agreements', 59 *International and Comparative Law Quarterly* (October 2010), at 941, 943. For the interplay between U.N. Security Council Resolution 1325 and CEDAW, see 'Women, Peace and Security: CEDAW and Security Council Resolution 1325: A Quick Guide'. Available at: www.unrol.org/files/CEDAWandUNSCR1325_eng.pdf. (last accessed in June 2011).

113 SC Res 1325, at paras 9, 10, 11 and 12.

114 Ibid at 943.

115 SC Res. 1325, at para 17.

116 Bell & O'Rourke (2010), at 946.

117 Figures provided by the authors show that before the adoption of Resolution 1325, 68 percent of a total of 399 peace agreements of a total of 585 peace agreements entered into between 1 January 1990 and 1 May 2010 were signed, while after the Resolution, 32 percent or 186 agreements were signed. Ibid at 955–956.

118 Bell & O'Rourke (2010), at 945.

119 They make this determination by deploying a quantitative analysis of the number counts of specific references made to women in peace agreements. This helps them assess whether the 'gender perspective' mandated by the Resolution has been adopted. Ibid at 945–946.

120 As the authors make explicit, this figure includes all references to women, including those which limited rather than furthered equality, and those with only small provisions. Ibid at 955.

121 When agreements mentioning women were disaggregated with reference to the timing of the Resolution 1325, 42 agreements mentioning women were reached before Resolution 1325 was passed, constituting 11 percent of all agreements signed before 1325, while 50 agreements mentioning women were reached after Resolution 1325 was passed, constituting 27 percent of all agreements signed after Resolution 1325. The results thus indicate a significant increase in references to women in peace agreements after Resolution 1325 was passed. Ibid at 956.

122 Ibid at para 4.

123 SC Resolution 1888, United Nations Security Council Adoption of Text Mandating Peacekeeping Missions to Protect Women, Girls from Sexual Violence in Armed Conflict (SC/9753), at Security Council 6195th Meeting, 30 September 2009. The text also calls on the strengthening of monitoring and reporting on sexual violence, the retraining of peacekeepers, national forces and police, and on boosting the participation of women in peace-building and other post-conflict processes, thus closely mirroring the principles underlying the U.N.'s policy on gender mainstreaming.

124 Paragraph 17 urges that 'the issues of sexual violence be included in all United Nations–sponsored peace negotiation agendas', and also that 'the inclusion of sexual violence issues from the outset of peace processes in such situations, in particular the areas of pre-ceasefires, humanitarian access and human rights agreements, ceasefires and ceasefire monitoring, DDR [demobilisation, demilitarisation and reintegration] and SSR [security sector reform] arrangements, vetting of armed security forces, justice, reparations, and recovery/development'. United Nations Security Council Resolution 1888, at para 17.

125 United Nations Security Council Resolution 1889 (S/Res/1889), adopted by the Security Council at its 6196th meeting (5 October 2009), (S/Res/1889), (S/Res/1889).

126 Gina Heathcote, 'Naming and Shaming: Human Rights Accountability in Security Council Resolution 1960 (2010) on Women, Peace and Security', *Journal of Human Rights Practice* (2012).

127 United Nations Security Council Resolution 2106 (S/Res/2106), adopted by the Security Council at its 6984th meeting, (24 June 2013), (S/Res/2106).

128 United Nations Security Council Resolution 2122 (S/Res/2122), adopted by the Security Council at its 7044th meeting, (18 October 2013), (S/Res/2122).

129 United Nations Security Council Resolution 2242 (S/Res/2242), adopted by the Security Council at its 7533rd meeting, (13 October 2015), (S/Res/2242).

130 Beijing Declaration and Platform for Action, Fourth World Conference on Women, A/CONF.177/20 (1995) and A/CONF.177/20/Add.1 (1995) (15 September 1995) at: Section E: Women and Armed Conflict Diagnosis.

131 Rashida Manjoo, 'Women, Peace and Security-Negotiating in Women's Best Interests', 7 *Global Policy Volume* (2) (2016).

132 Hence, intersectional theories became the preferred mode of feminist analysis in relation to accounting for the multiple dimensions of women's subordination in society, as chapter 4 goes on to illustrate.

3 The trajectory of wartime sexual violence: from marginalised phenomenon of wartime history to highly visible offence in international criminal law

Part I

Introduction

Sexual violence against women has been a greatly topical issue within recent years in both scholarship and the popular imagination. There have been important legal developments within international law which have provoked much academic, and in particular, legal commentary. On one level, the book contributes to this commentary. At the same time, it aims to contribute to a broader feminist theory which engages with questions of human rights, identity, gender, armed conflict, culture and violence.

This chapter provides the context for the analysis of key ICTY wartime sexual violence jurisprudence, as it contains a historical overview of distinctive events of gendered violence in armed conflict and illuminates some of the reasons for its traditional marginalisation from international law. Moreover, it provides a sense of the gendered dimensions of contemporary international wartime sexual violence jurisprudence by focusing on the key legal developments that have emerged from the international ad hoc tribunals for Yugoslavia and Rwanda. It does not conduct a comprehensive study of the historical roots of wartime sexual violence, but singles out for analysis a handful of ICTY and ICTR decisions adjudicated to date, as these have arguably dramatically altered the legal standing of wartime sexual violence in international law.

The chapter is primarily intended to give a general sense of how sexual violence crimes have evolved in modern-day international criminal law, in this way preparing the ground for analysis carried out in subsequent chapters. It provides a summary of the main legal developments emerging from the two international ad hoc tribunals, as they share similar legal characteristics, normative objectives, and are both considered international community projects. They stand in contrast to the more localised hybrid tribunals such as the Special Court for Sierra Leone,[1] the Extraordinary Chambers in the Courts of Cambodia,[2] the Special Tribunal for Lebanon[3] and the East Timor Tribunal[4] that were set up with the consent and complicity of the respective state affected. Most notably, the evolution of gender-based crimes is manifested through a discussion of the key legal developments shaping contemporary international criminal law in the area of wartime sexual violence. The feminist debate accompanying key wartime sexual violence advancements in international criminal law constitutes an integral part of the analysis.

Wartime sexual violence is obviously a feminist issue, as it is a crime that disproportionately affects women. As a topic, it has received prominence primarily as a result of the prosecution of gender-related crimes in international criminal tribunals. Its relevance as a subject of interest has been sustained by a plethora of legal successes delivered by international criminal tribunals, which have on numerous occasions successfully reinterpreted, or expanded international humanitarian law to encapsulate the gender-specific harms perpetrated against women. In this way, the tribunals are said to have advanced the twin feminist aims of gender equality and justice into the normative framework of international human rights law, whose key aim is the promotion of equality and anti-discrimination in all areas of public life, regardless of sex.[5]

The chapter provides a snapshot of these developments, while also asking what the prosecution of wartime sexual violence in international criminal law represents for women in the current political and legal moment. It shows how wartime sexual violence has been transformed from a perennially marginalised footnote of history to a widely recognised and theorised phenomenon of armed conflict. A constant theme of the book is to stress that socio-economic deprivation and institutional structures that naturalise women's subordinate status in society are as central in accounting for the widespread sexual abuse of women in armed conflict, yet are often occluded from the legal narrative, therefore invisibilising the underlying conditions of inequality that characterise many women's lives. Just as war has come to be accepted as an inevitable part of history, so too rape has come to be regarded as an unavoidable side product of war, a form of collateral damage, if not a 'just reward' for soldiers engaged in the battlefield. As radical feminist Susan Brownmiller has argued:

> War provides men with the perfect psychological backdrop to give vent to their contempt for women. The very maleness of the military – the brute power of weaponry exclusive to their hands, the spiritual bonding of men at arms, the manly discipline of orders given and orders obeyed, the simple logic of the hierarchical command – confirms for men what they long suspect, that women are peripheral, irrelevant to the world that counts, passive spectators to the action in the center ring.[6]

This segment does not focus upon sexual violence incidences stemming from World War II and it does not analyse the war crimes prosecutions at Nuremberg and Tokyo, as these have been theorised extensively elsewhere.[7] The Nuremberg International Military Tribunal and the International Military Tribunal for the Far East (IMTFE) are central in providing the current context underlying sexual violence prosecutions, as they ushered in the notion of individual responsibility and superior command responsibility for war crimes,[8] while at the same time highlighting the hidden, yet pervasive[9] incidences of sexual violence against women, such as the Rape of Nanking. Part III examines the genealogy of gender-specific provisions of international humanitarian law using a feminist legal perspective. It surveys the principal international humanitarian law treaties that regulate contemporary armed conflict and recognise it as comprising international customary law to show that these have not necessarily had the desired effect of providing for enhanced safeguards for female civilians in armed conflict. Moreover, it argues that the laws regulating armed conflict continue to perpetuate portrayals of women along fixed binaries, which always situate them in relation to men and in this way emphasise women's powerlessness. This part provides the critical legal context for the ensuing analysis, as it cautions against investing too much capital into a legal system that from its inception has reproduced hierarchical relations between men and women.[10] Despite its inherent shortcomings, however, international humanitarian law has been progressive in its ability to reimagine wartime sexual violence as one of the gravest offences against humanity.

Part IV focuses on the key ICTY and ICTR jurisdictional achievements accomplished in relation to wartime sexual violence by analysing the legal modalities through which these offences have been interpreted in international criminal law. It undertakes an analysis of recent developments to show how the subject-matter jurisdiction of the tribunals encompasses sexual violence under different categories of crimes. It also examines other significant legal developments, such as the creation of the Gender-based Adviser in the Office of the Prosecutor (OTP) as another manifestation of the seriousness with which gender-specific concerns are treated in international criminal law, while part V analyses how wartime sexual violence offences against women have been incorporated into the ICTY and reflects on the classification of sexual violence as a form of genocide in the ICTR Statute. Part VI reflects on the most significant legal achievements accomplished by the tribunals, examining in particular the development of the first-ever definition of rape in international law provided in the *Akayesu* case. In this vein, it focuses on specific aspects of ICTY wartime sexual violence jurisprudence, resulting, for instance, in the narrowing of the consent defence in wartime rape cases, which has been widely labelled as a significant victory for the current feminist moment. The chapter prepares the groundwork for the subsequent feminist analysis, which focuses in detail upon their significance as manifestations of a particular brand of feminism, known as 'governance feminism'.

Part II

Rape as an act outside of time: a brief historical overview of wartime sexual violence against women committed during the conflicts in Vietnam and Bangladesh

In her seminal book *Against Our Will: Men, Women and Rape* Susan Brownmiller provides a feminist politico-historical analysis of wartime rape. She places the phenomenon of rape within the context of social and biological realities to unveil its political purposes, and to counter the persistent myths surrounding it. Above all, she counters the perception that rape is a sexual act by showing that it is not inspired by sexual stimuli, but is often driven by political motivations that seek to dominate and degrade.[11] Brownmiller's work can be considered the forerunner, if not the authoritative feminist text on wartime sexual violence. Considered part of the second wave of U.S. feminism, a distinct strand of liberal thought, it is often perceived as representing the feminist perspective on rape and it has been highly influential in the development of reforms concerning rape laws.

It also furnishes contemporary feminism with the idea that wartime sexual violence against women is an extension of the everyday, a space so saturated with women's objectification – whether through pornography or prostitution as endemic social practices – that it constantly glorifies and naturalises violence against women in the private sphere.[12] There has been a notable turn in contemporary feminist scholarship towards the espousal of structuralist ideas in relation to the regulation of wartime sexual violence, which have located the root of the violence in 'oppressive' cultural traditions.[13] In the wake of the 'ethnic conflicts' of the 1990s and the ushering in of the era of 'human rights globalisation', this feminist trend has become more assertive, having assumed a prominent role in international treaty negotiations, diplomatic conferences, and in the drafting of international criminal statutes.

Current feminist investments in international criminal law are heavily rooted in U.S.-centric, Western liberal notions of women's role in society that locate sexual violence against women exclusively within the binary of female subjugation/male dominance. This book argues that the feminist structuralist focus on women's gendered injuries has had the effect of giving new life to imperial and protective subjectivities in international law. Dianne Otto has suggested that this might lead to undesirable consequence for the feminist movement, given that:

> [t]he extensive cataloguing of women's injuries and disadvantages, while clearly necessary for making women's human rights abuses legally cognizable, emphasizes women's helplessness, rather than their agency.[14]

The view of rape as an inevitable by-product of war has long held sway across a majority of the literature on the subject prompting more contemporary feminists to challenge the grain of dominant texts.[15]Certainly, as feminists have aimed to show, part of the explanation for the high incidence of sexual violence is found in the preponderance of inter-ethnic conflict and the disproportionate targeting of civilians in the post–Geneva Conventions era. Moreover, institutional cultures have long considered violence perpetrated by armies against civilians as 'heroic', resulting in a lack of legal accountability for acts of sexual violence. It is within this cultural context that stereotypical conceptions of female identity, which have variously portrayed women as property, chattel or as battle-camp trophies and their bodies as rewards of war, have found fertile ground. The reasons for sexual violence against women during wartime can also be ascribed to the intoxicating effect that victorious armies experience in perpetrating rape as part of a pattern of national terror and subjugation, as well as to the maleness of military institutions and the institutional hierarchies that create a culture of permissiveness for acts of sexual violence, where male bonding often consists of a spiritual connection felt in having exclusive ownership and control over weaponry, paired with the manly discipline of giving and obeying orders.[16]

In the field of war crimes, ideas around the legal characteristics of rape have a long pedigree dating back to Grotius, who is often seen as the 'father' of the laws of war.[17] Using rape as a crucial marker distinguishing 'civilised' from 'barbaric' states, Grotius asserted that the more civilised nations disallowed rape, as for him the distinction turned as much on how states condemned rape as on which states engaged in it.[18] Grotius, moreover, believed that rape of women indexed a hierarchy of states to the extent that rape and the official response to it became two means by which state behaviour was normatively ordered. Carrying distinctly Eurocentric undertones, this view perpetuated the idea that rape would not be committed by the more civilised Western armies, which were deemed more sophisticated than their 'barbarian counterparts'.[19] It is, therefore, interesting to note Brownmiller's observations that a simple rule of thumb as far as responsibility for rape is concerned was that 'the winning side is the side that does the raping'.[20] But given the colonial context, where the West did most of the winning, it is questionable whether this holds true. Certainly, this assumption would not apply to the Yugoslav context, given that the side deemed principally responsible for sexual violence crimes during the Yugoslav conflict were the Bosnian Serbs and by extension Serbia, the vanquished parties of the conflict.

Part III

The role of women in international humanitarian law – a feminist critique

Sexual violence has long been an integral part of armed conflict, and it has, frequently, although not always been deployed in systematic fashion, or used as a 'weapon of war'. In spite of the prohibition of sexual violence in humanitarian law for more than a century, customary international law has historically ignored and failed to punish gender crimes.[21] Moreover, the various and principal international humanitarian law treaties that regulate contemporary armed conflict and make up international customary law – the 1907 Hague Conventions and Regulations,[22] the four 1949 Geneva Conventions along with the annexes to these Conventions[23] and the two 1977 Additional Protocols to the Geneva Conventions[24] – have not necessarily had the desired effect of providing enhanced safeguards for female civilians in times of armed conflict. Neither the Hague Conventions, nor the Geneva Conventions and their Additional Protocols contain definitions of rape. Yet, as Michelle Jarvis has pointed out, despite the absence of any express reference to sexual violence it has always been possible to interpret the grave breaches provisions of the 1949 Geneva Conventions and Protocol I so as to include sexual violence. The category of 'inhumane treatment' has, for example, been defined as a grave breach pursuant to Article 147 of the Fourth Geneva Convention.[25] In the context of classical international criminal law,[26] rape was first explicitly formulated as a crime against humanity after World War II in Control Council Law No. 10, which was enacted by the Allied Control Council for Germany as the basis for the trial of non-major war criminals following World War II.[27] Yet it took as late as the drafting of the Geneva Conventions of 1949 for rape to be first explicitly recognised as an issue particular to women in wartime.[28] The Fourth Geneva Convention 'unequivocally and without precedent'[29] prohibits rape and forced prostitution, despite the absence of rape from the enumerated grave breaches of the Convention, which are subject to universal jurisdiction.[30] This was of great significance from a women's rights perspective, given that international law had been silent in relation to wartime sexual violence allegations at Nuremberg and Tokyo.

The prohibitions of the Geneva Conventions were later supplemented and extended with the adoption of two protocols – Additional Protocols I and II.[31] These primarily reiterate and cement the message that rape is prohibited in both international and internal armed conflicts.[32] Moreover, and in a significant shift away from proprietary and protective notions of women in Article 27 of the Geneva Conventions, Article 76 of Additional Protocol I, applicable to international armed conflicts, states that 'women shall be the object of special respect and shall be protected in particular against rape, forced prostitution and any other form of indecent assault'.[33] The semantic move away from a language of honour to female dignity and respect manifested itself further in Article 4(2) (e) of Additional Protocol II, which prohibits 'outrages upon personal dignity, in particular humiliating and degrading treatment, rape, enforced prostitution, and any other form of indecent assault'.[34] Moreover, and as quoted by the *Celebici* Trial Chamber, Article 4(1) of Additional Protocol II implicitly prohibits rape and sexual assault stating that all persons 'are entitled to respect for their person and honour'.[35] The two protocols also extend the protections of the Geneva Conventions to both international and internal armed conflicts, as well as to periods after a war ends, if the territory is still under foreign occupation.[36]

It, therefore, appears that in its more modern manifestations international humanitarian law has adopted a more progressive approach, by embracing 'dignity' instead of 'honour', although the former term is problematic from a feminist perspective because it still fails to express the fact that sexual assault is a violent crime, or that it is not solely targeted at women because of their reproductive capacities.[37] Moreover, it does not resolve feminist concerns about the overall portrayal of women within international humanitarian law.

In spite of the conceptual shift in the perception of women's legal status in times of armed conflict, international humanitarian law as a discipline has been subject to feminist critique since the early 1990s. Feminist legal scholars have argued that international humanitarian law fails to take into account the gendered experiences of women during times of armed conflict, denying women any sense of subjectivity by conceiving of female identity in wartime through a protectionist lens.[38] The most widely framed criticism has been encapsulated by Judith Gardam, who argues that the gendered hierarchy of armed conflict is mirrored in the language of international humanitarian law, which is firmly rooted in protections based on women's honour and in deeply essentialised sexual attributes, such as chastity and female modesty. Yet, women's honour, a concept constructed by men for their own purposes, has very little to do with the reality of sexual violence experienced by women in armed conflict.[39] But despite having established an unequivocal prohibition of rape, the second paragraph of Article 27 of the Fourth Geneva Convention has been a recurrent subject of feminist legal critique for its deployment of protective language, which aims to shield women 'against any attack on their honour, in particular against rape, enforced prostitution, or any other form of indecent assault'.[40]

The criticism has been that the law provides for women's protection from sexual crimes because of honour, not because of individual autonomy. In so doing, it fails to grasp the gendered reality of war and the more intense, personalised and psychological sense of harm felt by women as result of the sexual violence.[41] In a similar vein, Hillary Charlesworth has argued that Article 27 'assumes that women should be protected from sexual crimes because they implicate a woman's honour, reinforcing the notion of women as men's property, rather than because they constitute violence'.[42] Catherine Niarchos has criticised the idea of linking rape and honour for compromising women's 'true' injuries. As she has put it, 'rape begins to look like seduction with "just a little persuading", rather than a massive and brutal assault on the body and the psyche'.[43] Violations of honour and modesty are 'wholly inadequate concepts to express the suffering of women raped during war'.[44] This representation of women also has implications for the way in which sexual violence is later prosecuted, as rape as a mere injury to honour or reputation appears less worthy of prosecution than injuries to the person.

Nira Yuval-Davis has also contributed to this debate by suggesting that women have always been conceived of as the bearers of the 'collectivity's honour'.[45] In wartime narratives, the figure of the woman is often the symbolic bearer of the collectivity's identity and honour, whether in the form of 'Mother Russia', 'Mother Ireland' or 'Mother India'. But while women symbolise the collective, unity, honour and the raison d'être of specific national and ethnic projects, such as going to war, they are frequently excluded from active policy and decision-making processes, and therefore from the collective 'we' of the body politic.[46] Women therefore occupy an ambivalent position within the nation, by on the one hand being its symbol,[47] while at the same time constituting the 'Other' within society by virtue of their exclusion from key political processes. In this way, women retain their object position in international law. International humanitarian law has, further, deployed highly essentialised interpretations of women informed by adopting rules that focus on the biological differences of women from men and on the consequences that flow from this rigid distinction.[48] As Yuval-Davies has pointed out:

> Women's positions in and their obligations to their ethnic and national collectives, as well as to the states they reside in as citizens affect and sometimes even override their reproductive rights making their ability to bear children the focal point for their very existence. Women like men are members of the national collective, but, unlike men, they are bound by certain rules and regulations that apply specifically to them. These rules assume special

significance when considered against the fact that women are constructed as the 'biological reproducers' of the nation.[49]

The feminist sentiment is that the language of protection is reinforcing proprietary images of women, rather than focusing on the prohibition of violence more generally. The regime of 'special protection' in particular reveals a picture of women based on their perceived weakness, both psychological and physical, and their sexual and reproductive functions. Aside from the specific provisions designated for their protection, women remain largely invisible.[50] Moreover, a major shortcoming of international humanitarian law is that it overemphasises sexual violence, while failing to take into account the socio-economic dimensions characterising women's experiences of armed conflict, such as food insecurity and lack of medical and healthcare provisions, which are central to any comprehensive understanding of why women become vulnerable to begin with. The regime assumes that men and women have identical needs and that any potential problems that may arise can be dealt with according to the requirement of equal treatment by the law.[51] But, as feminists have argued, this system principally benefits the combatant, who is traditionally the central figure in armed conflict around which a majority of the legal provisions revolve. International humanitarian law still expressly assumes '[a] well-armed, well-dressed professional, from an organised group – a combatant predominantly engaged in an international armed conflict'.[52]

Part IV

Key developments in ICTY and ICTR wartime sexual violence jurisprudence

Janet Halley has noted that 'the specific criminalization of sexual violence in war has made an immense stride in recent years'.[53] The 1990s saw an explosion of law-making intended to govern armed conflict and witnessed a rapid development of international sexual violence prosecutions prompted primarily by the conflicts in the former Yugoslavia and Rwanda, which had gained notoriety for widely publicised incidents of rape, sexual mutilation and sexual humiliation of women. Both conflicts thrust into the open the stark reality of gender-based violence during armed conflict, ensuring that the international community would no longer ignore the issue.[54] Wartime sexual violence soon became a site for 'feminist lawmaking', as consistent and strongly organised feminist advocacy in the 1990s mobilised activists to engage with international humanitarian law as a means of addressing gendered harms.[55] It also influenced contemporary debates on transitional justice, prompting the discipline to recognise the importance of addressing gender issues in conflict situations and in their aftermath.[56]

The Yugoslav and Rwandan tribunals became pioneering institutions for wartime sexual violence adjudication due to their 'successful' prosecution of various forms of sexual violence as instruments of genocide, crimes against humanity, torture, persecution and enslavement.[57] The ICTY, in particular, has pioneered the idea of accountability for wartime sexual violence against women through its extensive jurisprudence.[58] Moreover, the creation of both tribunals embodied the feminist aspiration that wartime sexual violence would finally be visibilised by the law. Gabrielle Kirk MacDonald has, for example, noted that the establishment of the ICTY 'signalled the beginning of the end of the cycle of impunity'.[59] Both tribunals also appeared to provide the opportunity to move away from the notion that the rape was a crime against a man's property to acknowledging it as an attack upon female autonomy.[60] In particular, it was anticipated that the history of wartime sexual violence, which had been replete with reports of women being raped, sexually enslaved, impregnated, sexually mutilated, and subjected to multiple other forms of sexual violence, or mass violence, would finally be taken seriously and that violence against women would be criminalised.[61]

The ICTY and the ICTR statutes were adopted by the United Nations Security Council in 1993 and 1994, respectively, with the aim of defining their subject-matter jurisdiction, procedures, institutional roles and rules.[62] The tribunals are primarily driven by their statutes, which outline in detail the scope of their jurisdiction.[63] The statutes authorise prosecution and conviction in accordance with already existing forms of international criminal liability, but at the same time they modify these bodies of law both formally and substantively. They do not only select from the tradition on which they rely, but also authoritatively reinstate it. The statutes can therefore be likened to 'codes with crisp boundaries'.[64] Moreover, the tribunals promulgate their own rules of evidence and procedure, which were heavily driven by feminist efforts.[65]

The jurisprudence of the Yugoslav Tribunal has been particularly substantive in defining, delineating and developing substantive crimes. The ICTY has rendered decisions concerning the nature of modern-day armed conflict, such as the application and scope of Common Article 3 to the 1949 Geneva Conventions, while also 'breathing life' into the grave breaches regime by being the first institution to systematically apply it to sexual violence offences.[66] It has added significant definitional value to the Geneva Conventions through identifying comprised acts, such as rape and other sexual violence crimes, as well as distinguishing these acts from those comprised under the Torture Convention.[67] ICTY jurisprudence also firmly reflects the reconceptualisation of sexual violence as torture, which had begun within the context of international and regional human rights law.[68]

In addition, it has clarified when grave breaches may be applicable through an elucidation of the 'overall control test', which it used as a method for legally characterising the Yugoslav conflict. It found that the regime could apply in practice through the operation of the nexus requirement. In parallel strokes, it reinterpreted the 'protected person' category in order to crystallise which persons may benefit from its provisions. Moreover, it broadened the criteria serving to establish whether a widespread or systematic attack against a civilian population had occurred and it defined the prerequisite requirements necessary for proving the core crimes within the jurisdiction of the tribunal. In this way, it has also delineated what acts constitute forms of enslavement, as well as ruling on the constituent elements required to prove torture under international humanitarian law.[69]

Significantly, it has also provided detailed insight into when a superior can be held criminally liable for crimes committed by the subordinate by extensively developing the joint criminal enterprise theory of responsibility. According to Article 8 of the ICTY Statute, territorial jurisdiction is limited to the former Yugoslavia, but temporal jurisdiction is open-ended as to the events occurring in the territory after 1 January 1991.[70] Security Council Resolutions 1503 and 1534 provide that the ICTY and ICTR are to complete their proceedings by the end of 2010, although the Yugoslav Tribunal is still fully operational,[71] while the Rwandan Tribunal ceased to exist in December 2015.

At this point, it is relevant to note the circumstances that led to the creation of the Rwandan Tribunal. During the months of April to July 1994, between 500,000 and one million Rwandan men, women and children were slaughtered as part of a genocidal campaign against the Tutsi minority. This was typically accompanied by widespread massacres of moderate Hutus (who were willing to work with Tutsi). A circle of political leaders, threatened with the loss of political power, organised the killings with the help of Hutu militiamen and civilians.[72] One of the central patterns underlying the Rwandan genocide was the sexualised targeting of Tutsi women and girls, as part of a targeted and well-organised Hutu ethnic campaign against the Tutsi.[73] As a result of the events which took place in Rwanda during the spring of 1994, the ICTR was established by way of Security Council Resolution 955 of 8 November 1994.[74] Under the Statute, the ICTR has the power to prosecute Rwandan citizens responsible for serious violations of international humanitarian law, such as genocide and other such violations, committed in the territory of Rwanda and in neighbouring states between 1 January and 31 December 1994.[75] According to Articles 2 through 4, the tribunal has subject-matter jurisdiction over persons who committed genocide as defined in Article 2 of the Statute, persons responsible for crimes against humanity as defined in Article 3 of the Statute, and persons responsible for serious violations of Article 3 common to the Geneva Conventions of 12 August 1949, and for violations of Additional Protocol II, as well as the crimes defined in Article 4 of the Statute.[76]

From a gender-based perspective, the most substantive accomplishment of the ICTR has been its definition of rape in *The Prosecutor v. Akayesu*[77] and the recognition that consent is irrelevant for acts of a sexual nature within a nexus of genocide, armed conflict and crimes against humanity[78] This judicial insight, as pioneered in *Akayesu*, is becoming increasingly accepted in international criminal law, as related provisions in the Rome Statute similarly do not contain consent, thereby reflecting that the circumstances of coercion render consent irrelevant as a defence.[79]

ii) Gender integration through the position of Gender Adviser in the Office of the Prosecutor (OTP)

Much has been written about the creation and the appointment of Patricia Sellers to the position of Gender Adviser in the Office of the Prosecutor (OTP) by former Chief Prosecutor Richard Goldstone.[80] Charged with developing the law through formulating the approach of the OTP to the investigation and indictment of gender crimes, the post of the Gender Adviser is a prominent example of the mainstreaming approach espoused by the United Nations.[81] According to commentators, the creation of this role has led to an increase in awareness amongst ICTY staff of how to address gender issues more thoroughly and effectively by fostering gender expertise and integrating gender awareness throughout the organisation. In 1995, for instance, in response to staffing issues and in recognition of the need to hold perpetrators of gender-based crimes accountable, the tribunal established a 'sexual investigation team' composed exclusively of women with extensive experience of gender crimes.[82] After a few intense years of focusing on sexual violence the team was eventually dissolved, but only after the ICTY had gained sufficient gender awareness and expertise without having to rely upon this mechanism. The Gender Focal Point approach, moreover, enhanced the ability of prosecutors to bring successful charges against perpetrators of sexual violence, as ICTY staff members with gender expertise helped identify witnesses, analyse evidence, elicit testimony, and support those who testified.[83] Feminist activists also noted a correlation between participation rates of women and the existence of serious investigations into sexual violence, observing that this resulted in a 'gradual shift toward taking rape and other sexual violence crimes seriously and investigating them zealously'.[84] In fact, Goldstone went as far as to argue that if a woman had not been on the tribunal in its early years, there may not have been any indictments for gender-based crimes at all.[85] It is at the same time an example of the kind of 'governance feminism' that proved so influential to the adjudication of key ICTY wartime sexual violence cases. Another significant innovation of the tribunal in relation to the prosecution of wartime sexual violence was the drafting of Rule 34 of the Rules of Procedure and Evidence, which provided for the creation of a Victims and Witnesses Unit within the Registry, the tribunal's administrative organ that recommends protective measures for the victims and witnesses.[86] The purpose of this unit is to: 'provide counselling and support for [victims and witnesses], in particular in cases1 of rape and sexual assault'.[87] Moreover, it is supposed to give '[d]ue consideration . . . in the appointment of staff, to the employment of qualified women, 'thus reflecting the gender mainstreaming policies driving the contemporary legal institutions of the United Nations'.[88] An important innovation from a gender-based perspective has been Rule 96 of the Rules of Procedure and Evidence, governing evidentiary matters in cases of sexual assault. These rules prescribe a system of protection for victims or witnesses to be balanced against the rights of the accused, thus respecting universally accepted human rights standards.[89]

Part V

The classification of wartime sexual violence as a prosecutable offence in international criminal law

The ICTY's subject-matter jurisdiction is set forth in four articles, giving it jurisdiction over grave breaches of the Geneva Conventions of 1949 (Article 2), violations of the laws and customs of war (Article 3), genocide (Article 4) and crimes against humanity (Article 5). Women's advocates were particularly successful in having their demands that rape be explicitly listed as a crime against humanity met, as Article 5 defines crimes against humanity in armed conflict as '(a) murder; (b) extermination; (c) enslavement; (d) deportation; (e) imprisonment; (f) torture; (g) rape; (h) persecutions on political, racial, and religious grounds; [and] (i) other inhumane acts'.[90] Yet rape was omitted from both Articles 2 and 3, the provisions relating to grave breaches of the Geneva Conventions and other war crimes.[91] This was problematic from a feminist perspective, as rape could only be prosecuted as part of a widespread or systematic attack directed against a civilian population.

i) Sexual violence as a crime against humanity

The ICTY Statute is the first legal provision since Control Council No. 10 to expressly reference rape in the context of crimes against humanity. Article 5(g) confers on the tribunal the power to prosecute persons responsible for, inter alia, rape as a crime against humanity 'when committed in armed conflict, whether international or internal in character, and directed against any civilian population'.[92] According to the ICTY jurisprudence, as established in the *Kunarac* case, the following elements are required to establish a crime against humanity pursuant to Article 5 of the Statute:

(i) There must be an attack
(ii) The acts of the perpetrator must be part of the attack
(iii) The attack must be 'directed against any civilian population'
(iv) The attack must be 'widespread or systematic'
(v) The perpetrator must know of the wider context in which his acts occur and know that his acts are part of the attack
(vi) The crime must have been committed during an armed conflict.[93]

Indictments charging rape as a crime against humanity were issued in a number of other sexual violence cases arising from the context of the conflict in Bosnia-Herzegovina in accordance with the ICTY classification.[94] Moreover, the ICTY entered convictions for sexual violence as a crime against humanity constituting other expressly enumerated crimes under Article 5 of the ICTY, such as torture as a crime against humanity under Article 5(f).[95] Article 5(c) refers to 'enslavement' as a crime against humanity, which during times of armed conflict is often experienced in different forms and frequently encompasses detention and rape over prolonged periods of time, forceful marriage; or forced prostitution'.[96] This is notable, as the international community has been historically slow to act upon the connection between sexual violence and enslavement.[97] Chapter 5, for example, discusses the significance of the *Kunarac* case, where two defendants were found guilty of enslavement as a crime against humanity due to their treatment of women and girls as their personal property.[98] The tribunal in this case recognised both the physical as well as psychological elements of detention and the extreme sense of duress experienced by the women in this situation, which prevented any meaningful escape, as the women had nowhere to go and no means of survival in the prevailing wartime conditions.[99] The court, moreover, held that control of sexuality is a relevant factor in determining whether the crime of enslavement has been committed.[100] In addition, Article 5(h) of the ICTY Statute recognises that persecution can be a constituent act of a crime against humanity, and individuals have been convicted of sexual violence offences committed on political, racial and/or religious grounds.[101] Persecution has been defined in the jurisprudence of the tribunal as 'the gross or blatant denial, on discriminatory grounds, of a fundamental right, laid down in international customary or treaty law, reaching the same level of gravity as other acts prohibited in Article 5'.[102] Moreover, other acts of sexual violence excluding rape have been charged before the ICTY as inhumane acts, also a form of crime against humanity.[103] This was confirmed in the *Furundžija* decision.[104]

ii) Sexual violence as war crimes

War crimes have been broadly defined as 'violations of the laws and customs of war', although not all breaches of international humanitarian law result in criminal responsibility.[105] Recent developments in the prosecution of war crimes have confirmed the existence of two main categories of these crimes: grave breaches of the 1949 Geneva Conventions and of Additional Protocol I, applying to international armed conflict; and other violations of the laws and customs of war, which apply to both internal and international armed conflicts. In the ICTY, indictments have been issued by the Prosecutor on the basis of sexual violence as a grave breach by way of torture and/or inhuman treatment[106] and wilfully causing great suffering.[107] In practice, however, the OTP has increasingly avoided charging defendants with grave breaches to avoid the considerable time and expense involved in proving the existence of an international armed conflict.[108]

The ICTY, moreover, has jurisdiction over violations of the laws and customs of war under Article 3. Although the latter provides a non-exhaustive list, it does not make any reference to sexual violence. Nonetheless, the Prosecutor has issued indictments in which sexual violence is treated as a violation of the laws or customs of war applicable to international and internal armed conflict.[109] The extent to which sexual violence can be prosecuted as a violation of the laws or customs of war under Article 3 of the ICTY Statute was, specifically, considered in the *Furundžija* case.[110] The Trial Chamber here confirmed that Article 3 is an 'umbrella' rule that covers 'any serious violation of a rule of customary international humanitarian law entailing, under international customary or conventional law, the individual criminal responsibility of the person breaching the rule'.[111] The tribunal also found that 'rape and other serious sexual assaults' fall within the definition. *Furundžija* was, therefore, found guilty of violations of the laws and customs of war through committing outrages upon personal dignity, including rape.[112] This development was, moreover, confirmed in the *Kunarac* case, where the Trial Chamber convicted each of the three defendants of rape as a violation of the laws or customs of war.[113]

iii) Sexual violence as genocide

Genocide and genocidal acts are defined in the Convention on the Prevention and Punishment of the Crime of Genocide.[114] It was the first major human rights instrument of its kind adopted by the U.N.[115] Genocide is defined in Article II of the Genocide Convention as: 'any of the following acts committed with intent to destroy, in whole or in part a 'national, ethnic, racial or religious group', as such:

a) Killing members of the group
b) Causing serious bodily or mental harm to members of the group
c) Deliberately inflicting on the group conditions of life calculated to bring about the physical destruction in whole or in part
d) Imposing measures intended to prevent births within the group
e) Forcibly transferring children of the group to another group.

Genocide is a specific example of the broader category of crimes against humanity, but it differs from other crimes against humanity by the presence of a specific intent to destroy the specified group in whole or in part, making it difficult to prove the *mens rea* of the crime. Moreover, according to Article I of the Genocide Convention, genocide is a crime under international law whether or not it occurs during wartime or in peace.[116]

Before engaging with the monumental *Akayesu* decision in more detail another important ruling on sexual violence as a form of genocide merits attention, as it raises some interesting questions about women's agency in wartime, *The Prosecutor v. Pauline Nyiramasuhuko* case.[117] On 26 May 1997, the prosecutor of the Rwandan Tribunal filed an indictment accusing Pauline Nyiramasuhuko of genocide, crime against humanity and serious violations of common Article 3 common to the Geneva Conventions committed during the Rwandan genocide. Nyiramasuhuko was the former Minister of Family and Women's Development[118] in both the government of Rwandan President Juvénal Habyarimana that collapsed after his death on 6 April 1994 and the interim government that succeeded it.[119] Two years after the initial indictment, the prosecution was granted leave to amend it and to include charges of conspiracy to commit genocide, complicity in genocide and direct and public incitement to commit genocide.[120] The additional crimes against humanity included a rape charge. Nyiramasuhuko was the first woman to have been indicted by an international criminal tribunal, charged with rape as a war crime and crime against humanity, and the first woman indicted for genocide.[121] Specifically, she stood accused of having ordered male soldiers to actively rape and then burn Tutsi women.[122] According to Sherrie Russel-Brown, the *Nyiramasuhuko* case 'concretises' the precedent established in the *Akayesu* judgement by illustrating the intersectional nature of genocidal rape, which detaches it from the notion that it is a violation against a woman's honour, or a 'reward' for soldiers during war.

Certainly, in showcasing that women are indeed capable of committing rape as a form of genocide, this case opens up the possibility for seeing 'genocidal rape' solely as a gender-specific crime, or something that male soldiers generally commit against women during wartime. The fact that a Hutu woman, who might have been a Tutsi herself, could commit genocide raises not only important questions around notions of victimhood and agency that have informed the portrayal of women during armed conflict, but also around the conceptualisation of wartime sexual violence as an ethnically-driven act. Rather than showing that women can indeed commit the same crimes as men – that they can rape, or order rape and target women of a different ethnicity, this case ought to give pause for reflection in relation to the book's central question: Specifically, what does the prosecution of Pauline Nyiramasuhuko mean to women in the current legal and political moment? In convicting her of genocidal rape, do international criminal tribunals thereby view women as agents of war, or are the judgement and prosecution of this high-profile female figure to be understood as aberrations that only resulted in prosecution because of the high number of civilians raped and killed?

Part VI

The definition of rape in international criminal law: expanding rape and narrowing consent as a defence

i) Akayesu

Given that there was no definition of rape in either statute, both ad hoc tribunals made it their primary goal to elaborate the objective and subjective elements of rape. Moreover, to date, the most notable developments concerning the prosecution of sexual violence as genocide have occurred in ICTR wartime sexual violence jurisprudence,[123] most visibly and significantly, in the landmark *Akayesu* decision.[124] The accused, Jean-Paul Akayesu, served as the mayor of the Taba commune from April 1993 until June 1994. He was in charge of performing executive functions and maintaining public order, while maintaining exclusive control over the communal police and the gendarmes at the disposition of the commune.[125] Between 7 April and the end of June 1994, at least 2,000 Tutsis were killed in Taba, while he was in power. Hundreds of displaced civilians, the majority of them Tutsi, sought refuge in the town hall, whereupon the female civilians were taken out and subjected to sexual violence by armed local militia and the communal police. These acts of sexual violence were generally accompanied by explicit threats of death or bodily harm and sustained beatings, leading the displaced female civilians to live in constant fear of sexual violence, as a result of which their physical and psychological health deteriorated. With respect to the rape charges, the *Akayesu* Trial Chamber held that rape had to be first defined, as there had been no commonly accepted definition of this term in international law.[126] The first definition of rape in international law was formulated by the *Akayesu* Trial Chamber in September 1998 as:

> a physical invasion of a sexual nature, committed on a person under circumstances, which are coercive. Sexual violence, which includes rape, is considered to be any act of a sexual nature which is committed under circumstances which are coercive.[127]

The court acknowledged that rape was a form of aggression whose central elements could not be captured in a mechanical description of objects and body parts. It also acknowledged the conceptual approach to state-sanctioned violence adopted by the Convention against Torture as a more useful approach in international law.[128] Moreover, *Akayesu* signalled a breakthrough for holding that consent is irrelevant to sexual violence offences within a nexus of genocide, armed conflict and crimes against humanity. The insight proffered was that:

> lack of consent as an element of the crime of rape (or any other sexual violence crime for that matter) is immaterial within the supranational criminal law context, especially in light of the violent and oppressive context in which rape takes place during genocide, crimes against humanity or armed conflict, and should therefore be rejected.[129]

In this way, it departed from a majority of national jurisdictions, which have traditionally defined rape as 'non-consensual intercourse'. Navanathem Pillay, who as the only female judge in the case critically intervened to include wartime sexual violence charges into the Indictment, has justified this in the following way:

> I framed my decision in this manner because it was evident that, in the circumstances that were being described, there was no place whatsoever for the consideration of consent. I hoped that this ruling would remove the age-old practice of focusing on the conduct of the woman victim in order to establish the guilt of the perpetrator. That decision was not appealed. I was glad at the time. No one likes to be appealed![130]

In embracing legal regulation as the way forward, Pillay's words capture much of the contemporary feminist sentiment underlying wartime sexual violence prosecutions. While undoubtedly a welcome intervention from a feminist perspective, these words illustrate the rather uncritical approach espoused by feminist activists regarding consent. That lack of consent is not only immaterial to the offence, but next to impossible in circumstances that are inherently coercive regardless of their context has therefore been firmly embraced. From the book's perspective, this legal construction is problematic, as it precludes the idea that consent could have been given in a meaningful way. This critique is not meant to diminish in any way the profound conditions of duress and precariousness experienced by women during wartime, or to trivialise the great difficulties in successfully prosecuting rape cases in national courts, which almost always reflect a battle between the defence strategy and its evidentiary presumptions that consent was present and the prosecution's struggle in proving that the woman was the actual victim of rape.[131]

Trials often tell the same story, reproducing what is known about women from a male perspective. As Carol Smart has described it, 'women's sexual subjectivity has already been framed by the language of rape. Women "know" they are to blame for rape.'[132] This is because considerable deference is usually given to the claims of the defendant that he subjectively believed consent was present, therefore rendering the experience of the rape trial an often traumatic experience for women.[133] The rape trial also confirms what is already known about heterosexual sex, namely, that men have uncontrollable urges and natural desires to which women exercise passive consent. The rape trial, therefore, becomes another manifestation of the law's power. It confirms the perception of heterosexual acts as being lumped into the category of heterosexual acts, while same sex acts do not get the same legal recognition. In silencing all but one account of rape, the rapable, the biological and the sexed woman of legal discourse is produced. It is precisely because of these misgivings resulting from the law's perpetuation of deeply offensive gendered stereotypes that feminist investments in the law need to be questioned. Feminists need to be reminded not to fall into a similar trap of reproducing these gendered dichotomies in their spirited embrace of the law as the path leading to the promised land of gender justice and equality.

From an intersectional perspective, the *Akayesu* judgement highlighted genocidal rape by emphasising that it happened to women because of their ethnicity – in this case, specifically Tutsi women or Hutu women married to Tutsi men. The tribunal also recognised that these women were targeted both because of their ethnicity and because of the beliefs and opinions held by Hutus about Tutsi women.[134] Aside from emphasising the ethno-nationalist dimensions underlying the sexual violence-as-genocide attacks against women, th.e tribunal also visibilised the significance of gender amidst the genocide by recognising the subjectivity of the victims of genocidal rape. This has been singled out as a positive development by feminists, who have stressed that although the intent of genocidal rape might have been to destroy a particular individual – the Tutsi woman – the effect achieved, namely the destruction of the entire Tutsi group, was more significant. Thus, a key passage states:

> In light of all the evidence before it, the Chamber is satisfied that the acts of rape and sexual violence . . . were committed solely against Tutsi women, many of whom were subjected to the worst public humiliation, mutilated and raped several times, often in public, in the bureau communal premises or in other public places, and often by more than one assailant. These rapes resulted in physical and psychological destruction of Tutsi women, their families and their communities. Sexual violence was an integral part of the process of destruction, specifically targeting Tutsi women and specifically contributing to their destruction and to the destruction of the Tutsi group as a whole. . . . Sexual violence was a step in the process of destruction of the Tutsi group – destruction of the spirit, the will to love, and to life itself.[135]

Such lines of legal reasoning have been rather symptomatic of the way in which much of the feminist debate on wartime sexual violence has been conducted. Structural feminists in particular advocated the view that sexual violence attacks against women could not be divorced from their cultural context or their identity as members of a group. This, in turn, informed not only female legal subjectivity, but became the representational frame through which gender was constructed in wartime sexual violence jurisprudence. Moreover, it is evident from the passage above that the perpetrator's intent and the actual effect of the harm became closely intertwined in the court's legal reasoning. A significant element of the *Akayesu* judgement, certainly from a feminist viewpoint, was the ICTR's construction of rape as an act not so much directed against female autonomy but rather deployed as a tool of war, a violent act perpetrated against a member of a group with the intent of destroying that group. A similar reasoning has also been adopted in the subsequent *The Prosecutor v. Musema judgement*,[136] where the tribunal inferred specific intent to destroy the Tutsi group by finding that acts of serious bodily and mental harm, including rape and other forms of sexual violence, were often accompanied by humiliating utterances signalling a clear intent to destroy the Tutsi group as a whole.[137] As the Trial Chamber put it,

> In this context, the acts of rape and sexual violence were an integral part of the plan conceived to destroy the Tutsi group. Such acts targeted Tutsi women, in particular, and specifically contributed to their destruction and therefore that of the Tutsi group as such.[138]

But these interpretations raise an interesting point, namely, if rape is no longer defined as a violation of individual sexual autonomy, but rather an act targeting an ethnic group, does this reading not inherently depoliticise sexual violence as an act of war, divorcing it further from its socio-political context and the historical powers that helped shape it? Although it could be argued that treating rape as part of the ethnic targeting of a group makes it a less individualised and more contextualised offence, given that it could be conceived of as an attack on the socio-economic structures of society, it is counterproductive from a feminist perspective. In defining rape as an attack on an ethnic group, the act of rape becomes a culturalised event – it is no longer an attack against individual autonomy and agency and the woman herself, but a violation of the group as the proprietor of the female body.

ii) Furundžija

Given the progressive nature of the *Akayesu* judgement, it initially appeared as if the ICTY would adopt the same definition.[139] However, after having followed the holding of the *Akayesu* judgement in the *Celebici* Trial Judgement, the ICTY Trial Chamber came up with its own definition of rape in the *Furundžija* case, finding it necessary to further particularise the elements of rape along more traditional, if not mechanical lines. After surveying trends in national laws and other jurisprudence, it held that the 'objective elements' of rape, or the *actus reus* of rape in international law consist of the following:

i) the sexual penetration, however slight:
  a) of the vagina or anus of the victim by the penis of the perpetrator or any other object used by the perpetrator; or
  b) of the mouth of the victim by the penis of the perpetrator or any other object used by the perpetrator;

ii) by coercion or force or threat of force against the victim or a third person.[140]

As transpires from this wording, the *Furundžija* definition did not allow adequately for situations other than coercion, force or threat of force that could render sexual penetration non-consensual.[141]

iii) Kunarac

The Trial Chamber in *Kunarac* subsequently corrected this definition by finding that the *Furundžija* criteria, although appropriate to the circumstances of the case, were in one respect more narrowly stated than is required by international law. While agreeing with the *actus reus* elements of rape articulated earlier, the court found that paragraph (ii) of the *Furundžija* classification of the element needed to be interpreted to include consent.[142] It emphasised that while force, threat of force or coercion are relevant, these factors are not exhaustive, and focus needed to be placed on violations of sexual autonomy as a wider principle for penalising violations of this kind. The tribunal held that 'sexual autonomy is violated wherever the person subjected to the act has not freely agreed to it or is otherwise not a voluntary participant'.[143] Factors such as force, threat or taking advantage of a vulnerable person provided evidence as to whether consent was voluntary.[144] Guided by common law jurisdictions, which typically define rape by the absence of the victim's free will or genuine consent, the Trial Chamber identified three broad categories of factors to determine when sexual activity should be classified as rape:

i) the sexual activity is accompanied by force or threat of force to the victim or a third party;
ii) the sexual activity is accompanied by force or a variety of other specified circumstances which made the victim particularly vulnerable or negated her ability to make an informed refusal; or
iii) the sexual activity occurs without the consent of the victim.[145]

The decision emphasised the importance of recognising a victim's vulnerability or deception when in situations where he or she is unable to refuse sex due to such things as 'an incapacity of an enduring or qualitative nature' (such as a mental or physical illness, or the age of minority) or of a 'temporary or circumstantial nature' (such as being subjected to psychological pressure or otherwise being in a state of inability to resist).[146] The other key factors negating consent were held to comprise 'surprise, fraud or misrepresentation' leading to the victim's inability to offer an 'informed or reasoned' refusal. As the tribunal pointed out, 'In all of these different circumstances, the victim's will was overcome, or her ability to freely refuse the sexual acts was temporarily or more permanently neglected.'[147]

It was determined that sexual autonomy ought to be the standard for determining when sexual activity constitutes rape, leading the Trial Chamber to expand upon the parameters of rape under international law by proffering the following definition of its *actus reus*:

Rape is 'constituted by: the sexual penetration, however slight:

a) of the vagina or anus of the victim by the penis of the perpetrator or any other object used by the perpetrator; or
b) of the mouth of the victim by the penis of the perpetrator; where such sexual penetration occurs without the consent of the victim'.[148]

In this context, it was held that consent had to be given voluntarily as a result of 'the victim's free will, assessed in the context of the surrounding circumstances'. The *mens rea* of the offence was held to have been satisfied by demonstrating the 'intention to effectuate the sexual penetration and knowledge that it occurs without the consent of the victim'. The definition of rape as a violation of sexual autonomy in the *Kunarac* decision came close to the holding of the *Akayesu* Trial Chamber that rape is a physical invasion under 'circumstances which are coercive'.[149] In principle, this definition was also upheld on appeal. The *Kunarac* Appeals Chamber noted that 'the Trial Chamber had [appeared] to depart from the tribunal's prior definitions of rape', but that by emphasising the 'absence of consent as the condition *sina qua non* of rape', it had not divorced itself from the ICTY's prior jurisprudence; rather it had been concerned to elucidate the relationship between force and consent.[150] The Appeals Chamber clarified the court's holding in the following way:

> Force or threat of force provides clear evidence of non-consent, but force is not an element per se of rape. In particular, the Trial Chamber wished to explain that there are "factors [other than force] which would render an act of sexual penetration non-consensual or non-voluntary on the part of the victim." A narrow focus on force or threat of force could permit perpetrators to evade liability for sexual activity to which the other party had not consented by taking advantage of coercive circumstances without relying on physical force.[151]

However, the *Kunarac* Appeals Chamber added one significant observation:

> While it is true that a focus on one aspect gives a different shading to the offence, it is worth observing that the circumstances giving rise to the instant appeal and that prevail in most cases charged as either war crimes or crimes against humanity will be almost universally coercive. That is to say, true consent will not be possible.[152]

Given that the proven allegations against the appellants specifically concerned the rape of women held in de facto military headquarters, detention centres and apartments maintained as soldiers' residences, the *Kunarac* Appeals Chamber had to limit its findings accordingly. In this regard, it found that the circumstances had been so coercive as to negate any possibility of consent.[153] The *Kunarac* definition of rape was subsequently also adopted by the Trial Chamber in the *Kvocka* case.[154] By expanding the definition of rape, the *Kunarac* Trial Chamber precluded the notion of consent as relevant in circumstances of extreme duress in notable contrast to domestic criminal systems, which render the issue of consent central to rape trials. The potential for such problems to arise in proceedings before the ICTY has further been lessened by the existence of Rule 96, governing evidence in cases of sexual assault,[155] which states that a 'defence' of consent cannot be introduced in situations of threats or fears of violence, duress, detention or psychological oppression, therefore recognising the inherently coercive nature of armed conflict for women, which renders it difficult, if almost impossible to enact any form of resistance.[156] The *Kunarac* Trial Chamber concluded that this provision was consistent with a common sense understanding of the meaning of 'genuine consent'. In situations where the victim:

> [i]s subjected to or threatened with or has reason to fear violence, duress, detention or psychological oppression', or 'reasonably believed that if [he or she] did not submit, another might be so subjected, threatened or put in fear, any apparent consent which might be expressed by the victim cannot have been freely given'.[157]

The paragraph served to reinforce the requirements of consent in rape cases as 'absent until freely given' and satisfied the second limb of the Trial Chamber's definition. These gender-sensitive provisions, moreover, allowed it to deal promptly with the claims of two of the accused that some of the women and girls had, in fact, consented to sexual intercourse with them. On the basis of the evidence presented, the judges strongly rejected the argument made by the defendant that one of the victims had been his actual girlfriend, and that their relationship was consensual, an aspect of the decision elaborated upon more critically in chapter 6.[158] The *Kunarac* decision has provided significant clarification and elaboration of the appropriate elements of rape under international law, while emphasising wartime sexual violence as a violation of female autonomy in a nod to the spirit of *Akayesu*.

iv) Muhimana *and* Gacumbitsi

More recent ICTR jurisprudence suggests that this definitional divide has been successfully overcome. Thus, in *The Prosecutor v. Muhimana*,[159] the Trial Chamber found that:

> [t]he Akayesu definition and the Kunarac elements are not incompatible or substantially different in their application. Whereas Akayesu referred broadly to a 'physical invasion of a sexual nature', Kunarac went on to articulate the parameters of what would constitute a physical invasion of a sexual nature amounting to rape.[160]

In addition, in its appeal against the *Gacumbitsi* judgement,[161] the OTP requested that the Appeals Chamber find that non-consent and the perpetrator's knowledge thereof are not elements of rape as a crime against humanity or an act of genocide; instead consent was considered as an affirmative defence that could be raised by the accused subject to the limitations of Rule 96 of the ICTR Rules of Procedure and Evidence.[162]

The case concerned Sylvestre Gacumbitsi, who as mayor of the Rusumo commune had been accused of having publicly instigated the rape of Tutsi women and girls.[163] The Trial Chamber had convicted Gacumbitsi, inter alia, of instigating eight rapes (including that of one victim, who died after her genitals had been impaled with a stick) as a crime against humanity pursuant to Article 3(g) of the ICTR Statute.[164] Moreover, the appeals decision in this case effectively sustained the core insight of *Akayesu* in holding that the surrounding circumstances were so coercive as to negate any possibility of consent. It held that under coercive circumstances '[n]on-consent is not a separate element to be proven, but could be inferred from the context'.[165] The Appeals Chamber, moreover, further clarified the law by holding that the circumstances that prevail in most cases that encompass charges of either war crimes or crimes against humanity will almost 'universally be coercive rendering true consent impossible'.[166]

The *Gacumbitisi* Appeal Judgement has clarified that the prosecution may establish non-consent by proving coercive circumstances without having to introduce evidence of the victim's non-consent. This has widely been seen as a landmark improvement in comparison to the conduct of earlier proceedings in which victims were sometimes additionally humiliated by being asked whether they had consented even though they had only moments earlier testified about horrific incidences of sexual assault.[167]

v) Sexual assault

Aside from the substantive progress made in defining and crystallising rape in international law, the two ad hoc tribunals have made important advancements in relation to finding that sexual assaults fall within the scope of other crimes, punishable under international criminal law. The *Akayesu* Trial Chamber, for example, held that:

> [s]exual violence is not limited to physical invasion of the human body and may include acts which do not involve penetration or even physical contact.[168]

Moreover, it held that sexual violence including rape could be considered to be 'any act of a sexual nature which is committed on a person in circumstances which are coercive'.[169] Sexual violence was held to fall within the scope of 'other inhumane acts', set forth in Article 3(i) of the ICTR Statute as 'outrages upon personal dignity' set forth in Article 4(e) of the ICTR Statute, and 'serious bodily or mental harm' set forth in Articles 2(2) (b) of the ICTR Statute.[170]

The *Akayesu* Trial Chamber, consequently, found Jean-Paul Akayesu guilty of 'other inhumane acts' for the forced undressing of a woman outside the bureau communal after making her sit in the mud; for the forced undressing and public marching of another naked woman; for the forced undressing of a third woman and her two nieces and for forcing the women to perform exercises naked in public near the bureau communal.[171] The *Furundžija* and the *Kunarac* Trial Chambers also held that sexual assault and sexual harassment falling short of actual penetration were punishable acts under international humanitarian law.

Part VI

Conclusion

In overviewing key ICTY and ICTR developments, this chapter has shown that violence against women is today strongly articulated in international law and its effects mediated in the judgements of international criminal tribunals. This is of significance from a feminist legal perspective and wider international legal scholarship, as it showcases the juridicalisation of gender-based violence as a manifestation of the legitimatising function which international law has assumed in late modernity.[172] Wartime sexual violence as a previous footnote of history has travelled far, given its recognition today as one of the most serious violations of international humanitarian law. The legal advancements made in international criminal tribunals have given way to a more confident, if not more assertive institutional framework for the prosecution of wartime sexual violence against women. Despite significant obstacles along the way, the tribunals have made significant progress in crafting an international legal definition of rape that more closely corresponds to women' experiences of wartime, while taking into account the inherently coercive nature of wartime, which often precludes the exercise of any choice, or resistance.

Moreover, the tribunals have expanded the parameters of war crimes, crimes against humanity, the grave breaches provision of the Geneva Conventions and genocide in order to render sexual violence a justiciable offence in international criminal law, while at the same time elaborating the elements making up the rules and procedures in sexual violence cases. The analysis has shown that both tribunals have addressed crimes of sexual violence effectively and with special attention to the protection of victims, while balancing this against the rights of the accused to a fair trial. Gender issues have, therefore, become closely associated with notions of success in the popular discourse. This chapter has served as a platform for preparing the ensuing critical analysis, which aims to fire a warning shot in the way of feminist celebrations of the law by reiterating that the questions posed at the outset remain as urgent as ever.[173]

Notes

1 The Special Court for Sierra Leone was set up jointly by the Government of Sierra Leone and the United Nations. It was established for the purpose of trying those, who bear the greatest responsibility for serious violations of international humanitarian law and Sierra Leonean law committed in the territory of

Sierra Leone since 30 November 1996. For an overview see: The Special Court for Sierra Leone, established by an Agreement between the United Nations and the Government of Sierra Leone pursuant to Security Council Resolution 1315 (2000) of 14 August 2000. Agreement available at: www.sc-sl.org/LinkClick.aspx?fileticket=CLk1rMQtCHg%3d&tabid=176 (last accessed in June 2011).

2 This Special Court was created by the Cambodian National Assembly in 2001 to try the serious crimes committed by the Khmer Rouge regime during 1975–1979. The court is called the Extraordinary Chambers in the Courts of Cambodia for the Prosecution of Crimes Committed during the period of the Democratic Kampuchea (Extraordinary Chambers of ECCC). The U.N. ultimately reached an agreement with the Cambodian government in June 2003, which outlines how the international community will assists and participate in the Extraordinary Chambers. Overview available at: www.eccc.gov.kh/en/about-eccc/introduction (last accessed in June 2011); Information about the collaboration between the United Nations and the Cambodian government is also available on the specifically dedicated U.N. website, United Nations Assistance to the Khmer Rouge Trials (UNAKRT). Available at: http://unakrt-online.org/04_documents.htm (last accessed in August 2011).

3 The Special Tribunal for Lebanon was set up at the request of the Lebanese government to establish an international tribunal to try those individuals believed responsible for the attack in Beirut of 14 February 2005 on former Lebanese Prime Minister Rafiq Hariri and resulting in the death or injury to other persons. The Special Tribunal was thus established via Security Council Resolution 1664 in 2006 in agreement with the Lebanese Republic. For an overview of the activities of the court, see: www.stl-tsl.org/section/AbouttheSTL (last accessed in June 2011).

4 Also known as the Special Panels for Serious Crimes (SPSC) established by the United Nations acting as the transitional authority between the end of the Indonesian occupation in 1999 and the independence of East Timor in 2002, the Tribunal on 20 May 2005 completed more than four years of trials that had arisen out of the context of the 1999 violence following the referendum in which the East Timorese voted overwhelmingly in favour of independence from Indonesia. On 20 May 2005, the Tribunal completed more than four years of trials that had arisen out of the context of the 1999 violence following the referendum in which the East Timorese voted overwhelmingly in favour of independence from Indonesia. Although the work of the Tribunal was cut short by a decision of the United Nations to end the UNMISET missions of which it was part, it completed 55 trials, most involving relatively low-level defendants. Information available at: Berkeley War Crimes Studies Centre: http://socrates.berkeley.edu/~warcrime/ET.htm#SeriousCrimesUnit (last accessed in June 2011). For further information see: United Nations Transitional Administration in East Timor (UNTAET) UNTAET/REG/2001/25, Regulation on the Amendment of UNTAET Regulation No. 2000/11 on the Organization of Courts in East Timor and UNTAET Regulation No. 2000/30 on the Transitional Rules of Criminal Procedure 14 September, 2001.

5 The Preamble of the CEDAW, for instance states that: 'extensive discrimination against women' continues to exist. The persistence of discrimination continues, despite the states' obligations under the human rights covenants to ensure the equal rights of men and women, and despite the adoption of other international covenants, resolutions, declarations and recommendations promoting equality between women and men. See Convention on the Elimination of all Forms of Violence against Women (CEDAW), 1249 U.N.T.S. 13, 19 ILM 33 (1980), adopted by GA. Res. 180 (XXXIV) (18 Dec. 1979), entered into force: 3 September 1981 at Preamble.

6 S. Brownmiller, *Against Our Will: Men, Women and Rape* (London: Penguin Books, 1975), at 32.

7 For a discussion of the Laws and Customs of War on Sexual Violence after World War II, and the work of the International Military Tribunal for the Far East (IMTFE), also known as the Tokyo Tribunal, and the International Military Tribunal (IMT) held in Nuremberg see K.D. Askin & D. Koenig (eds.), *Women and International Human Rights* (Volume 1) (Ardsley, NY: Transnational Publishers, 1999), at 51–54. As Askin describes, gender-based violence during World War II was commonplace, and women were murdered, tortured, enslaved and otherwise abused, as were men. Yet unlike the treatment of most men, but consistent with the treatment of women in previous and subsequent wars, hundreds of thousands of women and girls were also raped, forced into sexual slavery, forcibly sterilised and subjected to other reproductive crimes, as well as subjected to sexual mutilation, sexual humiliation and forced to endure countless other forms of sexual violence and persecution. Nonetheless, when it came to hold the perpetrators and other responsible parties accountable for the gender-based crimes charges were conspicuously absent. In the post-war trials held at Nuremberg and Tokyo, although crimes against women were extensively reported and documented, these crimes were omitted from the jurisdiction of the International Military Tribunal (IMT) Charter, they were not charged in the indictment and they were not prosecuted. Thus, captured German documents presented at the Nuremberg War Crimes Tribunal in 1946 corroborate the routine use of rape as a weapon of terror, and detail, for instance, the sexual humiliation that German SS unleashed upon the Jewish women in the Warsaw ghetto, despite the stern prohibition against 'race' defilement – the injunction against contaminating Aryan 'blood' contained in the Nuremberg race laws of 1935 that extended under its own twisted logic to forcible intercourse, as well as to marriage or extramarital liaison. For a more detailed overview of sexual violence perpetrated against the female Jewish population at the hand of the Nazis during World War II see: Brownmiller (1975), at 31, 49–56. For a historical account of the rape of German women at the hands of the Soviet Red Army during the fall of Berlin in 1945, see Janet Halley's exposition of *A Woman in Berlin: Eight Weeks in the Conquered City: A Diary*, which she eloquently summarises and deconstructs the 'tight association of truth with moral certitude and of literary artifice with ideological spin'. In J. Halley, 'Rape in Berlin: Reconsidering the Criminalisation of Rape in the International Law of Armed Conflict', 9 *Melbourne Journal of International Law* (2008), at 78, 91. For a critique of the failure to prosecute wartime sexual violence at Nuremberg and Tokyo, see also C. MacKinnon, 'Turning Rape into Pornography', in *Reflections on the Universal Declaration of Human Rights* (The Hague: Martinus Nijhoff Publishers, 1999), at 160, 167.

8 For a discussion of the development of the superior command responsibility doctrine in the Nuremberg and Tokyo contexts, see: A. Zahar & G. Sluiter, *International Criminal Law* (Oxford: Oxford University Press, 2008).

9 The 'Rape of Nanking' after the nature of the atrocities was finally revealed to the world ten years after the event, soon passed into common usage as the worldwide metaphor for that city's invasion. The events leading to the 'rape of Nanking' stemmed from the Japanese Army's capture of China's then capital city in December 1937. Given that General Chiang Kai-shek had pulled out his National forces prior to the invasion, moving the capital westward to Hankow, any Chinese civilian with any means had fled leaving a defenceless city to the poorest classes and a handful of foreign missionaries, including some Americans who chose to stay. What happened next has been described by Brownmiller as: '[a]n orgy of wholesale assault against the remaining civilian population.' In a subsequent report compiled by the Nanking International Relief Committee, the missionary group that remained in the city, in June 1938, it found that among the injured females, 56 percent were between the ages of 15 and 29, although the terms and methods of

inquiry excluded rape per se. Subsequently, during the trial of General Iwane Matsui, the man in charge of the Nanking invasion, and one of the central defendants in the docket at Tokyo, it was established that 'approximately 200,000 cases of rape occurred within the city during the first months of occupation'. It was the considered opinion of the Tribunal at Tokyo that the invasion and wholesale destruction and looting of the city had been 'either secretly ordered of wilfully committed'. Although command responsibility for sexual violence was not tried as an independent crime, but as a crime tried in conjunction with other crimes, General Matsui was sentenced to be hanged for his part in the Rape of Nanking. For an in-depth analysis, see Brownmiller (1975), at 57–63. For a discussion of another very significant and entirely neglected narrative of World War II that only emerged decades later, see the discussion of sexual slavery and the so-called 'Comfort Women', in C. Chinkin, 'Women's International Tribunal on Japanese Military Sexual Slavery', 95 *American Journal of International Law* (2) (2001), at 335.

10 According to feminist legal scholars, the laws of war have primarily been concerned with the (male) combatants, despite the already long history of wartime sexual abuse against women. In Otto, (2006), at 318, 322.

11 For a critique of Brownmiller's work, see: A.J. Cahill, 'Feminist Theories of Rape: Sex or Violence?', in *Rethinking Rape* (Ithaca: Cornell University Press, 2001), at 16–28.

12 As Brownmiller puts it, 'The case against pornography and the case against toleration of prostitution are central to the fight against rape, and if it angers a large part of the liberal population to be so informed, then I would question in turn the political understanding of such liberals and their true concern for the rights of women. Or to put it more gently, a feminist analysis approaches all prior assumptions, including those of the great, unquestioned liberal tradition, with a certain open-minded suspicion, for all prior traditions have worked against the cause of women and no set of values, including that of tolerant liberals, is above review or challenge. After all, the liberal politik has had less input from the feminist perspective than from any other modern source: it does not by its own considerable virtue embody a perfection of ideals, it has no special claim on goodness, rather, it is most receptive to those values to which it has been made sensitive by others.' In Brownmiller (1975), at 390.

13 As Vasuki Nesiah has argued in her critique of American feminist scholarship in relation to their perception of Third World Women, the dominant U.S. feminist discourse about 'universally shared oppression' obfuscates global contradictions, and a discourse about the experience of oppression often participates in the imperially charged agenda of defining 'Third World' women as victims of oppression. In her contribution, Nesiah draws on Western feminist debates around Sri Lankan women who labour in transnational factories to argue that U.S. feminists remain complicit in masking global contradictions by insisting upon the notion of universalisation of oppression, a vision that privileges gender as the source of community and as a frame in which claims are articulated, thus preventing other critical issues pertinent to the Sri Lankan context, such as the disparity between the diverse ethnic composition of the country, which have been central to the Sri Lankan civil war, as well as complex class issues that cannot be negotiated along gendered registers, but are more strongly related to unequal power relations in society from emerging as a subject of debate. As Nesiah argues, 'By privileging gender as the source of community and the frame in which claims are articulated, they prevent other critical issues from being raised. The danger of basing feminist internationality on experiential discourse is that American feminists simply assume an international feminist community without interrogating their own investment in obscuring the structural conditions that separate women.' In V. Nesiah, 'Toward a Feminist Internationality: A Critique of U.S. Feminist Legal Scholarship', 16 *Harvard Women's Law Journal* (2003), at 189, 198–201.

14 Otto (2006), at 318, 350.

15 As Brownmiller argues, 'Rape in warfare is not bound by definitions of which wars are "just", or "unjust". Rape was a weapon of terror as the German Hun marched through Belgium in World War I. Rape was a weapon of revenge as the Russian Army marched through Berlin in World War II. Rape flourishes in warfare irrespective of nationality or geographic location.' Brownmiller (1975), at 32. It is perhaps interesting to note in view of Brownmiller's observation that if rape flourishes in wartime, regardless of nationality, or geographical origin, why it has become so central to the representation and framing of conflict in the post-1990s era particularly with respect to the Yugoslav and Rwandan conflicts.

16 As Brownmiller charts in her historical overview of rape across the centuries, as far back as the Ancient Greeks, rape was deemed an acceptable social behaviour within the rules of warfare, an act without stigma for warriors who viewed the women they conquered as legitimate booty, useful as wives, concubines, slaves, labour or battle-camp trophy. Thus, the phrase: 'To the victor belong the spoils' has applied to women since Helen of Troy. For a summary of these arguments see Brownmiller (1975), at 31–40.

17 Ibid at 35.

18 Doris Buss briefly analyses Grotius' writings in her critical evaluation of ICTR wartime sexual violence jurisprudence to suggest that these views, rooted in colonialist assumptions of so-called 'barbaric states' that gave Western powers license to intervene in the name of spreading civilisation as a guise for colonial domination and territorial expropriation, continue to inform much of present-day international legal scholarship. They have, thus, played a central part in the creation of a taxonomy between 'particularly Christian nations' that prohibit rape and 'barbaric nations', whose seemingly 'unappeasable appetites' signal their abject violator status, thus, allowing rape to flourish unchecked. In D. Buss, 'The Rwanda Tribunal and the Making of Ethnic Rape', presented at Sexual Abuse and Exploitation of Women in Violent Conflict Workshop', Emory University and Netherlands Defence Academy 17–19 June 2007 (copy with author), at 5.

19 For a postcolonialist critique of the laws of war, see F. Mégret, '"From Savages to Unlawful Combatants": A Postcolonial Look at International Humanitarian Law's "Other"', in A. Orford (ed.), *International Law and Its Others* (Cambridge: Cambridge University Press, 2006), at 265. As Mégret sees it, 'The move to codify the laws of war was certainly not triggered by colonial wars. It was the Battle of Solferino, a very European battle that prompted Henry Durant to write the famous souvenir that led to the first attempts at organizing services for the wounded in war. The wars that all delegates had in mind at the Hague Conference were the Franco-Prussian and Crimean conflicts. These were the wars that had demonstrated that 'as between disciplined troops the nations of Europe had practically reached an accord as to the maximum of severity with which warfare could be carried on – a consensus that now had to ratified into law. The laws of war were originally and superficially at least, part of a purely European story. Ibid at 270.

20 Brownmiller (1975), at 35.

21 See: K.D. Askin, *War Crimes against Women: Prosecution in International War Crimes Tribunals* (The Hague: Martinus Nijhoff, 1997), at 27 (original emphasis). For a summary of the historical trajectory of wartime sexual violence in international humanitarian law, see also: J. Campanaro, 'Women, War and International Law: The Historical Treatment of Gender-Based War Crimes', 89 *Georgetown Law Journal* (2000–2001), at 2557–2558.

22 See Convention Concerning the Laws and Customs of War on Land, 18 October 1907, 36 Stat. 2277, 3 Martens Nouveau Recueil (ser.3) 461 (hereinafter Hague Convention IV). In essence, Hague law governs the conduct of hostilities and

duties of combatants. Article 19 of the 1954 Hague Cultural Property Convention provides for the application of certain parts of the Convention to non-international conflicts.

23 The Conventions signed at Geneva on 12 August, 1949 consist of the following: Geneva Convention for the Amelioration of the Condition of the Wounded and Sick in Armed Forces in the Field, 6 U.S.T. 3114, 75 U.N.T.S. (hereinafter First Geneva Convention); Geneva Convention for the Amelioration of Wounded, Sick and Shipwrecked Members of the Armed Forces at Sea, 6 U.S.T. 3217, 75 U.N.T.S. (hereinafter Second Geneva Convention); Geneva Convention (III) Relative to the Treatment of Prisoners of War, 6 U.S.T. 3316, 75 U.N.T.S. 135 (hereinafter Third Geneva Convention); Geneva Convention (IV) Relative to the Protection of Civilians in Time of War, 6 U.S.T. 3516, 75 U.N.T.S. 287 (hereinafter Fourth Geneva Convention). The 1949 Geneva Conventions supersede the 1864, 1906 and 1929 Geneva Conventions. Prior to this the 1899 Hague Convention regulated the actions of participants in armed conflict. For an overview, see: J. Gardam, 'Women and the Law of Armed Conflict: Why the Silence?', 46 *International & Comparative Law Quarterly* (1997), at 55–80.

24 See Protocol Additional to the Geneva Conventions of 12 August 1949, and Relating to the Protection of Victims of International Armed Conflicts (Protocol I), 8 June 1977, 1125 U.N.T.S. 3, 16 I.L.M. (entered into force Dec. 1978) (hereinafter Additional Protocol I); Protocol Additional to the Geneva Conventions of 12 August 1949, and Relating to the Protection of Victims of Non-International Armed Conflicts (Protocol II), 8 June 1977, 1125 U.N.T.S. 3, 16 I.L.M. (entered into force Dec. 1978) (hereinafter Additional Protocol II).

25 M. Jarvis, 'An Emerging Gender Perspective on International Crimes', in G. Boas and W. Schabas (eds.), *International Criminal Law: Development in the Case Law of the ICTY* (Leiden: Brill Academic, 2003), at 169. Jarvis also draws on the Commentary to the Convention, which provides examples of 'humane treatment' in order to clarify the meaning of 'inhumane treatment'. Article 27 of the Convention requiring that protected persons must be treated humanely at all times would be such an example.

26 Classical international law comprises of the core offences, namely genocide, crimes against humanity and war crimes, as further specified under currently operative statutes of international criminal tribunals.

27 This provision on crimes against humanity covered '[a]trocities and offences, including but not limited to murder, extermination, enslavement, deportation, imprisonment, torture rape, or other inhumane acts committed against the civilian population, or prosecutions on political, racial, or religious grounds whether or not in violation of the domestic laws of the country where perpetrated'. See: Control Council Law No. 10, Dec. 20, 1945, Control Council for Germany, Official Gazette, 31 January 1946 at 50, reprinted in 6 Trials of War Criminals Before the Nuremberg Military Tribunals Under Control Council Law No. 10 at xviii. Art. II (1) (c) (1952).

28 The Geneva Conventions thus outline the protections owed by the state to specific groups, and each of the four Conventions contains a list of identical grave breaches, consisting of wilful killing, torture or inhuman treatment. See, for example, P.V. Sellers, 'Rape Under International Law', in B. Cooper (ed.), *War Crimes: The Legacy of Nuremberg* (New York, NY: TV Books, 1999), at 160–161; T. Meron, *Human Rights and Humanitarian Norms as Customary Law* (Broadbridge, Gloucesteshire: Clarendon Press, 1989), at 209, 265; Askin (1997), at 245.

29 Askin (1997), at 245.

30 Grave breaches have assumed the status of customary international law and are generally considered binding on all states, regardless of whether the states are parties to the Geneva Conventions or not. Ibid at 249. The high incidence of wartime sexual violence perpetrated against women during the conflicts of the 1990s have, moreover, prompted the International Red Cross Committee to

proclaim it as a harm that is '[w]ilfully causing great suffering or serious injury to body or health', and that it should therefore be encompassed within the grave breaches regime enumerated under Article 147 of the Fourth Geneva Convention. See: Fourth Geneva Convention, Art. 147.

31 See above at Additional Protocols I and II.

32 For a discussion, see Askin (1997), at 246.

33 Additional Protocol I, Art. 76. Article 85(4) (c), moreover, states that these '[p]ractices of . . . other inhuman and degrading practices involving outrages upon personal dignity' constitute grave breaches of Additional Protocol I, when they are based on 'racial discrimination'. Additional Protocol I, Art. 85 (4) (c).

34 Additional Protocol II, Art. 4(2) (e).

35 *Celebici*' Trial Chamber Judgement, at para 476. For an extensive discussion of the key legal developments of this case see chapter 5.

36 Askin (1997), at 247.

37 As Gardam has suggested, its rules exclusively address the situation of pregnant women, maternity cases and women at risk of sexual violence, but never women who might be combatants themselves. The common theme underlying the language of international humanitarian law is, thus, the protection of women in terms of their relationship with others and not as individuals in their own right. In J. Gardam and M. Jarvis (eds.), *Women, Armed Conflict and International Law* (The Hague: Kluwer International Law, 2001), at 94.

38 Gardam has argued that the legal regime applicable in times of armed conflict is in essence a category of rules based on the experiences of men that cannot respond to the situation of women. Given that women and men experience conflict in fundamentally different ways, the law takes the experience of men as the norm against which to construct the rules that are in turn inherently unjust to the experiences of women. These arguments have variously been made in: Gardam (1997), at 55–80; J. Gardam, 'Proportionality and Force in International Law', 87 *American Journal of International Law* (1993), at 391–413; J. Gardam & H. Charlesworth, 'Protection of Women in Armed Conflict', 22 *Human Rights Quarterly* (2000), at 150.

39 Gardam (1997), at 57.

40 Fourth Geneva Convention, Article 27.

41 The argument that rape '[o]ften results in traumatic, long-lasting psychological trauma that includes shock, paralyzing fear of injury or death, and a profound sense of loss of control over one's life' has frequently been used by feminist activists and scholars to show that the psychological consequences are compounded when the rape is committed during wartime. See for instance S. Healey, 'Prosecuting Rape under the Statute of the War Crimes Tribunal for the Former Yugoslavia', 21 *Brookings Journal of International Law* (1995), at 327, 336–337. But as previously argued and drawing on Brown's second strand of depoliticisation, this instantaneous coupling of corporal violation with psychological effect is a form of 'personalisation', which refers to the substitution of 'emotional and personal vocabularies for formulating solutions to political problems'. Thus when historically induced suffering is reduced to 'difference', or a problem of personal feeling, the field in which the 'political battle' and 'political transformation' ought to take place gets replaced with an agenda of emotional practices. In Brown (2006), at 15–16. The problem, as Brown points out in the context of tolerance discourses, is that women are all-encompassed by the sense of their psychological suffering, which is seen as an overwhelmingly destructive of their lives, making it seem as if rape was almost 'a fate worse than death'. Karen Engle has made this argument in the context of her reading of Ernest Hemingway's classic *For Whom the Bell Tolls* about the Spanish Civil War, suggesting that the view that rape is destructive and shameful to women enjoys wide concurrence in feminist scholarship, a tendency that reinforces the woman-as victim narrative of war without allowing for the

possibility of conceiving of women in more hybrid and multiple ways, as perpetrators of wartime violence for instance. See: K. Engle, 'Judging Sex in War', 106 *Michigan Law Review* (2008), at 941. Engle's argument might have some purchase, as Johanna Bourke has shown that even as late as the 1960s feminists were more likely to argue that rape was '[n]ot the worst thing that could happen to a woman'. In Bourke (2007), at 427.

42 H. Charlesworth, 'Feminist Methods in International Law', 93 *American Journal of International Law* (1999), at 379, 387.

43 C. Niarchos, 'Women, War and Rape: Challenges Facing the International Tribunal for the Former Yugoslavia', 17 *Human Rights Quarterly* (1995), at 649, 674.

44 Ibid.

45 This is most clearly visible when considering the modalities by which international humanitarian law has traditionally defined gender-specific crimes, such as rape as a crime of honour rather than a form of torture. Strict cultural codes, which are even more prominent in a situation of armed conflict, are often developed to keep women in this inferior position. See: N. Yuval-Davies, *Gender and Nation* (London: Sage Publications, 1997), at 39.

46 Ibid at 47.

47 In times of armed conflict women are associated in the collective imagination with women and children and it is supposedly for the sake of 'women and children' that men go to war. Their association with children also ties them with collective, as well as with the familial future. Wars come to be justified on the basis that they are fought for women and children in the reassurance that those who fight on their behalf i.e. men will come home to a safe hearth where women eagerly await their return. Ibid at 45.

48 Gardam & Jarvis (2001), at 94.

49 Yuval-Davis (1997) at 8. Similarly, Gardam has argued that international humanitarian law, in addressing the situation of pregnant women, maternity cases and women as victims of, or at risk of sexual violence, projects a common theme of protection for women, which is construed in terms of their relationship with others, but does not capture them as individuals in their own right. In J. Gardam & M. Jarvis (eds.), *Women, Armed Conflict and International Law* (The Hague: Kluwer International Law, 2001), at 94.

50 Despite the fact that 42 provisions of the four 1949 Geneva Conventions and Additional Protocols specifically deal with the effects of armed conflict on women, 19 concern women from the point of view of their reproductive capabilities. The underlying rationale of these provisions is the protection of the unborn child and small children, not the concern with the well-being of women because they are women. In Gardam (1997), at 67.

51 Christine Chinkin has widely discussed the different impact of armed conflict on men and women, arguing that women experience conflict differently as they are mainly non-combatant victims of violence in all forms of warfare, whether international or internal, religious, ethnic or nationalistic. In C. Chinkin, 'Peace and Force in International Law', in D. Dallmeyer (ed.), *Reconceiving Reality: Women and International Law* (Washington, DC: The American Society of International Law, 1993), at 204.

52 Gardam & Jarvis (2001), at 98.

53 J. Halley, 'Rape in Berlin: Reconsidering the Criminalisation of Rape in the International Law of Armed Conflict', 9 *Melbourne Journal of International Law* (2008), at 78.

54 In the context of the Yugoslav conflict, the international community started to take note in earnest of sexual violence, more specifically rape against women in 1992, when Bosnian Muslim women who had arrived in refugee camps in Croatia began reporting that they had been raped by Serbian men. These reports then

led to EC-initiated investigations, which found that close to 20,000 women had been raped during the war. Although estimates vary, this figure provided by the EC Investigative Mission into the Treatment of Muslim Women in the Former Yugoslavia is generally treated as authoritative. The figures can be found in the Report to EC Foreign Ministers (Warburton Mission II Report), para 14 (February 1993). Others estimate the numbers as ranging from 30,000 thousand to 50,000 women. A. Bell-Fiakoff, 'A Brief History of Ethnic Cleansing', *Foreign Affairs* (Summer 1993), at 110, 119.

55 The term 'feminist lawmaking' here is borrowed from Janet Halley and relates to her description of feminist advocacy leading to the incorporation of wartime sexual violence into the statutory framework of international criminal law. J. Halley, 'Rape at Rome: Feminist Interventions in the Criminalization of Sex-Related Violence in Positive International Criminal Law', 30 *Michigan Journal of International Law* (2008–2009), at 1, 8.

56 For a discussion of how gender structures the accountability mechanisms of transitional justice, see: K. Campbell, 'The Gender of Transitional Justice: Law, Sexual Violence and the International Criminal Tribunal for the Former Yugoslavia', 1 *The International Journal of Transitional Justice* (2007), at 411–432.

57 For an extensive analysis of the key developments in ICTY and ICTR wartime sexual violence jurisprudence see K.D. Askin, 'Prosecuting Wartime Rape and Other Gender-Related Crimes under International Law: Extraordinary Advances, Enduring Obstacles', 21 *Berkeley Journal of International Law* (2003), at 288.

58 From a jurisprudential point, the creation of the ICTY most certainly signalled a landmark shift in the way wartime sexual violence cases would be approached by future international criminal tribunals. Security Council Resolution 808 recalled that: 'persons who commit or order the commission of grave breaches of the Geneva Conventions are individually responsible or liable in respect of such breaches'. Emanating from the international law principle of individual responsibility for international crimes, Article 6 of the International Criminal Tribunal thus set forth the Tribunal's competence *ratione personae* or personal jurisdiction. This was to prove a cornerstone of the ICTY Statute, as the ICTY Appeals Chamber thereafter consequently ruled that no one who participated in serious violation of international humanitarian law could be made exempt from the Tribunal's jurisdiction. For a discussion, see: P. Viseur Sellers, 'Individual (s') Liability for Collective Sexual Violence', in K. Knop (ed.), *Gender and Human Rights* (Oxford: Oxford University Press, 2004), at 154.

59 Gabrielle Kirk MacDonald, 'The International Criminal Tribunals: Crime and Punishment in the International Arena', 7 *International Law Society Association Journal of International and Comparative Law* (2001), at 667, 673.

60 For a further discussion of this issue see, for example: A. Wald, 'What's Rightfully Ours: Toward a Property Theory of Rape', 30 *Columbia Journal of Law & Social Problems* (1997), at 459.

61 For a more extensive discussion see Askin (2003), at 297.

62 See International Criminal Tribunal for the former Yugoslavia, S.C. Res. 827, U.N. SCOR, 48th Sess., 3217th mtg. At 29, U.N. Doc. S/827/1993 (1993) (hereinafter Security Council Resolution 827). See also: Statute of the International Criminal Tribunal for the Former Yugoslavia, Art. 7(1), annexed to the Report of the Secretary-General pursuant to Paragraph 2 of the Security Council Resolution 808 (1993), U.N. SCOR, 48th Session, U.N. Doc S/25706 (1993) (hereinafter ICTY Statute). See International Criminal Tribunal for Rwanda, S.C. Res. 955 U.N. SCOR, 49th Sess., 3453d mtg. At 15, U.N. Doc. S/955/1993, Annex (1994) (hereinafter ICTR Statute).

63 The ICTY statute, for instance, grants the Tribunal subject-matter jurisdiction over genocide, crimes against humanity and war crimes. See: Arts. 6, 7(1), 7(3) of ICTY Statute.

64 Halley (2008–2009), at 8.

65 International Tribunal for the Prosecution of Persons Responsible for Serious Violations of International Humanitarian Law Committed in the Territory of the Former Yugoslavia Since 1991, Rules of Evidence and Procedure, U.N. Doc. IT-32/Rev, (13 June 2006). 303 K. Roberts, 'The Contribution of the ICTY to the Grave Breaches Regime', 7 *Journal of International Criminal Justice* (2009), 743. Article 3(3) of the ICTR Statute also provides that rape, enforced prostitution and any kind of indecent assault can constitute a grave breach of the Geneva Conventions 1949.

66 K. Roberts, 'The Contribution of the ICTY to the Grave Breaches Regime', 7 *Journal of International Criminal Justice* (2009), 743; Art. 3(3) of the ICTR Statute also provides that rape, enforced prostitution, and any kind of indecent assault can constitute a grave breach of the Geneva Conventions 1949.

67 Roberts (2009), at 743.

68 See, *The Prosecutor v. Furundžija* (IT-95–17/1), Trial Chamber Judgement, 10 December 1998.

69 For a more detailed overview see K.D. Askin, 'Reflections on Some of the Most Significant Achievements of the ICTY', 37 *New England Law Review* (2002–2003), at 903.

70 Art. 8 ICTY Statute; also see Security Council Resolution 827, at para 2, which specifies that temporal jurisdiction extends from 1 January 1991 'and a date to be determined by the Security Council upon the restoration of peace'. This open-ended provision entitled the ICTY jurisdiction over a conflict as recent as the conflict in Kosovo in 1999. For a discussion, see: K.D. Askin, 'The ICTY: An Introduction to Its Origins, Rules and Jurisprudence', in *Essays on ICTY Procedure and Evidence* (The Hague: Kluwer Law International, 2001), at 16.

71 See: United Nations Security Council Resolution 1503 (S/Res/1503) on the Completion Strategy of the ICTY and the ICTR, adopted by the Security Council at its 4817th meeting, (28 August 2003) U.N. Doc. S/Res/1503 (2003); United Nations Security Council Resolution 1534 (S/Res/1534) on the State Cooperation of States with the ICTY and ICTR, adopted by the Security Council at its 4935th meeting, (16 March 2004) U.N. Doc. S/Res/1534 (2004).

72 For a detailed summary leading to the events that precipitated Rwanda into genocide, such as the fact that Rwanda had been ruled by President Juvenal Habyarimana (himself a Hutu) and a close circle of supporters since 1973, and that while popular for a long time, Rwanda's economic decline by the end of the 1980s led to challenges to his previously monopoly-like hold on power in Rwanda at the hands of the National Republican Democratic Movement (MRND) and at the same time by external threat of invasion by the Rwandan Patriotic Front (RPF) (a group based in Uganda and mostly made up of Tutsi refugees – Tutsis had previously ruled Rwanda before and during the colonial era, but were driven from power by a revolution beginning in 1959), to the fact that this led to concerted actions and hate campaigns against Tutsis and all Hutus allied with them as 'accomplices' of the invaders, culminating eventually in a series of killings that would set the pattern for genocide of 1994, which was rapidly precipitated when Habyarimana's plane was shot down as he was returning from a peace conference in Tanzania on 6 April 1994., see: B. Nowrojee, 'Shattered Lives: Sexual Violence During the Rwandan Genocide and its Aftermath', 39 *Human Rights Watch/Africa*, (1996). As the report states, the killing of Habyarimana served as a pretext to initiate the massive killings that had been planned for months, both of Tutsis and of those Hutus who were opposed to Habyarimana. Ibid at 13.

73 The members of the Interhamwe (a Hutu paramilitary organisation) were conditioned to see women as 'cockroaches': unworthy seductresses, who wanted to undermine, feminise and weaken Hutu men and their identity. This led feminists to argue that in this conflict Tutsi women's gender intersected with their ethnicity

in potent ways that led to the use of sexual violence against women as a tool of genocide itself. See for example: F. De Londras, 'Prosecuting Sexual Violence in the Ad-Hoc Tribunals for Rwanda and the Former Yugoslavia', 6 *UCD Working Papers in Law, Criminology & Socio-Legal Studies* (2009), at 3. For a critique of the intersectional farming of gender and ethnicity in ICTR decisions, see D. Buss, 'The Rwanda Tribunal and the Making of Ethnic Rape', presented at Sexual Abuse and Exploitation of Women in Violent Conflict, Emory University and The Netherlands Defence Academy workshop, 17–19 June 2007, Amsterdam, NDL; revised and presented at American Society for Law, Culture and Humanities, annual conference, March, 2008, San Francisco.

74 The government of Rwanda specifically requested the creation of the Tribunal because of its desire to avoid 'the risk of being accused of administering an "expeditious victor's justice", its belief that genocide [is] a "crime against humanity calling for collective efforts to prevent, stop and punish it"; and its hope that a "free and fair international tribunal would contribute to ally the fear of retribution . . . would facilitate much needed national reconciliation . . . and [is] indispensable in building a legal system based on the rule of law'". See: S.L. Russell-Brown, 'Rape as an Act of Genocide', 21 *Berkeley Journal of International Law* (2003), at 350, 366.

75 ICTR Statute at Preamble.

76 Ibid at Arts. 2,3 and 4. Article 8, moreover, provides that the ICTR has concurrent jurisdiction with national courts, over which it has primacy. Ibid at Art. 8.

77 *The Prosecutor v. Akayesu* (ICTR-96-4-T), Judgement (2 September 1998), at para 598.

78 For a discussion see C. MacKinnon, 'The Recognition of Rape as an Act of Genocide – Prosecutor v. Akayesu' (Guest Lecture Series of the Office of the Prosecutor, 27 October 2008, The Hague) reprinted in 14 *New England Journal of International and Comparative Law* (2) (2008), 101. She describes the recognition of consent as 'meaningless' for such types of violations as a 'tremendous breakthrough'.

79 See Rome Statute. 'Taking advantage of a coercive environment' is recognised as a form of force in the ICC definition of rape and enforced prostitution as crimes against humanity. International Criminal Court, Elements of Crimes arts. 7(1) (g)-1, 7(1) (g)-3, ICC-ASP/1/3 (9 September 2002). The same phrase is part of the definition of force in the war crime of rape, enforced prostitution and sexual violence. Ibid. at Arts. 8(2) (b) (xxii)-1, 8(2) (b) (xxii)-6. Consent is not mentioned in any of these sections. The elements of crime defining rape focus on force, threat of force, coercion or a coercive environment, not non-consent. Ibid at Art. 7(1) (g)-1, 8(2)(b)(xxiii)-1. The ICC does have a procedural mechanism to address the issue of consent under certain circumstances, with the burden of proof on the defendant. See International Criminal Court, Rules of Procedure and Evidence, Rules 70,72 ICC-ASP 1/3 (9 September 2002) (hereinafter Rules of Procedure and Evidence).

80 Richard Goldstone drew wide praise from feminist activists for his supportive approach towards women's issues and was applauded for the creation of the position of the Gender Focal Point and for responding to outside pressure to investigate rape and other forms of sexual violence. For a discussion see: Mertus (2008), at 1303–1305.

81 In addition to promoting a gender-integrated approach across the ICTY, Sellers also devised the approach of the OTP to gender issues within the office itself. For an overview, see: R. J. Goldstone & Estelle A. Dehon, 'Engendering Accountability: Gender Crimes under International Law', 19 *New England Journal of Public Policy* (2003), at 121, 123.

82 As Mertus describes it, drawing upon her interview with Nancy Paterson, a leader of the team, sexual crimes at the time were still within the ambit of other teams, but a specialised team was needed to ensure that that rape and other forms of

sexual violence were not overlooked. Many of the investigators, for instance, were police officers who had never done sexual violence investigations before. Mertus (2008), at 1304 (original emphasis).

83 As Mertus notes, the inclusion of individuals, whether female or male, with gender expertise was crucial for capacity building throughout the OTP on related issues. Acknowledging that as a mechanism it was far from perfect, the ICTY made a concerted effort to integrate gender throughout the investigatory teams and in other parts of the tribunal. Thus, in four successful prosecutions in specific cases and long-term staff development, insisting on gender analysis had a lasting impact. Ibid at 1305.

84 Bedont & Hall Martinez (1999), at 75–76.

85 Mertus quoting Goldstone in Mertus (2008), at 1306.

86 International Tribunal for the Prosecution of Persons Responsible for Serious Violations of International Humanitarian Law Committed in the Territory of the Former Yugoslavia Since 1991, Rules of Procedure and Evidence, at Rule 34, U.N. Doc. IT/32/Rev. 38 (13 June 2006).

87 Ibid at rule 34 (A) (ii).

88 The unit thus has child care facilities, provides support for accompanied persons, and supports efforts to relocate witnesses and attendance allowances, such as flat fees paid to witnesses for costs incurred from being absent from home. Rule 34 (B).

89 Thus, Article 20 (1) of the ICTY Statute, requires the Trial Chamber to 'ensure that a trial is fair and expeditious and the proceedings are conducted in accordance with the rules of procedure and evidence, with full respect for the rights of the accused and due regards for the protection of victims and witnesses'. See: Rule 96 of the Rules of Procedure and Evidence of the ICTY, Evidence in Cases of Sexual Assault, IT32/Rev. 21, 12 July 2001, at Art. 20.

90 For a discussion, see Niarchos (1995), at 1315.

91 See ICTY Statute, Arts. 2–3.

92 See ICTY Statute, Art. 5.

93 *The Prosecutor v. Kunarac* (IT-96–23-T & IT-96–23/1-T) Trial Chamber Judgement (22 Feb. 2001), at para 410. (hereinafter *Kunarac* Trial Chamber Judgement).

94 See for example: *The Prosecutor v. Meakic* et al., Amended Indictment (IT-95–4), 2 June, 1998; *The Prosecutor v. Kunarac* et al; *The Prosecutor v. Kos, Kvocka, Prcac, Radic and Žigic* (IT-98–30/1); and *The Prosecutor v. Nikolic* (IT-94–2).

95 The Trial Chamber, for instance, entered convictions for torture as a crime against humanity stemming from sexual violence in *Kunarac*. See *Kunarac* Trial Chamber Judgement, at paras 883 (count I) and 888 (count 33).

96 In Gardam & Jarvis (2001), at 25–30.

97 A striking example of this would be the failure of the international community to recognise and redress committed against women and girls who were forced into military sexual slavery by the Japanese army during World War II. See: C. Chinkin, 'Women's International Tribunal on Japanese Military Sexual Slavery', 95 *American Journal of International Law* (2) (2001), 335.

98 *Kunarac* Trial Chamber Judgement, at paras 883 (count 18) and 886 (count 22). As will be illustrated subsequently, the accused claimed exclusivity over some of their detained victims, ordering them to cook and perform other household chores. In some cases they ultimately sold them.

99 Ibid at paras 728–745 and 746–782.

100 This has also been specified in the following indictments: *The Prosecutor v Tadic* (IT-94–1) Trial Chamber Opinion and Judgement, 7 May 1997, where the defendant was found guilty of crimes against humanity by way of persecution, based on inter alia, rapes and other forms of sexual violence, at paras 718, 726 and 730. The *Tadic* judgement forms part of the more in-depth case law analysis of chapter 5. *The Prosecutor v. Miloševic*, Kosovo Second Amended Indictment,

(IT-02–054-T), 29 October 2001; *The Prosecutor v. Miloševic*, Croatia Indictment (IT-01–50-I), 1 October 2001); *The Prosecutor v. Miloševic*, Bosnia Indictment (IT-01–51) 22 November 2001: *The Prosecutor v. Karadžic & Mladic* (IT-95–5-I), 24 July 1995; *The Prosecutor v Plavšic & Krajišnik*, Consolidated Indictment (IT-00–39 & 40, 9 March 2001); *The Prosecutor v Brdanin &Talic*, Prosecutor's Corrected Version of Fourth Indictment (IT-99–36-I, 10 December 2001; and *The Prosecutor v. Stakic*, Second Amended Indictment (IT-97–24-PT), 31 August 2001.

101 *The Prosecutor v Krajišnik* (IT-00–39), concerning the trial of Momcilo Krajšnik, who was a member of the Bosnian-Serb leadership including the president of the Bosnian-Serb Assembly during the war, where the Trial Chamber determined that the persecutory acts included rapes and other forms of sexual violence committed against Bosnian Muslim and Bosnian Croat civilians driven from their homes by Serb forces in 1992, at (amongst others) paras 291, 304, 306, 309, 327, 333, 372, 461 and 463. The *Prosecutor v. Kvocka* (IT-98–30/1) case, where three of the accused were convicted of persecution as a crime against humanity for acts which included rapes and sexual assaults, at paras 752, 755, 758, 761 and 763 (count 1), but subsequently, one of the defendants, Kvocka, was acquitted on appeal for persecutions as crimes against humanity to the extent that the conviction related to rapes and sexual assaults; see: *The Prosecutor v. Kvocka* and 3 others (IT-98–30/1-A), 28 February 2005, at paras 6, 329–334, 402, 407 and Disposition; *The Prosecutor v. Krstic* (IT-98–33), at paras 617–618; 653, 687–688. Here, the sexual violence formed part of the basis of the conviction for Krstic for persecution as a crime against humanity. He was the chief of staff and later commander of a Bosnian-Serb army corps. He was also convicted of genocide of Bosnian Muslim men in the Srebrenica area; *The Prosecutor v. Stakic* (IT-97–24) case, where rapes and sexual assaults committed by Serb forces against Bosnian Muslim and Bosnian Croat civilians formed part of Bosnian Muslim civilian leader, of persecutions as crimes against humanity, at paras 133, 234–236, 240–241, 244, 264, 415. (The prosecution failed to prove its case of genocide, the basis of which included rapes and sexual assaults. (See: Trial Judgement, at paras 536, 537544–561)., *The Prosecutor v. Todorovic* (IT-95–9/1), Sentencing Judgement, 31 July 2001, where the accused, Todorovic, a former Serb police chief in Bosnia-Herzegovina pleaded guilty to persecution as a crime against humanity for different forms of underlying conduct, including sexual assault of non-Serb civilians detained in various detention camps in Bosnia-Herzegovina, at paras 12, 14, 37–40.

102 See *Kunarac* Trial Chamber Judgement, at para 621.

103 See *The Prosecutor v. Kvocka* (IT-98–30/1), Judgement, 2 November 2001, and *The Prosecutor v. Nikolic*, First Amendment Indictment (IT-94–2), 4 November 1992.

104 *The Prosecutor v. Furundžija* (IT-95–17/1), Trial Chamber Judgement, 10 December 1998, at para 175.

105 See R. Provost, *International Human Rights and Humanitarian Law* (Cambridge: Cambridge University Press, 2002).

106 See *The Prosecutor v. Kvocka* (IT-98–30/1), Judgement, 2 November 2001, and *The Prosecutor v. Nikolic*, First Amendment Indictment (IT-94–2), 4 November 1992.

107 *The Prosecutor v. Meakic et al.*, Amended Indictment (IT-95–4), 2 June 1998, and *The Prosecutor v. Nikolic*, First Amendment Indictment (IT-94–2), 4 November 1992.

108 Jarvis (2003), at 170.

109 See for example: *The Prosecutor v. Delalic* (IT-96–21-A) (torture and cruel treatment); *The Prosecutor v. Meakic et al.* (cruel treatment); *The Prosecutor v. Kunarac* (IT-96–23-T & IT-96–23/1-T) (torture, rape, outrages on personal dignity); *The Prosecutor v. Furundžija* (IT-95–17/1-A), (outrages upon personal dignity); *The Prosecutor v. Karadžic & Mladic* (IT-95–5-I), Indictment, 24 July 1995,

(outrages upon personal dignity); *The Prosecutor v. Kvocka* (IT-98–30/1) (torture and outrages upon personal dignity).

110 See *The Prosecutor v. Furundžija*, Decision of the Trial Chamber on the Preliminary Motion of the Defence (IT-95–17/1) 29 May 1998; see also *The Prosecutor v. Furundžija* (IT-95–17/1), Trial Chamber Judgement, 10 December 1998, at para 168.

111 *The Prosecutor v. Furundžija*, at paras 132–133.

112 Ibid at para 274.

113 *Prosecutor v. Kunarac* (IT-96–23-T & IT-96–23/1-T), at paras 883 9 counts 4, 10, 12 and 20), 886 (count 24) and 888 (count 36). In addition, two of the defendants were convicted of torture as a violation of the laws or customs of war based on sexual violence. 356 Convention on the Prevention and Punishment of the Crime of Genocide, 12. 12 January 1951, 78 U.N.T.S. 277, (hereinafter Genocide Convention) (last accessed in June 2011).

114 Convention on the Prevention and Punishment of the Crime of Genocide, 12. 12 January 1951, 78 U.N.T.S. 277, (hereinafter Genocide Convention) (last accessed in June 2011).

115 The Genocide Convention was primarily drafted in response to World War II and the atrocities committed by the Nazis. A Polish lawyer, Raphael Lemkin, coined the term 'genocide' to describe the destruction of a nation or of an ethnic group. He defined genocide as both the 'mass killings of all members of a nation', and the 'coordinated plan of different actions aiming at the destruction of essential foundations of the life of national groups, with the aim of annihilating the groups themselves'. See: Healey (1995), at 364.

116 Genocide Convention, at Art. 1.

117 *The Prosecutor v. Pauline Nyiramasuhuko & Arsénes Ntahobali Case* (ICTR-97–21-I).

118 For a summary of the status of women in Rwandan society, see: 'Shattered Lives: Sexual Violence and the Rwandan Genocide and Its Aftermath', (1996), at 19–25. As the report describes it, traditionally the role of Rwandan women in society has centred around their position as wives and mothers, while their ability to seek opportunities beyond the home has been greatly limited by the idealised image of women as child-bearers. Women were thus mostly valued for the number of children they could produce, and prior to the genocide the average number of children per woman was 6.2, one of the highest rates in the world. Ibid at 20. Moreover, the traditional and legal constraints placed on women by society had been compounded by a lack of knowledge on the part of women themselves about their rights and a lack of power to enforce them. Significantly from the point of view of this book, high levels of poverty generally contributed further to the secondary status of women. It is thus of interest to note that before the genocide Rwanda was classified among the 25 poorest nations in the world, with 94 percent of its population engaged in subsistence agriculture. At the time, women constituted 51.3 percent of the population. Given those socio-economic conditions it is rather unsurprising to note that women were significantly under-represented in education and politics; thus in the 1980s girls represented some 45 percent of the students in primary school, but by secondary school age, boys outnumbered girls 9 to 1 and by university level, men outnumbered women by 15 to 1. Consequently, within political life, the constitution guarantees the right of all citizens to participate in politics without distinction based on sex or other enumerated grounds. Yet, few women participated in political life prior to the genocide, except often to vote in accordance with the wishes of their husbands. In parliament, women's participation, moreover, never rose above 17 percent. Ibid at 21. Today, it should be pointed out, Rwanda has one of the highest figures of female MPs in the world. This is a direct legacy of the Rwandan genocide in which a large number of men perished. Against this socio-political background of

pre-genocide Rwanda, it is perhaps all the more remarkable that Pauline Nyiramasuhuko rose to the level of Health Minister.

119 For a summary of these events, see: 'Shattered Lives: Sexual Violence and the Rwandan Genocide and Its Aftermath' (1996), at 12–19.

120 The additional indictment was filed on 1 March 2001. See: *The Prosecutor v. Pauline Nyiramasuhuko & Arsénes Ntahobali Case* (ICTR-97–21-I), Amended Indictment for March 1, 2001).

121 The allegations of rape, sexual assault and other crimes of a sexual nature formed part of the factual bases of the charge against Nyiramasahuko for genocide. Ibid at count 2. For an in-depth discussion of the case, see also: S.L. Russell-Brown, 'Rape as an Act of Genocide', 21 *Berkeley Journal of International Law* (2003), at 350, 353.

122 For a summary of some extracts of the eyewitness testimony in this case, see: Russell-Brown (2003), Ibid.

123 There has been some limited consideration of the issue in *Furundžija* with the Trial Chamber noting that under the ICTY Statute rape could constitute genocide. The ICTY's prosecution of sexual violence charges as genocide might have also been hampered by the International Court of Justice ruling in the *Bosnia v. Serbia* genocide case.

124 This was a historic judgement, as the ICTR became the first international criminal tribunal to define rape as an act of genocide and to find an individual guilty of genocide on the basis, inter alia, of acts of rape and sexual violence. For a discussion see: Russell-Brown (2003), at 350–351.

125 Indictment, (ICTR-96–4-T), Jean-Paul Akayesu, at paras 3–4.

126 *The Prosecutor v. Jean-Paul Akayesu* (ICTR-96–4-T) Trial Chamber Judgement, 2 September 1998 (hereinafter Akayesu Trial Chamber Judgment), at para 686. For a discussion see also: K. L. Fabian, 'Proof and Consequences: An Analysis of the Tadic & Akayesu Trials', 49 *De Paul Law Review* (1999–2000), at 981.

127 *The Prosecutor v. Jean-Paul Akayesu* (ICTR-96–4-T) Trial Chamber Judgement, 2 September 1998 (hereinafter Akayesu Trial Chamber Judgment), at para 97.

128 The definition was enthusiastically greeted by many women's groups for not relying upon a mechanical description of body parts and for its clarification of the many concerns raised in the early debate around genocidal rape. In Askin (2003), at 288.

129 A.-M. De Brouwer, *Supranational Criminal Prosecution of Sexual Violence: The ICC and the Practice of the ICTY and ICTR* (London: Intersentia, 2005), at 455 (original emphasis).

130 N. Pillay, 'Address-Interdisciplinary Colloquium on Sexual Violence as International Crime: Sexual Violence: Standing by the Victim', 35 *Law & Social Inquiry* (4), (2009) at 847, 849.

131 For an analysis of rape prosecutions in the domestic criminal justice system, see: J. Temkin, *Rape and the Legal Process* (Oxford: Oxford University Press, 2005).

132 C. Smart, *Law, Crime and Sexuality* (London: Sage Publications, 2005), at 84.

133 As Smart has put it, the trial is virtually the same ordeal as the rape itself, as it is humiliating, depersonalising and terrifying. The only difference between the experience of the trial and the rape itself is that the former takes place in the presence of witnesses. Ibid.

134 Russell-Brown (2003), at 350, 352.

135 *Akayesu* Trial Chamber Judgment, at paras 731–732.

136 *The Prosecutor v. Musema* (ICTR-98–39-A), Trial Chamber Judgement, 6 April 2000, (hereinafter *Musema* Trial Chamber Judgement).

137 The accused, Alfred Musema-Uwimana, was the director of the Gisovu Tea Factory, one of the most successful tea factories of Rwanda. He was also a member of the governing council of the Byumba Préfecture and a member of the Technical

Committee in the Butare Commune. See: *Musema* Trial Chamber Judgement, at paras 12, 13–16. On 13 May 1994, a large-scale attack was launched at Muyira Hill against 40,000 Tutsi refugees. About 15,000 employees of the Gisovu Tea Factory dressed in their uniforms, as gendarmes, soldiers, civilians and members of the Interahamwe were among the attackers and were armed with firearms, grenades, rocket launchers and traditional weapons. Thousands of unarmed Tutsi men, women and children were killed during the attack, while others were forced to flee for their lives. Musema, as the person in charge of the operations and the figure of authority in the region, was held to have exercised de jure and de facto control over the Tea Factory employees. Ibid at paras 901–902 and 910–911.

138 *Musema Trial Chamber Judgement*, at paras 901–902 and 910–911.

139 Jarvis (2003), at 173.

140 *The Prosecutor v. Kunarac* (IT-96–23-T & IT-96–23/1-T) Trial Chamber Judgement (22 Feb. 2001) (hereinafter *Kunarac* Trial Chamber Judgement), at para 438. For a discussion, see also: L. Van den hole, 'A Case Study of Rape and Sexual Assault in the Judgements of the International Criminal Tribunal for Rwanda (Akayesu and Musema) and the International Criminal Tribunal for the Former Yugoslavia (*Celebici*, Furundžija, Kunarac, Todorovic, Sikirica and Kvocka)', 1 Eyes on the ICC (2004), 54 at 60.

141 *The Prosecutor v. Kunarac* (IT-96–23-T & IT-96–23/1-T) Trial Chamber Judgement (22 Feb. 2001) (hereinafter Kunarac Trial Chamber Judgement), at para 438. For a discussion, see also: L. Van den hole, 'A Case Study of Rape and Sexual Assault in the Judgements of the International Criminal Tribunal for Rwanda (Akayesu and Musema) and the International Criminal Tribunal for the Former Yugoslavia (Čelebići, Furundžija, Kunarac, Todorović, Sikirica and Kvočka)', 1 *Eyes on the ICC* (2004), at 54, 60.

142 It criticised the *Furundžija* classification on the basis that it held that the relevant act of sexual penetration constitutes rape only if accompanied by coercion or force or threat of force against the victim or a third person. The objective elements of rape were defined, again, as being committed by coercion or force or threat of force against the victim or a third person. The Trial Chamber pointed out that the *Furundžija* decision does not refer to other factors which would render an act of sexual penetration non-consensual or non-voluntary on the part of the victim. *Kunarac* Trial Chamber Judgement, at para 438.

143 Ibid at para 457.

144 Ibid at para 458.

145 Ibid at para 442.

146 Ibid at para 452.

147 Ibid at para 460.

148 Ibid.

149 See: *Akayesu* Trial Chamber Judgment, at para 97.

150 See *The Prosecutor v. Kunarac,* (IT-96–23-T & IT-96–23/1-T)-A, para 120 (12 June 2002) (hereinafter *Kunarac* Appeals Chamber Judgement). For a critical discussion, see also: W. Schomburg and I. Peterson, 'Genuine Consent to Sexual Violence under International Criminal Law', *101 American Journal of International Law* (Jan. 2007), at 121, 135.

151 See *Kunarac* Appeals Chamber Judgement, at para 129.

152 Ibid at para 130.

153 Ibid at para 132.

154 See *Kvocka* et al. (IT-98–30/1-T), Trial Chamber Judgement, (2 November 2001), at para 87.

155 Rule 96 provides: In cases of sexual assault:

i) No corroboration of the victim's testimony shall be required;
ii) Consent shall not be allowed as a defence if the victim:

a) has been subjected to or threatened with or has had reason to fear violence, duress, detention or psychological oppression, or
b) reasonably believed that if the victim did not submit, another might be so subjected, threatened or put in fear;

iii) before evidence of the victim's consent is admitted, the accused shall satisfy the Trial Chamber in camera that the evidence is relevant and credible;
iv) prior sexual conduct of the victim shall not be admitted in evidence.

See: Rule 96 of the Rules of Procedure and Evidence of the ICTY, Evidence in Cases of Sexual Assault, IT32/Rev. 21, 12 July 2001.

156 In accordance with the *Kunarac* Trial Chamber's definition of rape, consent is not a 'defence', but rather the absence of consent is an element of the offence. See *Kunarac* Trial Chamber Judgement, at para 463.
157 *Kunarac* Trial Chamber Judgement, at para 464.
158 Ibid at para 762.
159 See *The Prosecutor v. Muhimana* (ICTR-95–1B-T), Judgement.
160 Ibid at para 550.
161 See: *The Prosecutor v. Gacumbitisi* (ICTR-2001–64-T) (17 June 2004) (hereinafter *Gacumbitsi* Trial Chamber Judgement).
162 See: *The Prosecutor v. Gacumbitsi*, Appellant's Brief (ICTR-2001–64-A), at para 183.
163 He had, for example, threatened that in case of resistance, the women would be killed in a horrific manner by the insertion of sticks into their genitalia. In *The Prosecutor v. Gacumbitisi Indictment* (ICTR-2001–64-T), Count 5 (June 20, 2001).
164 *Gacumbitsi* Trial Chamber Judgement, at paras 198–222.
165 *The Prosecutor v. Gacumbitsi* (ICTR-2001–64-A), Appeals Chamber Judgement (July 7, 2006) (hereinafter *Gacumbitsi* Appeals Judgement) at paras 155–157. For a discussion see also: C. MacKinnon, 'The Recognition of Rape as an Act of Genocide – *Prosecutor v. Akayesu*' (Guest Lecture Series of the Office of the Prosecutor, 27 October 2008, The Hague) reprinted in 14 *New England Journal of International and Comparative Law* (2) (2008), at 101, 103.
166 *Gacumbitsi* Appeals Judgement, at para 150. Here, it quoted the *Kunarac* Appeals Judgement, at para 130.
167 See: Schomburg & Peterson (January 2007), at 121, 140.
168 *Akayesu* Trial Judgement, at para 688.
169 Ibid at paras 596–598 and 686–688.
170 Ibid at para 688.
171 Ibid at para 697.
172 See for example: K. Engle, 'Calling in the Troops: The Uneasy Relationship among Women's Rights, Human Rights and Humanitarian Intervention', 20 *Harvard Human Rights Journal* (2007), at 189–226.
173 As Doris Buss has cautioned, for example, the definition of rape in international law still tends to align itself most closely to what is generally considered the 'prototypical' kind of rape, namely 'stranger rape', even though in reality rape does not always take this form. In Buss, 'Prosecuting Mass Rape: Prosecutor v. Dragoljub Kunarac, Radomir Kovac and Zoran Vukovic', 10 *Feminist Legal Studies* (2002), at 91. For a further analysis of current definitions of rape in international law, see: F. de Londras, 'Prosecuting Sexual Violence in the Ad-Hoc International Criminal Tribunals for Rwanda and the Former Yugoslavia', UCD Working Papers in Law, *Criminology & Socio-Legal Studies* (06/2009), at 9.

4 Feminist approaches to human rights, gender, ethnicity, culture and conflict

Part I

Introduction

The previous chapters provided an overview of the salient themes and concepts underlying the book and detailed how gender-based violence has become a subject of interest for international law, while wartime sexual violence today is no longer a footnote of history but a fully recognised international crime. These chapters have sought to provide ground for the critical feminist analysis ultimately pursued. They have provided a bridge between a discussion of the key legal developments in the areas of gender-based violence and wartime sexual violence and their ensuing analysis. The present chapter constitutes the first of the two limbs in the transition from an analysis of the existing law and the theory surrounding violence against women to chapters 5 and 6, which provide the second limb in this transition, where the actual 'critical feminist' approach of the book is fully carved out.

The wartime sexual violence debate is a fusion of issues cutting across human rights, gender, ethnicity and culture. The present chapter overviews various feminist approaches to these intersecting discourses, highlighting their respective advantages and disadvantages from the point of view of pursuing an analysis of an issue such as wartime sexual violence. These will consist of four principal approaches that have been salient in recent feminist debates: first, liberal and universalist feminism; second, radical and structural feminism, or governance feminism as its more modern manifestation; third, poststructural and postcolonial feminism; and fourth, intersectionality approaches, which have significantly influenced the development of the feminist critique. These approaches provide the focus of parts II, III, IV and V, respectively. Part VI concludes and summarises the chapter. Inevitably, the analysis in this chapter implies a considerable degree of generalisation and selectiveness. This is defensible in so far as the chapter's objective is to trace the most salient feminist approaches to the analysis of human rights, gender, culture and armed conflict, as they have been manifested in feminist scholarship and activism in recent years. References will be made in this chapter to the ways in which the overviewed approaches have dealt with the issue of wartime sexual violence in the Yugoslav context, where appropriate.

Part II

Liberal/universalist feminists

Although the 'liberal' and 'universalist' orientations in feminism are not, strictly speaking, identical, there is a significant degree of conflation and overlap between them as liberalism usually rests on strong universalist presumptions.[1] There is a long tradition of liberal feminism: indeed, 'first wave' feminists explicitly adhered to liberal, universalist ideology in their pursuit of equal rights for women. However, more recently liberal feminists began to pay attention to the 'endless variety', as well as the 'monotonous similarity' of gender oppression.[2] It is fair to say that such attention within liberal feminism has tended to concentrate on 'culture' or 'culture and religion' as the factors perpetuating the 'endless variety' of gender oppression.[3] Liberal feminists generally perceive culture and gender to be in antagonism.

The idea that cultural contexts play a key role in producing gender roles and expectations based on sexuality is exemplified by the approach adopted by Susan Moller Okin in her contested essay 'Is Multiculturalism Bad for Women?'.[4] Okin's central point is that the ascent of multiculturalism and celebration of cultural difference is profoundly anti-ethical to women's rights.[5] The crucial connection between gender and culture is manifested in the sphere of personal, sexual and reproductive life as the central focus of most cultures, since far more of women's time and energy goes into preserving and maintaining the personal, familial and reproductive side of life. The more a culture requires or expects of women in the domestic sphere, the less opportunity they have of achieving equality with men in either sphere.[6] On Okin's view, many societies appear to accept violence as appropriate discipline for certain kinds of behaviour and women who do not conform to traditional sexual expectation often become subject to violence from within their own communities. Most controversial, however, is Okin's premise that minority cultures are more hostile to women than the majority (i.e. liberal Western) culture. She writes:

> While virtually all of the world's cultures have distinctly patriarchal pasts, some – mostly, though by no means exclusively, Western liberal cultures – have departed far further from them than others. Western cultures, of course, still practice many forms of sex discrimination. . . . But women in liberal cultures are, at the same time, legally guaranteed many of the same opportunities and freedoms as men. In addition, most families in such cultures, with the exception of some religious fundamentalists, do not communicate to their daughters that they are of less value than boys, that their lives are to be confined to domesticity and service to men and children, and that their sexuality is of value only in marriage, in the service of men, and for reproductive ends. The situation, as we have seen is quite different from that of women in many of the world's other cultures, including many of those from which immigrants to Europe and North America come.[7]

Okin creates a monolithic picture of 'culture', which comprises all non-Western cultures, and which acknowledges no 'local traditions of protest, no indigenous feminist movements, no sources of political and cultural contestation'.[8]

Wendy Brown has argued that the fiction of autonomy's triumph in liberalism is made possible thanks to the strong Kantianism underlying liberalism's ideology, in which liberalism figures as uniquely capable of being 'culturally neutral and culturally tolerant'.[9] She explains that, within liberalism, the possibility of an 'optional relationship' with culture is secured by the conceit that 'the individual chooses what he or she thinks',[10] which posits culture as extrinsic to the subject. For liberal individuals in the West, culture is a mere 'background', a house one can enter and exit. In contrast, for non-liberal people, including ethnic and religious minorities within liberal societies, culture is not only fixed and static, but 'saturating and authoritative'.[11]

Mainstream human rights discourses share, by and large, the classical liberal vision of culture as exemplified by Okin. In international human rights law, the term 'culture' is synonymous and/or interchangeable with 'tradition'. U.N. instruments dealing with violations of human rights, such as those produced by the U.N. Office of the High Commissioner of Human Rights, use the formula of 'harmful traditional practices', notably when confronting such issues as female genital cutting and early marriage.[12] As Sally Engle Merry has noted:

> Labelling a culture as tradition evokes an evolutionary vision of change from a primitive form to something like civilization. In the evolutionary model, all cultures are positioned on a continuum from the private to the modern. Variations are exclusively temporal. So-called traditional societies are at an earlier evolutionary stage than modern ones, which are more evolved and more civilized. Culture in this sense is not used to describe the affluent countries of the global North but the poor countries of the global South, particularly in isolated and rural areas. When it does appear in discussions of European or North American countries, it refers to the ways of life of immigrant communities and/or racial minorities.[13]

Indeed, Brown has argued that the discourse of civilisation, although distinct from and much older than liberalism, is an additional dimension in the project of modernity and as such complements liberalism.[14] A civilisational discourse is, therefore, used across the political spectrum in order to define what is tolerable. In this way, the anxieties of neo-conservatives and right-wing Christians about the decline of Western civilisation coincide with those of liberal human rights activists and feminists, such as Okin, who advocate zero tolerance towards cultural practices such as female genital cutting or veiling. The question of 'What should be the attitude of the tolerant toward the intolerant?' is, therefore, deeply ingrained in civilisational discourse. Tolerance operates as a principle of demarcation, defining intolerable 'cultural' practices with the limits of tolerance as the limit of civilisation itself.

A related trope in feminism can be most relevantly located under the heading of liberal/universal feminism, and the distinct prioritisation on the part of many such feminists of practically-orientated activism and advocacy. Many scholars, who advocate a 'practical feminism' – that is a feminism that is orientated towards finding real-life solutions to 'real problems' and improving the lives of 'real women' – reject theory and theorising practices as at best irrelevant to their work and at worst dangerous and corrupting. Indeed, as Brown has argued, this crisis of feminist theory appears to reflect the broader contemporaneous 'pressure on theory . . . to apply, to be true, or to solve immediately real-world problems'.[15]

This is demonstrated in striking fashion in recent feminist mobilisations around international criminal tribunals, which have entailed significant recourse to practically orientated feminist work. In these instantiations, there has been a notable preponderance of 'simple theory preferences', which generally signifies some straightforward version of liberal or radical feminist theory, to the almost certain exclusion of postmodern and poststructuralist varieties. In the context of international(ist) liberal feminism especially, much of late twentieth-century feminist scholarship has been strikingly anti-theoretical.[16] The next part of the chapter dedicates itself to exploring the anti-theoretical turn in feminism in greater detail.

Part III

Radical feminists and governmentality feminists

This school of thought has dominated feminist discourse over the past two decades. As a theory, radical legal feminism first assumed prominence during the 1980s and it is rooted in the idea that society entrenches female subordination, which is contingent upon male domination.[17] In broad strokes, radical feminist theorists consider the law to be a reflection of historical evolution, which excluded women from the public world. Laws inscribe gender oppression, as they are directly reflective of society's patriarchal values and relationships of power. Since men have power over women, the laws reflect and reinforce these power relations particularly in the area of sexuality and sexual relations, as laws are constructed in such a way as to project the male view of the world. The law is never impartial, objective and rational.[18] Catherine MacKinnon, more than any other radical feminist scholar, has shaped this field by producing a plethora of foundational texts that have notably contributed to the visibility of this rich strand of feminist legal scholarship.[19] By foregrounding the '[c]oncrete conditions of all women as a sex',[20] she has, for example, in typical radical fashion defined sexuality as:

> [t]hat social process, which creates, organizes, expresses, and directs desire, creating the social beings we know as women and men, as their relations create society.[21]

On this strongly structuralist view, the social relations between the sexes are organised so that men dominate and women submit. This relation is sexual – in fact it is sex. Sexuality is, inherently gendered and gender is sexualised. Male and female are created alongside the axis of the eroticisation of dominance and submission – the man/woman difference and the dominance/submission dynamic, which in turn define each other. Inequality is always political and sexual in nature and is principally constructed on sexual difference within society. The state itself is male and is the instrument which hands the law the power to institutionalise male power. Therefore, 'if male power is systemic, it is the regime'.[22] The law, moreover, is the central mechanism that perpetuates the inferior position of women within society by preserving a hierarchical system based on gender and sex. As she has put it, 'The law sees and treats women as men see and treat women.'[23] The concept of gender difference, moreover, is an ideology which masks the fact that genders are socially constructed, coercively enforced and not freely consented to. Hence, the idea of gender difference helps keep the reality of male dominance in place. Further, gender as elaborated and sustained by behavioural patterns of application and administration is maintained as a division of power. These are considered to be the focal areas for understanding the space that gender occupies both in legal and non-legal contexts. At its crux, MacKinnon's theory is a theory of power. As a form of power, gender entrenches sex hierarchy as what men and women are – it is thus productive rather than reflective of sex. As Janet Halley has argued, this is one of the most radical elements of MacKinnon's theory. She interprets from these writings that:

> The reality of sex – the very idea that men and women exist and are bodily dimorphically different – and the consciousness in which that reality seems real, natural and inevitable are effects of power.[24]

In this articulation every single important term of sexuality, such as gender or sexual orientation, is a manifestation of the domination of *f* by *m* as what sexuality is. This set of ideas denotes 'power feminism', a neat and tight system, despite its constructedness and contingency. Moreover, MacKinnon's theory can be described as a consciousness theory in that power produces consciousness by recruiting 'all its subjects to the production and domination across the whole expanse of human life'.[25] But as Halley has argued, radical theories like this one pose a deep challenge to anyone seeking emancipation, as the very consciousness with which women perceive their being is based on 'the very wellspring of their desire', which is male domination. Only a transformation of consciousness propelled forward by women on behalf of women and working 'utterly without the leverage of any emancipatory "outside" – can possibly give any hope of release from m>f'.[26]

Moreover, radical feminism has been subject to equally impassioned critique from feminist historians, who have argued that theories of patriarchy fail to show how gender inequalities, or, indeed, how gender affects these areas of life that do not seem to be connected to it.[27] Nicola Lacey has argued that radical feminism replays and reconfirms the very stereotypes of active and aggressive masculinity and passive and victimised femininity, which she regards as counterproductive to the feminist cause, as it reinforces rather than contributes to ending women's marginalisation in the legal sphere.[28] In spite of the extensive criticism, MacKinnon's ideas were still distinctly radical in the early days in sharp contrast to the notably dogmatic undertones they assumed in her later texts.[29]

i) The ascendancy of governance feminism through structural feminist interpretations of the Yugoslav conflict

Radical feminism became highly influential in the early and mid-1990s as the conflict in Yugoslavia unfolded. MacKinnon's voice strongly re-emerged in this context, assuming central prominence in feminist legal interventions around the conflict in Bosnia-Herzegovina.[30] Her highly evocative description of the atrocities committed against Bosnian Muslim women provided the central thrust to her argument that the Yugoslav war was 'genocidal' in nature, a war targeting women because of their ethnicity.[31] Most notably, MacKinnon saw a convergence between ways of thinking about women and ways of thinking about international law and politics. The more a conflict could be framed as a civil war, as domestic, as private, the less effective the human rights system was. As she has put it:

> The closer the fight comes to home, the more "feminized" the victims become, no matter what their gender, and the less likely is it that international human rights will be found violated, no matter what was done.[32]

In this vein, MacKinnon attributed the violence committed during the Yugoslav war to the Serbs, whereas 'feminine' Croatia and Bosnia were to be treated like '[w]omen – women gang-raped on a mass scale'.[33] The discourses generated by MacKinnon about ethnic responsibility seen through a cultural lens were significant because they produced an interesting trend in feminist legal scholarship, namely the entanglement of gender and ethnicity as a central technique for making sense of the sexual violence committed against (specifically Bosnian Muslim) women during the Yugoslav conflict. The interlocking of gender and ethnicity and, by extension, their depoliticisation became complete in one of her most frequently cited remarks on the intersectional nature of rape, gender and ethnicity during the Bosnian conflict:

> The systematic and instrumental nature of these rapes marks them. Progroms were one thing, designing and fielding the gas chambers was another. Rape as most women generally know it and these rapes have a similar difference. Auschwitz was industrial murder. Omarska has "industrial rape: intended planned, mass-produced, serially executed, instrumentalized". It comes close to the experiences of prostituted women, serially raped in what is called peacetime.[34]

Given that the Omarska camp was Bosnian-Serb–run,[35] MacKinnon concluded that sexual violence against women had not only been committed on an industrialised scale, but was entirely ethnically motivated, in fact coming close to a finding that it was genocidal in nature. By comparing the rapes at Omarska to the World War II progroms against the Jewish populations of Europe, this tactic of historical reduction allowed MacKinnon, a Western, U.S.-based legal scholar with little practical experience of the former Yugoslavia, to introduce her audience to the idea that the Yugoslav war was driven by ethnic motivations – particularly Serb aggression directed against non-Serbs – based on ancient rivalries that sought to exterminate the 'ethnic Other'.[36] MacKinnon raised the possibility that the specific character of Yugoslavia and of the Balkans, as embodied in the persona of the Serb was the root cause of conflict. Whether it was the propensity of the Serb for pornography, or the patterns of patriarchal, pastoral and communal life with its own mythical views of heroism and a specific code of shame the blame for the high incidence of sexual violence against women during the conflict could always be located in culture.[37]

ii) Governance feminism and its impact on the interpretation of gender and ethnicity in ICTY wartime sexual violence jurisprudence

One of the most notable consequences of the radical feminist perspective on the Yugoslav conflict and its centre-stage status in much of the surrounding literature was the ascendance of 'governance feminism'. As Janet Halley has described it, this is not just a benign form of feminism, but rather 'a feminism grown up, professionalized and adept at wielding power for the good of women globally and locally. In short, it is a feminism that 'rules' and 'wants to rule'.[38] A form of organised feminism, 'governance feminism' assumed particular prominence in the formation of new international criminal tribunals over the course of the 1990s. It produced an interesting, if not unexpected trend in feminist legal scholarship of creating an overwhelmingly coalitional, if not consensual style of agreement, which was not a 'median liberal view' that split the difference between the conservative and leftist feminist ideologies, but instead a version of 'updated radical feminism' strongly committed to a structuralist understanding of male domination and female subordination.[39] It has, certainly, been of critical importance in propelling feminism from a discipline at the margins to its current institutional status – firmly considered part of the 'academic and bureaucratic life of international law in the twenty-first century'.[40]

The term 'governance feminism' was initially coined by four U.S.-based legal feminists, Chantal Thomas, Prabha Kotiswaran, Hila Shamir and Janet Halley, in part because it captured the strong resemblance of the 'new, muscular' NGO formations adopted by feminists in their political engagement with the law.[41] These feminists were particularly struck by the paradox that feminists working on male and sexual wrongs against women in the NGO mode that typically views the international and national legal orders as heavy, consolidated, top-down sovereign powers nevertheless ambitiously jumped on the bandwagon of this sovereign power in order to produce absolute results.[42] According to Halley, such feminists:

> seek to wield the sovereign's sceptre and especially his sword. Criminal law is their preferred vehicle for reform and enforcement; and their idea of what to do with criminal law is not to manage populations, not to warn and deter, but to end impunity and abolish.[43]

Halley has produced two key findings about the sovereign power wielded by feminists in the formation of contemporary international criminal tribunals:

1) Almost without exception, the 'consensus' feminist stance that dominates the law review literature and pervades the activist literature is 'structural-feminist', and it also overwhelmingly animates both argumentation and rule preference.[44]
2) The substance of this structuralist feminist vision evolved over the course of the 1990s without producing a literature of internal dissent. While the legal agenda initially started out as a fairly simple commitment to assure that international humanitarian law and international criminal law expressly and implicitly prohibit rape in war and that the international criminal tribunals prosecute it vigorously, over the course of the decade feminists who were active in this field discovered ways of implementing their 'structuralist' view of rape not merely as a tool of belligerent forces (Croat vs. Serb, Serb vs. Muslim, Hutu vs. Tutsi), but as part of a global war against women. Women were not seen as a particular group of humanity, but a universe of their own. In the new feminist, universalist worldview, humanitarian law and international criminal law norms relating to armed conflict could be about women.

The result of the second feminist imprint in particular was not only a much stronger representational practice, but also a much bolder reform agenda, which involved 'annexing' human rights law to international humanitarian law and international criminal law and vice versa, and extending the explicit prohibitions. The key terminology evolved from rape to sexual violence to sexual slavery to gender violence – 'beyond wartime rape' to 'everyday rape', beyond 'war as men define it' to 'war as women experience it'.[45] In this way, war became conceived of not as an event, but as a situation, the life of everyday. According to this feminist strand of thought, it made increasing sense to look at ethno-nationalist dimensions underlying the Yugoslav conflict, and to portray it as 'a war against women'.[46]

iii) Ethno-nationalist interpretations of gender in ICTY wartime sexual violence jurisprudence

One of the consequences of the structuralist turn in international legal feminist scholarship is that ethnic and gender stereotypes heavily inform identity representations in international wartime sexual violence jurisprudence. This process is symptomatic of a wider trend in late modern governmentality to depoliticise structural problems such as inequality, subordination and social conflict as personal and individual, on the one hand, and as neutral, religious, cultural on the other.[47] In the Yugoslav context in particular it has led to a view of the Serbs being particularly heinous rapists, or originators of a rationally conceived and systematically executed policy as a tool of war. The use of rape in the former Yugoslavia was often attributed to cultural values unique to the region.[48] But as feminist anthropologist Dubravka Žarkov has put it, when armed conflict is framed in ethnic terms, and is referred to as a war based upon 'ethnic hatred' and 'ancient ethnic rivalries', the danger is that such terminology will be merged with an Orientalist discourse of the 'Balkans'.[49] In her view,

> In such discourses the former Yugoslavia is represented as divided into two irreconcilable and incompatible parts: West and East. According to this argument, the western, Catholic modern part of the country strives for democracy and civil society, while the eastern, Orthodox, Muslim, traditional and even tribal, part is still satisfied with a communist totalitarian system.[50]

It is therefore conceivable that the representation of conflict as ethno-nationalist in ICTY wartime sexual violence jurisprudence, strongly informed by structural feminist ideas, has removed violence against women as a political and social phenomenon from comprehension of its historical emergence and from recognition of the powers that produced it. In casting 'group conflict' as rooted in ontologically natural hostility towards essential, religious, ethnic and cultural difference, such ideas have marginalised the significance of power and history in the Yugoslav context. Moreover, through their conceptualisation of the conflict as a space where competing identities vie for sovereignty based on identity claims, structural feminists have personalised conflict as an event along the lines of artificially constructed boundaries (such as ethnicity and territoriality) while removing factors such as economic violence and material conditions from the analysis.[51] The imputation of ethno-nationalist dimensions has, moreover, led feminist activists and scholars to label the Yugoslav conflict as a 'war on women',[52] which is an arguably distortive trope that renders the resulting jurisprudence a reductive narrative of 'ethnic war'.[53]

To conclude, radical feminism's key shortcoming, as most vividly encapsulated in MacKinnon's early writings, is its totalitarian approach to male domination as constitutive of female subordination. To borrow from Halley's method, everything about the relationship of *m* and *f* manifests domination and subordination.[54] On this account, every woman suffers, however differently, the same fate. Moreover, every woman's viewpoint is rooted in her own conscience and experience, which feminism 'unmodified' articulates. It suggests that any woman can transfer truth from feminism to law, if only she succeeds in obtaining redress for sexual injury she does so on behalf of all women everywhere.

Feminists critical of MacKinnon's theory of gender and of her prescription for using law to undo gender have objected to this reification of all women as spoken for through the body and speech of the one who happens to file the claim. They have contested the totalism of this model, alongside the idea of women having a single point of view, and the idea that by attaching these to the institutional system of rights adjudication and enforcement it will liberate women from male power. It is therefore relevant to evoke at this juncture Wendy Brown's question with reference to MacKinnon's discourse, namely:

> [W]hat does it mean to write historically and culturally circumscribed experience into an ahistorical discourse, the universalist discourse of the law? What happens when "experience" becomes ontology when "perspective" becomes truth, and when both become unified in the Subject of Woman and encoded in law as women's rights?[55]

This is the theoretical framework within which the book operates to ultimately query whether it might not be apposite at this moment in time to 'take a break' from feminism. Janet Halley's work is therefore of great importance to this project as, firstly, it criticises the dominant modalities of feminism, and, secondly, introduces the idea of taking decisions in the splits between theories. This is a form of contrapuntal analysis that is useful for this book, as attention to this type of argument may promote a more complex and insightful feminist analysis as well as make room for other discourses, which may provide refreshingly new insights pertaining to the questions that feminists engage with.

Part IV

Poststructuralist feminism – Judith Butler on gender

Given the difficulty of doing justice to a theory as complex as postmodernism, this part of the chapter restricts itself to a brief analysis of some salient aspects of Judith Butler's contributions to feminist thought. In this way it seeks to push the earlier critique further by distancing itself from the rigid models of gender, sex, subordination and culture embodied in liberal and radical modes of feminism. The term 'postmodern' has been described as an active verb from which to 'denounce some parts of the modern and to point out that other parts are lost or missing'.[56]

This school of thought is based on poststructuralist readings of Sigmund Freud and his theories of language. For Lacanians, the unconscious is a critical factor in the construction of the subject – it is the location, moreover, of sexual division and of continuing instability for the gendered subject. Language is the key to the child's induction into the symbolic order, as it is through language that gendered identity is constructed. But to Lacan language was not the everyday language spoken by people but was found in the symbolism accompanying it. According to Lacan, the phallus is the central signifier of sexual difference.[57] This approach stresses fragmentation, individuation and uncertainty and denies that the interests of women are all the same. On this view, there is no essential woman imbued with the characteristics and needs of every woman, regardless of age, race or class. Postmodern thinking has been vital to feminist attempts to trouble the limits of gender as a category of analysis and to make feminist expectations of gender into uncomfortable nodes for internal questioning. Poststructuralist feminism, as captured in the writings of Judith Butler, is of particular interest as it opposes the fixed nature of categorisations and adopts a fluid approach to gender and its location within certain extraordinary situations, such as armed conflict. It also represents a marked departure from radical feminism and liberal feminism in its rejection of universalising tropes surrounding female identity.

In contrast to the Anglo-American feminist schools of thought, Judith Butler's writings have been influenced by continental theories, such as Lacanian theory. Butler has been responsible for injecting feminism with new debates on gender meanings by allowing for a reconceptualisation of the category through the creation of new spaces for thinking about its relation to the law. Her writings probably offer the most distinctly alternative view of gender in current feminist literature. Butler's seminal text is *Gender Trouble: Feminism and the Subversion of Identity*,[58] where she illuminates the idea of gender identity as a free-floating concept, not connected to an essence, but rather to a performance. Butler believes that identities are constructed through gender performances. The question is not whether to do a gender performance, but what form the performance will take. By choosing to be different about it, gender norms and the binary understanding between masculinity/femininity might be disrupted. Therefore, what is required is a deconstruction of the categories of sex, gender and sexuality and a move towards alternative approaches to identity.[59]

Butler particularly contests the notion of gender as culturally constructed, and sex as biologically pre-determined. If gender is the cultural meaning that the sexed body assumes, then a gender cannot be said to follow from a sex in any one way. In spite, or precisely because of this binary understanding of the sex/gender distinction as 'a radical discontinuity', Butler does not believe that men will interpret their identities only through male bodies, or that women will view their identities only through the female body, for:

> when the constructed status of gender is theorised as radically independent of sex, gender itself becomes a free-floating artifice, with the consequence that the man and masculine might just as easily signify a female body as a male one, and woman and feminine a male body as easily as a female one.[60]

It follows that gender is not to culture as sex is to nature. Rather, gender is the cultural means by which a 'natural sex' is produced and established as a precursor to nature, it is 'a politically neutral surface on which culture acts'.[61] An essential part in radically rethinking the categories of identity lies in challenging the universal conception of the person as understood in social theory, and replacing it with historical and anthropological positions that understand gender as

> '[a] relation among socially constituted subjects in specifiable contexts.' The question becomes not so much one of what one is, or what gender is, but of what one does or performs at a particular time. Gender does not denote a substantive being, but a 'relative point of convergence among culturally and historically specific set of relations'.[62]

Gender, framed in postmodern terms, therefore, offers a site from which to problematise the identity categories that modernism produces. Implicit in the approach of post-feminism towards gender is a focus on subjects as the outcome rather than the source of historical processes and power relations. As illustrated above, this is reflected in Butler's arguments for performitivity, seeing gender as something one does, rather than something one is. This approach deconstructs gender and removes it as the sole focus of identity politics by tying it to other social categories, such as race, class, age, sexuality and disability. There is general agreement within postmodern feminist circles that gender does not stand alone as an analytical category and must be considered in relation to other salient practices of power. The goal of postmodernist thinking therefore is to incorporate gender practices with the aim of disrupting them altogether rather than recreating a better set.[63]

Part V

Intersectionality feminists

Intersectionality has been defined as 'signifying the complex, irreducible, varied, and variable effects which ensue when multiple axis of differentiation – economic, political, cultural, psychic, subjective and experiential – intersect in historically specific contexts'.[64] Within the last couple of decades, intersectionality has pervaded much of feminist theory and activism. It has even been argued that it is the most important contribution that women's studies in conjunction with related fields have made so far.[65]

From a methodological perspective, it has raised awareness of the intersection between power relations, cultural practices and gender roles, drawing attention to their intertwined nature. It is primarily concerned with subjectivity, referring to a particular paradigm based in individual categories,[66] and with the interplay of different power relations and/or systems of oppression in society. Furthermore, it has made a significant impact beyond feminism, notably in the international human rights arena. This part traces the origins of intersectionality, its international success, its relevance to a postcolonial feminist perspective and its drawbacks.

In its earlier stages, intersectionality was associated with mostly black and Latina feminist critique of mainstream feminist theory and law, which were seen as imposing the essentialist standard of the white, middle-class heterosexual woman.[67] Kimberley Crenshaw's seminal contributions finally introduced intersectionality into feminist legal scholarship in the early 1990s. She argued that the focus on traditional categories such as race and gender in anti-discrimination law and doctrine works to exclude those who are at the categories and intersections, especially black women.[68] According to Crenshaw, the aim of intersectionality was to 'bring together the different aspects of an otherwise divided sensibility'. She argued that:

> [r]acial and sexual subordination are mutually reinforcing, black women are commonly marginalized by a politics of race alone or a politics of gender alone, and a political response to each form of subordination must at the same time be a political response to both.[69]

Crenshaw's work has been of great influence in legal doctrine, practice and feminist legal activism across the globe. It now features prominently in international human rights and activism, at least since the start of the twenty-first century. Due to sustained feminist activism, as discussed previously, gender has, for example, made its way into the United Nations law and practice dealing with racial discrimination.[70]

It also featured prominently at the 2001 World Conference against Racism, Xenophobia and Related Intolerance, which was held in Durban, South Africa thanks to the feminist NGOs that had consistently advanced this agenda in the international legal arena.[71] The final text of the Declaration, adopted at Durban refers to the 'differentiated manner' in which 'racism, racial discrimination, xenophobia and related intolerance reveal themselves . . . for women and girls'.[72] At present, U.N. Human Rights Committees and Special Rapporteurs explicitly use intersectionality as a framework when dealing with gender issues. The concept was particularly salient in the work of former U.N. Special Rapporteur on Violence against Women, Professor Yakin Ertürk, and has been continued in the work of the previous U.N. Special Rapporteur, Rashida Manjoo.[73] In this way, intersectionality, which originally emerged as a theory at the margins of academic feminism, has now been widely accepted into international feminist activism and human rights discourse.

In its theoretical manifestations, intersectionality has tended to rely on terms frequently associated with geography such as vectors and crossings as metaphors for the description of the cumulative discrimination faced by minority women in society. As Crenshaw has put it:

> Intersectionality occurs when a woman from a minority group . . . tries to navigate the Main crossing in the city . . . The main highway is "racism road." One cross street can be colonialism, then Patriarchy Street . . . She has to deal not only with one form of Oppression, but with all forms, those named as road signs, which link together to Make a double, triple, multiple, a many layered blanket of oppression.[74]

On this view, an individual is treated as a composition of interlocking identity elements, such as gender, race, sexuality, religion and class. Governance feminism is in many ways an extension of intersectionality theory in that it explores the ways in which late modern subjects are constituted through discourses of power, class and race, albeit without ever using the term intersectionality. Of particular interest to this book is the impact of intersectionality theory on postcolonial feminist scholarship, which in turn is vital to the examination of the representational practices of the ICTY in its interpretation of wartime identities.

i) Structural bias critique and the opening up of the postcolonial feminist discourse

As noted previously, international feminist legal scholars such as Christine Chinking, Hillary Charlesworth, Rhonda Copeland, Charlotte Bunch and Catherine

MacKinnon have contributed notably to international feminist legal scholarship with their ideas underpinning many feminist reform projects of the law. In many ways their writings also represent the leading strand in feminist legal theory from the early 1990s onwards. It is useful to briefly resort back to the 'structural bias' critique of international human rights law, which has served as a springboard for many of the most distinct arguments in recent postcolonial feminist scholarship.[75]

Implicit in these critiques of international law is the idea that international law is male, and therefore inherently or 'structurally biased' against women, not only preventing their inclusion but even requiring their subordination. These feminists, each in their own registers, have advocated for an integration of women's human rights through a complete regime change. While universally applauded during the 1990s, 'structural bias' critique has subsequently come under sustained critique from other feminist scholars for its failure to explore the intersecting dimensions of female discrimination, which according to postcolonial feminist scholars cannot be divorced from the historical context in which they took shape. Moreover, their almost exclusive focus on the binary divisions of the law and the family as the main site of oppression is seen as misplaced for not taking into account government inaction as a force that frequently further perpetuates this oppression.[76]

In particular, the structural feminist embrace of cultural factors and practices as a way of accounting for gender-specific issues such as domestic violence, female genital mutilation or malnutrition is often deemed biased against Third World women in the sense that it does not conceive of their agency.[77] Most crucially, structural feminism has failed to conceptualise the multiplicity of women's voices within that group, which has become a renewed subject of interest in feminist legal scholarship not least because of the influence of postcolonial feminist ideas on current human rights discourses around gender-based violence. It is apposite to turn to some of the most notable contributions in postcolonial feminist scholarship, which further reinforce the idea earlier expressed by Crenshaw that discrimination is always multiple, yet also historically contingent and culturally constructed. In this way, postcolonial feminist scholars have pointed out some interesting modalities which also distinctly shape contemporary wartime sexual violence jurisprudence.

In one of the foundational postcolonial feminist texts, *Under Western Eyes: Feminist Scholarship and Colonial Discourses*,[78] Chandra Mohanty points to the absence of the histories of Third World women's engagement with feminism.[79] 'Feminist historiography' is her central method for understanding the connection between women as historical subjects and the re-presentation of women produced by hegemonistic discourses. Mohanty is particularly critical of Western feminist assertions that have reinforced the homogeneity of women based on their shared ground of oppression inevitably binding women together in a sociological notion of 'sameness' of oppression. Her most stringent critique of Western feminist discourse, however, is its conceptualisation of the Third World woman as a unitary subject with homogenous interests and goals. A majority of feminist texts are seen as having 'discursively colonised the material and historical heterogeneities' of the lives of women in the Third World, which reproduce a 'singular Third World Women' – an arbitrarily constructed, yet weighty trope in dominant Western humanist discourses.[80] Mohanty calls for women to form 'strategic coalitions across class, race and national boundaries', as the most useful way of exploring the links among the histories and struggles of Third World women against racism, sexism, colonialism, imperialism and monopoly capital.[81] This is because Western feminist political practice has foreclosed on the possibility of coalitions among Western feminists, working-class feminists and women of colour. In its prioritisation of certain issues – most notably gender-based violence – it has not accounted for those who might have entirely different concerns. In some ways, Mohanty's engagement with 'feminist historiography' is a rejection not only of the essentialised Third World woman frequently found in colonialist discourses; it is also a call for an intersectional understanding of the historical and political powers that constitute the varying vectors and crossroads of oppression that differently situated women experience around the world.

ii) *New intersectional understandings: postcolonial feminism and the rejection of the woman-as-victim paradigm*

Whereas earlier writings on the intersectional dimensions of oppression against women from the 'Global South' were primarily focused on their historical exclusion from the texts of international law, later postcolonial feminists sought to explore the more concrete threats to women shaped by very modern forms of violence, namely by way of economic globalisation and military intervention. Feminist legal scholars writing in this vein include Karen Engle, Diane Otto, Anne Orford and Ratna Kapur. Their common critique of contemporary feminist legal theory is that it has succumbed to the idea of women as unitary, monolithic subjects of international law, without acknowledging that gender is always shaped by intersecting vectors such as race, class and ethnicity and economic exploitation. Feminist legal theory has produced a limited and incomplete understanding of women's subjectivity, having denied women their agency as independently constituted subjects in international law. The universality and essentialism of the earlier feminist movements are seen as having contributed to the production of women as victims in much of contemporary feminist scholarship. While postcolonial feminists do not deny that the women's human rights movements were instrumental in raising awareness and setting international standards, they strongly reject the universal assumptions made about women and the lack of acknowledgment of the multiple dimensions of violence they face in everyday life. These writers, then, pose a direct challenge to modern international feminism's very foundation. Third World feminist critique has 'unconsciously affected' much of the feminist critique of international law through its introduction of the 'exotic other female' to the international stage.[82] Postcolonial feminists in particular have challenged the systems of knowledge that continue to inform feminist understandings of women and the subaltern subject in the postcolonial world.[83] Postcolonial feminism exposes the imperial and essentialist assumptions about Third

World women and culture that often characterise the debates on women's rights. Moreover, it challenges attempts to universalise women's experiences, primarily along the lines of gender, as these serve to exclude through cultural, religious or sexual 'Othering' the situation of women in the postcolonial world and their struggles for rights. Western feminist strategies espousing 'global sisterhood' in their search for universal solutions to women's concerns continue to ignore the colonial contexts on which these assumptions are founded.[84]

Ratna Kapur's writings reflect most strongly the contemporary postfeminist colonial critique of the international women's rights movement.[85] To Kapur, the depiction of the Third World woman as perpetually marginalised and underprivileged object of international law is reflected in the strategies adopted to remedy the harms that women experience, which in reality reinforce stereotyped and racist representations of 'Third World culture' and in doing so privilege the culture of the West.[86] The perception of the Third World woman in international legal scholarship is further reminiscent of colonialist representations, which regarded them as infantile, civilisationally backward and incapable of autonomy or self-determination. Moreover, the international women's human rights movement has reinforced the image of women as 'victim subjects', primarily through its focus on violence against women, which has had little to do with the actual promotion of women's rights. The focus on the 'victim subject' has strengthened gender and cultural essentialism and erased the problems, perspectives and concerns of women, who are marginalised on account of their race, class, ethnicity, religion or sexual orientation. Moreover, it has posited the Third World woman as the 'authentic victim' given that 'the look of starvation, helplessness and victimisation is remarkably familiar to our imaginations, irrespective of the reality'.[87]

The Violence against Women (VAW) campaign is one manifestation of cultural essentialism marking contemporary women's human rights discourse that has failed to encapsulate the lives and experiences of women as not only shaped by gender, but also by race, religion and class, therefore, never translating into a complex understanding of women's experiences.[88] Moreover, the campaign has reinforced a gratuitous connection between culture and violence in relation to the Third World, which is not invoked in a similar fashion when discussing violence against women in the West. This is reflected in the way certain crimes associated with the Third World, such as dowry murders and veiling have been deployed by the VAW movement to reproduce a totalising view of culture in its treatment of women, offering an overly simplistic image, if not total misrepresentation of the practice. As Kapur has remarked in relation to current feminist debates around veiling practices:

> The veil may not be a modern practice, yet the multiple meanings of the veil, through different cultural and historical contexts, get subsumed in rhetoric that focuses almost exclusively on veiling as an oppressive and subordinating practice. It is read in a uniform, linear manner as an oppressive practice because it erases women's physical and sexual identity and is symbolic of the subjugation of women in Islam. Yet, there is no universal opinion as to its function amongst those who wear the veil.[89]

Another prominent practice invoked by Western feminists – in relation to postcolonial India – is the image of the female body in flames, or the practice of sati, which is often collapsed with dowry murders as an entirely distinct phenomenon.[90] But what is frequently lost in such culturally essentialised discourses is how the subject in different cultural contexts comes to be constituted through oppositions between culturally totalising discourses and liberal rights discourses, which end up erasing the very subjectivity of the woman, whose rights are implicated or have been denied. In spite of its constant assertions that it is dealing with the 'real lives' of women, the VAW campaign has furnished accounts of the lives of these victims from the perspectives of outsiders. As Kapur argues, merely giving priority to the victim's voice as a response to this critique risks equating it with the 'truth' and produces an experiential politics that is too closely tied to identity politics, which has surrendered any commitment to a transformative vision of the world and women's lives in that world.

The effort to integrate cultural diversity into a gender analysis has, consequently, been a mixed bag for the women's human rights movement. The focus on violence against women has not only reinforced images of the Third World woman as 'thoroughly disempowered, brutalized and victimized; a representation that is far from liberating for women', but has foreclosed the possibility of imagining human rights discourses as reflecting a multitude of women's voices that draw strength from the fragmentation and multitude of experiences and thinking. Moreover, it has failed to analyse how the mechanisms of discursive engagement produce the victim subject and the forms of violence to which she may be subjected. Postcolonial feminists have inevitably been highly critical of radical feminism's essentialising tendencies, which have focused on the commonality of women's experiences, while failing to interrogate the extent to which the multiplicity of women's experiences displaces gender as the central category of analysis.[91] Moreover, Kapur's analysis has fleshed out the modalities by which contemporary women's human rights discourses continue to perpetuate unhelpful images of women by advocating for ways in which they ought to be, rather than reflecting on the ways in which they are.

The main theoretical contribution of postcolonial legal feminism lies in its interrogation of how colonial histories continue to discriminate in the postcolonial present. It exposes how scholars from 'the metropolis' including liberal feminists operate under hegemonistic historical narratives disguised by the idea of objectivity. Postcolonial theory, therefore, also poses a challenge to those feminists who speak in the name of postcolonial feminism by constantly trying to produce an 'authentic' identity, or a 'culturally distinctive position', as reinforcing binary divides between the 'us' and 'them', which homogenise the location and politics of Western feminism and play into the hands of right-wing agendas, who use the image of the 'woman victim' for their own political purpose.[92] It concludes that international law can only reinvent women's spaces through a radically reformed legal discourse that integrates an understanding of how women's subjectivities and experiences of violence are partly constituted and constructed in the arena of women's human rights in and through the discourse of the VAW campaign and the foregrounding of the 'victim subject'. This suggests that while solutions must be found outside of the law, it is still the most powerful tool for reinventing and re-politicising current women's rights discourses.

In various registers, contemporary legal feminist scholarship has been inspired by postcolonial feminist theory in its intersectional analysis of the representational practices deployed by international criminal tribunals with respect to wartime identities in the age of 'ethnic' conflict.[93] Doris Buss is one of the most prolific scholars to have engaged with ICTY and ICTR wartime sexual violence jurisprudence.[94] She has questioned whether there are limits to the strategy of seeing women and the human rights abuses they suffer within the work of international crimes tribunals. Her key argument is that wartime sexual violence against women has become visible in the emerging international criminal justice system largely through the attention placed on ethnicity as a key meta-narrative within which sexual violence against women materialises.[95] While the ICTY's analysis of gender-based violence produced an increased visibility of wartime violence against women, this has occurred against the backdrop of conflicts defined as 'ethnic', which were interwoven into the tribunal's jurisprudence.[96] The intersections of gender and ethnicity in the tribunal's jurisprudence reveal some of the mechanisms through which sexual violence and gender inequality are highly visible but only superficially so. As she has put it,

> In the Tribunal's reasoning, the focus on gender in the context of an overdetermined assessment of ethnic conflict becomes a means for occluding, rather than opening up the complex dimensions of violence against women.[97]

Buss illuminates that this tendency in much of international scholarship of understanding modern conflicts as 'ethnic', in particular when viewed in light of the complexity of the Yugoslav situation, can produce reductive and distorting effects. In overplaying the ethnic dimensions of conflict, the complex effect of political, economic and geo-political change that created the conditions for the wars in the region are simultaneously minimised. This raises concerns about what is lost and unseen when ethnicity becomes unquestionably the explanatory framework within which these conflicts are understood. Buss pauses to reflect on the fact that while wartime sexual violence against women has become both part of the public image of war, or the symbol of suffering, it has simultaneously been erased as an international concern. As she sees it:

> [M]issing from the various constructions of wartime rape is any sense of rape as an act of violence against women.[98]

Chapters 5 and 6 analyse in more detail the argument that ethnicity and race function as the dominant, arguably distorting lens through which gender crimes are seen and unseen in ICTY wartime sexual violence jurisprudence.[99]

Buss' analysis also ties in closely with the work of cultural feminist anthropologist Dubravka Žarkov, who has analysed the centrality of victim representations in media narratives around rapes and sexual assaults which in turn have shaped intersectional feminist legal interpretations of gender, ethnicity, the body and the nation in the breakup of Yugoslavia. As Žarkov has put it:

> Media representations of rapes and sexual assaults against women treated the female body as the map on which the new, sexual, geographies of ethnicity were drawn, this time in discursive terms.[100]

Žarkov has argued that victimisation accompanied both the violence against women and its legal remedies, as much as it accompanied the media representations and collective narratives during the breakup of Yugoslavia.[101] The victimised female body has been a particularly powerful tool in the deployment of media images, a potent metaphor in the violent production of collective identities that have made women in the Yugoslav war visible. A prominent example she has provided to illustrate this point is the way in which Croatian newspapers developed three distinctive stories about wartime rape.[102] The stories revolved around three central themes: the victims of rape, forced impregnation and about the rapists themselves. About half of the stories were about the victims of rape, and a majority of them were about the national and international activities around the issue, such as United Nations or European Union resolutions, international attempts to prosecute the perpetrators or assist the victims, and actions within Croatia, mostly by medical experts on treating trauma, thus indicating the international dimensions that helped visibilise rape in the popular discourse. Moreover, an overwhelming majority of the articles (largely supplied to the Croatian media through foreign sources)[103] were about raped Muslim women. Only a handful of the articles about rape surveyed mentioned that Croatian women had been raped at all, and only one or two went into describing the circumstances of the rape. By way of example Žarkov cites the following passage in the weekly daily *Danas*:

> With regard to the severity of the violence, Croatian women were no better off than Muslim women, but the scope of the violence against Muslim women surpasses everything ever seen in the history of wars.[104]

Aside from positing the 'unique' nature of the sexual violence against Bosnian Muslim women as a culturally loaded signifier of the Yugoslav conflict, the newspapers emerging in the Croatian media at the time usually mentioned the rape of Croatian women without providing any concrete details, while the rape of Serbian women was hardly ever mentioned, and if so, mostly to deny it. The underlying reason for these different representational practices might have been motivated by a desire to establish the difference between all Croats and Muslims, for:

> The visibility of the Muslim woman only as the rape victim produced her as having nothing in common with a Croat man or a woman. According to the Croatian press, Muslims and Croats belong to different levels of civilization, which simply do not touch each other.[105]

In this representation, rape becomes a question of 'humanity' – meaning that the raped Croat woman, if visible, would be a link to those 'dehumanized Others', both the Serb rapist and the raped Muslim woman. When rape becomes a question of humanity, to link the Croatian woman with 'those dehumanized Others' – with the Serb rapist, and the raped Muslim woman – would equal questioning her humanity. The dehumanisation of the Croatian woman needs to be prevented in order to preserve the humanity of the 'ethnic self', which is a crucial strategy whereby the victim is equated with the perpetrator, as the representation of Serb women in the Croatian press suggests.[106]

The danger of presenting violence against women as a ubiquitous practice along strictly ethnicised lines is that these practices produce certain women as victims only, denying them both subjectivity and agency while at the same time excluding women, who are deemed undesirable from the protective realm and, also, foreclosing male vulnerability. The act of sexual violence is given the power to produce dominant notions of both femininity and masculinity, creating the former through violence endured and the latter through violence perpetrated. That the Serbian press was similarly complicit in the production of women as victims viewed through highly essentialised readings of the woman's body has also been demonstrated by Žarkov and indicates that this was not a particularised representational practice, but rather ubiquitous regardless of ethnic context.

The ethnicised issue of forced impregnation became a particularly prominent theme in the Serbian press, as the children conceived of rape – whether born or unborn were defined as the source of 'ultimate torment' for the impregnated women.[107] These representations were on the one hand concerned with defining the Serbhood of the women, while at the same time seeking to define the Serbhood of the men. Both these directions speak about shifts at the intersections of gender and ethnicity – the practice of rape, specifically, defines women as both the female and the ethnic 'Other' at the same time, with gender and ethnicity appearing equally important. But the practice of forced impregnation, whereby the child's ethnicity is defined through the father, speaks of the gendered hierarchy of ethnicity and the primacy of gendered difference in 'ethnic conflict'. While gender and ethnicity are mutually productive, they at the same time produce each other in competing and conflicting ways. This is most strongly captured by the discourse of ethnic purity, which assumes that the child's ethnicity is produced by the man. The woman in such discourses is swept aside, as the right to determine the ethnicity of the child is deemed as the male preserve. According to Žarkov, this is what points away from the impregnated Serb woman, toward the Serb man, making him the ultimate victim of these impregnations: 'wronged' by seeing his ethnic stock contaminated and his lineage disrupted by Muslim men, he is the embodiment of Serbhood.[108]

Žarkov's is a powerful intersectional reading of the way in which female identity, bodily injury and culture emerge in the media discourses around the Yugoslav conflict with often regressive results for women. In order to have any emancipatory purchase, feminist theorising on wartime sexual violence against both women and men needs to deconstruct the 'fatal linkages' between male identity, male violence and male and female pleasure, as they produce highly problematic intersectional readings of gender, ethnicity, violence and the nation in the context of armed conflict. Žarkov cautions against the overwhelming visibility and presence of women as rape victims in public discourse along 'very specific, ethnicised identities of victims and villains', which are perpetuated through the use of universalised gendered and sexual identities that preclude the emergence of alternative notions of femininity and masculinity.[109] Her writings serve as vivid reminder of the centrality of popular narratives in the production of disenfranchised victim subjects, which are produced not only through the general sense of female subordination in armed conflict but are also shaped by conflicting forces of masculinity, which themselves are deeply contingent and hierarchical.

Yet, while intersectionality theories have undoubtedly provided highly useful insights into the multiple dimensions of identity underlying women's experiences, whether in their everyday lives or in times of armed conflict, they have been criticised for their insufficient emphasis on the broader and structural dimensions underlying female inequality, fragmenting both subjectivity and the forces that shape it. Prominent critical and feminist theorists, such as Judith Butler and Wendy Brown have argued that it is misleading to think of gender in isolation from race, or of race as free of all inflection of gender or sexuality.[110] Various strands of literature have, moreover, highlighted the pointlessness of constructing the individual as an atomistic, detached, 'relentlessly self-interested' entity.[111] Wendy Brown has, for example, argued that structural influences are always subsumed and internalised in the individual before individual identity components can be meaningfully articulated.[112] In addition, she has argued that the social powers constituting identity are not simply different powers, but different kinds of power, such as gender, sexuality, race, religion and so on, are not equivalent problematics.[113]

The concept of intersectionality, therefore, appears flawed, as it more often than not tends to presuppose that 'intersections' exist prior to the subject and are more or less equal in weight. More recent feminist theorising has asserted that 'intersectionality has reached the limits of its potential for the feminist project in law', with its value being confined to simply highlighting complex experiences before the law.[114] Joanne Conaghan has argued that intersectionality is:

> rather limited in its theory-producing power. In particular, while it acts as an aid to the excavation of inequality experiences at local level, it tells us little about the wider context in which such experiences are produced, mediated and expressed.[115]

To conclude, intersectionality has been successful at drawing attention to the problem of the marginalisation of certain identities and experiences in feminist politics, law and wider human rights discourses. However, intersectionality as an approach for feminist analysis has tended to concentrate on difference, while overlooking the persistent importance of gender structures across the intersections. It is questionable whether intersectionality has been able to capture the complexities inherent in experiences that do not conform to everyday norms, such as gendered experiences of war. Moreover, it appears that the concept's usefulness beyond its function of 'representing' experiences has been exhausted, as it appears to enhance, rather than destabilise the regulatory and identity-producing function of the law. It is conceivable that intersectionality may have reached its utility for feminism, and would benefit from giving way to other forms of engagement.

Part VI

Exploring gender's limits: the impact of economic globalisation, military intervention and structural violence

Although intersectional to the extent that it examines the confluence of power, gender, race and economic exploitation, Anne Orford's critical reading of recent intervention narratives is useful, as it reinstates critical legal theory in the face of dominant representations of power in current international legal texts. Orford analyses globalisation and economic injustice as central drivers of new liberal impulses, which are frequently interventionist in nature and directed at those with limited resistance, such as the people of the 'Global South'.[116] In this way, she is able to draw attention to economic injustice as the key driver of violence, if not the root cause of the disproportionate targeting of women for sexual violence offences in armed conflict. Moreover, she queries feminist conceptions of the law as operating through the creation of subjectivity and identity, or the constitution of sovereign states and international institutions, and suggests instead that it might be more helpful to understand power as operating beyond a 'juridical' or prohibitive model in order to think about the power relations involved in, and enabled by, the performance of humanitarian intervention.[117] Drawing on postcolonial theory, Orford argues that in the era of decolonisation, imperialism today manifests itself largely through its economic grip on power, rather than through territorial expansion. As she puts it:

> It is true that we do not today see reprised that form of imperialism premised upon the sovereignty of claiming of sovereignty over invaded or occupied territory by a foreign, colonial power. Yet, 'a largely economic' enterprise of imperialism continues in the form of exploitation of the colonised, their land and resources. Intervention has been preceded in places such as Bosnia-Herzegovina and Rwanda, and accompanied in Haiti, Kosovo and East Timor by the facilitation of this imperial enterprise. One of the overt aims of pre-conflict 'aid' programmes, and post-conflict reconstruction, has been the establishment of the necessary conditions to make foreign investment secure and profitable.[118]

Rather than reading international law and humanitarian intervention as a form of progress from a world of 'irrational tribal, premodern, failed states to one of free, democratic, developing states',[119] intervention and the power relations that sustain it need to be understood as part of the global history of global imperialism. Orford's approach is valuable, as it reinstates critique as an important methodological tool for any feminist inquiry that counters against the tendencies earlier described of analysing complex, structural problems through a 'simple theory' approach, which eschews critique as irrelevant to the facts on the ground, a luxury or the stuff of recreation amidst the problems facing 'real people in the real world'.[120] Taking aim at the pragmatic, goal-orientated, linear focus of international legal scholarship, which requires that all critique be directed towards policy and programmatic change, she argues that:

> The self-representation of international law as a discipline concerned with peace and security, decolonisation and humanitarianism reassures lawyers that there is no time to waste on dealing with theoretical irrelevancies, when our profession is engaged in more important life and death matters.[121]

On this view, theory and critique are seen as vacuous and narcissistic projects for their reflection of textual practices of the law without the provision of a corresponding plan for action. This is part of a broader pattern of negative reactions towards the use of cultural and critical theory to study issues of capitalism, globalisation, neo-imperialism and militarism both within the law and the social sciences more generally. The trend is, moreover, reflective of current trends in feminist scholarship and activism, which increasingly seeks 'real life' solutions to complex problems for which it might not have unique epistemic purchase.[122]

Orford proposes an approach that does not separate 'representation from reality', an abandonment of the disciplinary or generic rules of law that work to make stories of brutality appear legitimate and useful. Instead, cultural criticism is a necessary approach from which to understand 'the apparent naturalness and inevitability of both militarism and economic globalisation'.[123] In a similar vein to postcolonial feminist theorists, such as Spivak and Kapur, Orford is highly critical of a feminist theory that threatens to facilitate and enable colonialism, if it stages the key struggle in the globalised world as between 'male and female sparring partners'.[124] Indeed, as she puts it:

> A feminist analysis of intervention that focuses on gender alone, without analysing the exploitation of women in the economic 'South', would operate to reinforce the depoliticised notion of 'difference' that founds the privileged position of the imperialist feminist.[125]

Her analysis pays careful attention to the context of increasing economic integration in which humanitarian intervention takes place. Intervention, in particular, takes different forms in the contemporary context, and can denote the involvement by the international community in, say, the breakup of the former Yugoslavia by means of prohibitive economic measures taken against the country starting in the 1980s, or it can even take shape in the creation of international ad hoc tribunals, such as the ICTY, which has been viewed as an interventionist measure taken by the international community to remedy past wrongs.[126] Moreover, Orford's approach is insightful because it serves as a reminder that the ending of the Cold War has enabled the process of economic globalisation, which was in turn facilitated by the increasingly effective and rapidly shifting economic operations of international economic institutions such as the IMF, the World Bank and the World Trade Organization (WTO).[127]

This process has been very powerfully demonstrated by Balkans scholar Susan Woodward, who has shown that the engagement of the international community in the political and social life of Yugoslavia was extensive.[128] This external involvement gained in strength following the death of the former president of Yugoslavia, Josip Broz Tito, in 1980, who until then had managed to keep a tight grip on the central levers of power.[129] Yet with the death of Tito, the demise of the state became only a question of time, as in the 1980s all three of its key functions – its monopoly over the legitimate use of violence, its authority in the conferral and enforcement of rights, and its central function in the provision of protection to the population – began to break down. Moreover, a fiscal crisis and budget-cutting austerity programme of debt repayment signed with the International Monetary Fund (IMF) in the early 1980s undermined the government's ability to provide protections and guarantee minimum welfare.[130] The authority of the federal government was severely challenged by liberalising economic and political reforms and by republican politicians who opposed any loss of economic rights they had obtained during the decentralising reforms in the 1970s.[131] These developments resulted in a serious decline in the federal government's capacity to enforce rights and the weakness in authority was further undermined by parallel developments in two republics of Yugoslavia, Slovenia and Croatia, which by that stage had begun to secretly build separate armies.[132] As Woodward points out,

> There is no need for any historic of ethnic animosity or civil war to predict growing uncertainty, social chaos and potential violence under such circumstances.[133]

In this atmosphere of intense frustration with the political status quo, pseudo-nationalist sentiments, or 'a childlike yearning to be heard' found fertile ground to manifest themselves in tandem in the two largest republics, Serbia and Croatia.[134] Neither advocates of a free market, nor supporters of redistribution and equality were likely to be as popular under conditions of austerity and rising inequality as were states' right advocates who claimed that individuals had rights – national rights – to their earnings and employment.[135] Once political, cultural and economic elites called on Yugoslavs to think in terms of their ethnic identity and as members of a national instead of a Yugoslav community and claimed that their survival was threatened by other Yugoslav nations and that protection in insecure times lay with their own nation and its leaders, the gravity of the loss of an overarching Yugoslav state became 'crystal clear'.[136] In this situation of loss or renouncement of a Yugoslav identity paired with a debilitating economic crisis, the language of exploitation and victimisation based on 'ethnic belonging' found fertile ground.[137]

Yet the consequences of economic restructuring, and the central role played by international institutions in furthering that project have not been examined by international lawyers, who have often entirely ignored the historical context within which security and humanitarian crises emerge and military intervention takes place. While 'ancient ethnic hatreds', ethnic tensions, postmodern tribalism or emerging nationalisms are regularly treated as the causes of intervention, most international legal analyses do not ask whether such crises could be better understood as a consequence of ever more ruthlessly efficient divisions of labour and resources in the post-Soviet era.[138]

The argument of this book that ICTY wartime sexual violence jurisprudence has occluded from its analysis the nature of the economic order that was put in place in Yugoslavia as one of the key causes underlying the conflict does not seem far-fetched when considering the previous analysis. Moreover, the argument that identity categories such as gender and ethnicity exist in a vacuum that can be entirely divorced from the political, social and economic circumstances and the structural conditions characterising Yugoslavia in the pre-war era not only depoliticises the meaning of power and history in the constitution of these subjects, but also misrepresents the nature of the conflict, which, as previously shown, cannot be defined as solely 'ethnic' in nature.

Orford's approach is useful in so far as it has successfully delineated the limits of gender as a category of analysis for the complex power relations that inevitably underpin interventionist strategies – whether military, economic or 'humanitarian' in the present day. Her analysis, while distinctly feminist in its outlook is at the same time sceptical of feminism's capacity to provide the necessary framework for understanding the complex range of gendered experiences in extraordinary situations such as armed conflict. In moving away from subjectivity as a framework for understanding armed conflict by drawing attention to the material forces that determine discourses of power, Orford has raised pressing questions, perhaps inadvertently suggesting that it might be opportune for feminism to take a step back and reconsider its own investment with institutional power. In this way, her approach perhaps come closest to the book's ultimate suggestion that now might be the time for feminism to 'take a break' from itself in order to allow for new and fresh insights unperturbed by identity discourses to emerge and to find its seat at the table.

Part VII

Conclusion

This chapter has been concerned with providing an overview and analysis of the most salient contemporary feminist approaches to human rights, gender, ethnicity and culture. It has highlighted the advantages and disadvantages of these approaches, from the point of view of pursuing an analysis such as gender-based violence against women. The feminist approaches overviewed in this chapter comprised liberal/universalist feminists, radical and 'governance' feminists, post-structuralist feminists, postcolonial feminists and intersectionality feminists. This selection has implied a considerable degree of generalisation, which is justifiable to the extent that the approaches overviewed are considered to be the most salient or expressive points in contemporary feminist scholarship and activism dealing with human rights, gender, ethnicity, culture and armed conflict.

Although each of these approaches have undoubted merits, each also has some significant limitations for a project such as the present one. The liberal/universalist feminist approach is problematic because of its decoupling of gender and culture and its preference for 'simple theory', including a unified conception of the subject. Radical feminism, while undoubtedly instrumental in highlighting women's subordination and oppression as deeply embedded in the legal and power structures of the state, has overplayed the dominance of men over women and the struggle between men and women as the central mechanism for understanding the gendered dynamics of armed conflict. In so doing, it has reinforced the trend towards the culturalisation of identities in international law, which in turn has produced highly essentialised and reified stereotypes of women in ICTY wartime sexual violence jurisprudence. In its more contemporary manifestations radical feminism has been conceptualised as a form of 'governance feminism', which has largely produced consensus among feminist scholars and activists as to the legal reforms necessary to regulate sexual violence against women while often stifling critique from those who have queried these advances for women in the current and political and legal moment and have called into question feminism's belief in its unique epistemic purchase on the condition of women.

The intersectionality approach, arguably the most influential in the human rights arena, is useful for highlighting that gender alone does not account for the complexities that women find themselves in. This has been taken further by postcolonial feminist analysis, which has highlighted the intersection of gender, race and poverty in its analysis of the representational practices of international texts about 'Third World' women. It has, moreover, firmly located these practices in the postcolonial context, reinforcing the significance of history and the material dimensions of women's lives as essential for an understanding of how identities are produced in Western scholarship. However, intersectionality has been accused of further fragmenting subjectivity and, therefore, colluding with the classificatory impulse of the law. Furthermore, its theory-producing and practical resolution are to some extent limited, as postcolonial feminists in particular have tended to focus on the condition of the 'Third World' woman, while not paying much attention to women located in 'the in-between', such as Yugoslav women, who are neither seen as Western European nor as 'Third World' women, due to their geographical location in South-east Europe. While intersectionality has undoubtedly been deployed effectively to analyse the legal modalities used by the ICTY in its interpretation of wartime identities, it is not able to entirely account for the complex interplay of gender, ethnicity, the nation and armed conflict in relation to wartime sexual violence, as it focuses too closely on liberal notions of subjectivity and autonomy, which in themselves are contingent and limiting concepts.

Notes

1 Eg S. Mullally, *Gender, Culture and Human Rights: Reclaiming Universalism* (Oxford: Hart Publishing, 2006) distinguishes between 'universal' and 'universalist', the latter being imbued with negative connotations.
2 The phrase 'endless variety and monotonous similarity' (of gender oppression) was coined by Gayle Rubin: G. Rubin, 'The Traffic in Women', in R. Reiter (ed.), *Toward and Anthropology of Women* (New York: Monthly Press, 1975), at 157, 160.
3 There are, however, critiques that expose the heteronormative bias of liberal feminism, e.g. Brown (1995) is arguably among the stronger ones. See V. E. Munro, 'Feminism(s), Law and Liberalism(s)', in V.E. Munro (ed.), *Law and Politics at the Perimeter: Re-Evaluating Key Debates in Feminist Theory* (Oxford: Hart Publishing, 2007) for an insightful overview of feminist critiques of liberalism in general.
4 S. Okin, 'Is Multiculturalism Bad for Women?', in J. Cohen, M. Howard & M. Nussbaum (eds.), *Is Multiculturalism Bad for Women* (Princeton, NJ: Princeton University Press, 1999), at 1.
5 Ibid at 9.
6 Moreover, cultures have as one of their principal aims the control of women by men, whether in the founding myths of Greek and Roman antiquity, or Judaism, or Christianity and Islam: the history books are replete with stories of control and subordination of women, particularly strongly in traditions within formerly conquered or colonised nation-states found right across Africa, the Middle East, Latin America and Asia, in other words 'distinctly patriarchal' societies. Ibid at 12–14.
7 Okin (1999), at 16–17.
8 H. K. Bhaba, 'Liberalism's Sacred Cow', in J. Cohen, M. Howard & M. Nussbaum (eds.), *Is Multiculturalism Bad for Women?* (Princeton, NJ: Princeton University Press, 1999), at 79, 82.
9 W. Brown, *Regulating Aversion: Tolerance in the Age of Identity and Empire* (Princeton, NJ: Princeton University Press, 2006), at 151.
10 Ibid at 152.
11 Ibid at 154.
12 See: U.N. Office of the High Commissioner of Human Rights, Fact Sheet No.23 'Harmful Traditional Practices Affecting the Health of Women and Children'. Available at: www.unhchr.ch/html/menu6/2/fs.23.htm (last accessed in April 2011).
13 Engle Merry (2006), at 12.
14 Brown (2006), at 7.
15 W. Brown, 'At the Edge', 30 *Political Theory* (2002), at 556, 573.
16 For a discussion, see: T. Murphy, 'Feminism Here and Feminism There: Law, Theory and Choice', in D. Buss & A. Manji (eds.), *International Law: Modern Feminist Approaches* (Oxford and Portland, ON: Hart, 2005), at 67, 84.
17 This is expounded upon in one of MacKinnon's seminal texts: *Feminism Unmodified: Discourses on Life and Law* (Cambridge, MA: Harvard University Press, 1987).
18 Moreover cultural difference feminism as embodied in Gilligan's 'ethic of care' theory has emphasised that the law and its imagery entrench concepts such as rationality, objectivity and abstractness, or characteristics traditionally associated

with men. These stand in contrast to traits such as emotion, subjectivity and contextualised thinking, all typically associated with women. Gilligan argued that legal reform was of limited utility because the language of 'equal rights' and 'equal opportunities' and the strategies with which they are pursued, such as litigation and advocacy, all tacitly reinforce the basic organisation of society, which is male. In Gilligan (1982). Ibid at 12–15. Gilligan's ethics of care theory has been subjected to criticism from various feminist camps largely for its tendency to essentialise women's 'natural' characteristics, such as caring and nurturing, thus representing a throwback to the grand narratives characterising radical feminism. See: N. Fraser & J. Nicholson, 'Social Criticism without Philosophy', in J. Nicholson (ed.), *Feminism/Postmodernism* (New York and London: Routledge, 1990), at 33.

19 For an overview of MacKinnon's early rich contribution to feminist legal thinking: see for example: C. MacKinnon, 'Feminism, Marxism, Method and the State: An Agenda for Theory', 7 *Signs* (1982), at 515; C. MacKinnon, 'Toward Feminist Jurisprudence', 8 *Signs* (Summer 1983), at 640; C. MacKinnon, 'Pornography, Civil Rights and Speech', 20 *Harvard Civil Rights-Civil Liberties Law Review* (1985), at 1; MacKinnon (1987), at 81; C. MacKinnon, 'Prostitution and Civil Rights', 1 *Michigan Journal of Gender and Law* (1993), at 13; C. MacKinnon & A. Dworkin (eds.), *In Harm's Way: The Pornography Civil Rights Hearing* (Cambridge: MA: Harvard University Press, 1997), at 438–457. For an excellent critique and extensive overview of MacKinnon's work see: J. Halley, 'Before the Break: Some Feminist Priors', in *Split Decisions: How and Why to Take a Break from Feminism* (Princeton and Oxford: Princeton University Press, 2006), at 41–60. For a critical take on MacKinnon from an intersectional perspective, see also A. Harris, 'Race and Essentialism in Feminist Legal Theory', 42 *Stanford Law Review* (1989–1990), at 581; Nesiah (2003), at 189.

20 C. MacKinnon 'Feminism, Marxism, Method and the State: Toward Feminist Jurisprudence', 8 *Signs* (Summer 1983), at 640.

21 Ibid.

22 MacKinnon (Summer 1983), at 645.

23 Ibid.

24 Halley (2006), at 42.

25 Ibid at 43.

26 Ibid.

27 Scott (1986), at 1058–1059. Radical feminism has also been critiqued for its religious reliance on physical difference as a fixed and static demarcating factor of separation between genders and its insistence upon physical difference as a universal and unchanging aspect of womanhood. Other feminist scholars fault radical feminism for its reinforcement of women as monolithic entities who share a similar degree of repression. See, for example: Kapur (2005), at 101–105; Nesiah (2003), at 189–210.

28 N. Lacey, *Unspeakable Subjects* (Oxford: Hart Publishing, 1998), at 100.

29 Halley has described MacKinnon's early theory as an emancipatory method, whereas MacKinnon's later efforts of linking consciousness-raising with legal reform is where her early radicalism is eclipsed by what Halley denotes as MacKinnon's later 'dogmatism', which conceives of women's experience as the source of authority for the claim that sexuality is a form of power creating male superordination and female subordination. In Halley (2006), at 45, 46.

30 For feminist writings inspired by MacKinnon, see for example: Seifert (1996), at 35; B. Allen, *Rape Warfare: The Hidden Genocide in Bosnia-Herzegovina and Croatia* (Minneapolis: University of Minnesota Press, 1996); Barkan (2002), at 1–7; Stiglmayer (1994), at 82–164; R P. Barrett & L. E. Little, 'Lessons of Yugoslav Rape Trials: A Role for Conspiracy in International Courts and

Tribunals', 88 *Minnesota Law Review* (2003–2004), at 30; R. P. Barrett & L. E. Little, 'Lessons of Yugoslav Rape Trials: A Role for Conspiracy Law in International Tribunals', 88 *Minnesota Law Review* (2003–2004), at 30; R. C. Carpenter, 'Surfacing Children: Limitations of Genocidal Rape Discourse', 22 *Human Rights Quarterly* (2000), at 428. For a critique, see: J. Batinic, 'Feminism, Nationalism and the War: The "Yugoslav Case" in Feminist Texts', 3 *Journal of International Women's Studies* (1) (November 2001), at 1; V. Kesic, 'A Response to Catherine MacKinnon's Article Turning Rape into Pornography: Postmodern Genocide', 5 *Hastings Women's Law Journal* (1994), at 267.

31 This was exemplified in C. MacKinnon, 'Rape, Genocide and Women's Human Rights', in A. Stiglmayer (ed.), *Mass Rape: The War against Women in Bosnia-Herzegovina* (Lincoln, NA: University of Nebraska Press, 1994). In this collection of feminist essays on the Yugoslav conflict, MacKinnon's writings are superimposed on the Yugoslav context. Her other extensive interpretations of the Yugoslav conflict include: C. MacKinnon, *Are Women Human? Reflections on the Universal Declaration of Human Rights*, (The Hague: Martinus Nijhoff Publishers, 1999), which includes several chapters on the sexual violence committed during the Yugoslav conflict. For example: MacKinnon (1999), at 34; MacKinnon (1999), at 169; MacKinnon (1999), at 174.

32 Ibid at 139.

33 MacKinnon (1994), at 193.

34 'Rape as Nationbuilding' in MacKinnon (1999), at 169.

35 One of the most notorious cases involving the confinement of predominantly Bosnian Muslim civilians inside the Omarska camp was the *Prosecutor v. Tadic* decision (IT-94–1).

36 As she has put it, 'Serbian aggression against non-Serbs is as incontestable and overwhelmingly one-sided as male aggression against women in everyday life. Wars always produce atrocities, especially against women civilians. But there is no Muslim or Croatian policy of territorial expansion, of exterminating Serbs, of raping Serbian women. This is not a reciprocal genocide.' MacKinnon, 'Rape as Nationbuilding', *Are Women Human?*, at 161. For a critique see also D. Nadj, '"The Culturalisation of Identity in an Age of 'Ethnic Conflict" Depoliticised Gender in ICTY Wartime Sexual Violence Jurisprudence', 15 *International Journal of Human Rights* (5) (June 2011), at 647, 650.

37 MacKinnon has, for example, argued that pornography had saturated Yugoslavia before the war and was heavily consumed in Serbia in particular, thus normalising its consumption. As she put it, 'When pornography is this normal, a whole population of men is primed to dehumanize women and to enjoy inflicting assault sexually. . . . Pornography is the perfect preparation-motivator and instruction manual in one for the sexual atrocities ordered in this genocide.' Ibid, 164.

38 Halley (2006). See also J. Halley, 'Take a Break from Feminism?', in K. Knop (ed.), *Gender and Human Rights* (Oxford: Oxford University Press, 2004), at 57.

39 For an excellent discussion of 'governance feminism' in the context of international criminal tribunals see: Halley (2008–2009), at 1–2.

40 In J. Halley, 'Describing Governance Feminism', 29 *Harvard Journal of Law & Gender*, (2006), at 340.

41 Initially focused on issues such as sex trafficking, governance feminism began to gradually extend its reach into the two intersecting branches of international humanitarian and international criminal law, thus reflecting its engagement with positive law as a means of bringing about reform. Halley (92008–2009), at 5.

42 Classic examples would be: Dallmeyer (1993), at 143–157; Olsen (1993), at 157–171; Cook (1994), at 85–116.

43 Halley (2008–2009), at 5.

44 Interestingly, as Halley notes in one of her sub-finings, mainstream and often male international lawyers accepted governance feminism as authoritative on the 'badness of rape' and the need for many specific reforms to end the impunity of rapists. Ibid at 6.

45 Ibid.

46 As Halley adds, it made 'ever more sense to describe the war without any acknowledgment that men died in it'. Ibid (original emphasis).

47 Wendy Brown eloquently describes this phenomenon in her work on identity politics in Western liberal societies that under the guise of multiculturalism and tolerance institutes and perpetuates measures that discriminate and marginalise those the protection is aimed at even further. In Brown (2006), at 15.

48 In Todorova (2009), at 138. Also, as Catherine MacKinnon most controversially puts it in her discussion of rape as genocide during the Bosnian conflict, 'In this war, the fact of Serb aggression is beyond question, both here and in everyday life. 'Ethnic cleansing' is a euphemism for genocide. It is a policy of ethnic extermination of non-Serbs with the aim of 'all Serbs in one nation,' a clearly announced goal of 'Greater Serbia', of territorial conquest and aggrandizement.' This phrase most vividly encapsulates the way in which culture has been instrumentalised by feminists in their attempt at finding a way of rationalising rape by attributing it to a group of people in whose DNA it seemingly was to rape and abuse women. MacKinnon (1994), at 186.

49 D. Zarkov, 'Gender, Orientalism and the History of Ethnic Hatred in the Former Yugoslavia', in H. Lutz et al. (eds.), *Crossfires. Nationalism, Racism and Gender in Europe* (London: Pluto Press, 1995), at 105. Similarly, Maria Todorova in her extensive analysis of the etymological significance of the construct sees the Balkans as a geographical and cultural entity overwhelmed by a discourse that utilises it as a powerful symbol conveniently located outside of historical time. She describes its deployment as a trope highlighting the 'imbetweeness' of the region as neither fully European, nor Oriental and lists some of the slogans used in popular discourse to characterise and give meaning to the conflict in the former Yugoslavia such as 'the Balkan war', 'the Balkan conflict', the 'new Europe vanishing 'into the thick smoke of the stubborn Balkan fire', and 'today, Balkan is aflame in the name of Serbia's identity with itself' as symptomatic of a wider trend in discourses surrounding the conflict to 'Balkanise', or neatly compartmentalise the conflict into pre-defined, fixed and narrow understandings of the conflict. In M. Todorova, *Imagining the Balkans* (Oxford: Oxford University Press, 2009 updated edition), at 7, 54.

50 See Zarkov (1995), at 105.

51 As Anne Orford has argued in her critique of humanitarian intervention discourses, a feminist analysis that focuses on gender alone, without analysing the exploitation of women in the economic 'South', would operate to reinforce the depoliticised notion of 'difference' that founds the privileged position of the imperial feminist. In A. Orford, 'Misreading the Texts of International Law, *Reading Humanitarian Intervention* (Cambridge: Cambridge University Press, 2003), at 65. Orford's arguments are explored in further detail in the final segment of the chapter.

52 Kelly Dawn Askin and Dorean Koenig, for example, provide the following quote from leading human rights activist Aryeh Neyer to illustrate that sexual violence against women was a major impetus for the establishment of the ICTY: 'Among the crimes for which the wars in Croatia and Bosnia-Herzegovina became notorious is rape. Much of the public outcry for a war crimes tribunal arose from the outrage generated by the rapes committed during these conflicts. For a time, the war in Bosnia became synonymous with rape, acquiring a reputation for

uncommon ugliness in the process and helping to create and unprecedented awareness of rape as a common method of warfare and political repression worldwide.' Quote provided in K. D. Askin & D. Koenig, *International Criminal Law and the International Criminal Court Statute: Crimes against Women, Women and International Human Rights* (Volume 2) (Ardsley, NY: Transnational Publishers, 2000), at 5.

53 The term 'ethnic conflict' is deeply contested. As V.P. Gagnon points out in his insightful analysis of the roots causes underlying the Yugoslav conflict, 'There is no evidence of an automatic or logical shift from identification with particular ethnic ties to the kind of violence that took place in the 1990s.' To understand the behaviour of those people who were mobilised by the violence requires a much more complex and nuanced approach than the typical 'ethnic mobilisation' scenario. Moreover, the low mobilisation of people in Croatia and Serbia during the time of the conflict speaks to the fact that the images of ethnic war that were transmitted by the ruling party were not drawing or appealing to 'lived experiences' and meanings, which a large number of people in those places associated with their ethnic or national identification. In V.P. Gagnon, *The Myth of Ethnic War: Serbia and Croatia in the 1990s* (Ithaca, NY: Cornell University Press, 2004), at 178–179.

54 Halley (2006), at 57.

55 Brown (2006), at 131.

56 C. Di Palma & K. Ferguson, 'Clearing Ground and Making Connections: Modernism, Postmodernism, Feminism', in K. Davis et al. (eds.), *Handbook of Gender and Women's Studies* (London, Thousand Oaks, New Delhi: Sage, 2006), at 131.

57 For a summary of Lacan's thought see: Scott (1986), at 1063.

58 J. Butler, *Gender Trouble: Feminism and the Subversion of Identity* (New York, NY: Routledge, 1990). Another seminal text by Butler on a similar theme is: J. Butler, *Bodies that Matter: On the Discursive Limits of "Sex"* (New York, NY: Routledge, (1993).

59 Butler (1990), at 8.

60 Ibid at 10.

61 Ibid at 11.

62 Ibid.

63 Di Palma & Ferguson (2006), at 134.

64 Brah & Phoenix (2004), at 75–76.

65 L. McCall, 'The Complexity of Intersectionality', 30 *Signs Journal of Women in Culture and Society* (2005), at 1771.

66 Ibid at 1771 (emphasis added).

67 Examples of such scholarship include: K.W. Crenshaw, 'Mapping the Margins: Intersectionality, Identity, Politics, and Violence against Women of Colour', 43 *Stanford Law Review* (1991), at 1241; T. Grillo, 'Anti-Essentialism and Intersectionality: Tools to Dismantle the Master's House', 10 *Berkeley Women's Journal* 16 (1995); Harris (1990), at 581; C. T. Mohanty, 'Under Western Eyes: Feminist Scholarship and Colonial Discourses', 30 *Feminist Review* (1988), at 61; M. Kline, 'Race, Racism and Feminist Legal Theory', 12 *Harvard Women's Law Journal* (1989), at 15.

68 K.W. Crenshaw, 'Demarginalizing the Intersection of Race and Sex: A Black Feminist Critique of Anti-Discrimination Doctrine, Feminist Theory and Antiracist Politics', 129 *University of Chicago Legal Forum* (1989), at 139.

69 Crenshaw (1991), at 1283.

70 U.N. Committee on the Elimination of Racial Discrimination (CERD), General Recommendation XXV, Gender-Related Dimensions of Racial Discrimination (2000), U.N. Doc A/55/18, annex V at 152 (2000), at para 1.

71 Crenshaw had significant input in the drafting process of the Declaration and was part of the Expert Group Meeting on Gender and Race held by the U.N. Division for the Advancement of Women in Zagreb, Croatia prior to the 2001 World Conference. See: Gender and Racial Discrimination: Report of the Expert Group Meeting, 21–24 November 2000 Zagreb, Croatia. Available at: www.un.org/womenwatch/daw/csw/genrac/report.htm.

72 Declaration adopted at the World Conference Against Racism, Xenophobia and Related Intolerance, Durban, 2001. Available at: www.unhchr.ch/pdf/Durban.pdf, at para 69.

73 Former examples include: U.N. Commission on Human Rights, Towards an Effective Implementation of International Norms to End Violence against Women (2004), Report of the Special Rapporteur on Violence against Women, its Causes and Consequences, Yakin Ertürk, E/CN.4/2004/66, 26 December 2003, and U.N. Commission on Human Rights, Intersections of Violence against Women and HIV/AIDS (2005), Report of the Special Rapporteur on Violence Against Women, its Causes and Consequences, Yakin Ertürk, E/CN.4/2005/72, 17 January 2005. For an overview of the current Special Rapporteur, Rashida Manjoo's work, see, for example, U.N. Commission on Human Rights, Towards an Effective Implementation of International Norms to End Violence against Women (6 June 2011), Report of the Special Rapporteur on Violence against Women, its Causes and Consequences: Mission to the United States, Ms. Rashida Manjoo, A/HRC/17/26/Add.5. Available at: http://daccess-ddsny.un.org/doc/UNDOC/GEN/G11/138/26/PDF/G1113826.pdf?OpenElement. For a discussion of Manjoo's approach as U.N. Special Rapporteur, see also: D. Nadj and R. Manjoo, 'Bridging the Divide: An Interview with Professor Rashida Manjoo, U.N. Special Rapporteur on Violence against Women', 23 *Feminist Legal Studies* (3) (November 2015), at 329–347.

74 K.W. Crenshaw, 'Mapping the Margins: Intersectionality, Identity Politics and Violence against Women of Color', (2001) presented at the World Conference against Racism. Available at: www.hsph.haravard.edu/grhf/WoC/crenshaw.html.

75 For a discussion of different strands of feminism see: K. Engle, 'International Human Rights and Feminism: When Discourses Keep Meeting', in D. Buss and A. Manji (eds.), *International Law Modern Feminist Approaches* (London and Portland, ON: Hart, 2005), at 53.

76 Ibid at 55.

77 Ibid at 58.

78 C. Mohanty, 'Under Western Eyes: Feminist Scholarship and Colonial Discourses', in C. Mohanty, A. Russo & L. Torres (eds.), *Third World Women and the Politics of Feminism* (Bloomington, IN: Indiana University Press, 1991), at 51.

79 Much like Spivak, she argues that this vacuum has produced a generalised image about Third World feminism and the women it seems to encompass as singular, monolithic subjects in Western feminist texts, in particular. Also reprinted in C. Mohanty, 'Under Western Eyes: Feminist Scholarship and Colonial Discourses', in P. Williams & L. Chrisman (eds.), *Colonial Discourse and Postcolonial Theory* (New York, NY: Columbia University Press, 1994), at 196.

80 According to Mohanty, Western feminist writings on women in the Third World must be considered in the context of the global hegemony of Western scholarship, including the production, publication, distribution and consumption of ideas, as these writings resurrect colonialism all over again. Mohanty (1991), at 54–55.

81 Ibid at 2.

82 Engle (2005), at 57.

83 The Subaltern Studies Group emerged in the 1980s as a response to life in post-colonial and post-imperial societies in South Asia with the aim to attempt to formulate a new narrative of the history of India and the Subcontinent. Subalternity has been understood as engaging with the question of ideology and its implication on intellectual and economic history. It is also concerned with analysing how the colonial subject came to be constructed as 'the Other' or a '[r]emotely orchestrated, far-flung and heterogeneous subject' produced through the narrative of history as imperialism. One of the leading subaltern thinkers is Gayatri Chakravorti Spivak, who has argued that the Third World and its people have been mired in heterogeneous representations of the Other as a subject of Western, hegemonic ideology, whereby the 'Other' has been defined through what dominant discourses perceive it to be, while the 'real voice-consciousness of the subject's itinerary' has not been traced. For an exposition of Spivak's complex and salient ideas, see: G.C. Spivak, 'Can the Subaltern Speak?', in P. Williams & L. Chisman (1994), at 66–112. Moreover, Spivak's critique of the gender essentialism manifested in current 'hegemonic generalisations' about women is that it reinforces the idea of the subaltern as lacking either history or speech. Her aim is to recuperate the voice of the marginalised subject rather than to substitute it with Western feminist or Third World feminist voices, who believe they can speak on its behalf. As Spivak puts it, the 'subaltern cannot speak'. Ibid at 104.

84 As Anne Orford has convincingly shown in her analysis of humanitarian intervention narratives, central to each of the positions espoused by international legal scholars is that it involves forgetting the imperial history of international law. Those broadly opposed to humanitarian intervention, for example, argue that the emergence of a right of humanitarian intervention may allow increased interference by powerful states into the affairs of the weak, while those broadly in favour of intervention suggest that to advocate the protection of state sovereignty over human rights protection is to betray the universal principles of human rights protection and humanitarianism that underpin the U.N. system. Each of these views sees the era of late modernity as one in which decolonisation has successfully taken place, positing international law and postcolonial nation states as the end of anti-colonialist struggles. On this view, international law and the international community are essentially anti-colonialist, while ignoring a history in which the granting of formal political sovereignty to decolonised states coincided with the new techniques of international institutional control founded on limiting the economic sovereignty of those new entities. In Orford (2003), at 44–45.

85 See for example R. Kapur, *Erotic Justice Law and The New Politics of Postcolonialism*, (London: Glasshouse Press, 2005); Kapur (2002) in Ratna Kapur's writings reflect most strongly the contemporary postcolonial feminist critique of the international women's rights movement, at 525. To Kapur, the depiction of women as the victim subject has become the dominant focus of the global human rights movement', 15 *Harvard Human Rights Journal* (2002); R. Kapur, 'Post-Colonial Economies of Desire: Legal Representation of the Subaltern', 78 *Denver University Law Review* (2000–2001), at 85; R. Kapur, 'Postcolonial Erotic Disruptions: Legal Narratives of Culture, Sex, and Nation in India', 10 *Columbia Journal of Gender & Law* (2000–2001), at 333; R. Kapur, 'Unveiling Women's Rights in the War on Terrorism', 9 *Duke Journal of Gender, Law & Policy* (2002), at 211; R. Kapur, 'The "Other" Side of the Legal Regulation of Globalization Cross-Border Movements', 22 *Canadian Women's Studies* (2003).

86 R. Kapur, 'The Tragedy of Victimisation Rhetoric: Resurrecting the "Native" Subject', *International/Postcolonial Feminist Legal Politics* (2005), 97.

87 To a certain extent this view has also been reinforced by some postcolonial scholars in the Global South, who in their search for the 'authentic subject' have done

nothing to counter the representation of the Indian woman as the suffering impoverished and violated subject. Mehta's work is one example cited by Kapur. Ibid at 116.

88 As Kapur describes it, arguments that focus on sex discrimination do not reflect the fact that women do not experience discrimination exclusively on the basis of sex. Thus, the focus only on the category of gender is to obscure the ways in which particularly women in minority and disadvantaged communities experience multiple forms of subordination. More crucially, those who focus on gender as the exclusive and primary site of oppression have themselves typically not experienced other forms of subordination, such as religious, ethnic or caste subordination. These various forms of subordination therefore need to be understood not as distinct entities, but as rather intricately connected. Ibid at 101.

89 Ibid at 107.

90 As Kapur puts it, 'The body in flames is invariably associated with ancient Indian cultural practices, without any regard as to more obvious political, economic and social explanations.' Whereas the practice of sati relates to the immolation of the widow on her husband's funeral pyre, which was a traditional practice in some Indian communities, and was an exceptional rather than routine practice; dowry murders have never been part of, or sanctioned by any tradition in the Indian context. Ibid at 108.

91 Kapur has for example criticised MacKinnon's grand binary narrative of male dominance versus female oppression for its focus on the commonalities of women's experiences, and for her positing of a culturally essentialised woman victim as the authentic voice of all women. Moreover, she has critiqued MacKinnon's writings for their failure to focus on the way in which the legal systems have been shaped by social, economic and historical forces, and how the cultural context of the Third World is to the present day strongly mediated by the colonial encounter. MacKinnon's analysis has thus not contributed to the elimination of violence against women, but has merely provided ways in which to include women within the liberal discourses of equality without disrupting or challenging the metaphysical foundations and ontological limitations of rights discourses to women's empowerment. For an overview of Kapur's critique of MacKinnon, see Kapur (2005), at 104–107.

92 Kapur (2005), at 1–11.

93 This term has also been used by Anne Orford. In Orford (2003).

94 For specimens of her work see: D. Buss, 'Women at the Borders: Rape and Nationalism in International Law', 6 *Feminist Legal Studies* (2) (1998), at 171; D. Buss, 'Prosecuting Mass Rape: Prosecutor v. Dragoljub Kunarac, Radomir Kovac and Zoran Vukovic', 10 *Feminist Legal Studies* (2002), at 91; D. Buss & A. Manji (eds.), *International Law: Modern Feminist Approaches* (Oxford and Portland, OR: Hart, 2005); D. Buss, 'The Curious Visibility of Wartime Rape: Gender and Ethnicity in International Criminal Law', 25 *Windsor Journal of Access to Justice* (2007), at 3; D. Buss, 'The Rwanda Tribunal and the Making of Ethnic Rape', presented at Sexual Abuse and Exploitation of Women in Violent Conflict, Emory University and The Netherlands Defence Academy workshop, 17–19 June 2007, Amsterdam, NDL; revised and presented at American Society for Law, Culture and Humanities, annual conference, March 2008, San Francisco; D. Buss, 'Sexual Violence, Ethnicity, and the Limits of Intersectionality in International Criminal Law', in E. Grabham et al. (eds.), *Intersectionality and Beyond: Law, Power and the Politics of Location* (London: Routledge-Cavendish, 2009), at 105.

95 D. Buss, 'The Curious Visibility of Wartime Rape: Gender and Ethnicity in International Criminal Law', 25 *Windsor Yearbook of Access to Justice* (2007), at 1.

96 Ibid at 3.
97 In this context she has for example argued that a 'visible' victim fitting neatly into the dominant tropes of victimhood is typically the Bosnian Muslim woman whose ethnic identity has been constantly emphasised in the judgements (thereby implicitly highlighting her status as the voiceless, powerless and incapable victim of war), while the 'invisible' victim's ethnicity (usually Bosnian-Serb) would be less emphasised presumably for her association with the ethnic group widely regarded as responsible for the atrocities perpetrated during the Yugoslav war. Buss (2007), at 15; Buss (1998), at 171.
98 D. Zarkov, 'Sexual Geographies of Ethnicity', in *The Body of War: Media, Ethnicity and Gender in the Break-Up of Yugoslavia* (Durham and London: Duke University Press, 2007), at 116.
99 See also D. Zarkov, 'Gender, Orientalism and Ethnic Hatred in Former Yugoslavia', in H. Lutz et al. (eds.), *Crossfires: Nationalism, Racism and Gender in Europe* (London; East Haven, CT: Pluto Press, 1995); D. Zarkov, 'Towards a New Theorizing of Women, Gender and War', in K. Davis, M.S. Evans & J. Lorber (eds.), *Handbook of Gender and Women's Studies* (London: Sage Publishers, 2006), at 214.
100 Zarkov (2007), at 116.
101 See also Zarkov (1995); Zarkov (2006), at 214.
102 Zarkov (2007), at 129.
103 Only a handful of articles had reached the Croatian press through primary sources, stories on rape and raped women in Bosnia thus primarily came from Italian, French, German and British newspapers. Ibid at 129.
104 Article from the *Danas* weekly newspaper from 29 January 29 1993, at 65, reproduced in Zarkov (2007), at Ibid.
105 Ibid at 132.
106 As Žarkov shows, in Croatian media reports, the rape of Serbian women is mostly mentioned as a denial: Serb women were not raped at all, or rape was not committed on a mass scale in relation to them, and Muslim and particularly Croat forces did not commit any rapes or had committed only incidental rapes. Ibid at 132–133.
107 A headline in the daily newspaper *Politika*, for example, stated that, 'The mental murder' of forced pregnancies would assure that the 'dismembering of [women's] souls will never end'. (25 January, 23), or that 'Women would remain prisoners of these children forever, regardless whether they chose to abort or give birth. Thus, one woman, uncertain whether she aborted a child conceived from her husband or from the rapist, half-mad, screams at her own image in the mirror: "Baby-killer"' (26 January, 21) Cited in Zarkov (2007), at 122.
108 Ibid at 123. (Original emphasis).
109 Ibid at 182.
110 See: W. Brown, 'Suffering Rights as Paradoxes', 7 *Constellations* (2000), at 230, reprinted as 'Suffering the Paradoxes of Rights', in W. Brown & J. Halley (eds.), *Left Legalism/Left Critique* (Durham, NC: Duke University Press, 2002), at 420; Butler (1993).
111 Brown (1995), at 25.
112 See: Brown (1995, 1997, 2000).
113 Brown (1997); see also Brown (2000).
114 E. Grabham, 'Intersectionality: Traumatic Impressions', in E. Grabham, D. Cooper, J. Krishnadas & D. Herman (eds.), *Intersectionality and Beyond: Law, Power and the Politics of Location* (London: Routledge Cavendish, 2009), at 183, citing J. Conaghan, 'Intersectionality and the Feminist Project in Law', in E. Grabham et al. (eds.), *Intersectionality and Beyond: Law, Power and the Politics of Location* (London: Routledge-Cavendish, 2009), at 28.

115 Conaghan (2009), at 28–29.
116 Orford (2003), at 39.
117 Ibid at 40 (emphasis added).
118 Ibid at 47.
119 This is based on Orford's reading of humanitarian literature, which typically treats those who lead or inhabit target states as the 'other' of the international community: as 'disordered, chaotic, tribal, primitive, pre-capitalist, violent, exclusionary and child-like'. Drawing on Sartre's 'imperial conviction' that there is always some way of understanding an idiot, a child, a primate man or a foreigner, if only one has sufficient information, Orford argues that international texts treat as given that international lawyers and their audiences (in the West) can 'know' these primitive societies. Ibid at 47–48.
120 Ibid at 51.
121 Ibid.
122 Terry Threadgold, for example, critiqued the tendency emerging in feminist theory in the 1990s of supporting forms of feminist writing that privileged 'real' political action', which was imagined as non-theoretical over theoretical work seen as 'a kind of intellectual game'. In Orford (2003) citing Threadgold, at 52.
123 Ibid at 54.
124 Ibid at 65.
125 Ibid.
126 Makau Mutua, for example, has argued that the creation of the ICTY was a manifestation of the imperialism characteristic of international law, which punishes economically weaker states but does not reach the powerful ones. States signed up to the project of the ICTY because it was 'painless and temporary'; it was a tribunal with a limited mandate of prosecuting individual local offenders while letting powerful states 'off the hook'. In creating the tribunal, moreover, powerful states could no longer be accused of inaction. M. Mutua, 'Never Again: Questioning the Yugoslav and Rwanda Tribunals', 11 *Temple International & Comparative Law Journal* (1997), at 175. Criticism has also been voiced by political theorists such as Edward Herman and David Peterson, who regard Resolution 827 not only as *ultra vires*, but contend that the real purpose behind the ICTY's establishment was to use an alleged interest in justice to prevent peace, and to advance U.S. objectives in the Balkans, all of which required the use of force and the breaking of peace. See: E. Herman & D. Peterson, 'The Dismantling of Yugoslavia: A Study in Inhumanitarian Intervention and a Western Liberal-Left Intellectual and Moral Collapse', 59 *Monthly Review* (5) (2007).
127 Orford (2003), at 68.
128 S.L. Woodward, 'Violence-Prone Area or International Transition?', in V. Das & A. Kleinman (eds.), *Violence and Subjectivity* (Berkeley, CA: University of California Press, 2000); see also: S.L. Woodward, *Balkan Tragedy: Chaos and Dissolution after the Cold War* (S.L. Woodward The Brookings Institution: Washington, 1995). For an analysis of Woodward's writings, see also: Orford (2003), 87–96.
129 The death of Tito, of course, is only one event in a series of developments that ushered in the eventual demise of 'Titoism' as a central doctrine characterising the state of Yugoslavia. As historian Leslie Benson has documented, one of the most significant challenges the League of Communists faced during Tito's reign was the attempt to strike a balance between centralism and devolution. This resulted in three new constitutions in 21 years, endless tinkering with the state party machine, the transformation of a hitherto largely peasant society into a middling industrial power with gross deformations of Stalinism, and the failure to implement Tito's leitmotif of 'market socialism'. A stable allocation of authority between the Party and self-managing enterprises operating

on a profit-and-loss principle for their survival never materialised. Thus, 'direct democracy' as envisioned by Tito never translated into a concrete situation, leading to economic ruin and the absence of a democratic framework within which the Yugoslav federation could evolve. In L. Benson, 'The End of Titoism', in *Yugoslavia: A Concise History* (Basingstoke, Hampshire and New York, NY: Palgrave Macmillan, 2004), at 132.

130 Furthermore, hyperinflation and mass unemployment affecting 70 percent of the population between the ages of 15 and 25 created a great degree of uncertainty about survival itself amongst an even larger part of the population. In Woodward (2000), at 24.

131 This has been described by Spyros Sofos as 'a progressive confederalisation' that occurred as far back as 1974 when the new Yugoslav constitution legally sanctioned ethnic identities as the primary differentiation between the republics. By the mid-1980s against the backdrop of an increasingly severe economic situation and strengthening nationalist sentiment paired with large-scale migration from all republics of the former Yugoslavia abroad, virtually each republic and province, despite its multicultural and multi-ethnic composition, provided a framework for the promotion of the national identity and attainment of sovereignty of a specific ethnic group. While the Serbian leadership actively campaigned for the restoration of centralism and the restoration of Serbian control over the autonomous provinces of Kosovo and Vojvodina that had been granted their status following the enactment of the 1974 constitution, Slovenian communists pushed for political liberalisation and decentralisation, while in Croatia, there was hostility towards liberalisation of the political system and support for a decentralisation of the economy, with economic nationalism and the economic prospects that could be derived from these playing a central role. In Macedonia and Bosnia, on the other hand, the regional parties advocated the preservation of the Yugoslav federation, leading to a division, as Slovenia and Croatia supported provincial party leaderships against Serbian demands of decentralisation. This confrontational atmosphere led to a deep rift between republican elites and the republics more generally. It is also seen as having precipitated the declarations of independence of first Slovenia and then Croatia in 1991. In S. Sofos & B. Jenkins (eds.), *Nation and Identity in Contemporary Europe* (London and New York, NY: Routledge, 1996), at.9–32.

132 These separatist moves on the part of the two republics together with the growth of paramilitary groups aligned with emerging right-wing political parties in many parts of the country clearly ended the state's hitherto existing monopoly on the legitimate use of violence by early 1991. In Woodward (2000), at 12.

133 Ibid at 12.

134 In Serbia nationalism first manifested itself in the rhetoric used by President Slobodan Milosevic, who used the 'Albanian question' in Kosovo as a rallying cry with which to play on the fears of Serbs who saw their presence in Kosovo threatened largely due to demographic shifts in the region, which had produced a 90 percent majority of Albanians. In the latter case nationalism found its strongest advocate under the leadership of former Yugoslav National Army (JNA) general and historian Franjo Tudman, whose lifelong passion had been to deliver Croatian statehood. During the 1970s and under Tito's regime Tudman had twice been jailed for nationalism. In A. Silber & L. Little, *The Death of Yugoslavia* (London: Penguin Books, 1995), at 51–89.

135 In Woodward (2004), at 27.

136 All national groups in Yugoslavia were numerical minorities. Ibid at 29.

137 Historian Joel Malcolm has similarly argued that the Yugoslav economic system was only able to flourish and boom on borrowed money, leading to a total foreign debt of $33 billion by the end of 1988. But while it was certain that

internally there was a climate of profound political and economic malaise among the population added by strong apathy and distrust in the political institutions, it is nonetheless more than questionable whether Yugoslavia would have descended into violence had it not been for the involvement of the international community, according to Malcolm. In J. Malcolm, *Bosnia – A Short History*, (London: Palgrave Macmillan, 1994), 210.

138 Orford (2003), at 69.

5 The dynamics of 'ethno-nationalist conflict': the interface of gender and ethnicity in ICTY wartime sexual violence jurisprudence

Part I

Introduction

The book offers a critical feminist analysis of ICTY wartime sexual violence jurisprudence and the surrounding debate. This chapter forms the second strand in the transition from a discussion of the legal developments surrounding wartime sexual violence in international law presented in chapters 2 and 3 to a reflection on these developments adopted in chapters 4, 5 and 6, where the actual approach of the book is fully crystallised. The previous chapters have sought to demonstrate the long road travelled by feminists in gaining legal recognition for women's human rights and for gender-based violence to be considered as a serious human rights violation and a breach of international humanitarian law.

Chapters 1, 2 and 3 provided an overview of the evolution of gender-based violence and wartime sexual violence in international law and they clarified why gender-based violence is a feminist issue of currency in the contemporary legal moment. Chapter 4 constituted the first limb in the transition from the discussion of violence against women to their theoretical analysis by mapping out the salient feminist approaches that have shaped the theoretical understanding of this book. In highlighting their respective advantages and disadvantages, the book has clarified its position on the feminist spectrum by suggesting a more critical approach towards the study of armed conflict and wartime identity. It has shown that international law continues to perpetuate deeply entrenched images of women based on essentialised notions of female identity, which are dressed up as legal successes. This has prompted much debate in feminist circles about how to incorporate a more feminist perspective into the law. But, as argued previously, this has not necessarily been emancipatory for women, as feminist activism today is strongly informed by structuralist perspectives of women's subordination. The present chapter further analyses how wartime identities come into being in the jurisprudence. It provides the core context for the analysis of wartime sexual violence, as it scrutinises the key legal achievements accomplished by the ICTY in this area of the law. Primarily, the chapter examines the key dynamics of the Yugoslav war in order to convey a stronger sense of the nature of gender-based violence endured by women and the circumstances of extreme precariousness within which the sexual violence took place. The chapter proceeds with an overview of respective case law, interjected with some brief historical background of the events and patterns of wartime sexual violence that have defined the Yugoslav conflict in the popular imagination. It draws on feminist observations, which constitute an integral part of the discourse. In this way, it prepares the ground for the critical feminist analysis pursued in chapter 6.

As mentioned previously, the ICTY has adjudicated a host of cases in the area of wartime sexual violence that proved influential for future international criminal jurisprudence. Of the 161 individuals indicted to date, 78 had charges of sexual violence included in their indictments. Twenty-eight (more than one-third) were convicted of individual criminal responsibility for wartime sexual violence charges under Article 7(1) of the Statute, and four of them for added superior responsibility under Article 7(3) of the Statute. Moreover, 13 indictments have been either withdrawn or were terminated due to death, while 11 individuals have been acquitted of wartime sexual violence charges. There are 19 ongoing proceedings currently at pre-trial and trial stages, of which six have been referred to national jurisdictions, while one suspect still remains at large.[1] The chapter proceeds by presenting an overview of such developments. It does not, however, aim to cover them all.[2] Rather, the objective is to provide a sense of the evolving ICTY wartime sexual violence jurisprudence and its achievements to date, as seen from a feminist perspective. The chapter provides a platform for further reflection and analysis. The cases that constitute the central focus of the book are as follows: *Prosecutor v. Tadic*,[3] *Prosecutor v. Delalic*[4] (commonly referred to as Celebici after the name of the camp where the offences occurred), *Prosecutor v. Furundžija*,[5] *Prosecutor v. Kunarac*[6] and *Prosecutor v. Kvocka*).[7] These are considered to be the most significant cases to date in ICTY wartime sexual violence jurisprudence, as all bear the hallmarks of feminist advocacy and set precedents for the future prosecution of gender-based violence in international law.[8]

The common element underlying the judgements is that they address the particular phenomena that have characterised the Yugoslav conflict in its treatment of women: 'genocidal rape', systematic rape campaigns, forced pregnancy and mass detention of civilians in Serb-run 'rape/death camps' following ethnic cleansing campaigns against local civilian populations, which have been widely portrayed as motivated by a targeting of specific 'ethnic' identities. Moreover, the judgements have developed the jurisprudence on wartime sexual violence individually and as a whole, contributing to the 'remarkable presence and lifespan of the topic' in feminist discourses and beyond.[9] Part II addresses, in brief, the case selection criteria underlying this project. It provides a structural account of the internal and external forces of power that contributed to the collapse of the Yugoslav state. It also adopts a contrapuntal perspective in countering the common assertion transmitted in much of the contemporary scholarship on the Yugoslav conflict as originating in 'ancient ethnic rivalries'.

Part V analyses the structure of the camp as a political space in which the law is suspended and it looks to the significance of the findings of the Commission of Experts as an instrumental element in visiblising sexual violence in ICTY decisions. Part VI turns to the salient ICTY case law by providing a legal analysis of the *Tadic* decision and it elaborates on the significance of this judgement for international criminal jurisprudence more generally. Part VII analyses the *Celebici* judgement, considered one of the landmark decisions in international wartime sexual violence jurisprudence, for its acknowledgment of the serious and widespread nature of sexual violence, while parts VIII and IX chart the key developments arising out of the *Furundžija* and *Kunarac* cases, which together with the *Celebici* judgement have provided groundbreaking space for gender justice, due to their adjudication of sexual violence as a war crime and crime against humanity. They constitute part of a trilogy of cases emerging from the conflict in the former Yugoslavia.[10] Part X overviews the *Kvocka* case and its significance concerning the development of international criminal law with respect to its findings of individual responsibility for rape as part of persecution against the civilian population and torture for threats of sexual violence. Part XI summarises the chapter.

Part II

i) Case selection criteria

The case study focuses, exclusively, on sexual violence cases arising from the conflict in Bosnia-Herzegovina. The common elements underlying the incidences of sexual violence are, most notably, the circumstances of mass detention of civilians in camps or camp-like facilities, where sexual violence against women was commonplace, leading feminists to label them, variously, as 'death camps' and 'rape camps'.[11] The analysis of the camp as the space in which much of the conflict took place, moreover, is important for defying the commonly constructed portrayal of the conflict as 'ethnic' in nature, as is shown in the relevant section. The focus on the conflict in Bosnia and Herzegovina, specifically, is linked to the book's interest in exploring the portrayal of the Yugoslav war as being synonymous with rape and the raped woman as the metaphor for female identity. In this way, the cases selected provide a poignant insight into gendered experiences of wartime.

The common pattern underlying the cases selected for analysis is explored through a critical reading of the Final Report produced by the Commission of Experts. In a predominant number of cases, the detainees were civilians whose towns and communities had been initially rounded up by enemy forces. In most instances, they were later detained against their will and transported to detention-like facilities, such as sports halls or private residences and hotels, which was a commonly occurring phenomenon in the case of female detainees. Detainees would routinely be subjected to questioning and interrogation in adjacent hangars which functioned as makeshift interrogation facilities, where much of the violence, whether of a sexual or non-sexual nature was perpetrated, as is discussed in detail in the case law review.

Moreover, the cases featured in this analysis share in common a disproportionate targeting of women and girls for crimes of a sexual nature across a wide range of age groups. They showcase the systematic and widespread nature of sexual violence, which has prompted many feminists to label the rapes committed against women as 'mass rapes', if not 'genocidal rapes' – certainly, rape committed on an industrial scale.[12] As indicated previously, this view was almost universally espoused by feminists, regardless of whether they believed that rapes by Croats and Muslims ought to be distinguished from those committed by Serbs, or whether they believed that rape had been committed on all sides. These debates, far from aiding in the project of gender justice, have invoked problematic notions of gendered identity in armed conflict, doing little to dispel recurring gendered stereotypes in international law.

A further commonality of the cases discussed is their extensive elaboration of the various elements constituting sexual offences. The *Furundžija* case, for instance, has provided its own definitions of rape after finding that the elements of the crime were not sufficiently defined under existing international humanitarian law.[13] The cases also discuss superior command responsibility enshrined in Article 7 of the ICTY Statute, which is commonly regarded as a mechanism for ensuring individual responsibility on the basis of the position of the accused as superiors to the perpetrators of the crimes alleged.[14]

The case law analysed has been considered pivotal to the development of international criminal law and many commentators regard it as a monumental advance for women's human rights. Most importantly, the tribunal's work has been noted for its expansion of various definitions of sexual violence, enabling these acts to be brought within the remit of the Statute, while its wartime sexual violence jurisprudence is deemed as having reflected women's participation, therefore showcasing the potential for legal change through concerted feminist advocacy, as has already been indicated in chapters 2 and 3. Due to the wealth of material available on the conflict in Bosnia-Herzegovina, the analysis excludes the focus on sexual crimes committed in other parts of the former Yugoslavia. The conflicts in Croatia, Kosovo and to some extent in Macedonia are, consequently, not subject of the analysis.[15]

Part III

The Yugoslav ideal, its structural collapse and the role of external power

The conflict in Bosnia-Herzegovina was the most protracted of the conflicts that took place during the dissolution of the former Yugoslavia. This segment traces how popular legal and political discourses contributed to the idea of the conflict as ethno-nationalist, tied to the idea that the various Yugoslav peoples could not live together and that their common state consequently had to be divided.[16] This has prompted legal anthropologist Robert Hayden to argue that the disintegration of Yugoslavia into its warring components marked the failure of the imagination of the Yugoslav community.[17] The book asserts that this is a misconception, as Yugoslavia was founded on the notion of self-determination first espoused by former U.S. President Woodrow Wilson.

A predominant feature of President Tito's government was the creation of a Yugoslav identity, which throughout his time in power undermined nationalist or secessionist tendencies in the republics by maintaining a sense of apparent unity. This was in large part due to an inherent deference towards the Yugoslav constitution, as in the Yugoslav social system 'constitutional norms were more important than the convictions espoused by the ruling Communist Party', according to former Yugoslav Minister of Justice and legal scholar Tibor Varady.[18]

The Yugoslav ideology as such was therefore largely driven by a distinct sense of rationality, which from the state's very inception heralded a multicultural existence as the preferable option over a forced national identity. Schools, media, theatre and newspapers were not only permitted, they were in fact encouraged and supported by the ruling party. The Communist regime regarded nationalism as its biggest enemy, hence ensuring that everything considered nationalistic would be persecuted with all the instruments available to an authoritarian regime. An important consequence of this approach was the very strict prohibition of any attempt to protect or advocate the interests of a nation or of an ethnic group.[19] Any structuring of ethnic groups was considered a direct attack on the party itself. The party had a monopoly over identifying and redressing ethnic grievances, and any recognition or representation of a group identity was perceived as a disturbance of the one-party political system. Furthermore, structures at the national and regional levels were created, balancing the power of the Serbs, as the largest ethnic group within Yugoslavia, with those of the other ethnic groups, meaning that the Yugoslav state formed after World War II was '[u]ndeniably based on a concept of multi-ethnic coexistence'.[20]

Following the death of Tito in 1980 state structures began to crumble, allowing an atmosphere of uncertainty and anxiety to prevail with the voices of so-called 'nationalist' leaders, such as Slobodan Miloševic, Franjo Tudman, Ante Gotovina, Milan Babic, Alija Izetbegovic, Momcilo Kraijšnik, Radovan Karadžic and Ratko Mladic, finding fertile ground. But the rise of these political players was more a reaction of anxiety and clinging on to hope for a sense of familiarity and structure amidst a tide of sea change that enveloped Europe far beyond the borders of Yugoslavia, namely the collapse of communism and the demise of the Soviet Union. The clinging on to hope found its expression in the support of admittedly nationalist and exclusionary ideas, but these ideologies were not necessarily borne out of a primordial instinct, or 'ancient ethnic' rivalries, as has so often been stated in Western popular discourses. Indeed, the book seeks to further divorce the Yugoslav conflict from the representation in much scholarly literature of the Balkans as a violence-prone area characterised by seething ethnic feuds and rivalries.

That ethnicity was not the root cause of the conflict, but rather an artificially constructed and static attribute of interest, has been suggested by political theorist V. P. Gagnon, who has argued that the representation of the Yugoslav conflict in much of the dominant scholarship has been founded on a 'myth of ethnic war'.[21] As he has put it in relation to the escalation of violence in the region:

> In trying to account for this outburst, most western journalists, academics and policy-makers have resorted to the language of the premodern: tribalism,

> ethnic hatreds, cultural inadequacy, irrationality; in short, the Balkans as the antithesis of the modern West. Yet, one of the most striking aspects of the wars in Yugoslavia is the extent to which the images purveyed in the Western press and in much of the academic literature are so at odds with the evidence from the ground.[22]

On this view, ethnicity is conceived of as a fluid and relational process of identification based on social interactions founded on complex structural factors. The violence witnessed in 'ethnic conflicts' is not meant to mobilise people by appealing to ethnicity, but is aimed at fundamentally altering or destroying social interactions founded on intricate structural factors. It is, precisely, the inability of political elites to play the 'ethnic card' that leads them to rely on massive violence in order to demobilise and homogenise previously heterogeneous political space and silence the voices calling for fundamental shifts in the structures of power.[23] Following Gagnon's argument, it is therefore not altogether surprising that massive violence was deployed as a mechanism of destruction of previously heterogeneous communities that had co-existed side-by-side for decades, if not centuries, in particular regions such as in Bosnia-Herzegovina, as massive violence was the only means whereby such communities could be destroyed. In this way, the book provides an alternative viewpoint to a debate that has frequently insisted on its own correctness, while denying other perspectives the chance to find expression. As stated previously, the outbreak of the Yugoslav conflict cannot be divorced from its socio-political or economic context.[24] While the exact economic factors contributing to the demise of the Yugoslav state are too complex to enumerate, it is worth noting that several developments coincided to cripple the status and stature of Yugoslavia in international relations: the transformation taking place in Europe and the global order in the 1980s, including tougher fiscal measures adopted by international financial institutions towards their debtors, while institutions such as the European Union and the European Free Trade Association both substantially toughened their bargaining stance in relation to the renewal of association agreements with Yugoslavia. NATO taking a more aggressive stance towards the Eastern Mediterranean, in different registers, led to the perception in the Yugoslav defence establishment of the West as a growing security threat, eventually ushering in the demise of the state.[25] A perhaps most symbolic indicator of things to come amidst the atmosphere of deepening European integration was the message by the new U.S. ambassador to Yugoslavia that the country was no longer of any strategic significance to the United States.[26]

So the European Union played a crucial part in the breakup of the former Yugoslavia. In the same way that the economic crisis cannot be explained without grasping the impact of external economic shocks imposed through suddenly stiffening IMF loans in 1982, the physical return of workers and émigrés who had been living abroad to participate directly in support of anti-communist and nationalist forces and the actions of the international community cannot be omitted from a structural analysis of the dissolution.[27] Unlike much current legal scholarship, the author believes that the international community made the actual outbreak of violence more likely. Woodward has identified three ways by which foreign actors strengthened the causes of violence: by contributing to the weakness of the federal government and state capacity, by legitimising the people and ideas that would win, and by failing to do, much less understand the hard work needed to make peace when they accepted the peacemakers' role.[28] Through its analysis of select case law, the book offers an alternative account of the conflict by highlighting specific situations arising out of the Bosnian context that most vividly embody the nature of the brutality that pervaded much of the conflict, as seen through a feminist lens.[29] Specifically and rather uniquely, the conflict became synonymous with the practice of 'ethnic cleansing',[30] alongside terms such as 'mass rape', 'genocidal rape' and 'rape as a weapon of war', as the next segment goes on to assess.[31]

Part IV

The terminology of 'ethnic cleansing' as central to the framing of sexual violence crimes in ICTY wartime sexual violence jurisprudence

How sexual violence is framed in tribunal decisions becomes crucial to the representation of identity in wartime. As has been shown, language and the deployment of specific terminology play a central role in how armed conflict is conceptualised and understood in the popular imagination. One of the most 'hypervisible' terms associated with the Yugoslav conflict in both feminist and non-feminist discourses was the phrase 'ethnic cleansing'. While not a term of law, it was frequently invoked in feminist legal debates around the different prosecution strategies to be adopted by the ICTY in order to ensure that rape would be prosecuted as a form of genocide. Over time, the boundaries within which the concept was invoked became increasingly blurred, as some equated ethnic cleansing outright with genocide, while at other times the connection was less certain.[32] The term 'ethnic cleansing' was quickly deployed by feminists and non-feminists alike to describe many of the events that occurred in Bosnia-Herzegovina. This stands in contrast to its early origins, which conceptualised it as an administrative matter characteristic of behaviour displayed by Kosovo Albanians in the then Yugoslav autonomous province of Kosovo towards the Serbian minority.[33]

Today, 'ethnic cleansing' as a strategy of war is exclusively associated with ethnonationalist, collateralised motivations believed to have been at the heart of the Serbian war strategy, with Serbia as the commonly identified aggressor of the conflict, whose hubristic thinking led it to believe that a 'Greater Serbia' on Serb-inhabited land within Bosnia-Herzegovina would become a reality. The term took on a life of its own and became symbiotic with the portrayal of the conflict itself. The Commission of Experts has described the practice as follows:

> With respect to the practices by Serbs in Bosnia and Herzegovina and Croatia, "ethnic cleansing" is commonly used as a term to describe a policy conducted in furtherance of political doctrines relating to "Greater Serbia". The

> policy is put into practice by Serbs in Bosnia-Herzegovina and Croatia and their supporters in the Federal Republic of Yugoslavia. The political doctrine consists of a complex mixture of historical claims, grievances and fears and nationalistic aspirations and expectations, as well as religious and psychological elements. The doctrine is essentially based on ethnic and religious exclusivity and the dominance of Serbs over other groups in certain historically claimed areas. This doctrine breeds intolerance and suspicion of other ethnic and religious groups and is conducive to violence when it is politically manipulated, as has been the case.[34]

The portrayal of ethnic cleansing as a practice was first mentioned by Tadeusz Mazowiecki, then Special Rapporteur of the former Commission of Human Rights, who deployed the term to characterise various 'terrorising measures' pursued during the Yugoslav war.[35] The most common measures of terror identified by Mazowiecki and later widely used by the ICTY to characterise the strategies used by Bosnian-Serb soldiers or armed civilians involved: robbery, terrorisation and intimidation in the street;[36] massive deportation campaigns of the civilian population; detention and ill treatment of the civil population and their transfer to prisons and camps; shootings of selected civilian targets and blowing-up and setting fire to homes, shops and places of business;[37] destruction of cultural and religious and monuments and sites;[38] mass displacement of communities;[39] and discrimination of refugees on the basis of ethnic difference. Most importantly, the report identified rape and other forms of sexual abuse, such as castration as specific elements of ethnic cleansing.[40] This led to the finding by the Commission of Experts that rape had been used most frequently against women of different ethnic origins, and that it had been committed systematically.[41] These findings also gave rise to the suggestion that special women's camps had been established for the purpose of sexual violence, and that rape had been committed with the intent of making women pregnant for the purpose of mutating the ethnic composition of the offspring.[42]

Part V

The camp as the space of 'bare life'

The camp as a specific political-juridical structure is of particular interest to this book, as it is within so-called 'rape camps', although not exclusively, where many of the crimes of a sexual nature against women took place. The Italian philosopher Giorgio Agamben has extensively theorised the camp as the place in which the most absolute *condition inhumane* ever to appear on Earth has been realised. Agamben has called the camp the 'hidden matrix and nomos of the political space in which we still live'.[43] He has linked the establishment of the camp as the site of violence to the state of exception, which is not born out of ordinary law, but is rather the space in which the law is suspended. It is in the suspension of the law, or in the creation of martial law that we find the constitutive nexus between the states of exception and the concentration camp, as occurred in Prussia in the mid-nineteenth century with the institution of the Schutzhaft (protective custody), which provided the juridical foundation for the internment of individuals, regardless of any relevant criminal behaviour and exclusively to avoid threats to the security of the state.[44] The derivation of the Nazi Lager can be traced back directly to the institution of the Schutzhaft, which provided the precedent for interning people without cause or reason.[45]

Following the work of Agamben, the author understands the camp as 'the space that opens up when the state of exception starts to become the rule'.[46] In it, the state of exception, which was essentially a temporal suspension of the state of law, acquires a permanent spatial arrangement that, as such, remains constantly outside the normal state of law. Agamben's theorisation on the state of exception and the camp as its embodiment is of central importance, as the camp epitomises the tragedy of the Yugoslav conflict more vividly than any other site of violence. The parallels of what he describes in relation to the atrocities committed in the Nazi Lagers during World War II are striking when reflected against the atrocities that marked the conflict in Bosnia-Herzegovina. The events that took place inside the camps will always be beyond human comprehension, but what is more crucial is the understanding that the camp as the structure in which the state of exception is manifestly realised, in other words the camp as the space in which the law is completely suspended, is today no longer an aberration but the norm. The camp is the space in which the people who enter it move about in a zone of distinction and indistinction between the outside and the inside; it is the space in which its inhabitants have been stripped of every political status and reduced completely to naked life. The camp is also the most absolute biopolitical space that has ever been realised – a space in which power confronts nothing other than pure biological life without any mediation. The camp is the paradigm itself of political space in which politics becomes biopolitics and the *homo sacer* becomes indistinguishable from the citizen.[47]

The atrocities committed in so-called 'rape' or 'death camps' became a synonymous feature of the Yugoslav conflict.[48] The deployment of certain terminology to describe the events has, moreover, become central to the manner in which the conflict has been portrayed in the public discourse, taking on a life of its own and heavily influencing the legal modalities through which a majority of cases have been prosecuted. Determinations about those who carried responsibility for the oversight of the camps became crucial in framing culpability, and in inscribing victimhood on their inmates. These debates were reflective of a wider trend in popular discourses around the Yugoslav conflict of framing it as a 'uniquely' heinous conflict, a metaphor for the barbaric and tribalist proclivities of the region and its inhabitants, which became central to the way the conflict was depoliticised in the wider scholarship. But as Agamben has noted,

> The state of exception, which used to be essentially a temporary suspension of the order, becomes now a new and stable spatial arrangement inhabited by that naked life that increasingly cannot be inscribed into that order. The

> increasingly widening gap between birth (naked life) and nation-state is the new fact of the politics of our time and what we are calling "camp" is this disparity.[49]

In other words, the camp as a 'dislocating localisation' is the hidden matrix of the politics in which we still live; it is now firmly inside the political system, it is the new biopolitical nomos of the planet. This perspective directly contradicts the labels commonly associated with the Yugoslav conflict, which have rendered it a unique phenomenon in late modernity. Agamben in this way provides a counterargument to the frequently essentialised and deeply culturalised stereotypes associated with the Balkans as a region, while at the same time showing the brutality of the camp as a space where little, if any, agency is ever possible, given that those who perpetrate atrocities on the inside can rely on the suspension of the law to absolve them from any sense of culpability. That this is now a regular state of affairs, as evidenced by the discriminatory treatment of the Roma, or the treatment of African migrants fleeing from political unrest in their home countries into EU member states such as Italy, or the ethnic cleansing of the Rohingya in Myanmar, which lend Agamben's writings additional potency. This is a challenging perspective, as it defies the common perception that latent ethnic divisions or perceived cultural attributes lie at the root of conflict. It is instead late modernity, which normalises the state of exception and divides people into categories of life and 'bare life' that is today the spectre of political life everywhere.

i) The findings of the commission of experts

Eighty percent of the rapes committed during the Yugoslav conflict are said to have occurred in detention camps. The Commission early on identified Bosnian Serbs as operating the camps, where grave breaches and other violations of international humanitarian law, including killing, torture and rape had reportedly occurred on a large scale.[50] The camps ranged in size from small detention centres designed to temporarily house a few prisoners to camps that housed a large number of prisoners for varying durations and purposes and under different control.[51]

With respect to the camps established in Bosnia-Herzegovina under Bosnian-Serb control, the Commission linked this war strategy to broader political motives inextricably tied to ethnic identity stating that:

> The Bosnian Serbs use camps to facilitate territorial and political control of a geographic region and to expel and eliminate other ethnic and religious populations from that area.[52]

This links the space of the camp to the practice and policy of ethnic cleansing, as the Commission ascertained in its findings that camps are ultimately 'intended to achieve "ethnic cleansing".'[53] The common methodology preceding the rapes was of women being selected randomly at night with rapes being carried out in a manner that would instil terror in the women's prisoner population.[54] In its identification of the methodologies adopted, the Commission implied that women did not have much agency in either choosing to obey orders or in resisting them, as presumably this would have resulted in their deaths. Early on, in the texts produced by international institutions rape was conceived of as part of a broader strategy designed to instil terror and fear in the prison population.

ii) Patterns of rape and the centrality of ethnicity

A series of interviews was carried out by the Commission in Croatia and Slovenia in March 1994 for which 146 witnesses from Bosnia and Herzegovina were interviewed. Some 31 of those interviewed had been raped, and two had been suspected by the Commission to have been raped, but were unwilling to speak of their own experiences.[55] The information gathered was specifically based on 223 interviews that were made available to the Prosecutor of the ICTY.[56] As a result, five distinct patterns of rape and sexual assault could be identified based upon the Commission's database and the interviews conducted.

Pattern I: This was identified as taking place before any widespread or generalised fighting broke out in the region. It typically involved individuals or small groups, who committed sexual assault in conjunction with looting and intimidation of the target ethnic group.[57] The Commission chose to illustrate this pattern through the interview of a gang-raped woman, who had been raped by eight men in front of her six-year-old sister and her five-month-old daughter for, as it appears ethnic reasons, as one of the men involved was instructed to rape her as she was 'an Ustaša'.[58] Moreover, when she reported the crime to the local authorities the reply was that nothing could be done as she was Croat. The Commission presented the first pattern of relatively small-scale violence through the instrumentalisation of the most violent manifestation of rape, namely 'gang rape', which in turn was portrayed through an ethnic lens, as the violence seemingly originated in the ethnic identity of the victim.

Pattern II: This involved individuals or small groups committing sexual assaults in conjunction with fighting in an area, often including the rape of women in public.[59] During the attacks of towns and villages, forces would round up the population and then divide it by sex and age. Some women were raped in their homes, as the attacking forces secured the area, while others were raped publicly, following which they were later transported to camps.

Pattern III: This concerned the sexual assault of people in detention mainly because individuals or groups had easy access to their targets. Once the local population had been rounded up, men were either executed or sent off to camps, while women were sent off to separate camps generally.[60] This pattern also involved numerous allegations of gang rape, commonly accompanied by beatings and torture.[61] The Commission for the first time also identified sexual violence against men based on interviews conducted with 15 people, whose major allegations related to the same detention camp; there were numerous male witnesses who attested to sexual violence in the camps, while reportedly all of the women had been raped.[62] This pattern is significant for the imputation of superior command responsibility, as the women were sometimes gang raped in the presence of the camp commander, who had allowed guards from the external ring of security around the camp, as well as soldiers who were strangers to the camp access for the specific purpose of rape.[63] With respect to the sexual assaults on men, it was reported that prisoners were forced to bite other prisoners' genitals, while 10 of those interviewed had witnessed deaths by torture and seven of the group had survived or witnessed mass executions.[64]

Pattern IV: Adding another dimension of terror to sexual violence, it identified individuals or groups committing rapes against women for the purpose of terrorising or humiliating them, often as part of the policy of 'ethnic cleansing'. This pattern perhaps most starkly illustrates the ethnic dimension accompanying sexual violence, serving as precursor to the way sexual violence would later be interpreted in the judgements.[65] Some captors, moreover, stated that they had raped women for the purpose of impregnating them, presumably to change the ethnic composition of the offspring. As a result, pregnant women were detained until it was too late for an abortion.[66]

Pattern V: This involved the detention of women in hotels or similar facilities for the allegedly sole purpose of sexually entertaining soldiers, rather than causing a reaction in the women, as the Commission puts it rather cryptically. What differentiated this pattern from the foregoing ones was that women were reportedly more often killed than exchanged, unlike women in other camps, and that the women were of mixed ethnicity.[67]

The Commission found that the largest number of reported victims had been Bosnian Muslims and the largest number of alleged perpetrators Bosnian Serbs. Interestingly, there had been few reports of rape and sexual assault between members of the same ethnic group.[68] This led the Commission to conclude that a 'systematic rape policy' existed in certain areas, but that it remained to be proven whether such overall policy existed, which was to apply to all non-Serbs. Moreover, it found that some level of organisation and group activity were required to carry out many of the rapes, suggesting that rape and sexual assault should be examined in the context of the practice of 'ethnic cleaning', while finding that grave breaches of the Geneva Conventions had occurred throughout the territory, alongside numerous other violations of international humanitarian law. These findings and legal modalities influenced much of the subsequent adjudication of wartime sexual violence cases. The next segment overviews in detail the most significant ICTY wartime sexual violence cases adjudicated upon to date. To some extent these have already been touched upon, a degree of overlap is inevitable.

Part VI

The Tadic *case: paving the way for the inclusion of specific references to sexual violence*

The significance of the *Tadic* case for the development of contemporary international criminal law cannot be overstated. It was expected to be the first international criminal case in history to prosecute rape separately as a war crime, and not solely in conjunction with other crimes.[69] Moreover, the case paved the way for the future inclusion and specific reference to sexual violence in the indictments presented at trial, and perhaps most significantly it defined the scope of customary international law pertaining to internal and international armed conflict, the applicability of crimes against humanity, and the scope of the grave breaches to the 1949 Geneva Conventions. It reconceptualised the principal international humanitarian law treaties that regulate contemporary armed conflicts, and recognised them as comprising customary international law.[70] It was also the *Tadic* decision that established that international humanitarian law increasingly governs non-international, or internal armed conflict alongside international armed conflict.[71] Moreover, it produced findings regarding the legitimacy of the tribunal and made the armed conflict in the former Yugoslavia more justiciable by defining it as partly international in scope.[72] It also extensively developed the joint criminal enterprise theory of responsibility with the Appeals Chamber having first articulated the theory based largely on jurisprudence derived from the post–World War II Nuremberg Trials.[73] From a gender perspective, the case was deemed pivotal for the reclassification of rape and other forms of sexual violence as priority crimes in the ICTY.[74]

i) The first signs of feminist governmentality

One of the most remarkable illustrations of feminist intervention and subsequent prosecutorial responsiveness occurred in the very first trial of the ICTY. Judge Odio-Benito – described as the only woman on the ICTY trial court panel – questioned the Prosecutor on the treatment of rape as a lesser offence than other crimes directed predominantly against men, such as beatings. This led Chief Prosecutor Richard Goldstone to promptly write a letter to several feminists, who had previously issued an *amicus curiae brief* on the same matter.[75] 'In the letter Goldstone acknowledged that the affidavit did not sufficiently reflect the ICTY's policy of equating rape with other serious violations of international law and went on to promise that rape and other sexual assaults would be prosecuted under the Statute's provisions for torture, inhumane treatment, wilfully causing great suffering or serious injury to body, inhumane acts, alongside other provisions that adequately encompassed the nature of the acts committed and the intent formulated.'[76] Goldstone's relenting signalled that feminists had finally gotten a purchase on the events, as they were successful in winning him over for their cause. His endorsement of feminist organisational strategies became evident in his later reflections on his time as Chief Prosecutor. As he has put it:

> There has been substantial progressive development of humanitarian law as a consequence of the establishment of the ICTY. Of real importance are the developments in the law with respect to gender offenses. From my first week in office, from the middle of August 1994 onwards, I began to be besieged with petitions and letters, mainly from women's groups, but also from human rights groups generally, from many European countries, the United States and Canada, and also from non-governmental organizations in the former Yugoslavia. Letters and petitions expressing concern and begging for attention, adequate attention, to be given to gender-related crime, especially systematic rape as a war crime. Certainly, if any campaign worked, this one worked in my case.[77]

As Janet Halley has commented somewhat sardonically, this episode of feminist intervention is both a story of 'intense legal drama', a moment from which feminist activism emerged from the sidelines with 'spectacular sudden success'. Feminism had arrived, 'active and alert, in the persons of Judge Odio Benito, Judge Pillay and the NGOs . . . but it was scrambling for a place at the table'.[78]

ii) The 'globalisation of human rights'

The *Tadic* case, further, exemplified the 'globalisation of human rights' by showcasing the increasing penetration of international law into the domestic sphere of national legal systems. Tadic was arrested in Germany following the request of the Prosecutor under Rule 9 of the Rules of Procedure and Evidence. Under Rule 10 of the Rules of Procedure and Evidence, the court has the right to ask domestic courts, such as the German courts, to defer to the competence of the tribunal.[79] Germany had indicted Tadic for war crimes in the Balkans prior to turning him over to the ICTY, so, his extradition to The Hague on the basis of 'crimes against humanity' jurisdiction appears to have constituted an 'act of solidarity'.[80] The act of extradition also exemplifies the promotion of normative instantiations in the name of human rights, independent of the affected state, in the name of promoting a 'global rule of law and justice'. As Ruti Teitel has argued, the contemporary globalisation of rights enforcement, however sporadic, challenges the immediate post-war emphasis on international institutions, as well as the more particularist local understandings of justice.

The *Tadic* trial is of monumental significance from a range of perspectives, including for the far-reaching precedent it set for the future prosecution of gender-based crimes under international law. In reaching its verdict, the ICTY Trial Chamber included specific references to sexual violence and convicted Tadic of crimes of a sexual nature. It also allowed for anonymous testimony of three victims of sexual assault to be brought forward without having their identities disclosed to Tadic or his counsel.[81] However, the trial is also emblematic of the difficulties inherent in sexual violence prosecutions, as even anonymity proved insufficient for a victim identified as 'F'. Tadic had been charged with the rape of this prisoner at the Omarska camp, but as soon as the proceedings began, the rape charges were dropped because victim 'F' was too afraid to testify. This shows that despite all the successes achieved in instituting protective measures for victims, there were still inadequacies in the system.

iii) The facts and background

The case dates back to the start of the war in Bosnia-Herzegovina, May 1992, when Bosnian-Serb forces attacked Bosnian Muslims and Croat population centres in the municipality of Prijedor.[82] As part of the attack, most of the population was forced from their homes and more than 3,000 people were confined to detention in the Omarska camp, a former mining complex. The accused Duško Tadic, a low-ranking official at the Omarska camp and member of the Bosnian-Serb forces operating in Prijedor, participated in killings outside Omarska camp and acted as one of the ringleaders. About three weeks after the Serb forces took control of the government authority in the region, they began interning prisoners in the Omarska camp while continuing to round up Muslims and Croats in surrounding towns. Amongst the detainees were many local Muslim and Croat intellectuals, professionals and political leaders.

Of the approximately 3,000 prisoners there were approximately 40 women in the camp, while the other prisoners were men.[83] Most of the women were confined to the administration building where most of the interrogations took place. Living conditions were described by the prosecution as brutal, with overcrowding a common feature, as well as little or no facilities for personal hygiene provided for the prisoners.[84] Prisoners had no change of clothing, no bedding and received no medical care. Moreover, severe beatings were commonplace with camp guards physically abusing prisoners, using all types of weapons during these beatings, including wooden batons, metal rods and tools, rifle butts and knives amongst others.[85] Both female and male prisoners were beaten, tortured, raped, sexually assaulted and humiliated. Many, some of whose identities were never established, did not survive the camps. After collecting thousands of Bosnian Muslims and Croats in late May 1992, Serbian groups including Duško Tadic later entered villages in which Muslim and Croat residents had remained during the siege continuing to kill villagers and driving others away from their homes.

iv) Wartime sexual violence charges

Many parts of the second amended indictment addressed sexual violence against females and males.[86] They alleged that Tadic, a Serb, had participated in the killing and 'maltreatment' of Bosnian Muslims and Croats within and outside Omarska camp. Approximately 40 women were in Omarska, where both female and male prisoners were 'beaten, tortured, raped, sexually assaulted and humiliated'.[87] Similarly, in the Trnopolje camp the indictment alleged that female detainees had been subjected to sexual violence.[88] Count 1 of the indictment charged Tadic with a crime against humanity, specifically with persecution on political, racial and/or religious grounds for taking part in a 'campaign of terror, which included killings, torture, sexual assaults, and other physical and psychological abuse'.[89] He was also charged for his participation in the torture of more than 12 female detainees, including several 'gang rapes'.[90] Counts 2–4 alleged that Tadic had subjected victim F to 'forcible sexual intercourse' inside one of the buildings attached to the Omarska camp, thereby, causing great suffering to her as a grave breach of the Geneva Conventions recognised by Article 2(c) of the Statute of the Tribunal.[91] For these acts he was charged with a grave breach for inhuman treatment (count 2), 'forcible sexual intercourse' as inhuman treatment (count 2) and a violation of the laws or customs of war recognised by Article 3 of the Statute and Article 3(1) of the 1949 Geneva Conventions,[92] and rape as a crime against humanity (count 4) as recognised by Article 5(g) and 7(1) of the ICTY Statute. To prove a crime against humanity for purposes of Article 5, the prosecution had to demonstrate that the alleged acts or omissions were part of a 'widespread or large-scale or systematic attack directed against a civilian population', specifically the Muslim and Croat populations of the Prijedor municipality.[93]

v) Opinion and judgement

Tadic was found guilty of his participation in a general, widespread and systematic campaign that included beatings, torture, sexual assaults and other physical and psychological abuse directed at the non-Serb population in the Prijedor region.[94] He was found guilty of crimes against humanity for criminal acts of persecution including crimes of sexual violence such as rape, which were considered constituent elements of a widespread or systematic campaign of terror against the civilian population. But the prosecution did not have to prove that rape itself was widespread or systematic; it only had to show it as one of many types of crimes committed on a widespread or systematic basis underlying the aggressor's campaign of terror. Moreover, the Trial Chamber did not analyse gender-based discrimination as a form of persecution, but only focused on persecution on religious or political grounds.[95] The chamber signalled a potential limitation to the prosecution of gender-based crimes by holding that while persecution was a required element of crimes against humanity, it was more important to highlight the ethnic dimensions of the crime rather than to address its gendered elements. It did, however, accept that rape may come within the purview of possible persecutorial acts in certain situations.[96] Moreover, Count 5 referred to other abuses of a sexual nature, namely the beating of several male prisoners while ordering them to perform sexual acts upon each other, amounting to gross and humiliating treatment and therefore to torture.[97] The court also noted that during the confinement in the camps, 'both male and female prisoners were subjected to severe mistreatment, which included beatings, sexual assaults, torture and executions'.[98] Moreover, women at Omarska camp were 'routinely called out of their rooms at night and raped'.[99] This statement was supported by testimony of a medical worker in Trnopolje, who personalised the rape through a description of its imputed impact on the victims in the following way:

> The very act of rape, in my opinion – I spoke to these people, I observed their reactions – it had a terrible effect on them. They could, perhaps, explain it to themselves when somebody steals something from them, or even beatings or even killings. Somehow, they sort of accepted it in some way, but when the rapes started they lost all hope. Until then they had the hope that this war could pass, that everything would quieten down. When the rapes started, everybody lost hope, everybody in the camp, men and women. There was such fear, horrible.[100]

This quote underlines the decision's potency, as the Trial Chamber instrumentalised gender-based violence as an act constitutive of personal feeling exceeding all other types of harm. It also abstracted the political context in which these acts were committed by conceptualising rape as a uniquely terrifying experience that reiterates the victim's inferiority vis-à-vis the assailant precluding any possibility of agency. The tribunal also found Tadic guilty of persecution for his indirect participation in 'a campaign of terror, which included killings, torture, sexual assaults, and other physical and psychological abuse'.[101] Although it was not proven that Tadic himself had committed sexual violence, his participation in the general campaign of violence described meant that under customary international law his direct individual criminal responsibility and personal culpability for assisting, aiding and abetting or participating in a covered criminal act were invoked.[102] Therefore, Tadic's culpability was based on his participation in the seizure and imprisonment of the people within the camps, his knowledge of a policy that criminally discriminated against and persecuted non-Serbs, and his perpetration of sexual mutilation of Harambasic, one of the male detainees.[103]

vi) Summary

Much has been made in feminist circles of the significance of the *Tadic* judgement, and of the fact that its adjudication bears the mark of feminist advocacy.[104] Thanks to this case, for example, witness testimony no longer needs to be corroborated, as the tribunal's Rules of Procedure and Evidence, especially sub-rules 89 (C) and (D) permit the introduction of 'any relevant evidence having probative value . . . unless its probative value is substantially outweighed by the need to ensure a fair trial'.[105] Feminists have interpreted this as sign that the ICTY takes the testimony of female witnesses seriously, as a result bolstering the credibility of victims of sexual violence in rape proceedings.

Moreover, this case has been praised for allowing feminist judicial activism to influence proceedings, a development which feminists have generally welcomed. But as Halley has remarked, 'The ICTY has actually held that experience as a feminist activist in international legal work can be a qualification for service as a judge on the court.'[106] While Halley's assessment might seem harsh, it nonetheless raises questions around whether female judges ought to be included in high-profile sexual violence trials merely on account of their gender, and whether these types of feminist interventions necessarily produce desirable results for women.

It is certain that the *Tadic* judgement has ushered in the notion of individual accountability in modern-day international criminal proceedings and has significantly expanded the ICTY's subject-matter jurisdiction through its determination of the Yugoslav conflict as international in character. As such, it is an unprecedented legal finding. The judgement not only reconceptualised the parameters of modern-day armed conflict, but it also introduced a wider international audience to the idea that the conflict had been fought along ethno-nationalist lines. Not only is this a powerful legal tactic, it is arguably also a strand of depoliticisation whereby wartime identities and their actions could easily be imbued with ethnic motivations. From the book's perspective, this simplification of political events has been problematic, as it has reduced the understanding of armed conflict to a clash between those, who have culture, and those 'whom culture has'.[107]

Part VII

The Furundžija *judgement: the recognition of rape as torture*

i) Facts and background

This case occurred against the backdrop of the armed conflict between the Croatian Community of Herzeg-Bosna ('HZ-HB'), which considered itself an independent political entity inside the Republic of Bosnia-Herzegovina and the armed forces of the government of the Republic of Bosnia-Herzegovina from around 3 July 1992 through at least mid-July 1993.[108] The conflict between these two sides ought to be understood against the backdrop of the declaration of independence by the Republic of Bosnia-Herzegovina, which had been announced on 6 March 1992. The conduct of war underlying the Croatian military strategy reflects to a large degree the modus operandi of the Bosnian-Serb forces engaged in the conflict, so from the outset of the hostilities in January 1993, the Croatian Defence Counsel (the HVO) attacked villages predominantly inhabited by Bosnian Muslims in the Lašva River Valley region in central Bosnia-Herzegovina, which resulted in the death and wounding of numerous civilians. The additional acts perpetrated against the local population included forceful detention, transportation from their places of residence, the performance of sexual labour, sexual assault and other physical and mental abuse.[109]

The general allegations against Anto Furundžija concerned his role as the local sub-commander of a paramilitary unit of the HVO, known locally as the 'Jokers', whose members had a 'terrifying reputation'.[110] During the attacks carried out by forces under his command, a civilian woman of Bosnian Muslim origin, identified as Witness A, was arrested and taken to the headquarters of the Jokers. The headquarters were located in the town of Nadioci in a building termed the 'Bungalow', where Furundžija, who was the only accused on trial because he was the only indictee in the custody of the tribunal, verbally interrogated Witness A, while another, Accused B, physically assaulted her. Both were sub-commanders of the Jokers, thus potentially subject to individual responsibility pursuant to Article 7(1) of the Statute for violation of Articles 2 and 3 of the Statute.

ii) Rape as torture and a violation of customary law

The interrogators forced Witness A to stand nude before a group of laughing soldiers. During the initial phase of interrogation, Accused B repeatedly ran a knife up the victim-witness's inner thigh and threatened to stick it inside her and cut her sexual organs if she failed to cooperate.[111] Over the course of the day, Accused B proceeded to rape Witness A several times in multiple ways, such as orally, vaginally and anally, often in the presence of Furundžija and others. The prosecution charged Furundžija in the Indictment with two counts of violations of the laws or customs of war: torture and 'outrages upon personal dignity, including rape'.[112] The defendants also interrogated and beat Witness D, a Bosnian-Croat male member of the HVO who had already endured beatings at the hands of Furundžija's subordinates, as he was suspected of assisting Witness A and her sons, in the same room where Witness A was being raped and otherwise abused.[113] Furundžija, in his position of command, was present during part of the sexual violence, as Witness A was being subjected to oral and vaginal sexual intercourse with one of the lower-ranking soldiers. According to the prosecution, his role in verbally interrogating her during the infliction of the violence, as well as his words, acts and omissions, encouraged and facilitated the crimes. The tribunal found that the elements of rape in this case were met 'when Accused B penetrated Witness A's mouth, vagina and anus with his penis'; the rape was attributable to the accused because the Trial Chamber had also found that the crimes were committed as part of the interrogation process in which Furundžija participated. Although consent was not raised in this case, the Trial Chamber stressed that 'any form of captivity vitiates consent'.[114] The judges also noted the increased efforts by international bodies to redress 'the use of rape in the course of detention and interrogation as a means of torture, and therefore as a violation of international law'.[115] It further noted that when the requisite elements are met, rape might also constitute a crime against humanity, a grave breach of the Geneva Conventions, a violation of the laws and customs of war, and act of genocide.[116]

Moreover, in determining the appropriate definition of torture to implement in the case, the Trial Chamber adopted the definition of torture found in the Convention against Torture,[117] which imposes a 'state actor' requirement typically involving a large number of people in the torture process who perform different functions, which however minor, impose personal liability.[118] It stressed the different roles played by Furundžija and Accused B and highlighted the sexual dimension of the torture process in the following way:

> Witness A was interrogated by the accused. She was forced by Accused B to undress and remain naked before a substantial number of soldiers. . . . The interrogation by the accused and abuse by Accused B were parallel to each other . . . There is no doubt that the accused and Accused B, as commanders divided the process of interrogation by performing different functions. The role of the accused was to question, while Accused B's role was to assault and threaten in order to elicit the required information from Witness A and Witness D.[119]

The Trial Chamber further expanded the list of prohibited purposes behind the Torture Convention's definition of torture to include humiliation, stating:

> Among the possible purposes of torture, one must also include that of the humiliation of the victim. This proposition is warranted by the general spirit of international humanitarian law: the primary purpose of this body of law is to safeguard human dignity.[120]

At this juncture the act of rape is personalised and the psychological impact of the rape is propelled to the forefront of the court's interpretation of sexual violence, since it finds that Witness A was raped during the course of her interrogation in order to 'degrade and humiliate her'.[121] Moreover, the court concluded that the verbal interrogation by Furundžija, which was described as 'an integral part of the torture', as well as the physical perpetration by Accused B, 'became one process', and these acts caused severe physical and mental suffering to the victim.[122] For these crimes, the tribunal found Furundžija guilty of individual responsibility for the sexual violence as a co-perpetrator of torture and as an aider and abettor of outrages upon personal dignity including rape.[123] In a further significant finding from a gender perspective, the judges found that forcing a third party to witness rape also formed part of the torture of Witness D due to the psychological impact on the witness, who was interrogated and beaten while Witness A was being raped in his presence:

> The physical attacks on Witness D, as well as the fact that he was forced to watch sexual attacks on a woman, in particular, a woman whom he knew as a friend, caused him severe physical and mental suffering.[124]

This effectively brings in a third-party element as an aggravating factor to the rape as torture charge. In analysing the 'outrages upon personal dignity including rape' charge, the Trial Chamber reached the conclusion that Witness A 'suffered severe physical and mental pain, along with public humiliation, at the hands of Accused B in what amounted to outrages upon personal dignity and sexual integrity'. Despite the fact that Furundžija had not physically perpetrated the violence against Witness A, his 'presence and continued interrogation of Witness A' was found to have 'encouraged Accused B', therefore 'substantially contributing to the criminal acts committed by him'.[125] The judges sentenced Furundžija to 10 years of imprisonment for the torture conviction and to eight years of imprisonment for the outrages upon personal dignity conviction, which were to run concurrently instead of consecutively.[126]

iii) Post-traumatic stress disorder (PTSD) and the appearance of judicial bias

A number of delicate issues concerning gender-based advocacy arose during the trial with significant implications for the way in which future cases of wartime sexual violence would be prosecuted. One of the issues centred on the disclosure of statements that had been made to a rape counselling centre and the weight given to a victim's testimony in relation to her credibility when suffering from post-traumatic stress disorder (PTDS) or rape trauma syndrome (RTS).[127] The Trial Chamber held that there was no evidence to suggest that a witness suffering from extreme trauma cannot give accurate information or provide wholly reliable testimony.[128] The decision was upheld by the ICTY Appeals Chamber Judgement rendered on 21 July 2000.[129] This was significant in so far as it also signalled that the introduction of the witness's prior sexual history would not be permitted in court proceedings, as it could lead to judicial bias.

On appeal, however, the defence alleged that the presiding judge in the case, Florence Mumba, should be disqualified for appearance of bias.[130] The allegations were based on Mumba's past record as representative of Zambia to the United Nations Commission on the Status of Women (CSW), during which the Commission had strongly condemned rape and urged its prosecution and punishment. The defence further alleged that her outspoken feminist views made Judge Mumba predisposed to promoting a common feminist agenda.[131] The Appeals Chamber then reviewed domestic case law regarding the appropriate standard in determining judicial bias, finding that a general rule existed which required judges not only to be free from bias, but also from the appearance of bias.[132] Ultimately, the Appeals Chamber determined that there was no basis for the allegations that her position and role as a member of the CSW had even created the appearance of bias. In fact, the Appeals Chamber concluded that, even if Judge Mumba shared the goals of objectives of the CSW of promoting and protecting the human rights of women, 'she could still sit on a case and impartially decide upon issues affecting women'.[133] The Appeals Chamber effectively ruled that it is not a disqualification for a judge to share the view that rape is reprehensible and a terrible crime and it determined that, in principle, judges should be entitled to a presumption of impartiality.[134]

iv) Summary

The precedent set by this case was the recognition of rape and serious sexual assault as self-standing war crimes. Rape was charged as a war crime based on article 4(2)(e) of the Additional Protocol II to the Geneva Conventions, which enumerates rape as a war crime under the rubric of 'outrages upon personal dignity'.[135] Rape was also for the first time deemed to be a part of customary law, as all substantive offences prohibited by Article 4 of Additional Protocol II were defined as breaches of customary law, thus enhancing the protections already afforded to civilians by common Article 3. Moreover, from a feminist perspective, the tribunal's rejection of the idea that gender advocacy backgrounds could impact female judicial thinking and that female judges are inherently biased against men in sexual violence cases has been seen as an important step in the development of 'progressive' wartime sexual violence jurisprudence. Finally, the case introduced concurrent sentencing, both for the 'outrages upon personal dignity', as well as for the torture charges for sexual violence offences.

Part VIII

The Celebici *judgement*

Considered a landmark decision, this case had significant implications regarding superior command responsibility, the treatment of various forms of sexual violence committed against male detainees, and the development of the law of torture when victims are tortured by means of rape. Aside from its significant gender implications, the case assumed added significance for the fact that it was the first at the ICTY to charge and try multiple accused at the same time.[136] The case is also reflective of the wider trend in international law of 'human rights globalisation', as two of the defendants, Zejnil Delalic and Zdravko Mucic, were arrested in Germany and Austria under Rule 40 of the Rules of Evidence and Procedure on 18 March 1990.[137] Further, the decision is emblematic of the patterns described by the Commission of Experts in its findings as to the strategies underlying the commission of wartime sexual violence. It is also reflective of the sexual violence committed within the confines of detention-like situations, specifically within camp life, or so-called 'rape camps'. The case also examined the psychological impact of rape, suggesting that it often leads to 'social ostracism' from the community. In this way, the tribunal linked the individualised nature of rape to a form of communal harm.

i) Facts and background

This case is based on the events that took place at the detention facility in the village of Celebici located in the Konjic municipality in central Bosnia-Herzegovina during May to November 1992.[138] All charges centre on acts perpetrated within the Celebici prison camp during the attack on the municipality.[139] This was a largely inter-ethnic community that assumed military significance during the conflict in large part due to its large arms factory and strategic location as the transport link between Sarajevo and Mostar, the two largest cities in Bosnia.[140] Another factor behind the strategic importance of Konjic was its location on the fault line between the areas which Croats and Serbs considered within their spheres of influence; the Bosnian Croats were thus laying claim to the entire area of Herzegovina, while Serbs were primarily interested in the eastern Neretva valley.[141]

The defendants belonged to a force consisting of predominantly Bosnian Muslims and Bosnian Croats, who took control of several villages inhabited by Bosnian Serbs in and around Konjic starting at the end of May 1992.[142] As part of their military campaign the attackers forcibly expelled Bosnian residents from their homes and held them at collection centres. Most women and children were held in local schools or in other locations, while most of the men and some women were taken to a former Yugoslav People's Army (JNA) facility in Celebici, referred to as the Celebici camp. The Indictment alleges that detainees in the camps were 'killed, tortured, sexually assaulted, beaten and otherwise subjected to cruel and inhuman treatment'.[143]

The accused included Zejnil Delalic, the commander of the camp and therefore in a position of authority; Zdravko Mucic, the de facto commander of the camp; Hazim Delic, a subordinate who worked in the camp; and Esad Landžo, who acted as guard. Crucially, three defendants, Delalic, Delic and Mucic, were charged with both individual responsibility, as well as superior command responsibility for failing to prevent, halt or punish crimes committed by subordinates acting under their authority. They had 'wilfully caused great suffering or serious injury to body or health' as a grave breach of the 1949 Geneva Conventions under Article 2 of the Statute, and were charged with cruel treatment as violations of the laws or customs of war under Article 3 of the Statute for acts committed by their subordinates, which included subjecting two male detainees to abusive treatment by having a burning fuse cord placed around their genitals. The three accused were also charged with superior responsibility for the grave breach of inhuman treatment and for cruel treatment as a violation of the laws and customs of war when subordinates forced two male detainees to perform fellatio on each other.[144]

ii) Multiple rape as torture

Mucic and Delic were also charged with individual responsibility for their direct involvement in sexual violence crimes, while Landžo, who did not hold any position of authority, was charged solely with individual responsibility. The charges also included various forms of sexual violence brought against the three accused arising from the actions of Hazim Delic as deputy commander of the Celebici camp, who alongside his accomplices subjected a Bosnian-Serb woman and store owner in Konjic, Grożdana Cecez to repeated incidents of forcible sexual intercourse. During this period, she was allegedly raped by three different men in one night and on another occasion she was raped in front of four other men.[145] Specifically, counts 18 to 20 concern torture as a grave breach punishable under Article 2(b) of the Statute and a violation of the laws and customs of war. The Trial Chamber emphasised that in order for rape to be included within the offence of torture it had to meet each of the elements of this offence contained in the Convention Against Torture, and held that when any form of sexual violence satisfied these elements, it may constitute torture.[146] In defining the elements of torture as constitutive of rape, it stressed that rape is:

> [a] despicable act which strikes at the very core of human dignity and physical integrity. The condemnation and punishment of rape becomes all the more urgent where it is committed by, or at the instigation of, a public official, or with the consent and acquiescence of such an official. Rape causes severe pain and suffering, both physical and psychological. The psychological suffering of persons upon whom rape is inflicted may be exacerbated by the social and cultural conditions and can be particularly acute and long lasting. Furthermore, it is difficult to envisage circumstances in which rape, by, or at the instigation of a public official, could be considered as occurring for a purpose that does not, in some way, involve punishment coercion,

> discrimination, or intimidation. In the view of this Trial Chamber this is inherent in situations of armed conflict.[147]

According to the evidence adduced at trial, Delic interrogated Ms. Cecez upon her arrival at the camp. During the course of the interrogation, Delic repeatedly raped her as he questioned her to the whereabouts of her husband. Three days later, he subjected her to multiple rapes when she was transferred between buildings in the camp, and he again raped her in the camp two months later.[148] The Trial Chamber held that 'the acts of vaginal penetration by the penis under circumstances that were coercive, quite clearly constitute rape'.[149] Moreover, it found that the rapes committed by Delic caused severe pain and suffering and they were committed against Ms. Cecez for the purpose of obtaining information about the whereabouts of her husband, to punish her for not providing information, to punish her for the acts of her husband, and to coerce and intimidate her into cooperating.[150]

The Trial Chamber also emphasised that Delic used sexual violence as an instrument of terror and subordination, given that he committed the rapes with the aim of 'intimidating not only the victim, but also other inmates, by creating an atmosphere of powerlessness'.[151] Specifically he subjected a detainee (Witness A), another Bosnian-Serb woman, to repeated incidents of forcible sexual intercourse, both vaginal and anal in nature. From about 15 June 1992 until the beginning of August 1992 Witness A was raped over a period of six weeks starting with her initial interrogation, after which she was raped every few days.[152] Hence, the court concluded that Delic had repeatedly raped Witness A for the purpose of intimidating, coercing and punishing her, and these rapes caused severe mental and physical pain and suffering. The tribunal found him guilty of torture for the *actus reus* of forcible sexual penetration.[153] Sexual violence as an instrument of terror was closely connected with 'powerlessness' as the Trial Chamber suggested. Thus, Witness A, the female victim, in an instant was rendered powerless presumably for the fact that she was a woman. This stands in notable contrast to the manner in which gender-based violence against men is construed, interpreted and prosecuted by the court.

iii) Superior command responsibility

Another development arising from the judgement concerned the Trial Chamber's examination of the scope of criminal responsibility for military commanders or for other persons having superior authority. The court explained that holding a superior criminally responsible for unlawful conduct of subordinates was a 'well-established norm' of international customary law and conventional law.[154] It identified three essential elements of command superior responsibility, which involves the failure to act when there is a legal duty to do so, as follows:

i) The existence of a superior-subordinate relationship;
ii) The superior knew or had reason to know that the criminal act was about to be or had been committed; and

iii) The superior failed to take the necessary and reasonable measures to prevent the criminal act or punish the perpetrator thereof.[155]

These elements led the judges to conclude that persons in positions of authority, whether in civilian or within military structures, may incur criminal liability under the doctrine of superior command responsibility on the basis of 'their de facto as a well as de jure positions as superiors'.[156] The absence of formal legal authority to control the actions of subordinates did not preclude the imposition of such responsibility.[157] The most significant element underlying criminal accountability was whether the civilian or military commander had 'effective control' over subordinates committing the crime, 'in the sense of having the material ability to prevent and punish the commission of the crimes'.[158] In cases in which knowledge is impossible to ascertain for lack of evidence, be it through the absence of a paper trail or lack of eyewitness testimony, the prosecution will typically attempt to establish knowledge through circumstantial evidence.[159] The Trial Chamber determined that the appropriate standard in deciding whether the superior had 'reason to know' of crimes committed by subordinates was inquiry notice, meaning whether the information had been available so as to put a superior on notice about possible criminal activity by subordinates.[160]

The Appeals Chamber in fact further elaborated upon this standard by giving an example of inquiry notice, as a superior who 'has received information that some of the soldiers under his command have a violent or unstable character, or have been drinking prior to being sent on a mission, may be considered as having the requisite knowledge'.[161] Hence, the Trial Chamber was careful to stress that a superior could only be held criminally responsible for failing to take such measures as are within his powers', meaning that the measures required but not forthcoming had to be within his 'material possibility'.[162]

iv) Summary

This case was significant from a gender perspective, as superior responsibility for crimes committed by subordinates was held not to be limited to war crimes, but was also applicable to other crimes, including crimes against humanity and genocide. Similarly, superior responsibility was not confined to military leaders but deemed to have been used to hold civilian leaders accountable for crimes of sexual violence committed by subordinates which the superior negligently failed to prevent or punish.[163] The precedent from this case was important in so far as it could be used in the future to hold superiors responsible for failing to adequately train, monitor or supervise and punish subordinates who commit rape.[164] It also added further protection to women and girls, recognising their 'extreme vulnerability' when separated from their families and held in detention facilities, where they might be at high risk of sexual violence. The case was also considered to be of importance for its interpretation that 'pain and suffering', a required element of torture, can be psychological in nature.

Part IX

The Kunarac et al. *judgement: finding 'mass rape' as a phenomenon of the conflict in the former Yugoslavia*

Considered a landmark decision in the area of wartime sexual violence, the *Kunarac* judgement was rendered by Trial Chamber II of the Yugoslav Tribunal on 22 February 2001.[165] This decision is considered groundbreaking primarily for its determination that the rape of Muslim women amounts to a crime against humanity, therefore, highlighting the significance of ethnicity in the Trial Chamber's reasoning.[166] The decision also held that conduct constituting sexual slavery and rape classifies as enslavement, qualifying as crimes against humanity situations when victims were held in facilities and repeatedly raped over a period of days, weeks or months. The judgement, therefore, rendered the first ICTY rape as a crime against humanity conviction and the first-ever conviction of enslavement in conjunction with rape. It made extensive holdings regarding the element of enslavement, and it further clarified the elements of rape and torture under international law.[167] The case is further noteworthy in that it is the first case solely to focus on the rape, mistreatment and torture of women during the Yugoslav conflict. Moreover, as Doris Buss points out, it is the first case to consider the phenomenon of 'mass rape' in the context of Bosnia and Herzegovina.[168] The accused were eventually each charged with and convicted of various forms of gender-based crimes, including rape, torture, enslavement and outrages upon personal dignity. The labelling of the sexual violence in Bosnia-Herzegovina as committed on a mass scale gave the event its headline-grabbing moment. Defining rape as 'mass rape' is what distinguished it from other crimes, while at the same time shocking an until-then largely complacent Western world and mobilising feminist activism.[169]

i) Facts and background

The original indictment centred on eight accused charged with various forms of sexual violence committed during the siege of the municipality of Foca by Serb forces in April 1992.[170] The population of the town was gathered together by the military, following which Muslim and Croatian men were separated from women and children and taken to separate detention facilities.[171] These detention centres had been set up at the local high school and sports hall. For the Muslims detained in Foca conditions were described as extreme, with facilities reportedly unhygienic, little food made available to the detainees, and routine abuse of prisoners being commonplace.[172] Women and children were typically collectively held, and in these facilities, they were subjected to 'systematic' rape, 'gang rape' by Serb soldiers, with some women and young girls being subject to public rape, while others were routinely taken out of the facilities to be raped and then returned. Yet others were permanently removed from the facilities to be held elsewhere for sexual access whenever their captors demanded it.[173] The three defendants were involved, in different capacities, with those rapes as well as with the removal of the group of women and girls, most of who were in the age range of 12 to 20, from these centres to local houses and apartments, where they were raped by the defendants and by other soldiers. Some of these women were detained for several months and were subjected to constant rapes, taken as the 'property' of the individual defendants, and made to perform household chores such as cleaning and cooking.[174] After a period of time, some of these women and girls, including a 12-year-old girl, were then sold to other soldiers.[175]

ii) The sexual violence charges

The three defendants were charged with rape as a crime against humanity under Article 5 (g) of the ICTY Statute and as a violation of the laws of war under Article 3, and rape as torture, constituting both a crime against humanity under Article 5 (h) and a violation of the laws of war under Article 3. In addition the defendants were charged with enslavement as a crime against humanity as per Article 5(c) and with outrages upon personal dignity under Article 3. As Buss comments,

> The multiple charges are significant, as in most cases, the multiple charges of rape (as a crime against humanity and as a violation of the laws and customs of war) and torture (also as a crime against humanity and as a violation of the laws and customs of war) are made in respect of the same incident.[176]

The fact that multiple charges were brought is therefore significant, as it constitutes a recognition that wartime rape occurs in different contexts, for different reasons and with various impacts on the victims.[177] The Trial Chamber found that individual acts of rape committed against Muslim women specifically by the accused amounted to crimes against humanity, and were part of a larger policy to terrorise Muslims, evict them from their residential areas, and convert the region into a Serb stronghold.[178]

iii) Expanding on existing rape definitions and the issue of consent

One of the most contentious issues arising during the *Kunarac* trial – certainly from a feminist perspective – was the allegation made by two of the defendants that some of the sexual activity between them and individual Muslim women was consensual. Despite the coercive circumstances of the situation, the tribunal nonetheless decided to consider consent in this instance, as Kunarac had raised the defence under Rule 96, of mistake of fact, thinking that the woman had consented. According to the evidence, one witness took an active part in initiating sexual activity with Kunarac after being threatened that if she did not seduce and sexually please him, she would suffer severe consequences. The Trial Chamber, after considering the overall pattern of conduct of the accused, and the relative position of the victims, refused to accept that consent had been given. It stated unequivocally that it was proven 'beyond reasonable doubt' that although witness D.B. had had sexual intercourse with Kunarac in which she had taken an active part by '[t]aking off the trousers of the accused and kissing him all over the body before having vaginal intercourse with him', the conclusion had to be that 'she had only initiated the sexual intercourse with Kunarac because she was afraid of being killed by "Gaga", if she did not do so'.[179]

The judges, therefore, rejected Kunarac's claim that he did not know that D.B. only initiated sex with him because she feared for her life. They found it entirely unrealistic that Kunarac could have been confused by D.B.'s actions, particularly against the backdrop of the ongoing war and her detention by enemy forces.[180] Not only does this passage have implications for female agency in wartime by presuming that under circumstances of coercion consent is almost always impossible, but it also speaks to the broader motivations and policies underlying the conflict in this way reducing this instance to another unfortunate side effect of the conflict.

A more interesting segment for purposes of determinations of female autonomy during wartime is presented in the charges against the co-accused Vukovic of rape and torture for certain instances of sexual violence committed against women and girls in Foca. Much like Kunarac, Vukovic strongly contested the allegations of sexual torture against him, arguing that even if it were proved that he had committed rape he 'would have done so out of a sexual urge, not out of hatred'.[181] This is perhaps the most emblematic of the expressions produced by a defendant in an ICTY sexual violence case. The defendant's claim that he did not commit the rape for a prohibited purpose necessary for establishing torture and the Trial Chamber's response to it are instructive in that the defendant's interpretation of events is eschewed in favour of a reading of the conflict as entirely ethnic, and therefore beyond any discussion of agency. The tribunal explains that

> all that matters in this context is his awareness of an attack against the Muslim civilian population of which his victim was a member, and for the purpose of torture, that he intended to discriminate between the group of which he is a member and the group of his victim.

It is this reified, if not flawed, legal reasoning of wartime identity that gives rise to the critique of this book. Although the judges stressed in their reasoning that torture could be committed for any number of reasons and that one of the prohibited purposes merely needed to be part of the motivation behind the torture, not necessarily the principal motivation, it is clear that ethnicity was seen as the central catalyst driving the perpetrator's actions.[182] Moreover, in imputing ethnic motivations to the act, the Trial Chamber did not have to engage with a chain of potentially intricate and complex set of events that might have established that the sexual interaction between the defendant and the woman had happened on entirely consensual basis that was not at all prompted by fear or duress. The tribunal found Vukovic guilty of torture as a war crime and a crime against humanity for sexual torture.

iv) Sexual violence as an 'outrage upon personal dignity'

The third defendant, Kovac, was charged with 'outrages upon personal dignity' for sexual violence committed against women and girls held in enslavement conditions.[183] Particular emphasis was placed on the fact that the suffering did not have to be long-lasting to qualify as an 'outrage upon personal dignity', as long as the humiliation or degradation was 'real and serious'. Moreover, it was held to be immaterial whether the victim had recovered or had overcome the effects of such an offence.[184] But here, as in previous paragraphs, the perceived psychological impact of the sexual violence on the woman is implied in the language used by the tribunal. In convicting Kovac of outrages upon personal dignity for occasions in which women and girls were made to dance nude on a table together – and at times individually in front of him and others – for their seeming entertainment, the Trial Chamber suggested that Kovac knew that having to stand naked on a table while being watched was 'a painful and humiliating experience' for the three women involved, a factor further exacerbated by their young age.[185] The court looked to the effect of the crime, while implying that it would inevitably cause a 'psychic wound' in the victim, which suggests that her body is 'already and always violated', regardless of whether the act might have brought sexual gratification to the perpetrator, or possibly even the victim herself.[186]

v) Enslavement as a crime against humanity

Most of the women in this case were 'enslaved' for weeks or months, and during this period they were systematically and repeatedly raped during all or part of their time in captivity. On some occasions they were given keys to the house where they were held, and at other times they would find the door of where they were staying open. The Trial Chamber here had to determine whether the absence of physical barriers was relevant to the psychological or logistical barriers present. Hailed as one of the most groundbreaking aspects of the *Kunarac* decision, extensive findings were made in relation to enslavement with reference in particular to the Slavery Convention, which has consistently defined slavery as 'the status or condition of a person over whom any or all of the powers attaching to the right of ownership are exercised', thus codifying customary international law. The *actus reus* element of the crime was defined as 'the exercise of any or all of the powers attaching to the right of ownership over a person', while the *mens rea* was defined as the 'intentional exercise of such powers'.[187] The sub-elements of the offence were determined to include control and ownership; the restriction or control of an individual's autonomy; freedom of choice or freedom of movement; the accrual of some gain to the perpetrator; absence of consent or free will; exploitation; 'the exaction of forced labour or compulsory labour or services, often without remuneration and often, though not necessarily, involving physical hardship', including sex, prostitution, trafficking in persons, assertion of exclusivity, subjection to cruel treatment and abuse, and control of sexuality.[188]

The judges found that free will or consent is impossible or irrelevant when certain conditions are present, such as the 'threat or use of force or other forms of coercion: the fear of violence, deception, or false promises; the abuse of power; the victim's position of vulnerability; detention or captivity, psychological oppression or socio-economic conditions'.[189]

The judgement emphasised that control over a person's sexual autonomy, or obliging a person to provide sexual services, may be proof of enslavement, but such indicia are not elements of the crime. The facts of the case demonstrate that the enslavement and rape were inseparably linked, and that the accused enslaved the women and girls as a means to effectuate continuous rape. Since a primary but not necessarily exclusive motivation behind the enslavement was to hold the women and girls for sexual access at will and with ease, the crime would most appropriately be characterised as sexual slavery. According to Askin, for example, it is regrettable that the term 'sexual slavery' was never used in the judgement.[190]

The Appeals Chamber Judgement of 12 June 2002 upheld and reinforced the Trial Chamber Judgement's holdings concerning rape, torture and enslavement.[191] Indeed, the Appeals Chamber rejected the assertion that resistance, force or threat of force are elements of rape, as such factors are simply evidence of non-consent and it found that not only may rape constitute torture, but also that rape is an act that 'establishes per se the suffering of those upon whom it was inflicted'.[192]

vi) Summary

While the *Kunarac* judgement has undoubtedly advanced the scope of gender-based violence further by redefining sexual violence as a form of slavery and therefore a crime against humanity and by narrowing the consent defence to a degree which suggests that in situations of wartime it is almost impossible for a woman to meaningfully consent, there are a number of problematic side-effects from a critical feminist perspective. Firstly, the case implies that torture against women can only be committed in the form of rape. Secondly, it reinforces the sense that women are tortured in ways different to men, given that rape as form of torture is closely interlinked in the judgement with the female experience, while male sexual violence as a form of torture is ignored. This creates a reified category of women, the presumption being that all women suffer torture in the same way, while precluding the possibility that the torturers could be women themselves in this way, denying female agency. A feminist critical reading suggests that the preservation of separate definitions and special acknowledgments about women reiterates persistent stereotypes. This is not helped by the fact that for an act to classify as torture in international law it has to be committed at the hands of a public official. The case is also relevant for highlighting the intersectional nature of gender and ethnicity in wartime and it has notably contributed to the culturalised and depoliticised interpretation of gender in ICTY wartime sexual violence jurisprudence.

Part X

The Kvocka *judgement: rape as persecution in the context of a joint criminal enterprise*

This case is of significance from a gender-based perspective for its finding that rape can be used as a form of persecution incurring individual liability and for rendering important holdings in relation to threats of sexual violence as constituting torture. This case also defined standards of liability for any foreseeable, consequential or incidental rape crimes when committed during the course of a joint criminal enterprise, in this way extensively developing the joint criminal enterprise theory of responsibility.[193] This was taken further in the present decision, which specifically examined the common purpose doctrine/joint criminal enterprise theory in the Nuremberg case law and applied the theory of responsibility to persons knowingly working in the Omarska prison camp in Bosnia.[194] This legal technique and modality has become a preferred charging preference in ICTY indictments, and has been especially used when charged in conjunction with persecution.[195] Participation in a joint criminal enterprise, for example, had been a prominent feature in the Miloševic trial.[196]

i) Facts and background

The case centred around five defendants who worked or regularly visited the Omarska prison camp, which had been established by Bosnian Serbs in Prijedor in May 1992 with the purported aim of suppressing an uprising of Bosnian Muslims and Bosnian Croats in the region. The camp operated for approximately three months in 1992 during which over 3,000 men and approximately 36 women were detained. Mistreatment and inhumane conditions were pervasive, and crimes such as murder, torture, rape and persecution were rampant. Counts 1–3 of the Amended Indictment charged the five accused with persecution and inhuman acts as crimes against humanity and with outrages upon personal dignity as a war crime. The persecution count alleged that the accused persecuted non-Serbs detained inside the camp through several means, namely: murder, torture and beating, sexual assault and rape, harassment, humiliation and psychological abuse, and confinement in inhumane conditions.[197]

In addition, counts 14–17 charged one of the accused, Mladjo Radic, a guard shift leader in the camp, with rape, torture and outrages upon personal dignity for the sexual violence he allegedly committed personally against women detained in the Omarska prison camp.[198] In relation to gender-based violence, the Trial Chamber found that 'female detainees were subjected to various forms of sexual violence' in the camp,[199] while pointing out that sexual violence covered a broad range of acts including rape, molestation, sexual slavery, sexual mutilation, forced marriage, forced abortion, enforced prostitution, forced pregnancy and forced sterilisation.[200]

ii) Joint criminal enterprise responsibility

The case is of further significance for building upon the development of the common purpose/joint enterprise theory contained in the *Tadic* Appeals Chamber Judgement, and its holding that such theory of responsibility is implicitly included within Article 7(1) concerning individual responsibility of the Statute of the tribunal.[201] The *Kvocka* Trial Chamber specified that a joint criminal enterprise may exist:

> whenever two or more people participate in a common criminal endeavour. This criminal endeavour can range anywhere from along a continuum from two persons conspiring to rob a bank to the systematic slaughter of millions during a vast criminal regime comprising thousands of participants. Within a joint criminal enterprise there may be other subsidiary criminal enterprises. . . . Within some subsidiaries of the larger criminal enterprise, the criminal purpose may be more particularized: one subset may be established for purposes of forced labor, another for purposes of systematic rape for forced impregnation, another for purposes of extermination, etc.[202]

Based on the brutality of the crimes and their pervasiveness throughout the camp, the Trial Chamber ultimately concluded that Omarska camp operated as a joint criminal enterprise established to persecute non-Serbs contained therein, thus imputing the ethnic dimension to the act.[203] There was no direct physical element that could be ascribed to the perpetrators. Consequently, the three accused were not convicted of having physically perpetrated the crimes, mistreating the detainees, aiding in the establishment of the camp, or exercising any significant influence over abusive policies in the camp. However, they undoubtedly knew that a range of crimes were committed on an everyday basis and that the camps functioned to gather, persecute and eliminate non-Serbs.[204] Because the defendants continued to show up for work every day in the Omarska camp, despite being aware of the criminal activities committed therein, their efforts were held to have contributed significantly to the continued and effective functioning of the camp, which facilitated the commission of the crimes, even allowing them to continue at ease. Through these actions they incurred criminal responsibility for participating in the criminal enterprise.[205]

An interesting detail emerged in the judicial reasoning with regard to the fact that although there was no evidence admitted at trial to indicate that the defendants had knowledge of the rapes or other forms of sexual violence, it was nonetheless evident that by knowingly working in the camp where criminal activity was rampant, the participants had assumed the risk of incurring criminal responsibility for all foreseeable crimes, including rape crimes. As the Trial Chamber has put it:

> Any crimes that were natural and foreseeable consequences of the joint criminal enterprise . . . can be attributable to participants in the criminal enterprise if committed during the time he participated in the enterprise.[206]

Holding that sexual violence in the camp was patently foreseeable and virtually inevitable under the circumstances, it reasoned that:

> In Omarska camp, approximately 36 women were held in detention, guarded by men with weapons, who were often drunk, violent and physically and mentally abusive and who were allowed to act with virtual impunity. Indeed, it would be unrealistic and contrary to all rational logic to expect that none of the women held in Omarska, placed in circumstances rendering them especially vulnerable, would be subjected to rape or other forms of sexual violence. This is particularly true in light of clear intent of the criminal enterprise to subject the targeted group to persecution through such means as violence and humiliation.[207]

This led the court to conclude that participants in a joint criminal enterprise, whether aiders and abettors or co-perpetrators, may be held liable for any natural or foreseeable crimes committed while they participate in the criminal enterprise.[208] The judgement is remarkable in that it implies that any such act committed in detention, whether in a large facility where many women are formally detained or in a house where a small group or even one woman is unlawfully kept, may constitute a criminal enterprise if individuals knowingly participate with others in criminal activity.[209] Indeed, the decision is highly significant for its implication that extra measures may be needed to protect women for rape in such situations. Thus, the Trial Chamber specified that:

> If a superior has prior knowledge that women detained by male guards in detention facilities are likely to be subjected to sexual violence, that would put him on sufficient notice that extra measures are demanded in order to prevent such crimes.[210]

The implication here is that the extensive evidence of wartime rape generated by media reports is now virtually universal knowledge, therefore it is expected that women are always in grave danger of being subjected to sexual violence and that this is particularly true during periods of hostility and or mass violence. The decision can be interpreted as imposing a burden on those detaining females to ensure that adequate protections are devised to prevent sexual abuse, and to monitor facilities where there is a likelihood that such crimes might take place.[211] While this development is, on the one hand, undoubtedly attentive to women's needs, it at the same time has the potential to produce overly protective gendered images, as it reinforces the idea that in situations of detention women will inevitably fall victim to sexual violence, thus precluding any sense of female agency. The judgement is also notable for recognising that persecution takes many forms and is not limited to physical violence. According to the tribunal:

> Just as rape and forced nudity are recognized as crimes against humanity or genocide if they form part of an attack directed against a civilian population

> or if used as an instrument of genocide, humiliating treatment that forms part of a discriminatory attack against a civilian population may, in combination with other crimes, or in extreme cases alone, similarly constitute persecution.[212]

This is significant from a gender-based perspective in so far as it recognises the psychological impact of sexual violence as a form of persecution, reiterating the conceptual finding in *Akayesu* that sexual violence manifests itself in multiple forms and can constitute a crime against humanity, despite the absence of any manifest physical contact.

iii) The charges against Radic

An important aspect of the decision concerned the ruling on the rape and torture charges against Radic, a guard shift leader in the camp. The allegations against him ranged from groping, blatant threats and attempts at sexual violence to the outright commission of rape. Finding that Radic had committed sexual violence against some women in the camp, the chamber recalled the definition of sexual violence promulgated in Akayesu as 'any act of a sexual nature, which is committed on a person under circumstances, which are coercive'.[213] It found that 'the sexual intimidations, harassment, and assaults committed by him clearly fell within this definition, given that he had physically perpetrated rape against women detained in the camp'.[214]

Interestingly, in its determination that rape and other forms of sexual violence constituted torture, the Trial Chamber imbued the decision with distinct ethnic undertones, stressing that the rape and other forms of sexual violence were committed '[o]nly against the non-Serb detainees in the camp, and solely against women, making the crimes discriminatory on multiple levels'.[215] It also stressed that Radic intentionally raped and attempted to rape, and that these acts in and of themselves 'manifest[ed] his intent to inflict severe pain and suffering', amounting to torture. Finding that the accused had intentionally inflicted severe pain and suffering on the women by subjecting them to groping, harassment and threats of rape, the Trial Chamber concluded that these acts too satisfied the requirements of torture.[216] From a feminist perspective, this case was not a wholesale victory, as the relegation of a rape to an arguably more potent category in international law dented its earlier recognition as a standalone crime against humanity. Ultimately, the tribunal convicted Radic of sexual violence under the persecution charge, while the sexual violence as torture charges were not similarly subsumed, leading to Radic's concurrent conviction for rape as a form of torture constituting a war crime.

iv) Summary

The *Kvocka* case has had considerable implications for securing criminal responsibility for sex and gender crimes committed either during a joint criminal enterprise or as part of a persecution scheme. This is especially important given the ICTY trend of indicting leaders and subordinates under the joint criminal enterprise theory and using the persecution as a catch-all category to cover a broad range of crimes, such as murder, torture, rape, deportation and destruction of homes or religious facilities, without indicting each crime separately.[217] Moreover, in this case as in each of the above cases, a female judge was a member of the Trial Chamber hearing the case, and occasionally it was a female intervention that facilitated the judicial redress process and impacted the development of gender crimes. As some have argued, the presence of qualified female judges, prosecutors, investigators, translators, defence attorneys and facilitators (for example in the Victim and Witnesses Unit) has improved the record in affording redress for gender-related crimes.[218] Yet a critical feminist analysis might suggest the contrary and argue that this is yet another manifestation of 'governance feminism' that has not been entirely emancipatory for women across the board.

Part XI

Conclusion

This chapter has highlighted wartime sexual violence as a fusion of issues cutting across human rights, gender, ethnicity and culture. Through a review of the salient wartime sexual violence cases generated by the conflict in Bosnia-Herzegovina, it has provided both an analysis of the legal accomplishments of the tribunal, while also conveying a sense of the space and circumstance within which this type of violence found expression. The chapter has, moreover, shown that the interpretation of sexual violence and gendered identity is strongly mediated by legal terminology, which has potent effect in determining subjectivities. How armed conflict is interpreted and history is narrated in popular discourses can have a powerful impact on the construction of its actors in the popular imagination, allowing little room for critical refection, much less for divergence from dominant narratives.

While monumental legal successes have been accomplished by the ICTY, gender has been closely entwined with culturalised notions of ethnicity. Women therefore continue to be defined along recurring traditional stereotypes, which have not been altered despite the most sustained feminist advocacy. But as shown previously, the portrayal of female identity in this way might have been perpetuated by feminists themselves. The various feminist judicial interventions described in this chapter have demonstrated that this is a type of feminism feeling more comfortable in its own skin – it is what Janet Halley has termed a form of 'governance feminism' that now feels at ease with power. The book contends that governance feminism has failed to interrogate the ontological essence of the Yugoslav conflict, and it has not meaningfully engaged with the root causes of conflict. Perhaps this was an unrealistic expectation, given the ICTY's institutional nature and its symbolic location with a new global order situated at the 'end of history'.

A contrapuntal analysis was provided in part III of the chapter in its discussion of the internal and external forces of power that contributed to the collapse of the

Yugoslav state and its institutions. This segment sought to complicate the prevailing narrative around the Yugoslav conflict as based on 'ancient ethnic rivalries' by examining closely the multiple structural and financial causes that contributed to the breakdown of the Yugoslav state and its institutions. In this way, the chapter was able to complicate the parameters of the debate by suggesting that the popular discourse has sought to camouflage, or 'depoliticise' pervasive, fundamental and deeply entrenched social problems, such as inequality and subordination. Moreover, part IV critically assessed the role of language as reflected in the use of terminology such as 'ethnic cleansing', which helped frame the idea of an 'ethnic conflict' in the law. It was suggested that the deployment of such terminology warrants further complication.

This chapter has sought to further stimulate critical debate and provided a springboard for the final chapter, which explores in more detail what the institutionalisation of gender-based violence means for women in the contemporary political and legal moment. In this vein, it aims to address whether international criminal law ought to be the 'preferred vehicle' for feminist advocacy and whether the move to institutions, which resulted in a near 'seamless performance of consensus' within feminist argumentation and rule preference, is the way forward in achieving the twin feminist goals of gender justice and equality.[219] It is, therefore, worth recalling feminism's original roots, which did not set out to achieve consensus, much less find triumph through criminalisation, but rather to contest persistent structural inequalities against women. To quote Karen Engle:

> That many feminists now have a sense of achievement with regard to the development of international law in this area is surprising not only because feminists do not generally associate their efforts with success.[220]

The book aims to bring back critique as an opportunity for identifying a more nuanced analysis of power. Its aim is to reshape assumptions underlying dominant norms, rather than to come up with proposals for quick-fix reforms. Critique is an opportunity to examine positions, rather than remain trapped in the contemporary obsession with position-taking, as the next chapter goes on to demonstrate.

Notes

1 Key Figures of ICTY Cases 3/06/2011, available at: www.icty.org/x/file/cases/keyfigures/key-figures_110328-en.pdf (last accessed in June 2011). Three of the seven cases currently at trial and three of those awaiting trial (including that of the recently captured former Bosnian-Serb military leader Ratko Mladic) involve sexual violence allegations and charges. Moreover, four of six trial judgements subject to actual or potential appeal also involve sexual violence findings. For an overview, see: United Nations Department of Peacekeeping Operations: 'Review of the Sexual Violence Elements of the Judgements of the International Criminal Tribunal for the Former Yugoslavia, the International Criminal Tribunal for Rwanda, and the Special Court for Sierra Leone in the Light of Security Council Resolution 1820' (pdf file, copy with author).

2 ICTY sexual violence cases as of June 2011 include: *Tadic* (IT-94–1); Nikolic (IT-94–2); *Došen, Kolundžija and Sikirica* (IT-95–8); *Todorovic* (IT-95–9/1); Blagoje Simic (IT-95–9/9-T); Milan Simic (IT-95/9/2); Cesic (IT-95–10/1); Rajic (IT-95–12); Cerkez and Kordic (IT-95–14/2); Bralo (IT-9517); Furundžija (IT-95–17/11); Meakic et al.(IT-95–4); Blaškic (IT-95–14);Kupreškic et. al (IT-95–16) Cesic (IT-95–10/1); Delalic, Delic, Mucic and Landžo (*Celebici* case) (IT-96–23); Kovac, Kunarac and Vukovic (IT-96–23, IT-96–23–1); Zelenovic, "Foca" (IT-96–23/2); Stakic (IT-97–24); Krnojelac (IT-97–25)Kos, Kvocka, Prcac, Radic and Žigic (IT-98–30/1); Krstic (IT-98–33); Vasiljevic (IT-98–32); Brdanin (IT-99–36); Plavšic (IT-00–39 &40/1); Krajišnik (IT-00–39); Halilovic (IT-01–48); Banovic (IT-02–65/1); Rasim Delic (IT-04–83); Milutinovic et al. (IT-05–87); Mladic (IT-(IT-09–92).

3 *Prosecutor v. Tadic* (Trial Chamber) Case No IT-94–1-T (7 May 1997) (Judgement); *Prosecutor v. Tadic* (Appeals Chamber) Case No IT-96–21-A (15 July 1999) (Judgement) (collectively 'Tadic'').

4 *Prosecutor v. Zejnil Delalic*, Zdravko Mucic, Hazim Delic and Esad Landžo (IT-96–21-T), (16 November 1998) (Judgement); *Prosecutor v. Delalic et al Appeals Chamber*, Case No IT-96–21-A (20 February 2001) (Judgement) (collectively '*Celebici*').

5 *Prosecutor v. Furundžija* (Trial Chamber) Case No IT-96–23-T/1-T (10 December 1998) (Judgement); *Prosecutor v. Furundžija* (Appeals Chamber) Case No IT-95–17/I-T (21 July 2000) (Judgement) (collectively 'Furundžija').

6 *Prosecutor v. Kunarac* (Trial Chamber) Case No IT-96–23-T/1-T (22 February 2001) (Judgement); *Prosecutor v. Kunarac* (Appeals Chamber) Case No. IT-96–23-T/1-A (12 June 2002) (Judgement) (collectively 'Kunarac').

7 *Prosecutor v. Kvocka* (Trial Chamber) Case No IT-98–30/1-T (2 November 2001) (Judgement); *Prosecutor v. Kvocka* (Appeals Chamber) Case No IT-98–30/1-A (25 February 2005) (Judgement) (collectively 'Kvocka').

8 For a discussion see, 82. See also Askin (2003), at 88 and Askin (2002–2003), at 910.

9 This phrase is borrowed from Jelena Batinic's discussion of both local as well as international feminist debates on rape accompanying the Yugoslav conflict, which later significantly influenced the legal regulation and interpretation of these acts in the jurisprudence. In Batinic (2001), at 1.

10 See for example Askin (2002–2003), at 910.

11 As Catherine MacKinnon has put it, 'Serbian forces have exterminated over 200,000 Croatians and Muslims thus far in an operation they've coined "ethnic cleansing"'. In this genocide, in Bosnia-Herzegovina alone, over 30,000 Muslim and Croatian girls and women are pregnant from mass rape. Of the hundred 'Serbian-run concentration camps, about twenty are solely rape/death camps for Muslim and Croatian women and children.' In MacKinnon (1999), at 36.

12 Going as far as to equivocate the 'death camps' run by Serbs with the systematic extermination of Jews during World War II, MacKinnon in describing the pattern of rape committed in Yugoslavia has argued that: 'The systematic and instrumental nature of these rapes marks them. Pogroms were one thing, designing and fielding the gas chambers was another. Rape as most women generally know it and these rapes have a similar difference. Auschwitz was industrial murder. Omarska has industrial rape: intended planned, mass-produced, serially executed, instrumentalized. It comes close to the experiences of prostituted women, serially raped in what is called peacetime.' In C. MacKinnon, 'Rape as Nationbuilding' in MacKinnon (1999), at 176. This point has also been made in Nadj (2011), at 647.

13 *The Prosecutor v. Zejnil Delalic, Zdravko Mucic* (IT-96–21-T) (hereafter referred to as *Celebici* case), Trial Chamber Judgement, 16 November 1998, at para 478.

The Trial Chamber draws guidance on this question from the ICTR case, which has considered the definition of rape in the context of crimes against humanity. The *Celebici* Trial Chamber fully concurred with the *Akayesu* definition adopting the 'rape as a physical invasion of a sexual nature, committed on a person under circumstances, which are coercive' as its working definition in the present judgment.

14 Three of the accused, Zejnil Delalic, Zdravko Mucic and Hazim Delic, were charged with responsibility as superiors for all the criminal acts alleged in the indictment, with the exception of count 49 on plunder of private property where the charge of responsibility was limited to Zdravko Mucic and Hazim Delic. At para 330. The governing principles of 'command responsibility' have been incorporated into Article 7(3) of the Statute, which provides that: 'The fact that any of the acts referred to in articles 2 to 5 of the present Statute was committed by a subordinate does not relieve his superior of criminal responsibility if he knew or had reason to know that the subordinate was about to commit such acts or had done so and the superior failed to take the necessary and reasonable measures to prevent such acts or to punish the perpetrators thereof.' See 'Statute of the International Tribunal for the Former Yugoslavia' (Adopted 25 May 1993 by Resolution 827), Article 7(3).

15 For a summary of the conflict in Kosovo, see: *The Prosecutor v. Vlastimir Dordevic* (IT-05/87/1-PT), Fourth Amended Indictment, 9 July 2008, at paras 23–33. For a summary of attacks on ethnic Albanians within the Republic of Macedonia, see: *The Prosecutor v. Boškoski & Tarculoski* (IT-04–82).

16 R. Hayden, 'Imagined Communities and Real Victims: Self-Determination and Ethnic Cleansing in Yugoslavia', 23 *American Ethnologist* (November 1996), at 788.

17 Ibid at 788.

18 T. Varady, 'Minorities, Majorities, Law, and Ethnicity: Reflections of the Yugoslav Case', 19 *Human Rights Quarterly* (1997), at 18.

19 Ibid at 19.

20 Ibid.

21 Gagnon (2004).

22 Ibid at 1.

23 In surveys conducted in the early 1990s prior to the outbreak of the conflict in Bosnia-Herzegovina, only 18 of the 106 municipalities of the republic had populations that were 80 percent or more of a single group. The experience of living with others led Serbs in Bosnia to have a more positive view of ethnic pluralism than Serbs in homogenous Yugoslavia. In a similar survey undertaken in November 1989, 80 percent of the wider population surveyed considered inter-ethnic relations in the places where they lived to be positive, and 66 percent saw inter-ethnic relations in Bosnia-Herzegovina as the most stable in Yugoslavia. In Gagnon (2004), at 39–42.

24 By the mid-1980s against the backdrop of an increasingly severe economic situation and strengthening nationalist sentiment paired with large-scale migration from all republics of the former Yugoslavia abroad, virtually each republic and province, despite the multicultural and multi-ethnic composition of Yugoslavia's constituent entities, progressively provided a framework for the promotion of the national identity and attainment of sovereignty of a specific ethnic group, facilitating the fragmentation of the already delicate Yugoslav public sphere. While the Serbian leadership actively campaigned for the restoration of centralism and the restoration of Serbian control over the autonomous provinces of Kosovo and Vojvodina that had been granted their status following the enactment of the 1974 constitution, on the other hand the leaderships of the provincial parties were ardent supporters of decentralization, meaning that Slovenian communists pushed for political liberalisation and decentralisation, while

in Croatia, there was aversion towards liberalisation of the political system and support for a decentralisation of the economy with economic nationalism and the economic prospects that could be derived from there playing a central role. In Macedonia and Bosnia, on the other hand, the regional parties advocated the preservation of the Yugoslav federation leading to a 'bipolar' division as Slovenia and Croatia supported provincial party leaderships against Serbian demands of decentralisation. This confrontational atmosphere led to a deep rift between the republican elites and the republics more generally. This rift precipitated the declarations of independence of first Slovenia and then Croatia. On 25 June 1991, Slovenia declared its formal independence, thereby effectively seceding from the Socialist Federal Republic of Yugoslavia (SFRY). By the time full-out war broke out between the Serbian and Croatian military forces, Slovenia had thus already ceased to be a part of Yugoslavia. In Sofos & Jenkins (1996), at 261–263. For a detailed overview of the breakup of Yugoslavia, see also: Little & Silber (1995).

25 In the same year Soviet reform was looking westward under Mikhail Gorbachev's new foreign policy of a 'European home', a Vatican campaign under the helm of a Polish pope began for new converts and the end of communism in eastern Europe, and moreover, economic and cultural contacts between Slovenes and Croats and their neighbours in Italy and Austria began to take on institutional forms. In Woodward (2000), at 30–33.

26 It is well documented that following the collapse of the Soviet Union, Yugoslavia had lost its strategic importance to Washington as U.S. geo-political and interests shifted to the Middle East. Thus, preoccupied with the Persian Gulf War and the future of the disintegrating Soviet Union, the United States was satisfied to leave the handling of the Yugoslav crisis to the European Community. When fighting began in 1991, Secretary of State, James Baker explained the U.S. lack of interest by saying: 'We don't have a dog in that fight.' Quote provided in E. O'Ballance, *History of the Yugoslav Crisis* (1995), at 31.

27 The rationale behind the new fiscal austerity policies underlying IMF loans and World Bank assistance to Yugoslavia was political reform, as Woodward points out, ibid.

28 Woodward (2000), at 32.

29 According to the Commission of Experts, the conflict in Bosnia and Herzegovina constitutes the third phase of the conflict beginning on 6 March 1992, following its declaration of independence. It simultaneously involved fighting between Croatian and Bosnian government forces, Bosnian government and Serb forces, and Croatian and Serbian forces. For an overview of the history of the Yugoslav crisis, see also: O'Ballance (1995), at 20.

30 For a discussion see: D. Petrovic, 'Ethnic Cleansing-An Attempt at Methodology', 5 *European Journal of International Law* (1994), at 342.

31 For a summary of the events characterising the conflict in Bosnia-Herzegovina, see in particular *The Prosecutor v. Zejnil Delalic, Zdravko Mucic, Hazim Delic and Esad Landžo* (IT-96–21), (hereinafter the *Celebici* case) Trial Chamber Judgment, (16 November 1998), at paras 104–108. It is interesting to note that the Trial Chamber uses the term 'ethnic cleansing' only in the context of Serb war strategies, never in the context of Croat or Bosnian Muslim campaigns. The following paragraph, describing the Yugoslav National Army campaign illustrates this neatly: 'There is substantial evidence that the JNA was openly involved in combat activities in Bosnia and Herzegovina from the beginning of March and into April and May of 1992, aided by various paramilitary groups. The offensive was designed by a campaign designed to drive non-Serbs out of desired territory, a practice gaining notoriety under the term "ethnic cleansing"'. Ibid at para 213. The Final Report of the Commission of Experts has described the policy of 'ethnic cleansing' in the following way: 'Considered in the context of the

conflicts in the former Yugoslavia, 'ethnic cleansing' rendering an area ethnically homogenous by using force or intimidation to remove persons of given groups from an area'. 'Ethnic cleansing' is contrary to international law. Further, 'ethnic cleansing' has been carried out by means of murder, torture, arbitrary arrest and detention, extra-judicial executions, rape and sexual assaults, confinement of civilian population in ghetto areas, forcible removal, displacement and deportation of civilian population, deliberate military attacks or threats of attacks on civilians and civilian areas, and wanton destruction of property. Those practices constitute crimes against humanity and can be assimilated to specific war crimes. Furthermore, such acts could also fall within the meaning of the Genocide Convention. Ibid at para 56.

32 As Karen Engle details, 'The understandings of rape range from a relatively straightforward interpretation of the rapes as systematic rather than isolated events, to detailed explanations of ways that rapes were systematic, for example, through efforts of forcibly impregnating or socially ostracising Bosnian Muslim women'. In K. Engle, 'Feminism and Its (Dis)Contents: Criminalizing Wartime Rape in Bosnia and Herzegovina', 99 *American Journal of International Law* (2005), at 788.

33 Petrovic's article charts the origin of the term to mass media reports of the early 1980s, which discussed the establishment of 'ethnically clean territories' in Kosovo after 1981. At the time, the term related to administrative and non-violent matters and referred mostly to the behaviour of Kosovo Albanians towards the Serbian minority in the autonomous province within the Socialist Federal Republic of Yugoslavia. But as Petrovic notes, the term derived its current meaning during the war in Bosnia and Herzegovina, and was also used to describe certain events in Croatia. Although it is impossible to definitively establish who was first to employ the term and in what context, it is believed that military officers in the former Yugoslav People's Army played a central part, and that the expression 'ethnic cleansing' has its origin in military vocabulary. In Petrovic (1994), at 343.

34 The Commission goes on to describe the manner in which the policy of 'ethnic cleansing' is carried out by Serbs in Bosnia as consistent throughout a certain geographic area represented by an arc ranging from northern Bosnia and covering areas in western and eastern Bosnia adjoining the Serb Kraijna area in Croatia. It goes on to state that the practice of 'ethnic cleansing' is carried out in strategic areas linking Serbia proper with Serb-inhabited areas in Bosnia and Croatia. It argues that this strategic factor is highly relevant to understanding why the policy has been carried out in certain areas and not others, thus imputing ethnic motivations to this practice. Final Report of the Commission of Experts, established pursuant to Security Council Resolution 780 (1992) U.N. Doc. S/1994/674/ Add. 2 (Vol.1), annex II), para 2 (May 1994), at paras 29–32.

35 Mazowiecki submitted two series of reports in total. One series of four reports was submitted pursuant to the Commission Resolution 1992/S-1/1 of 16 August 1992. They were the reports of 28 August 1992, U.N. Doc. E/CN./1992/S-1/9 – hereinafter referred to as First Mazowiecki Report I; 27 October 1992, U.N. Doc. E/CN.4/1992/S-1.10 – hereinafter referred to as the Second Mazowiecki Report I, 17 November 1992, U.N. Doc A/47/666 and S/24809 – or the Third Mazowiecki Report I; and 10 February 1993, U.N. Doc. E/CN.4/1993/50, or the Fourth Mazowiecki Report I, and another series of six reports pursuant to paragraph 32 of Commission Resolution 1993/7 of 23 February 1993.These were the reports of 5 May 1993, U.N. Doc. E/CN.4/1994/3 – hereinafter referred to as First Mazowiecki Report II; 19 May 1993, U.N. Doc. E/CN.4/1994/4 – hereinafter referred to as Second Mazowiecki Report II, 19 May 1993, U.N. Doc. E/CN.4/1996/6-hereinafter referred to as Third Mazowiecki Report II, 6 September 1993, U.N. Doc. E/CN.4/1994/8 – hereinafter referred to as Fourth

Mazowiecki Report II, 17 November 1993, U.N. Doc. E/CN.4/1994/47 – hereinafter referred to as the Fifth Mazowiecki Report II; 21 February 1994, U.N. Doc. E/CN.4/1994/110 – hereinafter referred to as Sixth Mazowiecki Report II.

36 Fourth Mazowiecki Report II, at 8, point 26.

37 First Mazowiecki Report I at 4, point 15; Third Mazowiecki Report I, at 6, point 9; Fourth Mazowiecki Report II, at 2, point 11.

38 First Mazowiecki Report I at 4, point 16: 'Attacks on churches and mosques are also part of a campaign of intimidation use to force Muslims and ethnic Croats to flee Bosnian territory'; Fourth Mazowiecki Report II, at 8–9, points 26 and 29; Sixth Mazowiecki Report II, at 5, point 13. This point in particular illustrates that ethnicity as driving force underlying the conflict played a central role in the Commission's research methodology.

39 Fifth Mazowiecki Report II, at 4, point 15.

40 Third Mazowiecki Report I, at 12, point 27: 'Rape is another repugnant feature of ethnic cleansing'; Report of the Team of Experts on their Mission to Investigate the Allegations of Rape in the Territory of the Former Yugoslavia from 12 January to 23 January 1993, Annex II to Fourth Mazowiecki Report I, at 73, point 62: 'In Bosnia-Herzegovina and in Croatia, rape has been used as an instrument of ethnic cleansing.' These Reports strongly set the tone for a characterisation of wartime sexual violence through an ethnic prism.

41 For an analysis, see Second Interim Report of the Commission of Experts, U.N. Doc. S/26545 of 6 October 1993, points 68 and 69.

42 This pattern of 'women's camps' or 'rape camps' led to the declaration of the U.N. Security Council in its Resolution 798 (1992) on 18 December 1992 U.N. Doc. S/RES/798 (1992) that it was 'appalled by reports of the massive, organized, and systematic detention and rape of women, in particular Muslim women, in Bosnia-Herzegovina', and demanded that 'all detention camps, in particular camps for women, should be immediately closed'. This passage has decidedly structuralist overtones in its portrayal of the camps as 'women's camps', thus creating the impression so roundly criticised by Halley of the Yugoslav conflict being a 'war against women', which the author has also discredited. As for the use of rape as a strategy of impregnating women, see for example, Rape and Sexual Abuses by Armed Forces, Amnesty International, January 1993, AI Index: EUR 63/01/93, at 5.

43 G. Agamben, 'What is a Camp?', in *Means without an End: Notes on Politics* (Minneapolis: University of Minnesota Press, 2000), at 37.

44 As Agamben has noted, the Schutzhaft was a juridical institution of Prussian derivation that Nazi jurists sometimes used as a measure of preventive policing. The camps were at first officially described by the SS as 're-education camps', but they were soon renamed as 'concentration camps' taking the name from camps set up by the British during the Boer War (1899–1902) to 'concentrate' Boer farming families during the conflict. See: http://reocities.com/vienna/strasse/8514/holocaust.html. The legal origin of the term Schutzhaft lies in Prussian law on the state of siege that was passed in 4 June 1851 and was subsequently extended to the whole of Germany, except for Bavaria, in 1871, as well as the earlier Prussian law on the 'protection of personal freedom' (Schutz der persönlichen Freiheit) that was passed on 12 February 1850. Both these laws were extensively used during World War I. It was also thanks to the Schutzhaft that in May 1933 Heinrich Himmler was able to create a 'concentration camp for political prisoners' at Dachau and to immediately entrust it to the SS, as this suspension of the law allowed him to place it outside of the jurisdiction of the criminal law, as well as prison law, with which it neither then or later had anything to do with. Agamben (2000), at 38.9.

45 The derivation of the Nazi Lager can be traced back directly to the institution of the Schutzhaft, which provided the precedent for interning people without cause or reason. With the creation of the first concentration camp in Dachau in May 1933, which occurred in a space of exception in which the law had been suspended; soon more camps were added (such as Buchenwald and Sachsenhausen) that remained virtually always operative. The number of inmates varied at times and during certain periods (in particular between 1935 and 1937, before the deportation of the Jews began) it decreased to 7,500 people, but the camp, as such, had become a permanent reality in Germany. Ibid.

46 Ibid at 38.9 (original emphasis).

47 Ibid at 40.1.

48 The term 'rape camp' has been used by some commentators, despite not appearing in the judgements. See for example Barrett & Little (2003–2004), at 30. For a critique of the deployment of this terminology see Engle (2005), at 778.

49 Agamben (2000), at 42.3.

50 According to the Commission, there were a total of 715 camps, most of which were subsequently closed. Of the 715 camps, 237 were operated by Bosnian Serbs and the former Republic of Yugoslavia; 89 were operated by the government and army of Bosnia-Herzegovina; 77 were operated by Bosnian Croats, the government of Croatia, the Croatian army and the Croatian Defence Council; four were operated jointly by the Bosnian government and Bosnian Croats, and there were another 308 camps for which it was not definitively established under whose control they were. See: Final Report of the Commission of Experts (Yugoslavia), Pursuant to Security Council Resolution 780 (1992), U.N. Doc. S/1994/674, 27 May 1994, Part IV Substantive Findings, part E, at para 55.

51 As the Final Report states, 'Owing to the nature of the several conflicts and the military structure of the warring factions, the control of the camps varies. At different points in time, the same camp may be controlled by the army, the central Government, local and police authorities, the police, various military groups and local armed civilians.' Ibid at paras 110–128, also at annex III. The use of pre-existing structures, such as municipal buildings, administrative offices, schools, sports arenas within the occupied areas and larger facilities on the outskirts of those areas, such as factories and warehouses, was specifically designed to facilitate control of these structures, as the use of pre-existing facilities allowed for quick and easy control and displacement of the targeted population of a conquered geographical region by one of the warring factions. As the Report further notes, the camps were frequently used to detain the civilian population that has been forcibly replaced from particular regions. The detention is either preceded or followed by armed engagements in these regions. Ethnicity is invoked in this context in relation to the finding that 'wholesale detention of persons from another ethnic or religious group occurs even in situations in which there is nothing to suggest that internment of civilians is necessary for any valid legal purpose.' Ibid at paras 129–150 and annex III). Moreover, in pattern b) the Report identifies the purpose of the different facilities as having specific purposes such as mass killing, torture, rape and exchange and holding of civilian prisoners. Ibid at paras 231–252 and annexes IX and IX.A. Interestingly in pattern J, the Report notes that at the larger camps, beatings, more severe torture and killings escalate when there has been a Bosnian-Serb military setback and when there are Serb casualties. The Report does not seem to identify an identical occurrence when the setback is on the Croatian or Muslim side, and when the casualties are Serbs. Ibid at point j.

52 Ibid at para 57, point 3.

53 Ibid at paras 129–150, 151–182 and annex V.

54 Women and children and men over the age of 60 were usually separated from other detainees and taken to separate camps.

55 Final Report of the Commission of Experts (Yugoslavia), Pursuant to Security Council Resolution 780 (1992), U.N. Doc. S/1994/674, 27 May 1994, Part IV Substantive Findings, part F at para 65. It is also remarkable to note that only one of the men from Bosnia and Herzegovina interviewed was a victim of sexual assault committed in a detention facility. The Report also includes statistics on where the rapes took place, finding that among the women 66 had been raped in their homes, while 13 had been raped while in detention. Among the additional male and female interviewees, there were 21 witnesses to additional cases of rape or sexual assaults, meaning that a total number of 55 persons in the pilot study had either been victims or witnesses to rape or sexual assault. A large number of the women, 77 'victim-witnesses' interviewed, were from Croatia, of whom 11 had been victims of rape. In addition, there were six men from Croatia, who had been victims of sexual assault. Interestingly, in the case of all but one man, the violations occurred predominantly in a detention context, whereas in the case of the women, seven had been raped in their own homes. There is an interesting dichotomy between the rape of men as being performed in the public space and the rape of women as confined to the private sphere of the home even in times of armed conflict. But the rape of women in their own homes could also suggest that the boundaries of agency, choice and consent could be further blurred, as is perhaps more difficult to ascertain whether consent was freely given or not within the confines of the home, in which presumably there is not the same level of terror and intimidation as in a camp-like environment. However, the Commission concluded that the women raped in their homes had been subjected to multiple and/or gang rapes involving up to eight soldiers in yet another strategy emblematic of the conflict. Such constructions have been strongly criticised by feminist scholars, as outlined in chapter 2. Moreover, of the four women raped in detention, one was raped on almost daily basis, thus adding a systematic, planned quality to the rapes. Among the other men and women interviewed from Croatia, nine were witnesses to additional cases of rape or sexual assault, thus involving a total of 27 persons from Croatia who were either victims of or witnesses to rape and sexual assault. Ibid at paras 66–67.

56 Although there had been insufficient time between the end of the interview process, which had commenced on 31 March 1994 and was finalised in the Final Report on 30 April 1994 for a detailed analysis to be conducted, the information gathered by the Commission supported the findings that five distinct patterns of rape and sexual assault could be identified based upon its database and the interviews conducted. Ibid at paras 67–70.

57 The common elements underlying this pattern are described as involving growing tension in area leading members of different ethnic groups to control the regional government and beginning to terrorise their neighbours. Typically, this would involve two or more men breaking into a house, intimidating the residents, stealing their property, beating them and often raping the women present. As the Commission describes it, often there would be a 'gang atmosphere' where the abuses are part of the same event and all the attackers participate, even if they do not sexually assault the victim. Ibid at para 70.

58 The 'Ustaša' movement was created by the former leader of the Croatian Party of the Right, Ante Pavelic, who in 1929 following trials against prominent member of the Croatian Peasant Party fled Croatia to form the fascist Ustasha (Insurgent) movement in Mussolini's Italy. During the Second World War, Pavelic's Ustaša followers treated the Serbs as the Nazis treated the Jews, as vermin to be exterminated. This practice was not imposed by the occupying forces, but

sprang out of the Ustasha's own ideology, which incorporated a conception of Croats as a pure Aryan race. For a detailed account of some of the practices deployed by the Ustašas against the Serb population of Yugoslavia see: Benson (2004), at 53, 78.

59 Ibid at para 70.

60 As the Commission outlines, soldiers, camp guards, paramilitaries and even civilians were allowed to enter the camps, pick out the women, take them away and rape them, and then either kill them or return them to the site.

61 According to survivors' accounts, women were also raped in front of other internees, or other internees were forced to sexually abuse each other. Ibid at para 70.

62 The Commission refers to the women as 'women victims', whereas the men are referred to neutrally.

63 In one case, according to witness testimony, a woman died after being in a coma for a week as a result of the 'sadistic rapes' by guards. Ibid.

64 Further incidents collected by the Commission involved prisoners being lined up naked, while Serb women from outside undressed in front of male prisoners. According to witness testimony, if a prisoner was found to have an erection, his penis was cut off, and it was reported that a Serb woman took such a measure in one instance, thus adding an ethnic dimension to the atrocity. Moreover, another ex-detainee told of having electric shocks administered to his scrotum, and of seeing a father and son who shared his cell being forced by camp guards to perform sex acts on each other. Ibid at para 70.

65 But as the Commission is careful to point out, survivors of the camps felt that they had been detained for the specific purpose of being raped, as evidence suggested that all of the women had been raped quite frequently and often in the presence of other internees. These rapes were frequently accompanied by beatings and torture.

66 The Commission highlights this pattern through the interview with a Muslim woman who had been raped by her neighbour near her village for six months for the ostensible purpose of giving birth to a 'chetnik' boy, who would then be groomed to kill Muslims when he grew up.

67 According to one of the witnesses, all women were raped when the soldiers returned from the front line every 15 days, and they were compelled to oblige because the women in another camp had reportedly been exhausted. Ibid at para 70.

68 As the Commission summarises, in Bosnia, some of the reported rape and sexual assault cases committed by Serbs, mostly against Muslims, are clearly the result of individual or small group conduct without evidence of command direction or an overall policy. However, many more seemed to have been part of an overall pattern whose characteristics included: similarities among practices in non-contiguous geographic areas; simultaneous commission of other international humanitarian law violations; simultaneous activity to displace populations; common elements in the commission of rape were identified as designed to maximise shame and humiliation not only to the victim, but also to the victim's community; and the timings of the rapes. One factor which led to the conclusion was the large number of rapes, which had occurred in places of detention, which were analysed by the Commission as not appearing to be random but as indicative of a policy of encouraging rape supported by a deliberate failure of camp commanders and local authorities to exercise command and control over the personnel under their authority. Ibid at para 71.

69 See for example S. Murphy, 'Sexual Violence in Decisions and Indictments of the Yugoslav and Rwandan Tribunals: Current Status', 93 *American Journal of International Law* (1999), at 101; Askin (2003), at 288.

70 As Kirsten Campbell describes it, the final indictment '[a]rticulates the legal wrong that the court adjudicates'. The indictment is thus of significance in delineating the legal harm under adjudication. In Campbell (2007), at 421.

71 See *Prosecutor v. Tadic*, Decision on the Defense Motion for Interlocutory Appeal on Jurisdiction, 2. Oct. 1995 (IT-94–1-AR72], at paras 96–137. This aspect of the decision was further discussed in Chapter 4 in order to demonstrate that the 'internationalisation' of the armed conflict also had implications for the manner in which gender crimes were prosecuted. For a more extensive discussion of the definition for both of the concepts of international and non-international armed conflict provided in Tadic, see: D. Kritsiotis, 'The Tremors of Tadic', 43 *Israel Law Review* (2010), at 262.

72 For a discussion see: I. Bantekas & S. Nash, *International Criminal Law* (London: Routledge-Cavendish, 2003); I. Bantekas & S. Nash, *International Criminal Law* (London: Routledge-Cavendish, 2007).

73 See Tadic, (IT-94–1-A), Appeals Chamber Judgement, 15 July 1999.

74 The background to this is former Prosecutor Richard Goldstone's decision to seek transfer of jurisdiction for Tadic from a German court to the ICTY. At the time, the affidavit gave 'decidedly secondary consideration' to the conditions affecting women and to the severity of rape, for example treating it as a less serious offence than beatings. Quite poignantly, the affidavit described an episode in which one man was forced to bite off the testicle of another as 'what was worse', presumably than the rapes also alleged. I quote here from Halley's excellent article on some of the background stories, which are reflective of entrenched institutional attitudes towards wartime sexual violence prosecution prompting later feminist intervention. For a critical analysis of the feminist interventions leading to the shift in attitude towards the prosecution of wartime sexual violence in the *Tadic* case, see Halley (2008–2009), at 13–15.

75 The feminist advocacy groups were all of U.S.-origin and included the International Women's Human Rights Clinic, the Harvard Human Rights Program and the Jacob Blaustein Institute. The aim of the affidavits issued by these institutions was to warn against the trivialisation of gender-based violence in international criminal proceedings, and to urge the ICTY to adopt a more serious, thus punitive approach toward the prosecution of such offences. For an overview of some of the background feminist advocacy see: R. Copelon, 'Surfacing Gender: Re-Engraving Crimes against Women in International Humanitarian Law', 5 *Hastings Women's Law Journal* (1994), at 243, 253–254.

76 This is taken from Copelon's article quoting the letter from Justice Richard Goldstone, Prosecutor to Rhonda Copelon, Felice Gaer & Jennifer Green (22 November 1994). Ibid at 253–254.

77 R. Goldstone, 'The United Nations' War Crimes Tribunals: An Assessment', 12 *Connecticut Journal of International Law* (1997), at 227, 231.

78 The reference to Judge Pillay is related to her instrumental role as the only woman on the Tribunal in the Akayesu case. In Halley (2008–2009), at 17.

79 These provisions allow the ICTY to exercise its primary jurisdiction in connection with proceedings already instituted in a state in a case, where, inter alia, what is at issue is closely related to, or otherwise involves significant or factual legal questions which may have implications for investigations or prosecutions before the International Criminal Tribunal. *Prosecutor v. Tadic*, (IT-94-1 T), Trial Chamber Opinion and Judgement, 7 May 1997, at paras 6–7.

80 Teitel (1998–1999), at 294.

81 For an extensive discussion on the admittance of anonymous testimony see Fabian (1999–2000), at 1010.

82 *Prosecutor v. Tadic*, Initial Indictment, (IT-94–1-I) (13 February 1995), at para 1. This is also consistent with the findings of the Final Report of the Commission

for Experts, which noted as a common pattern underlying the wartime tactics deployed by the Bosnian Serbs during the conflict that during the rounding-up process of local populations of villages, towns or cities, local religious, political, civic, professional, business leaders and prominent personalities in particular would be singled out for the worst abuses. Ironically, the captors themselves would frequently be made up of local civil servants, political leaders and particularly the police, who participated and were involved in the rounding-up process. See: Final Report of the Commission of Experts (Yugoslavia), Pursuant to Security Council Resolution 780 (1992), U.N. Doc. S/1994/674, 27 May 1994, Part IV Substantive Findings, part E, at paras 129–150, 151–182, at part j).

83 Ibid at para 2.3.

84 Ibid at para 2.5.

85 Ibid at para 2.6.

86 *Prosecutor v. Tadic Indictment* (Amended) (IT-94–1-T) (Dec. 1995) (hereinafter referred to as the Indictment).

87 Ibid at paras 2.3 and 2.6.

88 Ibid at para 2.7.

89 Ibid at para 4.

90 Ibid at para 4.3.

91 Ibid at para 5.

92 Ibid at paras 4.2, 4.3.

93 In a passage synonymous with the overall portrayal of the Yugoslav conflict as embedded in long-standing ethnic tension and hostility, the ICTY describes the immediate events leading to outbreak of the conflict as follows: 'In opština Prijedor during the days following the take-over of the town of Prijedor by JNA forces on April 30, 1992 . . . Serb nationalist propaganda intensified. The need for the 'awakening of the Serb people' was stressed and derogatory remarks against non-Serbs increased. Muslim leaders who attempted to speak on the radio were barred while SDS leaders had free access to it. Even more propaganda against Muslims and Croats began in earnest after an incident in the Hambarine region on May 22, 1992. Examples include statements that a Croat doctor castrated newborn Serb boys and was performing sterilisation surgery on Serb women and that a Muslim doctor intentionally administered the wrong drug in an attempt to kill his Serb colleague.' This description thus sets the tone for a visualisation of the events in the run up to the Yugoslav conflict being ethnically motivated with rival fractions divided into clearly bounded entities with fixed and unmoving political agendas. *Prosecutor v. Tadic*, (IT94–1-T), Opinion and Judgement, (IT-94–1-T) (7 May 1997), at para 93.

94 On 11 November 1999, Tadic was sentenced to 25 years' imprisonment. The sentence was later reduced by the Appeals Chamber to a maximum of 20 years. International Criminal Tribunal for the Former Yugoslavia, Fact Sheet on ICTY Proceedings, November 2000, 698. The court stated that the crime of persecution encompasses acts of varying severity from killing to a limitation on the type of professions open to a targeted group. The court also addressed the issue of whether a single act can constitute a crime against humanity, finding that a single act by a perpetrator taken within the context of a widespread or systematic attack against the civilian population entails individual criminal responsibility and that an individual perpetrator need not commit numerous offences to be held liable. *Prosecutor v. Tadic* (IT94–1-T), Opinion and Judgement, at para 704.

95 After reviewing customary law and the ICTY Statute, the chamber concludes that 'what is necessary is some form of discrimination that is intended to be and results in infringement on an individual's fundamental rights' and that 'this discrimination must be on specific grounds, namely race, religion or politics' in order to constitute persecution. Ibid at para 697.

96 The 1996 I.L.C. Draft Code the chamber states that there is now a recognition in international criminal law that 'the inhumane act of persecution may take many forms with its most common characteristics being the denial of human rights and fundamental freedoms to which every individual is entitled without distinction' as recognised in the Charter of the United Nations (Articles 1 and 55) and the International Covenant on Civil and Political Rights (article 2). One expert then provided additional examples of the term persecution, which is defined as 'oppression, harassment or the imposition of mental or physical harm based on discrimination', namely 'murder; manslaughter; rape; assault; battery; theft; robbery; destruction of property and a variety of crimes related to unlawful interference with fundamental legal rights'. Ibid at 703.

97 For this act, Tadic was charged with individual direct responsibility for forcing two male prisoners at Omarska camp to commit sexual acts on another prisoner and sexually mutilate him during June–July 1992, as a grave breach under Article 2(b) (torture or inhuman treatment); a grave breach under Article 2(c) (wilfully causing great suffering or serious injury to body or health); a violation of the laws and customs of war under Article 3 of the Statute and Article 3 (1) (a) of the Geneva Conventions of 1949 (cruel treatment), and a crime against humanity under Article 5(i) (inhumane acts). Ibid at para 6.

98 *Prosecutor v. Tadic*, (IT94–1-T), Opinion and Judgement, (IT-94–1-T) (7 May 1997), at para 154.

99 Ibid at para 165.

100 Ibid at para 175.

101 The 'campaign of terror' refers to Tadic's participation, alongside Serb forces, in the attack, destruction and plunder of Bosnian Muslim and Croatian residential areas, the seizure and imprisonment of thousands of Muslim and Croat residential areas, the seizure and imprisonment of thousands of Muslims and Croats under brutal conditions in camps located in Omarska, Keraterm and Trnopolje and the deportation and/or expulsion of the majority of Muslim and Croat residents of opština Prijedor by force or threat of force. During this time Serbian Tadic engaged in criminal acts including killings, torture, sexual assaults and other physical and psychological abuse. Ibid at para 377.

102 The concept of individual criminal responsibility and personal culpability for assisting, aiding and abetting, or participating in the commission of a criminal endeavour stands in contrast to the direct commission of a criminal endeavour or act, which also has a basis in customary international law. The chamber provides as an example Article 4(1) of the Convention Against Torture and Other Cruel, Inhuman or Degrading Treatment or Punishment, which uses the phrase 'complicity or participation in torture' to indicate culpability and Article III of the International Convention on the Suppression and Punishment of the Crime of Apartheid, which cites as culpable those who 'participate in, directly incite, or conspire in [or] directly abet, encourage, or cooperate in the commission of the crime'. Ibid at para 666.

103 In the judgement, Tadic was found unanimously guilty of count 1.

104 The term feminist advocacy here refers to the work of 'inside feminists', who were instrumental in introducing gender-based reforms. For an in-depth discussion see Halley (2008), at 82.

105 *Prosecutor v. Tadic*, (IT94–1-T), Opinion and Judgement, (IT-94–1-T) (7 May 1997), at para 536. Moreover the chamber concluded that corroboration is not part of customary international law and need not be required by the ICTY. Ibid at para 539. For an in-depth analysis of the Rules of Evidence and Procedure and the use of anonymous witness testimony in the Tadic trial, see: Fabian (1999–2000), at 1010. Rule 96 (1) also dispenses with the need for corroboration in cases of sexual assault stressing that this 'accords to the testimony of victims of a sexual

assault the same presumption of reliability as the testimony of victims of other crimes, something long denied to victims of sexual assault by the common law'. See: Rule 96 of the Rules of Procedure and Evidence of the ICTY, Evidence in Cases of Sexual Assault, IT32/Rev. 21, 12 July 2001.

106 Halley (2008–2009), at 35.

107 Brown (2006), at 20–21.

108 *The Prosecutor v. Anto Furundžija* (IT-95-17/1), (2 November 1995), Initial Indictment, at paras 2–3.

109 The crimes listed are all variously indictable as grave breaches of the Geneva Conventions prosecutable under Article 2 of the Statute, given the Tribunal's finding that a state of international armed conflict and partial occupation existed in the Republic of Bosnia-Herzegovina on the territory of the former Yugoslavia and/or as crimes against humanity. Ibid at paras 5–7.

110 Ibid at para 72.

111 Count 13 concerns 'rape as torture' on account of the defendant's act of rubbing his knife against Witness A's inner thigh and lower stomach and his threat of putting a knife inside her vagina should she not tell the truth. Ibid at para 82.

112 See *The Prosecutor v. Anto Furundžija*, Amended Indictment, (IT-95-17/1-PT), 2 June 1998, in which counts 1–11 and 15–25 against additional accused are redacted. Furundžija was charged under Article 3 of the ICTY Statute with count 13, Violation of the Laws and Customs of War (torture), and count 14, Violation of the Laws or Customs of War (outrages upon personal dignity including rape). Count 12 was withdrawn. Torture and outrages upon personal dignity are prohibited by Common Article 3 of the 1949 Geneva Conventions, and thus fall under Article 3 of the Statute. The Prosecution thus pressed the following charges: torture or inhuman treatment as a grave breach of the Geneva Conventions under Article 2(b) of the Statute; and as a violation of the laws or customs of war for outrages upon personal dignity including rape, as recognised by Article 3 of the Statute.

113 *Furundžija* Trial Chamber Judgement, at paras 124–130.

114 Ibid at para 271.

115 Ibid at para 163.

116 Ibid at para 172.

117 Article 1 of the Convention Against Torture defines torture as: 1. 'Any act by which severe pain or suffering, whether physical or mental, is intentionally inflicted on a person for such purposes as obtaining from him or a third person information or a confession, punishing him for an act he or a third person has committed or is suspected of having committed, or intimidating or coercing him or a third person, or for any reason based on discrimination of any kind, when such pain or suffering is inflicted by or at the instigation of or with the consent or acquiescence of a public official or other person acting in an official capacity. It does not include pain or suffering arising only from, inherent in or incidental to lawful sanctions. 2. This article is without prejudice to any international instrument or national legislation which does or may contain provisions of wider application.' See: Convention against Torture and Other Cruel, Inhuman, Degrading Treatment or Punishment, 10 December 1984, Art. 1, S. Treaty Doc. No. 100–20, 1465 U.N.T.S. 85, 114 (entered into force 26 June 1987), Art. 1.

118 In describing the torture process organically, the Chamber noted that a large number of people are typically involved in the torture process by performing different functions, thus rendering them liable for torture, regardless of how minor the role was. More specifically, the Trial Chamber identified a process of division and distribution inherent in the process of torture in order to: 'compartmentalize and dilute' the moral and psychological burden of perpetrating torture by

assigning to different individuals a partial and sometimes relatively minor role in the torture process. Tasks are divided along the lines of one person ordering the carrying out of the torture, another organising and administering the whole process, another one preparing the tools for executing torture, while somebody provides medical assistance in order to prevent the detainee from dying as a consequence of the torture, and yet another one procures the information gained as a result of torture in exchange for granting the torturer immunity from prosecution. *Furundžija* Trial Chamber Judgement, at para 253.

119 Ibid at paras 124, 130.

120 Ibid at para 162.

121 Ibid at paras 124, 130.

122 Ibid at para 264.

123 Ibid at paras 269, 275. The Trial Chamber distinguished a co-perpetrator from an aider or abettor, concluding that one who participates in torture and 'partakes of the purpose behind torture' is a perpetrator, whereas one who does not share the intent but 'gives some sort of assistance and support with knowledge that' torture is being inflicted is an aider or abettor. Ibid at para 252. Further, the assistance must not only have occurred with knowledge, it must also 'have a substantial effect on the commission of the crime'. Ibid at paras 234–235. Thus, to be a perpetrator or co-perpetrator of torture, an accused must 'participate in an integral part of the torture and partake of the purpose behind the torture'. To be an aider or abettor of torture, there must be some assistance 'which has a substantial effect on the perpetration of the crime and with knowledge that torture is taking place'. Ibid at para 257.

124 Ibid at para 267 (ii).

125 *Furundžija* Trial Chamber Judgement, supra note 147, at para 273.

126 In imposing the concurrent sentencing, the Trial Chamber reasoned: 'Witness A was tortured by means of sexual assault and beatings, and the Trial Chamber has considered this to be a particularly vicious form of torture for the purpose of aggravating the sentence imposed under Count 13 [torture]. On the other hand, in assessing the sentence imposed under Count 14 [outrages upon personal dignity, including rape], the Trial Chamber has [already] considered the fact that the sexual assault and rape amounted to a very serious offence. Therefore, the sentence imposed for outrages upon personal dignity including rape shall be served concurrently with the sentence imposed for torture.' Ibid at para 295.

127 These concerns were raised in two amicus briefs submitted to the ICTY by a group of international human rights lawyers, of which feminist advocates were very prominent. See *Prosecutor v. Furundžija*, Amicus Curiae Brief on Protective Measures for Victims or Witnesses of Sexual Violence and Other Traumatic Events, Submitted on behalf of the Center for Civil and Human Rights, Notre Dame Law School, November 6, 1998 (prepared by Kelly Askin, Sharielle Aitchison, and Teresa Phelps); Amicus Curiae Brief Respecting the Decision and Order of the Tribunal of July 16, 1998 Requesting that the Tribunal Consider its Decision Having Regard for the Rights of Witness "A" to Equality, Privacy and Security of the Person, and to Representation by Counsel, November 4, 1998 (prepared by Working Group on Engendering the Rwandan Criminal Tribunal, International Women's Human Rights Law Clinic & The Centre for Constitutional Rights). This would be another instantiation of what Janet Halley has classified as 'governance feminism', which is evident in the vocal support lent by feminist groups to the rights of the victim to have sensitive information regarding her mental state protected from scrutiny of the tribunal.

128 *Furundžija* Trial Chamber Judgement, supra note 147, at para 109. This has been lamented by some feminists as being too narrow a holding in that it doesn't address whether a patient-client relationship exists in international law, which

would make medical or psychological records or statements made during a counselling session outside the scope of compellable evidence. See Askin (2003), at 331.

129 *Prosecutor v. Furundžija*, Judgement, IT-95–17/1-A, 21 July 2000 (hereinafter Furundžija Appeals Chamber Judgement).

130 Ibid at para 164 (Fourth ground of appeal).

131 The Appeals Chamber noted that Rule 15(A) of the Rules of Procedure and Evidence of the Tribunal address the issue of impartiality and provides: 'A Judge may not sit on a trial or appeal in any case in which the Judge has a personal interest or concerning which the Judge has or had any association which might affect his or her impartiality. The Judge shall in any such circumstance withdraw, and the President shall assign another Judge to the case.' Ibid at para 191 (quoting ICTY Rules of Procedure and Evidence 15 (A)).

132 Ibid at para 189. Consequently, the Appeals Chamber adopted the following principles to direct it in interpreting and applying ICTY Rule 15 (A): '(A) A Judge is not impartial if it is shown that actual bias exists. (B) There is an unacceptable appearance of bias if: i) a Judge is party to the case, or has a financial or proprietary interest in the outcome of a case, or of the Judge's decision will lead to the promotion of a cause in which he or she is involved, together with one of the parties. Under these circumstances, a Judge's disqualification from the case is automatic; or ii) the circumstances would lead a reasonable observer, properly informed, to reasonably apprehend bias.' Ibid at para 190.

133 Ibid at para 200. The Appeals Chamber also noted that Article 13(1) of the ICTY Statute requires that 'due account' be taken of human rights, international law and criminal law experience of the judges in deciding the composition of the chambers of the tribunals. It considered that Judge Mumba's experience in international human rights law and in gender issues gained as a member of the CSW was relevant in her election to the tribunal, reasoning that a judge should not be disqualified 'because of qualifications he or she possess, which by their very nature, play an integral role in satisfying eligibility requirements . . . It would be an off result if the operation of an eligibility requirement were to lead to an inference of bias'. Ibid at paras 204–205.

134 Ibid at paras 196–197. It has to be pointed out that this challenge was only raised after the Trial Chamber had rendered a guilty verdict against the accused. Because Judge Mumba's qualifications and professional background were public and easily accessible, the Trial Chamber concluded that the defence had waived its right to complain and thus dismissed those ground of appeal on this basis. In spite of this, it decided to consider the merits of the case, 'given its general importance'. Ibid at paras 173–174.

135 See: Additional Protocol II, Art. 4(2)(e).

136 *The Prosecutor v. Delalic, Indictment* (IT-96–21-I), 19 March 1996 (hereinafter *Celebici* Indictment), at para 33.

137 Ibid at para 30.

138 *The Prosecutor v. Zejnil Delalic, Zdravko Mucic* (*The Prosecutor v. Delalic et al.*), (IT-96–21-T)-(hereafter referred to as '*Celebici*' case), Trial Chamber Judgement, 16 November 1998, at para 3.

139 Zejnil Delalic is alleged to have exercised authority over the prison camp in his role as first co-ordinator of the Bosnian Muslim and Bosnian Croat forces in the area, and later as Commander of the First Tactical Group of the Bosnian Army, whereas Esad Landžo and Hazim Delic are primarily charged with individual responsibility in accordance with Article 7(1) of the Statute, as direct participants in certain of the crimes alleged, including acts of murder, torture and rape. Zdravko Mucic and Zejnil Delalic are thus primarily charged as superiors with responsibility in accordance with Art. 7(3) of the Statute for crimes committed by their subordinates,

including those alleged to have been committed by Esad Landžo and Hazim Delic. Several counts in the Indictment also charge Hazim Delic in his capacity as superior with individual criminal responsibility. Ibid at paras 4–5. The geographical, demographic and political structures of the Konjic municipality can be found starting at para 120 of the judgment. *Celebici* case (IT-96–21-T).

140 Formerly known as the Socialist Republic of Bosnia-Herzegovina, it was divided into territorial units of self-management, which each had their certain level of autonomy. Each of these municipalities (opština) was governed by a municipal assembly, consisting of members directly elected by the local population, which in turn elected an executive council from its own members. In Bosnia-Herzegovina there were 109 such municipalities in total. Ibid at para 120.

141 Ibid at para 122.

142 It is interesting to note that the Trial Chamber acknowledges in its summary of the demographic proclivities that the mix of ethnicities in Konjic lived together 'harmoniously' and in an 'integrated fashion' until the escalation of tension and outbreak of hostilities in 1992. Ibid at para 121.

143 *Celebici* Indictment at para 2.

144 Ibid at para 26.

145 A description of the sequence of events taking place during this period of time is provided at para 24 of the Indictment.

146 *Celebici* Trial Chamber Judgement, at para 496.

147 Ibid at para 495.

148 Ibid at paras 937–938. He was thus charged with the commission of torture and rape as grave breaches of the Geneva Conventions punishable under Article 2 (b) of the Statute; torture and rape as violations of the laws or customs of war punishable under Article 3 of the ICTY Statute and Article 3(1) (a) under the Geneva Conventions. The additional accusations against him were torture and rape as violations of the laws or customs of war under Article 3 of the Statute and torture as a form of cruel treatment under the Geneva Conventions (Article 3 (1)(a).

149 Ibid at para 940.

150 Ibid at para 941.

151 *Celebici* Trial Chamber Judgement, at para 941.

152 The charges against Delic in this respect include the torture and rape of Witness A as grave breaches under Article 2(b) of the Statute, two counts of torture and rape as violations of the laws and customs of war under Article 3 of the Statute and as a form of torture and a form of cruel treatment under Articles 3(1) (a) and Article 3(1) (b) of the Geneva Conventions. *Celebici* Indictment, at para 25.

153 Ibid at paras 475–96, 965–65.

154 Ibid at para 1066.

155 Ibid at para 346.

156 As the Chamber noted, 'The mere absence of formal legal authority to control the actions of subordinates should therefore not be understood to preclude the imposition of such responsibility.' Ibid at para 354.

157 Ibid at 354.

158 Ibid at 378.

159 Knowledge can be inferred in a number of ways, including through a consideration of the number, type or scope of illegal acts; the location of the commander; the 'tactical tempo of operations'; and the modus operandi and similar acts. Ibid at para 386.

160 The Trial Chamber clarified that the 'information needed to be such that it by itself was sufficient to compel the conclusion of the existence of such crimes'. Ibid at para 393.

161 In *Prosecutor v. Delalic* (IT-96–21-A) Judgement, 20 February 2001, at para 238 (hereinafter *Celebici* Appeals Chamber Judgement).

162 *Celebici* Trial Chamber Judgement, at para 395.
163 The ICTY Appeals Chamber Judgement rendered on 20 February 2001, upheld the findings of the *Celebici* Trial Chamber Judgement. See *Celebici* Appeals Chamber Judgement.
164 This was reiterated in the *Kvocka Trial Chamber Judgement*, which is analysed subsequently.
165 *Prosecutor v. Kunarac, Judgement* (IT-96–23-T & IT-96–23/1-T) (22 Feb 2001) (hereafter the Kunarac Trial Chamber Judgement).
166 For a discussion of the ethnic dimension underlying the decision see Buss (2002), at 91.
167 For a discussion of the significance of this holding for wartime sexual violence jurisprudence see for example: C.S. Maravilla, 'Rape as a War Crime: The Implications of the International Criminal Tribunal for the Former Yugoslavia's Decision in Prosecutor v. Kunarac, Kovac & Vukovic on International Humanitarian Law', 13 *Florida Journal of International Law* (2001), at 321.
168 In Buss (2002), at 91.
169 For further discussion of the importance of the public discourse of wartime rape as part of the 'storytelling' of the war, see Buss (1998), at 187.
170 For an in-depth discussion of the events leading to the violent overthrow and siege of Foca see the *Prosecutor v. Gagovic*, Indictment (IT-96–23-T), 1 December 1999 & It-96–23/1-T, 3.
171 Prior to the war in Bosnia-Herzegovina, 52 percent of the 40,513 inhabitants of the Foča municipality were Muslim. After the conflict, approximately 10 Muslims remained. In Kunarac Trial Chamber Judgement, at para 47.
172 Ibid at paras 31–33.
173 *Prosecutor v. Kunarac*, Amended Indictment (IT-96–23-T), 1 December 1999 & (IT-96–23/1-T), 3 March 2000. Given that the ICTY Statute does not explicitly list sexual slavery as a specific crime, Article 5 covering crimes against humanity lists rape and enslavement as two of the acts justiciable as crimes against humanity in the ICTY. Thus, the crime of holding women and girls for sexual servitude was charged and prosecuted under the provisions of the ICTY Statute granting the tribunal jurisdiction over rape and enslavement as crimes against humanity.
174 Ibid at paras 40–43.
175 As the Trial Chamber emphasises, the girl was never seen again. Ibid at para 42 and paras 775–780.
176 Buss (2002), at 94.
177 As Buss points out the fact that rape is classified as a crime against humanity, which is defined as a 'widespread and systematic' attack on the community committed with knowledge by the perpetrator 'of the wider context in which his acts occur' suggests that in the Yugoslav context, charges of crimes against humanity are directed at 'ethnic cleansing'. Ibid.
178 This decision will be more extensively discussed in Chapter 6. One example by which the Trial Chamber attributed ethnic motivations to the underlying offence was through statements made by Dragoljub Kunarac such as that 'the rapes against Muslim women were one of the many ways in which the Serbs could assert their superiority and victory over the Muslims'. This passage reveals the tendency of the Trial Chamber to read acts of sexual violence through an ethnic lens. See *Kunarac* Trial Chamber Judgement, at para 583.
179 Ibid at paras 644–645.
180 Ibid at para 654.
181 Ibid at para 816.
182 As the Chamber points out, there is no requirement in customary international law that the conduct must solely be perpetrated for one of the prohibited

purposes of torture, such as discrimination. The prohibited purpose need only be part of the motivation behind the conduct and need not be the predominant or sole purpose. Ibid at para 816.

183 An outrage against personal dignity has been defined as an act that is 'animated by contempt for the human dignity of another person. The corollary is that the act must cause serious humiliation or degradation to the victim.' This was determined in the *Prosecutor v. Aleksovski*, Judgement (IT-14/1-T) 25 June 1999, at para 56 (hereinafter *Aleksovski* Trial Chamber Judgement). The *Aleksovski* Trial Chamber made extensive findings with regard to this offence. See at paras 54–57 in particular.

184 *Kunarac* Trial Chamber Judgement, at para 501.

185 Ibid at paras 773–774. According to the ICTY Statute, to be charged under this category, it is not necessary to show that the perpetrator specifically intended to humiliate the victim, as long as he knew that his act or omission would have such an effect. Ibid.

186 The ICTR Trial Chamber had previously recognised in the *Akayesu* Judgement that serious humiliation was a clearly foreseeable consequence of forced nudity. Moreover, forced nudity could be classified as crime against humanity, thus not being restricted to 'outrages upon personal dignity', or even war crimes charges. In *Akayesu*.

187 In *Kunarac* Trial Chamber Judgement, supra at note 147 at para 540.

188 Moreover, the Trial Chamber retained discretion in considering duration as a factor in determining whether somebody had been enslaved. Ibid at para 542–543.

189 Ibid at para 542. This finding was made in regards to enslavement, although it is widely considered that one can never consent to such crimes as slavery and torture.

190 In Askin (2003), at 340.

191 See: *The Prosecutor v. Kunarac* (IT-96–23-T/1-A) (12 June, 2002) (Appeals Chamber Judgement).

192 Ibid at para 150.

193 The Appeals Chamber in the *Tadic* decision first articulated the theory based largely on jurisprudence derived from the post–World War II Nuremberg Trials. See *Prosecutor v. Tadic* (IT-94–1-A), Appeals Chamber Judgement, (15 July 1999).

194 See *Kvocka et al.* (IT-98–30/1-T), Trial Chamber Judgement, (2 November 2001).

195 See for example, *Prosecutor v. Miloševic* (IT-02–54–1), First Amended Indictment (Croatia), 23 October, 2002; *Prosecutor v. Miloševic* (IT-02–54–1), Indictment (Bosnia), (22 November 2001); *Prosecutor v. Šešelj* (IT-03–67), Indictment, 14 February 2003; *Prosecutor v. Borovcanin* (IT-02–64), Indictment, (6 September 2002); *Prosecutor v. Blagojevic et al.* (IT-02–60-I), Amended Joinder Indictment, 27 May 2002; *Prosecutor v. Nikolic* (IT-02–60-I) Indictment (26 March 2002); *Prosecutor v. Meakic et al.* (IT-02–65-I) Consolidated Indictment (29 November, 2002).

196 *Prosecutor v. Miloševic* (IT-02–54–1), Prosecution's Second Trial Brief (Croatia and Bosnia Indictments) (31 May 2002); *Prosecutor v. Miloševic* (IT-99–37-PT), Prosecution's Pre-Trial Brief Pursuant to Rule 65ter (E)(i), (26 November 2001). For a discussion see also Askin (2002–2003), at 911.

197 *Prosecutor v. Kvocka*, Amended Indictment (IT-98–30/1-I), 21 August 2000, at para 25. (hereinafter *Kvocka* Indictment).

198 The charges were count 14, torture as a crime against humanity; count 15, rape as a crime against humanity; count 16, torture as a violation of the laws and customs of war; and count 17, outrages upon personal dignity as a violation of the laws or customs of war. Ibid at para 42.

199 Ibid at paras 108.

200 Ibid at paras 180, 343.

201 *Tadic* Appeals Chamber Judgement, at paras 185–229. The Krstic Trial Chamber further held that this theory of responsibility need not necessarily be explicitly pled in the Indictment. *Krstic* Trial Chamber Judgement, at para 307.

202 *Kvocka* Trial Chamber Judgement, at para 307.

203 The Trial Chamber relied on 'an enormous amount of evidence', which helped it conclude beyond a reasonable doubt that Omarska camp functioned as a joint criminal enterprise. The crimes committed in Omarska were not atrocities in the heat of the battle; they consisted of a 'broad mixture of serious crimes committed intentionally, maliciously, selectively, and in some instances sadistically against the non-Serbs detained in the camp'. Ibid at para 319.

204 The Trial Chamber found that in addition to other elements of the joint criminal enterprise, knowledge of the abuses could also be gained through the ordinary senses. Even if the accused were not eyewitnesses to crimes committed in Omarska cap, evidence of abuses could be seen by observing the bloodied, bruised and injured bodies of the detainees; by observing heaps of dead bodies lying in piles around the camp; and noticing the emaciated and poor conditions of the detainees, as well as by observing the cramped facilities or the bloodstained walls. Evidence of abuses could be heard from the screams of pain and cries of suffering, from the sounds of the detainees begging for food and water and beseeching their tormentors not to beat or kill them, and from gunshots heard everywhere in the camp. Evidence of abusive conditions in the camp could also be smelled as a result of the deteriorating corpses, the urine and feces soiling the detainees' clothes, the broken and overflowing toilets, the dysentery afflicting the detainees, and the inability of detainees to wash or bathe for weeks or months. Ibid at para 324.

205 Their individual degree of participation was reflected in sentencing. Although all were convicted of persecution as a crime against humanity, the three men who worked in the camp for a relatively short period of time or on occasion tried to assist certain detainees were given five- to seven-year prison sentences; the two men who physically participated in and sometimes instigated atrocities were given 20–25-year sentences. Ibid at paras 408, 464, 500, 566.

206 Ibid at para 327.

207 Ibid.

208 A similar holding was rendered in the *Krsti* case. Although the Trial Chamber was not convinced that many crimes, including rape, committed against refugees at Potočari were an 'agreed upon objective among the members of the joint criminal enterprise', nonetheless, the crimes were 'natural and foreseeable consequence of the ethnic cleansing campaign'. *Krsti* Trial Chamber Judgement, supra at note 227 at para 616. Indeed, not only were the crimes of murder, rape, beatings and abuses foreseeable, the circumstances essentially made the crimes virtually 'inevitable' due to the 'lack of shelter, the density of the crowds, the vulnerable condition of the refugees, the presence of many regular and irregular military and paramilitary units in the area and the sheer lack of sufficient numbers of U.N. soldiers to provide protection'. Thus, the accused was held responsible for 'incidental' rapes committed during the persecution of non-Serbs at Poto ari. Ibid at para 327.

209 *Kvocka* Trial Chamber Judgement, at paras 266, 306.

210 Ibid at para 318.

211 Ibid at para 190.

212 Ibid at para 190.

213 The Trial Chamber here quoted the *Akayesu* Trial Chamber Judgement, at para 688.

214 Ibid at para 559. The credibility of Witness K, who was found to have been raped by Radic, was challenged by the defence, primarily because she was interviewed by a journalist shortly after the crimes were committed and she did not

mention the rape crimes. However, the Trial Chamber stated that 'the fact that Witness K did not mention the rape incident in 1993 to a journalist is irrelevant, particularly in light of the sexual and intensely personal nature of the crime'. Ibid at para 552.

215 Ibid at para 560.

216 'The Trial Chamber takes into consideration the extraordinary vulnerability of the victims and the fact that they were imprisoned in a facility in which violence against the detainees was the rule, not the exception. The detainees knew that Radic held a position of authority in the camp, that he could roam the camp at will, and order their presence before him at any time. The women also knew or suspected that other women were being raped or otherwise subjected to sexual violence in the camp. The fear was pervasive and the threat was always real that they could be subjected to sexual violence at the whim of Radic. Under these circumstances, the Trial Chamber finds that the threat of rape or other forms of sexual violence undoubtedly caused severe pain and suffering. . . . and thus, the elements of torture are also satisfied in relation to these survivors.' Ibid at para 561.

217 See, for example, *Prosecutor v. Miloševic*, Second Amended Indictment "Kosovo" IT-02-54, 29 October 2001; *Kraijisnik & Plavšic*, Consolidated Amended Indictment (IT-00-39&40, 7), March 2002.

218 For the first time in over 50 years, the U.N.'s influential International Law Commission elected women (Paula Escaremeia and Xue Hanqin from China), and the International Court of Justice elected a female judge in 1995 (Rosalyn Higgins from the U.K.). According to Kelly Dawn Askin, these advances are 'revolutionary' in spite of their seeming modest nature, given that for decades no women held high, or even mid- or low-level positions of power in international law bodies or courts. In Askin (2003), at 296.

219 Halley (2008–2009), at 6. At the heart of governance feminism is its preoccupation with a subordination theory: a distinction between something m and something f, a commitment to be a theory about, and a practice about the sub ordination of f to m; and a commitment to work against the subordination of f. This encompasses a range of liberal, radical, cultural and other feminisms, and is to a large degree co-extensive with Brown's term 'feminist foundationalism'. Halley (2006).

220 Engle (2005), at 778–779.

6 The value of critique and the representation of female identity in ICTY wartime sexual violence jurisprudence

Part I

Introduction

The book pursues a critical feminist analysis of wartime sexual violence, as it is constructed in ICTY wartime sexual violence jurisprudence and the surrounding debate. So far, it has been concerned with laying out the legal and theoretical background for the analysis. To recap, Chapters 1 and 2 provided a detailed summary of recent developments concerning gender-based violence in international human rights law by charting the key developments that contributed to its visibility and incorporation into contemporary international criminal law. At the same time, they provided a sense of the crucial advocacy work delivered by various feminist groups in gaining recognition for women's human rights and acknowledging gender-based violence as a serious violation of international human rights law. These chapters constituted the first pillar in the transition from a discussion to a more critical analysis of wartime sexual violence. Yet, they adopted a critical feminist analysis of certain concepts such as the gender mainstreaming policies prevalent within United Nations institutions in order to showcase the feminist concerns animating this project. The argument that these developments might have not been uniformly emancipatory for delivering the twin feminist aims of gender justice and equality first found expression there.

Chapter 3 provided a sense of wartime sexual violence as a long-standing historical phenomenon by focusing on the events that triggered the establishment of the ad hoc tribunals for Rwanda and Yugoslavia and that helped to propel this issue to the forefront of the international agenda. The attention with which wartime sexual violence was treated starting in the early 1990s stood in notable contrast to the response to earlier widespread reports of sexual violence, as the analysis of the handling of sexual violence during the Vietnam War and the Bangladeshi conflict has shown. In addition, the chapter provided a sense of a key feminist critique of international humanitarian law in order to illustrate the patriarchal notions informing the laws of armed conflict, which have largely regarded women as objects rather than subjects. At the same time it demonstrated the monumental work accomplished by the ad hoc tribunals in redefining international humanitarian law and expanding the tribunal statutes in order to make acts of sexual violence justiciable in international criminal law. In this way, the tribunals have provided landmark definitions of rape, redefined classical categories of international criminal law, such as crimes against humanity to incorporate multiple forms of sexual violence against women and men. They have made significant accommodation for a gender-based perspective by instituting gender-based legal advisers and by allowing feminist activists to develop wartime sexual violence jurisprudence through *amicus curiae* submissions and other initiatives. As such, the tribunals have, inevitably, been hailed by both feminist and non-feminist scholars as unparalleled successes, while little concern has been raised about what these legal accomplishments might mean for the substantive equality of the women concerned.

Chapter 4 has furnished the book with its theoretical underpinnings for the analysis of wartime sexual violence jurisprudence carried out in this chapter. It has canvassed the various feminist approaches to the study of human rights, gender, culture, the law and armed conflict. In highlighting their respective advantages and disadvantages, the book has suggested a more critical approach towards the study of armed conflict and wartime identity. It has shown that feminist activism around the issues of gender-based violence and wartime sexual violence is strongly informed by structuralist perspectives of women's subordination, which have permeated both feminist rule preference and legal strategy. While it remains true that international law perpetuates deeply entrenched images of women based on essentialised notions of female identity, which are often dressed up as legal successes, it is also true that feminists themselves have been complicit in this process in their quest for quick-fix solutions at the expense of more strategic, long-term feminist goals. While there has been much debate in feminist circles about how to incorporate a more feminist perspective into the law, there has been little focus on what these developments might mean for women beyond the courtroom.

Chapter 5 has constituted the second limb in the transition from the legal developments surrounding gender-based violence to a more critical account by charting in detail the landmark cases of sexual violence prosecuted in the ICTY to date and by reflecting on their key jurisprudential achievements. It has overviewed the key patterns underlying acts of wartime sexual violence against women, reflecting on the fact that the conflict has often been described as a systematic war against women. It has also shed light on the detention camp as a space which symbolised the violence against civilians during the Yugoslav armed conflict, yet today may well be part of a new political reality. In this way, the book has distanced itself from the almost universally endorsed idea that the conflict in Bosnia-Herzegovina was a uniquely evil event, characteristic of an entire cultural landscape and its inhabitants. The chapter focused on a number of select cases drawn from the Bosnian conflict to flesh out their notable contribution to the evolution of international wartime sexual violence jurisprudence.

The chapter represents the final transition from a discussion of the legal developments surrounding wartime sexual violence, developments in international criminal law set out in the previous chapters, to their feminist evaluation pursued here. It ultimately crystallises the actual critical feminist approach adopted by the book as not exclusively based on one type of feminist theory. Rather, it consists of a series of insights garnered across various strands of contemporary feminist, as well as non-feminist theorising.

Together, these insights are conducive to the type of critical feminist analysis of wartime sexual violence jurisprudence and the surrounding debate pursued. This chapter crystallises the overall approach of the book by explaining its constitutive elements, which are categorised as follows.

Part II of the chapter aims to assert the value of critique as itself a worthwhile transformative academic and political strategy, in contrast with some feminist preoccupations with legal reform and the theory/practice division. Part III addresses the problem of the perceived crises of normativity and subjectivity informing much of the debate in current feminist scholarship by arguing that the absence of a unified subject need not block certain feminist pursuits. Part IV gives an indication of how such a narrative pursuit might proceed, with particular reference to the idea of counterpoint, which helps to clarify the narrative and academic strategy of the book. Part V aims to highlight the two salient trends in ICTY wartime sexual violence jurisprudence: the reading of gender identity through an ethnic lens, and the portrayal of women as either victims or mothers. As noted in chapters 1 and 2, these two trends constitute the focus of the chapter because they form the 'feminist' core of the debate. Part VI focuses on demonstrating the intersection of gender and ethnicity in key ICTY decisions by showing that dominant feminist readings of wartime identities have produced a problematic narrative of gendered identity in wartime. To this end, this part of the chapter provides an account of the rhetoric of female victimhood as tied to ethnic identity, as it shines through the judgements and the dominant feminist discourses surrounding it. Part VII turns to the opponents of these interpretations of female victimhood and of the idea that the Yugoslav conflict was in essence a 'war against women', highlighting how these as well are more often than not articulated within the same conceptual framework. Part VIII takes a step back, in order to consider the limitations of the currently prevailing preoccupation with the intersection of gender and ethnicity, as well as with notions of autonomy and consent. It adds another dimension to the analysis highlighting what the current feminist rhetoric might eclipse – namely the possibility of conceptualising wartime agency in different terms. Part IX emphasises the desirability of admitting the possibility that women's subordination and inequality might not be analytically resolvable by feminism alone. It implies making room for analytical axes other than feminism, sometimes even those apparently incompatible with it, which will be an important aspect of the critique pursued in this chapter. Part X proposes an alternative framework which is not necessarily inspired by feminist thinking, or reliant on the increased regulation of gender-based violence as the way forward in conceptualising gendered identity in wartime. Part XI summarises and concludes the chapter.

Part II

The value of feminist critique

Much of feminist scholarship, in particular the structuralist/universalist strand, shares numerous reservations about critique. But conceding to these anxieties is neither intellectually justifiable nor politically desirable. Wendy Brown's defence of the value and purpose of critique serves as a key element in the ensuing explanation of such an approach.[1] She notes that 'anxiety about critique, reduction of it to dismissal or mere negativity, is ubiquitous in contemporary political and legal theoretical culture today'.[2] This observation is certainly applicable to international feminist circles. Brown and Halley argue that critique:

> is variously charged with being academic, impractical, merely critical, unattuned to the political exigencies at hand, intellectually indulgent, easier than fixing things or saying what is to be done-in short, either ultra-leftist or ultra-rhetorical, but in either case without purchase on or in something called 'the Real World'. Critique is thus characterized as an abandonment of politics, in so far as it is an abandonment of the terms and constraints of real political life, a flight to an elsewhere, politically and theoretically.[3]

Brown confronts these misconceptions by examining the historical trajectory of critique in Western thought. She argues that critique has its origins in the ancient Greek *krisis*, which was a 'jurisprudential term identified with the act of making distinctions on acts that were considered essential to judging and rectifying an alleged disorder in or of the democracy'.[4] This stands in contrast with contemporary views of critique as evading judgement and therefore being 'either destructive or irrelevant'.[5] But despite critique's uncomfortable quality, this does not mean suspension of political values or normative judgement. It gives one an opportunity to examine positions, rather than remain trapped in the contemporary obsession with position taking. Critique is therefore not a process of rejection, but of thorough scrutiny and re-engagement. As Brown has noted, it is precisely the importance and omnipresence of the object of critique that does not allow us to reject or dismiss it as insignificant.[6] Rather, critique is a practice of continued re-evaluation, the ultimate aim being the object's transformation.

Similarly to Brown and Halley, Nicola Lacey has rejected the dichotomy of feminist critique/feminist strategy by arguing that critique itself is a strategy.[7] She has argued that it is misleading to measure the success of the feminist legal project in terms of straightforward legal reform, which is often the case, as legal reforms tend to be perceived as the most tangible indication of feminist progress – certainly feminist advocacy around the establishment of the ICTY, the drafting of its Rules of Evidence and Procedure, and the vociferous lobbying for the inclusion of acts of gender-based violence into the tribunal's statute exemplify this trend.

Not all 'feminist' problems can be matched with legal solutions. This is especially evident from the fact that many such solutions, introduced for the benefit of women, have turned out to be rather anti-emancipatory, inevitably generating new forms of subordination and discipline, in which women are even further away from the ostensible feminist goal of liberation and empowerment.[8] To the extent that such new forms of repression are largely invisible and difficult to pinpoint, feminist critique that does not see theory and practice as radically divorced becomes all the more appropriate.

Lacey's conception of 'critique as strategy' means that feminist critique is in a way a form of political action, a 'discursive intervention in the production of dominant meanings, albeit one, which still has an uneven hold'.[9] In this way, it implies 'a broader conception of the political' underlying the legal and a sharpened 'sense of the questions we need to confront'.[10] Critique also has close connections with modalities of feminist theory that engage with law as a discourse and gendering practices[11] involving a reconfiguration of feminist theorising to identify a more nuanced analysis of power.[12] Through generating critique of the dominant norms, such feminist aspirations are more long-term: it is to transform assumptions underlying the norms, rather than coming up with proposals for quick-fix reforms. As Wendy Brown has put it:

> Theory's most important political offering is [the] opening of a breathing space between the world of common meanings and the world of alternative ones, a space of potential renewal for thought, desire and action. And it is this that we sacrifice by capitulating to the demand that theory reveal truth, deliver applications, or solve each of the problems it defines.[13]

As has been discussed previously, there are noticeable tendencies in recent feminist theory to ignore or underestimate the material dimensions of women's subordination, such as the oppression of capitalism and the gendered division of labour. This has been analysed in previous chapters with reference to Susan Woodward's, Nira Yuval-Davis' and Anne Orford's work on the structural factors underlying the outbreak of conflict in Yugoslavia. The argument of the book is that these dimensions are persistent and omnipresent as ever, despite having been erased in the resulting jurisprudence. The material dimensions affecting gendered realities in societies experiencing war remain relatively unaffected by decades of feminist advocacy. Although the author doesn't directly engage with materialist critiques and modalities of feminism, materialist concerns do not vanish altogether through its preoccupation with discursive practices. It is more accurate to characterise its method, which is indebted to Wendy Brown's work, as an engagement with 'existing discourses'. Such an engagement aims to highlight how framing issues through certain discursive practices 'presumes the creature it needs to explain'[14] and erases the materialist questions of structural conditions in which subjectivity is formed. The framing of wartime sexual violence issues as human rights claims under available legal frameworks has assigned deep political social problems to a rather impoverished analytical spectrum, which evades power and history, understood in a broader, more materialist sense. Rather than ignoring the materialist and structural dimensions, the aim is to bring them to light.

Part III

Questions of normativity and subjectivity in feminist theory

There is currently a widespread perception that feminist theory is experiencing a crisis of normativity, which is commonly blamed on postmodernist tendencies to fragment female subjectivity, which is considered to be extremely counterproductive to the attainment of feminist goals.

In a seminal essay written more than a decade ago, Wendy Brown locates what she describes as a 'palpable feminist panic'[15] caused by postmodernist deconstructions of the subject in a strong modernist ethos, even a certain 'foundationalism', prevalent in mainstream feminism. The link between feminism's modernist ethos and its panic in the face of 'something called postmodernism' that does away with singular, unified notions of women can be understood through Foucault's discussion of the confessional subject, who is presumed to contain 'truth' as a secret with which to purge his soul through confession. To the extent that feminism hails breaking the silence about women's oppression as a way to liberation, the voicing of women's experiences acquires '[a]n inherently confessional cast'.[16] This is what makes staunchly modernist feminists express concerns such as those articulated by an earlier critic of postmodern feminism, Christine di Stefano:

> To the extent that feminist politics is bound up with a specific constituency or subject, namely women, the postmodernist prohibition against subject-centred inquiry and theory undermines the legitimacy of a broad-based organized movement dedicated to articulating and implementing the goals of such a constituency.[17]

Essentialism as such is not the problem here. Rather, it is the particular type of essentialism: the equation of subjectivity with truth, normativity and perhaps most problematically, politics. The problematic conflation of subjectivity and politics is also characteristic of the scholarship of Seyla Benhabib, a leading Habermasian feminist: she cannot conceive of politics 'without positing [in some form] norms of autonomy, choice and self-determination'.[18]

The core of Brown's argument against strongly modernist, or what she calls feminist foundationalist concerns about the crisis of the subject is that 'gender can be conceived as a marker of power, a marker of subjects, an axis of subordination without thereby converting it to a "center of selves" understood as foundational'.[19]She cites as an example the fact that even the most radical post-structuralists do not claim that pervasive gender subordination structures do not exist because feminists cannot agree on 'who or what "woman" is or what it is that she wants'.[20] There is a clear distinction between politics and ontology, a fact that seems to have escaped those feminists who decry the destabilisation of the subject as paralysing normative pursuits. As Brown and Halley reiterate, critique promises perspective, rather than objectivity. It is then exactly the perspective of critique that sustains normative feminist engagement with political, social and legal issues – in so far as perspective is offered by the normative technique of counterpoint, which provides the impetus for the ensuing analysis of the wartime sexual violence debate.

Part IV

Counterpoint as a methodological tool for analysis

As explained previously, there is a widespread perception that feminist normativity is in crisis, which tends to be linked with a crisis of subjectivity. How then might feminism be normative – how might it engage in critique and political lobbying – in the absence of unifying truth claims about the subject whose putative interest it purports to represent? Brown's own vision that

> [d]ispensing with the unified subject does not mean ceasing to be able to speak about our own experiences as women, only that our words cannot be legitimately deployed or construed as larger or longer than the lives they speak from.[21]

is, therefore, useful, as the destabilisation of the universal woman does not mean the silencing of women's voices. One possibility of perspective is found in the normative technique of counterpoint, which provides the impetus for the ensuing analysis of ICTY wartime sexual violence jurisprudence. The book is therefore guided by the idea of counterpoint, which was advanced by Wendy Brown as a 'provisionally proposed technique for holding together the inherent slide of gender on the one hand and the powers comprising regimes of male dominance on the other'.[22]

Counterpoint can be described as an anti-hegemonic, open-ended and tactical practice of multiplicity that does not rely on methodological techniques such as dialectics, which seeks out the opposition and contradiction in texts. The aim of counterpoint is to bring out the complexity that cannot emerge through a single representational practice. It does not seek to harmonise or find solutions to intricate problems, but seeks to provide an elsewhere to dominant narratives, thus, contesting dominance and power through the work of juxtaposition.[23] In this way, counterpoint can provide a technique for resisting both the essentialist and fragmenting impulses in a manner that does not simply put the two into opposition, but uses one to complicate the other. Specifically, counterpoint as a methodology reflects the normative aspiration that feminist scholarship would benefit from the sort of engagement that seeks to complicate and interrogate discursive modalities and understandings prevalent at a particular time. As Brown explains, such a complication does not necessarily carry a contradiction; rather it is driven by anti-hegemonic sensibilities.

This is exactly what this chapter sets out to do. It adopts contrapuntal strategies in both its structure and substantive approach to the analysis. It gives an account of gendered identity as constructed in ICTY wartime sexual violence jurisprudence. This account represents the dominant position espoused by various feminist groupings in the current wartime sexual violence debate. This analysis particularly focuses on the *Prosecutor v. Kunarac* decision, for it provides fertile ground for the critical feminist analysis pursued. Not only does it encapsulate the full range of gendered experiences occurring in wartime. Its depiction of gendered identity has also elicited a wide range of feminist reactions this book seeks to put into perspective. First, an account of the standard portrayal of female identity in international law and its attendant discourse is provided. Secondly, the opposite position is put forward, in counterpoint to the dominant one. Third, these are complicated by a more in-depth analysis of the parameters of the debate, which purports to interrogate the underlying assumption on which both positions rest. Fourth, a final counterpoint is advanced in an attempt to reformulate the frames of the debate. Throughout this analysis reference is made to related wartime sexual violence jurisprudence and the specific feminist discourses that surround it. Before proceeding with this analysis, the rest of the present chapter explains the remaining two background elements in this segment of the book.

Part V

The representation of female identity in ICTY wartime sexual violence jurisprudence

This segment considers the first of two trends informing current ICTY wartime sexual violence jurisprudence, i.e., the preoccupation of the legal trial with reproducing and naturalising dominant social norms and practices, including those that normalise women's inequality. International wartime sexual violence jurisprudence, as has been argued, rests on dichotomised and hierarchical gendered subjectivities that are brought into being through the law. Returning to the critique first advanced by Dianne Otto, the book argues that far from constructing a unitary trope of 'woman', three recurring subjectivities emerge, overlapping frequently and producing complex and productive interrelationships.[24] The recurrent subjectivities are that of the 'wife and mother' who needs 'protection' during both times of war and peace and is more often an object than a subject of international law; second, the woman who is formally 'equal' with men, at least in the realm of public life; and thirdly, the 'victim' subject produced by colonial narratives of gender, as well as by notions of women's sexual vulnerability.[25] The chapter is predominantly concerned with demonstrating how the subjectivity of the 'wife and mother' and the 'woman as victim' materialise, for the woman who is formally equal to men has been largely absent from ICTY wartime sexual violence jurisprudence possibly because very few women occupied high-ranking military or political posts during the Yugoslav conflict.[26] The forthcoming analysis demonstrates that although the representations of men and women in the judgements appear to be fluid, as different subjectivities are seemingly showcased, the gendered duality whereby male dominance depends on his dissimilarity with the feminine 'Other' is resurrected.[27] The analysis shows that these gendered identities and their attendant hierarchies have 'displayed an uncanny ability to survive' despite the vocal feminist lobbying and advocacy for gender justice and equality. In short, they have repeated women's marginalisation and exclusion from full humanity.

i) Gendered wartime identity in the Kunarac *decision*

The Prosecutor v. Kunarac case provides the focus for this chapter, as it showcases the central modalities by which gendered identities came into being in ICTY wartime sexual violence jurisprudence.[28] To refresh the more detailed account provided in chapter 4, the case concerned the 'systematic' rape including 'gang' rape by Serb soldiers of Bosnian Muslim women held inside local high schools and sports halls that had been transformed into detention centres during the Serb takeover of the town of Foca in central Bosnia-Herzegovina in April 1992.[29] Some women and girls were subjected to public rape, while others were routinely taken out of the facilities to be raped and subsequently returned. Other women, in turn, were permanently removed from the facilities and held elsewhere for sexual access whenever their captors demanded it. The ICTY ruled the rape of women to be a crime against humanity, and held that both sexual enslavement and rape qualify as crimes against humanity when victims held in circumstances of detention are subjected to repeated rape over days, weeks or months.

The judgement rendered the first rape as crime against humanity conviction and the first-ever enslavement in conjunction with rape conviction. Furthermore, it made extensive holdings regarding the element of enslavement, while at the same time further clarifying the elements of rape and torture under international law. Moreover, the case was significant, for multiple charges against the defendants were brought, with rape being variously charged as a crime against humanity, a violation of the laws and customs of war, and a form of torture. It was classified as a crime against humanity and a violation of the laws and customs of war. The fact that multiple charges were brought was significant because it constituted a recognition that wartime rape occurs in different contexts, for different reasons, and with various impacts on the victims.

Jurisprudentially, the *Kunarac* case has been widely seen as a success amongst feminist advocates and scholars; yet the law continues to present a very partial idea of the body through the representation of the female identity as inevitably rooted in victimhood. The first indicative paragraph to illustrate the notion of women as victims and their lack of agency is as follows:

> Numerous witnesses stated that soldiers and policemen would come constantly, sometimes several times a day; they would point at women and girls or call them by their names and take them out for rape. The women had no choice but to obey those men and those who tried to resist were beaten in front of other women. The girls and women were generally taken for a few hours and returned, sometimes overnight, and some of them were taken away every day. After about 10–15 days, most of them were transferred to Partizan Sports Hall.[30]

Female victimhood is implied here through a purported absence of choice to resist the rapists. Moreover, in referring to women in the same breath as girls, which is achieved rather effectively through the use of the passive verb to describe the women's ordeal, any sense of resistance or autonomy is precluded. This is emphasised in the following passage:

> Some women who had testified before the Trial Chamber had been taken out so often by so many soldiers, that they were consequently unable to assess with precision the number of times they had been raped.[31]

The deployment of the passive verb to characterise the treatment of women is once again evident in this passage. Moreover, the inference that soldiers had 'easy access' to the women suggests that the women offered very little resistance, reinforcing a sense of objectification, a rendering of women as passive recipients of the violence constituted through the corporeal aspects of their existence. The passage not only vividly embodies the women's subjectivity in international law as defined by victimhood, but also reinforces their sense of helplessness and suffering, notions closely intertwined with gendered identity during this conflict.

While this passage illustrates the indiscriminate nature of rape and the incalculable harm suffered by the women, at the same time the women here are presented as the opposite of the abstract, rational individual subject of international law. The emphasis on their inability to remember the precise details, or number of rapes implies that they might have been overtaken by emotion, or humiliation – characteristics commonly associated with women and suggestive of the often infantilised victim subject of international law, who is utterly subjugated by her male bearer of 'civilization', in this instance the male captor, as the central protagonist of this war, thus, reinforcing the protectionist and proprietary notions of women described earlier.[32] While it is undoubtedly true that victims of sexual violence suffer from memory loss and sometimes cannot remember exact details when faced with the formal and utterly oppressive atmosphere of the courtroom, it appears as if the women's gap in memory and their inability to remember facts are central to their very subjectivity as women. In this way, the tribunal characterises female identity through a deeply essentialised lens.

ii) Contested wartime agency and the case of witness FWS-87

One of the key testimonies during the trial came from witness FWS-87, a woman who had been transported from the nearby town of Buk Bjela to Foca High School in July 1992. After testifying to having endured multiple rapes inside the Foca High School and Partizan Sports Hall detention camps for several weeks, the witness was then transferred to a private residence in the town where the abuse continued under the authority of Dragoljub Kunarac.[33] Following her stay in the private residence provided by the defendant, the witness was subsequently transferred to yet another private apartment belonging to Radomir Kovac in the Lepa Brena block. While testifying about the almost daily oral and vaginal rape she had to endure at the hands of Kovac in this instance, she also recalled several incidents in which she was made to strip in front of him and another soldier, Jago Kostic, who were both armed at the time.[34] A startling passage indicative of the sense of emotional harm experienced by the witness during her time of captivity inside the residence attests to a situation of extreme duress, where

> [o]n another occasion, Radomir Kovac forced her alone to undress, climb on a table and dance to music. While he was watching her, he pointed a gun at her. FWS-87 was frightened and ashamed; she had the feeling that Radomir Kovac owned her.[35]

The description of the emotional impact of the sexual abuse carries protectionist undertones, for although designed to reinforce the sense of trauma experienced by the witness, the passage portrays female identity through the female body as the soldier's property. It reinforces a sense of déjà-vu, indirectly sustaining the historical treatment of sexual violence by the law, which was marked by a complete absence of registering female subjectivity as anything other than rooted in bodily corporeality, given that its essence was 'damage to the proprietary value of virginity or chastity to an 'owning' male rather than recognition of a woman's interest in her own sexual freedom'.[36]

The passage reinforces the proprietary notions of the female body as the central objective of the offence while devaluing any sense of the violation as a harm against female subjectivity. The tribunal, therefore, instrumentalises the female body as a mechanism for keeping intact firmly entrenched gendered subjectivities resting on dominant hierarchies inherent in the very nature of the law. Female autonomy in this rendering is not about exercising any meaningful choice, but is an interest which the disembodied subject has in controlling access to, '[a] rather curious object to which she stands in a position of ownership – her body'.[37] The feeling of emotional harm experienced by the victim is not generated through a violation of her autonomous self, but through the idea of the injury to the body, as a proprietary value that has been interfered with. The emphasis on the corporeality of the harm obscures its emotional implications, as an emphasis on shame and humiliation does not encompass the full range of emotions experienced during the process of violence. Female subjectivity in this rendering has come full circle: in drawing attention to the gendered harm experienced by the witness the tribunal has drawn attention to the sense of precariousness and vulnerability of women in wartime. An alternative and more fruitful judicial strategy might have been to underline the women's survival instinct in the face of such extreme circumstance. Yet, instead the judges chose to focus on female identity as closely linked to a sense of helplessness, lack of agency and victimhood, a strategy that forecloses any possibility of courage, if not outright heroism in having survived the ordeal described on these pages.

iii) Complicating identity the intersection of gender and ethnicity in Kunarac

A rather effective legal modality deployed by the Trial Chamber was its overdetermination of gender and ethnicity as two intersecting axis of subordination that constantly combine to create the impression that the women were raped or otherwise sexually violated due to their ethnic belonging. In a passage concerning allegations that some of the women might have consensually engaged in sexual relations with their captors, witness FWS-191 denies these allegations by stating that '[i]t is inconceivable that FWS-87, or for that matter "any Muslim girl" could have moved around Foca freely'.[38]

This statement is significant from an intersectional perspective, as it emphasises the sense of victimhood and powerlessness as inextricably tied in with Muslim identity in wartime Bosnia-Herzegovina. The witness in question was seemingly unable to move around freely both on account of her gender, as well as her ethnic identity, which together combine to deny her any sense of agency or choice in her interactions with the Bosnian-Serb soldiers. The implication here is that a Bosnian Muslim woman could not have meaningfully consented to any social, let alone sexual interaction with her captors because her gendered identity, evidently entirely informed by her ethnic affiliation, prevented her from exercising any meaningful choice in this situation.[39] The intersectional construction of sexual violence in ICTY jurisprudence is taken up again in the analysis of the *Celebici* judgement, at which point a contrapuntal perspective on the intersectional tendencies of ICTY wartime sexual violence jurisprudence is presented.

As seen from the analysis of the *Kunarac* judgement so far, much of the testimony about the female experience of war hinges on statements made by witness FWS-87, whose ethnic identity has been made central in producing the main narrative on wartime sexual violence. The next segment aims to demonstrate how the Trial Chamber presumes that Bosnian Muslim women lacked agency in all kinds of situations, whether coercive or not, by highlighting a number of passages that portray the witness in a rather different way, therefore complicating her identity rather significantly to suggest that she was indeed able to make informed choices, in spite of the apparently coercive circumstances of the situation. In an insightful passage Kunarac describes taking witness FW-87 aside for a talk in the Karaman's house after hearing that she had been transferred there instead of having been taken back to the Partizan detention facility.[40] Upon taking her upstairs and inquiring about her well-being, given his impression that she looked like a 'depressed vegetable', the witness expressed that she 'did not expect him just to want to talk, but expected to be raped by him like the others did'.[41]

This passage is interesting for a number of reasons. Firstly, it complicates the picture provided in the Trial Chamber judgement of the existence of a linear story of female agency or lack thereof, juxtaposed against the binary of an utter sense of male domination and oppression of women. Upon closer inspection of the statement, a sense that the interaction between Kunarac and the witness might have been rather multifaceted and not entirely driven by fear and coercion is created. Rather than a sense of female victimhood, the impression here is of the male protagonist captor acting in a sensitive fashion towards the woman's needs, not only because it suggests that he did not intend to physically harm her, but more so because he goes as far as to express concern about her well-being. While this statement is to be read with great care, as it is entirely based on the defendant's subjective recollection of events, this situation nonetheless suggests the possibility of male compassion. Theirs could possibly have been a relationship of intimacy, which would overthrow the sense created so far of an interaction driven by male domination and female submissiveness. The passage, in subtle ways, complicates the picture of male oppression and female victimhood presented throughout the judgement.[42]

iv) The testimony of Radomir Kovac

The projection of FWS-87 as a passive victim of war without any sense of agency was most strongly challenged by the testimony of the co-accused, Radomir Kovac, whose account strongly suggested that he and the woman were not only engaged in mutual sexual relations, but were in fact in love with each other.[43] This was corroborated by the testimony of numerous witnesses, who stated that FWS-87 looked 'happy' with Kovac and that the two were actually engaged in a consensual romantic relationship.[44]

It is significant at this juncture to remark upon the fact that the defence introduced the testimony of seven female witnesses who were privy to the 'intimate' relationship between the defendant and the witness and were therefore able to comment on its nature. According to one witness, for example, Kovac would regularly refer to the girl as 'my little one', which in the witness's mind suggested that theirs was a romantic relationship based on intimacy, if not love, but certainly not founded on duress.[45]

In a rather startling passage, which yet again invokes the close intersection of ethnicity and gender in this situation, witness DM, a cousin of the defendant's father, claimed that Kovac came to visit her with a girl, FWS-87, going as far as to introduce her as his girlfriend at the end of November 1992 after months already spent in captivity.[46] Another witness testimony, that of DH, a cousin of Radomir Kovac who lived in the same apartment block after the latter had moved in the autumn of 1992, goes even further to suggest that Kovac lived on the top floor with a girl whom he introduced as his girlfriend, thus indicating that theirs was not a relationship based on captivity and sexual violence, but was one of mutual co-habitation.[47]

A further witness, who was unrelated to Kovac by virtue of family ties, was witness DV, a nurse who worked with his unit during the war. In one seemingly insignificant yet highly nuanced glimpse into their relationship, she recalls an incident during which she provided him with medicine and sanitary towels, which he had requested for his 'girlfriend'.[48] The witness stated that he looked 'in love at the time'. Moreover, upon seeing the accused and FWS-87 on a couple of other occasions when she went to his apartment, DV had come to the conclusion that he and the girl had a good relationship, also making reference to the letter he had received from the girl to which the witness had been privy.

In yet another piece of key testimony, this time from witness DN, the owner of Café Linea and a childhood friend of the accused, Radomir Kovac, accompanied by Kostic and two girls, came to the café and sat with the witness for a while. Kovac then introduced one of the girls, allegedly FWS-87, as his girlfriend, prompting his childhood friend to exclaim that it seemed 'incredible' that she 'could be a Muslim'.[49] The witness went on to concede that having a girlfriend of this ethnic background was 'highly unusual' in those days for a Serb and noting that the two girls were the only Muslim customers in the café.[50] While this passage highlights the strong intersection of gender and religion as constitutive of female wartime identity, it also complicates the linear wartime narrative presented through its assertion that female agency was indeed not only possible, but distinctly present in this case. Given the challenges and prejudices faced by an inter-ethnic couple (especially male Bosnian Serb and female Bosnian Muslim), it is even more remarkable that these two chose to be together. This could indicate that witness FWS-87 had exercised her will and choice by engaging in a seemingly romantic relationship with a man deemed her enemy not only by those in her local community, but also by outraged international feminists of various stripes who could not conceive of such scenarios either in peace or in wartime.[51]

Another significant witness for the prosecution, witness DO, a friend of Kovac, recalled seeing the latter sometime in November 1992, at which point the accused told him about his girlfriend, admitting that he was in love with witness FWS-87.[52] The witness also recalled seeing Kovac in the presence of FWS-87 at the Café Leonardo in December of the same year, the only occasion in which he exchanged a few words with the girl. According to witness DO all appeared to be in 'good mood'. On another occasion Kovac, who at this point had been wounded in combat, urged him not to say anything about the injuries to his girlfriend so that she would not be worried, while later Kovac told him that he had received a letter with a heart drawn on it from one of the girls, who he had seen off in Montenegro, in which she expressed her gratitude to him, although the witness conceded not having read the letter personally.

The examples highlighted variously illustrate that agency and choice in wartime are decidedly more complicated than what transpires in standard interpretations of wartime sexual violence jurisprudence. This suggests that while the picture is far more complex than the resulting judgements indicate, the law itself continues to portray women in monolithic fashion, as victims of their circumstances who are utterly unable to exercise any sense of individual agency, for they are entirely subjected to male domination and control in situations of armed conflict. Yet, as the highlighted passages suggest, female agency was present and alive, even amidst these scenarios of extreme coercion. In this light, a range of female voices, who were not victims but women with jobs, with incomes generating a living for themselves – even in times of utter instability and precariousness of life – were illuminated.

The witness testimonies presented came from women who worked as nurses, journalists, bar owners and administrators, highlighting the fact that even in wartime women had a voice and a purpose unrelated to their sexuality. The voices of these witnesses coupled with their sense of agency firmly contradict the predominant wartime gender identities constructed in international law. It is unfortunate that these women's voices were not given greater weight in the resulting jurisprudence of the tribunal, as they could have potentially explained the material and structural dimensions that contributed to one set of women being viciously assaulted for sexual and other motives, while another set of women was seemingly able to pursue professions with relative normality, in spite of the situation surrounding them. It is precisely the voices of these women and the constructions of these female identities which ought to have been pronounced to far greater effect in the decisions in order to demonstrate the multiple and varied nature of gender identity in times of armed conflict.

The next segment aims to highlight another set of passages where the identity of the woman as mother is most strongly pronounced before turning its attention to the dominant feminist representation of wartime sexual violence, as part of the contrapuntal analysis pursued by the book. The following passage arises out of the testimony by witness FWS-75, who spoke about her time in captivity in the apartment of Radomir Kovac for a period of one month. As described in the Trial Chamber judgement:

> During that time, the girls had to perform household work, such as cleaning up, cooking and washing men's clothes. When the men were not present, they would be locked in an apartment.[53]

The *woman-as-mother* figure is implicit in this passage, which portrays women through entrenched gender stereotypes prevalent in the private sphere – the women here are not only sexually violated, they are also enslaved through having to perform household chores typically associated with motherhood and childrearing. It is this portrayal that defines them, as the Trial Chamber does not provide any information about what these women might have done prior to their captivity – whether they pursued professions, went to university, or what role they played in the local community prior to the outbreak of the conflict.

Another 19-year-old witness, A.S., is described as having been continuously raped while she lived at Kovac's apartment and as having had to 'perform household duties – moreover, she was not free to go where she wanted to go'.[54] This passage merges both entrenched gender subjectivities into one narrative: the woman here is both respectively victim, by way of the continuous rape subjected to, as well as mother, by way of the fact that she is made to perform domestic duties typically associated with motherhood and the private sphere.

Another passage in relation to A.S.'s experience brings out the gendered dimensions of wartime sexual agency, as seen by the Trial Chamber, more strongly:

> A.S . . . had the impression that Kovac had control over what happened in the apartment. Jago Kostic would rape her anytime he wanted, orally and vaginally, and she had no choice but to comply with his demands; he would also sometimes beat her and once threatened to cut her throat. Both women had to obey every command, because the two men were armed at all times with knives, rifles or pistols. The apartment was locked and there was no access to the outside world. The women had to do housework like cleaning the apartment and the men's clothes, as well as serving them food and drinks.[55]

In this passage the two recurring subjectivities emerge, overlapping frequently and producing complex and productive interrelationships. The 'wife and mother' in need of protection during wartime is clearly evident in the contours of this passage as the object, but not the subject of international law. Secondly, the victim and her attendant sexual vulnerability emerges strongly in the passage, for it is implied that she is at the constant mercy of her captor, who rapes her anytime he wants, leaving her no choice but to comply with his demands. Furthermore, the women's utter subjection and final humiliation is magnified through the Trial Chamber's emphasis on the men, who are portrayed as being in complete control of the situation.

A further passage, arising out of the testimony of witness FWS-87, magnifies the recurring gendered subjectivities illustrated above, thereby further entrenching gender stereotypes in wartime Bosnia:

> FWS-87 testified that she was taken to the apartment of Radomir Kovac together with A.S., FWS-75 and A.B. FWS-87 further described that A.S. would be raped by Jago Kostic, while FWS-87 herself would be raped by Radomir Kovac. FWS-87 also confirmed that the women had to do household chores during their stay in the apartment and that they were locked up in the apartment without any contact to the outside world. FWS-87's testimony also supports A.S.'s statement that the two women were sold together by Radomir Kovac for 500 Deutschmarks each to two Montenegrin soldiers and were subsequently taken to Niksic and Podgorica in Montenegro.[56]

Both the stereotypes of the woman, as victim, as well as the woman as mother, are amplified in this passage by tying them to sexual slavery and trafficking. The portrayal of women is not only objectified through their representation as the soldier's chattel, it is also implied that the women lack any sense of control over their future predicament, as it is a foregone conclusion that they will be traded as sexual merchandise to yet another set of male captors, in this case Montenegrin soldiers. More attention needs to be drawn to alternative narratives, or possibilities of an elsewhere amidst the stories of wartime ruin and oppression, which rather than disempowering women could actually enhance their agency and draw attention to their subjectivity and autonomy as fully constituted subjects of international law.

Part VI

The dominant feminist position on gendered identity and the Yugoslav conflict

As already widely discussed throughout the book, the dominant strand in feminist thinking on wartime sexual violence has centred on 'governance feminism', which has been especially prevalent in the way feminist voices that have emerged across contemporary international institutions. The move to institutions therefore led to a strong feminist consensus that wartime sexual violence against women is best addressed through international criminal prosecution. Hence, feminist advocacy placed strong faith in the mechanism of the criminal trial as the preferred vehicle for addressing gender injustice. The consolidation of feminist thinking was in large part due to a structuralist-feminist worldview, which permeated much of feminist argumentation and rule preference.[57] This is manifested most clearly in the 'move to institutions' advocated by Catherine MacKinnon, who had very dogmatic ideas about the meaning of the rapes in Bosnia-Herzegovina. The most problematic aspect about the ideas espoused by MacKinnon was that they presumed that there were 'essential ethnic differences' between Serbs, Croats and Bosnian Muslims, that women were powerless victims, incapable of defending themselves or speaking out to defend others, or, even less likely, that they could take sides and participate in the war.

Most feminist international legal scholars and practitioners have viewed the ICTY's treatment of sexual violence as an important step forward in the long road to gender justice and equality. However, there was strong disagreement among 'governance feminists' as to how to approach the rapes in Bosnia-Herzegovina. The question was whether rape was an act of genocide against Bosnian Muslims, or whether it was merely a tool in a wider 'war against women', thus, an attack on women as a universal group, regardless of their ethnicity. Catherine MacKinnon was one of the most vocal proponents of the position that rape in the Balkans by Serbs was 'genocidal'.[58] The *Kunarac* judgement in the numerous passages highlighted above embodies the prevailing feminist sentiment of MacKinnon, for it suggests that women were raped not only because they were women, but also because they were Muslim women. The constant sense of duress implied in these scenarios would therefore suggest to a structuralist feminist like MacKinnon that the ultimate motive behind the rapes was the elimination in whole or in part of Bosnian Muslim women as a distinct ethnic and religious group. Much of MacKinnon's writings in the 1980s argued that the distinction between everyday heterosexual sex and rape embodied in the legal definition of rape was a product of male dominance and therefore incoherent and inherently suspect.[59] In the 1990s, she transposed this critique onto the Balkan context by attempting to articulate an international legal understanding of rape that would distinguish not between everyday heterosexual sex and rape, but between 'everyday' wartime rape and the rape committed by Serbs. As previously described, she did so by referring to the Holocaust as a seemingly useful analogy to the events in the Balkans.[60] Moreover, in attacking those who opposed her, MacKinnon asked:

> If all men do this all the time, especially in war, how can one pick one side in this one? And since all men do this all the time, war or no war, why do anything special about this now? This war becomes just a form of business as usual. But genocide is not business as usual-not even for men.[61]

MacKinnon's reasoning was that the extent of the rapes against Bosnian Muslim women by Serbian men was systematic and extraordinary. Much of the passages highlighted in the *Kunarac* judgement reiterate this view through their heightened emphasis on the systematic, if not industrialised nature underlying the sexual violence. The feminists who advocated distinguishing the rapes of Bosnian Muslim women as genocidal were encouraged by the jurisprudence emerging from the tribunal, which created the sense that the rapes were widespread, organised and systematic, in addition to being attacks based on ethnicity, which formed the core argument of this position. At the start of the war, when MacKinnon termed the Bosnian-Serb rape of both Croats and Muslims as genocidal, she explicitly reiterated the ethnic component in distinguishing the rapes by Croats and Muslims from those by Serbs:

> This genocidal war has been repeatedly mischaracterized as a 'civil war', aggressor equated with victim 'all sides' blandly blamed for their 'hatred' . . . But there is no Muslim or Croatian policy of territorial expansion, of exterminating Serbs, of raping Serbian women.[62]

Again, reading through the *Kunarac* judgement, the sense of this being a war fought against women marches hand in hand with the idea that the intent of the Serbs was to destroy Bosnian Muslims, and that mass rape committed by the Serbs was just another part of war. According to some structuralist feminists the intent of the rapes themselves would not have to be the destruction of a group – as long as the rapes were widespread or systematic and used in a war of genocide, the nexus would be assumed.[63] Hence, the legal modality of the Trial Chamber employed in this case of constantly emphasising the widespread and systematic nature of the rape inflicted on the women in both the detention camps and the sports facilities clearly resonates with the structuralist feminist worldview espoused by legal feminist scholars such as Catherine MacKinnon. The judgement in the *Kunarac* case then easily leads to another highly problematic assumption about gendered identities during the Yugoslav conflict and particularly espoused by radical feminists, namely that the effect of the rapes on Bosnian Muslim women was social ostracism, which in turn rendered the impact of the rape on Bosnian Muslim women 'unique'. Askin, for example, has noted that the consequences of rape:

> [m]ay be "particularly severe in traditional patriarchal societies, where the rape victim is often perceived as soiled and unmarriageable, thus, becoming a target of social ostracism." . . . Adding to the trauma and humiliation is the fact that for many women, and to a more extreme extent traditional Muslims, chastity is essential to maintain family honor. Stealing the virginity of a Muslim woman, even if by rape, causes the survivor to be considered unworthy of a man, casting shame and disgrace on the entire family.[64]

The overdetermination of gender and shame along the axis of culture is also evident in the passage above describing FWS-87's 'utter sense of humiliation' when she was forced to perform an erotic dance for Radmir Kovac in a state of undress, which evoked a strong sense of shame in the witness for reasons related to her ethnic background. As Karen Engle has rightly pointed out, arguments such as Askin's suggest that such effects like shame and humiliation '[a]re intended by the Serbian rapists' as a means of specifically targeting Muslim culture and religion. More problematically, the argument uses the presumed effects to impute intent. As Engle has put it:

> That the Muslim communities might respond differently from the ways suggested by the stereotype, even with acceptance, is not considered. The cultural effects – and therefore intended effects – of rape are overdetermined in this argument.[65]

This segment has sought to illuminate how the interpretation of gendered identity in wartime is heavily informed by cultural stereotypes purportedly rooted in fixed ethnic traits, and it has shown how this representation is in turn reproduced in the dominant feminist discourses surrounding wartime sexual violence in armed conflict. The jurisprudence emerging from the tribunal sustains, rather than dismantles, firmly entrenched gender subjectivities in international law by failing to complicate the parameters upon which such assumptions are built. The concern of the book is to demonstrate how female victimhood replicates itself in the relevant jurisprudence and how dominant feminist discourses sustain these notions. Structuralist feminists were not alone in treating women as victims of war; on the other side of the debate were feminists, who saw all Bosnian Muslim women as rape victims. Their ideas further perpetuated the notion of women as eternal victims of war. The second strand of the counterpoint technique presents an alternative position to the dominant one in order to show that despite its purported difference, it is largely similar given the limited parameters within which it operates.

Part VII

The 'all women as victims' alternative and the Celebici *judgement*

A notable strand in feminist thinking around wartime sexual violence in the Yugoslav conflict, which shared many of advocacy goals of the more radical structuralist feminist school of thought, argued at the time that the focus on rape as genocide was fallacious, as the evidence of rape against women was so overwhelming that it could be safely assumed that the rapes were committed on all sides, regardless of ethnicity. These feminists, of whom Rhonda Copelon was perhaps the most visible, regarded women on all sides of the war as victims, rather than as political participants, or even military participants in the war, and saw the sexual violence perpetrated against women as an extension of the everyday. As Copelon has put it,

> With regard to crimes against women, there is unfortunately not so sharp a difference between war and everyday life. Torture and rape in conflict

> situations have too much in common with rape in the marital bedroom, battering in the home, and gang rape in bars and streets . . . These are examples of egregious gender violence that is committed on a widespread or systematic scale and involves policies of legitimation, whether policies of active encouragement or policies of knowing omission, invisibilization, and toleration.[66]

This stance of perceiving wartime violence as a symptom of everyday aggression against women led Copelon to argue that in the context of the Yugoslav conflict all women had been victimised equally, regardless of their ethnicity. For Copelon,

> Women are targets not simply because they "belong" to the enemy . . . They are targets because they too are the enemy . . . because rape embodies male domination and female subordination.[67]

While this is arguably a structuralist view, Copelon nonetheless sharply departs from MacKinnon's rhetoric in so far as she believes that the emphasis on genocidal rape does more harm than good to women, as it is 'factually dubious' as well as risky, for it renders the gendered nature of rape invisible once again.[68] In particular, she was critical of the limited and narrow understanding of genocidal rape espoused by feminists like MacKinnon, insisting that genocidal rape can happen on all sides in a war and is not confined to war, but also regularly occurs in peacetime. In the context of ICTY prosecution, Copelon's main goal was to have rape recognised as a crime against humanity whenever it was committed on a mass or large-scale basis. Specifically, she sought recognition of the harm being based on gender, not ethnicity, as long as the harm was large scale.[69]

This stance is best exemplified by the *Celebici* judgement, the first case to try multiple accused at the same time for charges related to sexual violence.[70] To refresh the details of this case, the defendants belonged to a force consisting of predominantly Bosnian Muslims and Bosnian Croats, who took control of several villages inhabited by Bosnian Serbs in and around Konjic starting at the end of May 1992.[71] As part of their military campaign, the attackers forcibly expelled Bosnian residents from their homes and held them at collection centres. At the same time, most women and children were held in local schools or in other locations, while most of the men and some women were taken to a former Yugoslav People's Army (JNA) facility in Celebici, referred to in the judgement as the Celebici camp.

It is interesting to note, that the aggressors this time were not Bosnian Serbs, but Bosnian Croats and Muslims, who had confined Bosnian-Serb civilians to detention camps. The Indictment alleged that detainees in the camps were 'killed, tortured, sexually assaulted, beaten and otherwise subjected to cruel and inhuman treatment'.[72] The accused included Zejnil Delalic, allegedly the commander of the camp and therefore in a position of authority; Zdravko Mucic, the de facto commander of the camp; Hazim Delic, a subordinate, who worked in the camp; and Esad Landžo, who acted as guard at the camp.

Amongst the civilians detained was Grožđana Cecez, a Serb woman who was subjected to repeated incidents of rape, which were later deemed to have constituted torture, given that they had been committed as part of her interrogation within the camp. The aim of this part of the analysis is to show – by way of highlighting relevant passages from the Trial Chamber judgement – how gender-based violence is perceived as systematic, yet gender-specific because it is targeted against the women because she is a woman. This interpretation of the act largely confirms Copelon's position, and while it provides a departure from the structuralist interpretation of gender identity in the *Kunarac* decision, it does little to dismantle the firmly entrenched stereotypes described above. While the view of violence against women as an extension of the everyday provides a departure from the 'ethnicised' and 'genocidal rape' discourse, it only adds an additional layer to the debate, but ultimately fails to provide an alternative to female subjectivity in wartime, continuing to produce it as firmly rooted in strongly dichotomised gendered narratives.

i) The surfacing of the woman-as-wife

As stated, one of the recurrent subjectivities produced in ICTY wartime sexual violence jurisprudence is of the woman-as-mother, who has surfaced strongly in the case law discussed so far. A related subjectivity in ICTY wartime sexual violence jurisprudence has been the woman-as-wife figure, who surfaces in the following segment:

> Ms. Cecez testified that, during the rape, Hazim Delic told her she was in Celebici prison-camp because of her husband and that she would not have been there if he had been around. Further, she testified that Zdravko Mucic had asked about the whereabouts of her husband.[73]

Two things are at play here: in demonstrating that rape amounts to torture, the woman's individuality is eclipsed through the persona of her husband, who is allowed to take centre stage in the interrogation, despite his physical absence. The woman materialises only through her belonging to a man, so, any sense that this crime could have been directed against the female autonomy of the woman is subsumed through the emphasis on her subjectivity as a wife, therefore, reiterating a familiar gendered stereotype in international law of the woman as in need of protection.

Interestingly, the defence in this case contended that the interrogation regarding the witness's husband ended before the alleged rape had begun and was not resumed after the rape. It argued that it would therefore have to be proven that the purpose of the alleged rape was indeed to obtain information.[74] This argument sought to reduce the elision between the gendered persona of the woman-as-wife from the actual sexual harm, suggesting (albeit probably unintentionally) that she might have been raped because she was a woman, not because she was somebody's wife. But the judges chose to follow the interpretation of events given by Ms. Cecez, according to which Delic had told her during the course of the rapes that 'the reason she was there, was her husband, and that she would not be there if he was'.[75]

It is a further passage in which the effect of the rape on the woman surfaces most vividly, implying that the rape is an act with extreme gendered consequences, if not a fate worse than death. In expressing what impact the rapes had on her, the witness describes it as follows:

> The effect of this rape by Hazim Delic was expressed by Ms. Cecez, when she stated: "he trampled on my pride and I will never be able to be the woman that I was."[76]

The passage proceeds by describing the emotional impact of the rape on the witness in the following way:

> Ms. Cecez lived in constant fear while she was in the prison camp and was suicidal. Further Ms. Cecez was subjected to multiple rapes on the third night of her detention in the prison camp – when she was transferred from Building B to a small room in Building A. After the third act of rape that evening she stated, "It was difficult for me. I was a woman who only lived for a man and I was his all my life, and I think that I was just getting separated from my body at this time."[77]

Several problematic interpretations of wartime female subjectivity are at play here: firstly, rape, although directed against only one individual, is described through its systematic nature, reiterating that it necessarily had to be committed multiple times and on a rather systematic scale in order to be perceived as serious. Secondly, and confirming Copelon's view, the rape committed here does not appear ethnically motivated, as barely any mention of the woman's Serbian ethnic identity is made in the relevant passages.[78] This would also confirm her earlier perception of the rapes being committed against all women, regardless of ethnicity. Moreover, given the ease, if not systematic nature with which the perpetrators went about raping implies that the act was considered an extension of the everyday, for a certain sense of routine within which the abusers operated left open for interpretation whether they might have engaged in similar conduct in the past, possibly even in the context of peace. Moreover, the tribunal makes explicit that the violence suffered by Ms. Cecez, in the form of rape, was inflicted upon her by Delic because she is a woman, therefore adopting a similar argument as Copelon.[79]

But perhaps most problematic is the portrayal of the woman-as victim, which most strongly surfaced in the judgement through the witness's utterance that as a woman, she 'only lived for man and that she was his all her life'. While this is undoubtedly a self-characterisation, it carries connotations about women which do little to dispel firmly entrenched gendered narratives of women in international law. Again, what emerges from the witness is a sense of utter female subjection, submissiveness and lack of agency. In this passage, Ms. Cecez, who was previously described as a shop owner, suggesting a strong sense of agency required for a less typically female profession, was entirely transformed into the victim subject produced not only by colonial narratives of gender, but – perhaps more prominently – by notions of women's sexual vulnerabilities, which seem all-consuming and all-defining. The Trial Chamber has, therefore, in the space of a few passages accomplished the objectification of the female wartime identity through its portrayal of the woman as both the wife and victim of war, respectively, but never as an agent in her own right.

Her testimony led the Trial Chamber to find that acts of vaginal penetration by the penis under circumstances that were coercive constituted rape.[80] The purpose of the rape was interpreted by the tribunal to have been to obtain information about her husband, who was considered to be a rebel; hence she was 'punished' for her inability to provide information about his whereabouts, and additionally, she was coerced and intimidated into providing such information in order to ultimately be punished for the activities of her husband.[81] While this passage, undoubtedly, was designed to showcase the serious nature of the violence in the tribunal's understanding, what is lacking is any sense of the rape as an act against the woman, despite the judge's best intentions.

While this judgement has presented another dimension underlying the war by focusing on rape of two women, as opposed to a large number of women, it has highlighted the more individualised nature of sexual violence. Moreover, in line with Copelon's argument, it has demonstrated that sexual violence during the Yugoslav conflict was not necessarily always ethnically motivated (at least where Serbian women were targeted), thus disproving one of the central arguments made by MacKinnon that this was genocidal rape committed by Serbs with the intent of eradicating the Bosnian Muslim and Croatian population. Her assertion that the Yugoslav conflict embodied rape as genocide, a rape directed against women 'because they are Muslim or Croatian, and that this was a part of a campaign by Serbia against non-Serbia'[82] does not stand up on close inspection of the present case. Moreover, through the description of the routine nature of the rape, the Trial Chamber has created a sense that within the context of Yugoslav society, the sexual violence could have well just been an extension of the everyday, thus giving valence to the idea espoused by a large number of feminists of the Yugoslav war being in its essence a war against women. In presenting the case law analysis of the *Celebici* judgement interspersed with Copelon's commentary as illustrative of a powerful strand in feminist discourses around the conflict, which sought to actively contradict the stance espoused by MacKinnon and the more radical feminist variety, the book has provided an argument in opposition to the dominant one. The next step is to seek to complicate the two dominant, albeit differently framed viewpoints by providing an alternative perspective that seeks to complicate the standard feminist discourses around wartime sexual violence and the Yugoslav conflict.

Part VIII

Surfacing the margins of female agency and resistance in ICTY wartime sexual violence jurisprudence

To a large part wartime identities have already been complicated in the in-depth analysis of the *Kunarac* judgement, which, among other things, sought to demonstrate that while the narrative of the women-as-victim defined along fixed lines surfaces strongly, any sense of her agency or power as a female is marginalised from the Trial Chamber's legal reasoning. This part of the chapter seeks to map out the critical feminist insight that underlies its main analysis, for this strand has been highly significant in helping to illuminate the margins of ICTY wartime sexual violence jurisprudence. Most notably, it has complicated the picture of ICTY wartime sexual violence, in this way challenging many of the perceived feminist successes, which had previously gone largely unchallenged. Karen Engle's and Doris Buss' takes on dominant feminist interpretations of ICTY wartime sexual violence jurisprudence have been particularly indispensable to this project.

Karen Engle, specifically, has critiqued both the direct and indirect roles that feminists played in the '(re)consideration' of the international criminalisation of rape. As she saw it, the dominant feminist strands in the debate could be located in two distinct camps: those that argued that rapes should be primarily understood as an instrument of 'genocide' and therefore distinct from 'everyday rapes' espoused by the second feminist camp, and already illuminated upon previously.[83] Engle's contribution to the debate is particularly useful as it questions the premises and assumptions upon which the two dominant strands have been built. Most significantly, it criticises the institutionalisation of the feminist viewpoint of there being 'essential' ethnic differences between Serbs, Croats and Bosnian Muslims, and the portrayal of women as powerless victims. As she has put it, these representations have reinforced a sense of women as 'powerless victims, incapable of defending themselves or speaking out to defend others, but also of taking sides or participating in the war'.[84]

She has introduced the idea that the international criminalisation of rape might not have been as path-breaking or progressive as the doctrinal recognition would suggest. She has, moreover, suggested that the approach of the United Nations, and particularly the ICTY – largely at the urging of feminists – has at times treated women as part of the same concept of 'women and children' that has long been deployed as a mechanism to provide women with special protection they are seen to need during wartime. In so doing, she has raised the possibility that feminist advocates might have unwittingly – also because of their own disagreements – denied much of women's sexual and political agency in ways that have ultimately manifested themselves in the approach adopted by the tribunal. Moreover, Engle has complicated the way in which political agency and choice manifest themselves in the tribunal's jurisprudence, and has argued that both feminist camps have treated most women as victims of war, having done little to dismantle prevailing gender stereotypes in international jurisprudence. She has pointed out the legal modalities by which Bosnian Muslim women in particular were seen as rape victims,[85] suggesting that silence was often interpreted as a sign of victimisation, a testament to the trauma of rape with strong connotations of shame, which defined the Bosnian Muslim woman, as because of her silence, she was assumed to have been raped. In other words, the rape of Bosnian Muslim women often became 'the sole factor' by which they were defined.[86]

In her analysis of ICTY wartime sexual violence jurisprudence, Engle has mapped out, very helpfully, the three key cases that define international law in the area of wartime sexual violence jurisprudence, *Celebici*, *Kunarac* and *Furundžija*, in which the OTP successfully prosecuted rapes alleged to have been committed on all sides, while at the same time concentrating its efforts on the *Kunarac* case that viewed rape as 'systematically aimed' at Bosnian Muslims.[87] In concentrating its efforts on a case denoting the 'systematic' attack against women civilians, the Trial Chamber has simultaneously highlighted (without even producing a finding of genocide) that the rapes of Bosnian Muslim women were 'different' from the rapes of Serbian and Croatian women, as only the former were found to have been systematic.

In the *Celebici* case, for instance, the fact that the women who were raped were Serbian is barely mentioned. It has also been noted by Engle that the various references to 'ethnic cleansing' through the 'wiping out of all traces of Muslim presence and culture', for instance, suggest that the Trial Chamber was inclined to represent the rape as inherently linked to ethnic cleansing, therefore imputing an ethnic dimension to the act of sexual violence. Perhaps most useful has been Engle's observation that the Rules of Procedure and Evidence are based on rather problematic assumptions about women's wartime agency, given in particular the limiting of consent as a defence to rape before the ICTY.[88] Indeed, the *Kunarac* Appeals Chamber 'softened' the effects of the requirement of the *mens rea* in its interpretation of the rule given that non-consensual and non-voluntary sexual relations had to be examined in light of the prevailing coercive circumstances of war'.[89] This has led Engle to suggest that the tribunal construed consent in a way that made it next to impossible to imagine that it could have been given in a situation that was inherently coercive and marked by duress.[90] As the book has previously shown, consensual relationships appear to have taken place in wartime Foca, if the numerous accounts are to be believed. Engle has also shown that another legal modality by which gender and ethnicity were heavily elided in the jurisprudence was rooted in the presumption that the lack of consent was connected to the identities of the Serb as the perpetrator and the Bosnian Muslim woman as the victim, reiterating the view of the author that the identities of victims and perpetrators were highly 'ethnicised' in the tribunal's legal reasoning. She has noted that:

> The presumption of coercion serves to deny at a formal level that Muslim women would have chosen, in the way that we normally use the term "choice" in these matters, to have sex with a male Serbian soldier during the war.[91]

Engle's view has therefore provided invaluable insight into current ICTY wartime sexual violence jurisprudence by pointing out the possible unintended consequences of a feminist activism that has been intent on the criminalisation of wartime sexual violence as a means of addressing gendered harms of the past. Much like Wendy Brown, Engle has queried whether feminist advocacy and its results are desirable in the current legal and political moment, given that it has produced a number of 'troubling' aspects, which she identifies as having resulted in 1) the entrenchment of reified understandings of 'ethnic difference'; 2) the 'minimization' of women's sexual, political and military agency; and 3) the 'replacement of a focus on gender with a focus on sex.'[92]

In posing these pertinent questions, Engle has complicated the idea that the legal successes achieved in the ICTY have necessarily produced a wholesale feminist victory. In particular, her contribution has shown that both dominant strands in feminist legal theory and activism, reflecting 'governance feminist' principles, have recreated, rather than critiqued the essentialised understanding of ethnic identity found in the prevailing scholarship and in popular discourses around the Yugoslav conflict. The danger, as she has shown, is that such approaches assume a 'biological notion of identity' in particular in relation to whether Bosnian-Serb rapes against Bosnian Muslim women were perpetrated with the intent of injecting Serb sperm into the lineage. By making 'biological identity' central to the jurisprudence, the ICTY has reproduced problematic and heavily contested notions around the meaning of gender, the nation, ethnicity and culture as heavily informed by essentialist constructions. Moreover, in using critique as her methodology for contesting ICTY jurisprudence, Engle has reiterated the importance of such a strategy for a feminist concern as topical as wartime sexual violence. Her contribution lies in not shying away from destabilising the normative and stable woman subject that 'governance feminism' most would like to utilise as part of its advocacy efforts. Elsewhere, Engle has critiqued 'structural feminism' for its reproduction of the binary divisions in international law, whether through its focus on the family as the main site of female oppression or on cultural rituals such as female genital mutilation, which she believes is responsible for the theory's 'ultimate demise'.[93]

Engle's analysis has provided an 'elsewhere' to the dominant gender subjectivities and wartime narratives created in international law by interrogating the powers that go into producing these 'sexed' identities. In so doing, she has provided a counterpoint argument, a different insight and perspective to much of the current debate informing feminist legal theory and activism around the issue of sexual violence. She has queried whether the perceived legal victory achieved by feminist activism by way of the criminalisation of sexual violence has been desirable for a broader understanding of gendered identity in wartime, or whether such a trend has in fact produced unintended consequences that have not resulted in gender justice, or gender equality as the twin feminist paradigms in much of the current debate around this issue. Moreover, Engle's insight has pointed out the legal modalities underlying the perpetuation of dichotomised gendered stereotypes in ICTY wartime sexual violence jurisprudence, therefore demonstrating that international law more often recreates problematic binaries and an axis of subordination based on sex. Despite the invaluable insights provided, the book believes that Engle's critique remains within the liberal paradigm, which posits female autonomy and normativity as central to female subjectivity.

Although she complicates the idea of the unified female subject in international law through her willingness to use critique as a place from which to destabilise the normative aims of feminist theory and activism, her analysis makes little room for analytical axes other than feminism. In her desire to promote female agency, by, for example, showing that women might indeed be involved at the heart of political and military power in times of war, Engle has utilised agency as a way of arguing for a different gendered subjectivity to the one constructed in much of the dominant feminist scholarship. However, the insistence on female agency as a lens for understanding women's roles in wartime can itself be rather reductive, as it still fails to answer how the underlying structural, systemic, socio-economic and societal dimensions in a pre-conflict sphere contribute to the outbreak of sexual violence in wartime. Although the focus on female agency to a certain extent subverts and contests the male dominance of the law, it does not explain why conflict is construed as 'ethnic' in nature, why sexual violence is institutionalised, or why the 'international community' decided to establish the ICTY. This approach does little to engage with the socio-political dimensions underlying conflict, which this book believes is central to reaching an understanding of how gendered and ethnicised identities come into being in the resulting jurisprudence.

Moreover, autonomy as a concept is heavily rooted in classical liberal notions of autonomy, which in themselves are contested. As Wendy Brown has argued in relation to the depoliticising discourse of liberalism, its 'most profound achievement' is in its 'excessive freighting of the individual subject with self-making, agency and a relentless responsibility for itself' supplemented with the important ideological 'reduction of freedom to rights, and equality to equal standing before the law'.[94] The emphasis on female agency and rights might create the illusion that deep social problems are (fully) redressable through individual legal litigation, as they are, in essence, matters of 'remarks, attitudes, and speech'.[95] Engle's focus on agency and choice somewhat runs the risk of eclipsing the possibility of conceptualising political agency in different terms. Her approach, moreover, works within the dominant institutional mechanisms of international criminal justice without fully questioning the power dimensions that underlie them. In a way, while Engle's critique is, undoubtedly powerful and highly relevant, it remains located within a liberal discourse.

Part IX

Questioning the limits of seeing gender through an ethnic lens

Another powerful voice countering much of the mainstream feminist discourses around the Yugoslav conflict has been that of Doris Buss, who has gone further than Engle in problematising the notion of conflict being ethnic by arguing that this has had a 'distorted' and 'reductive' effect on producing and understanding conflict as the complex effect of political, economic and geo-political change that played a significant role in creating the conditions for the wars in the Yugoslavia.[96] Her main contribution lies in showcasing, through various nuanced analyses of key ICTY cases, the legal modalities by which wartime sexual violence jurisprudence has become visible in the emerging international criminal justice system largely through the attention placed on ethnicity as a key meta-narrative within which sexual violence against women materialises.[97]

Buss has queried the limits of seeing women and their gender-specific abuses within the framework of international criminal tribunals. Moreover, she has gone further than other feminist observers of the ICTY in viewing the 'hypervisible' treatment of women in international law as a consequence of a new context in which 'international liberal legality' reigns supreme. She has, therefore, located the fault line of international criminal justice in its ambition to compartmentalise identity categories, such as that of the victim and perpetrator, into neat legal boxes which insist on heteronormativity as their defining standard. The critique is invaluable as it raises concerns about what is 'lost' or 'unseen' when ethnicity becomes unquestionably the explanatory framework within which these conflicts are understood.[98] Elsewhere, Buss has described the difficult questions posed by the feminist movement as to the strategies to be used in mobilising international legal attention on the mass rape of women. The question was whether to showcase the intersecting forms of oppression against women in order to draw attention to their fate in wartime, or whether to dispense with an intersectional analysis in favour of preventing the destabilisation of female subjectivity in international law.[99] Buss' work has focused on the way in which gendered and ethnicised subjectivities intersect in both ICTY and ICTR jurisprudence. This is briefly elaborated upon in the case law analysis below in order to complicate the legal modalities deployed by the ICTY in its approach to wartime identities.

The Prosecutor v. Radislav Krstić *case and notions of Bosnian Muslim patriarchy*

The Prosecutor v. Radislav Krstic case arose out of the circumstances related to the fall of the Srebrenica enclave to the Bosnian-Serb army on 13 July 1995. Krstic was the Chief of Staff/Deputy Commander of the Drina Corps of the Bosnian Serb Army (VRS) and he was accused of having aided and abetted in the genocidal attack against the Bosnian Muslim civilian population of the United Nations–protected Srebrenica, as well as having aided and abetted murder as a violation of the laws or customs of war; aided and abetted extermination; and aided and abetted persecutions on political, racial and religious grounds as crimes against humanity.[100] Krstic was accused of having had knowledge of the genocidal intent of some of the members of the VRS Main Staff. He was allegedly aware that the Main Staff had insufficient resources of its own to carry out the executions and that, without the use of the Drina Corps resources, the Main Staff would not be able to implement its genocidal plan. Moreover, he knew that by allowing the Drina Corps resources to be used he was making a substantial contribution to the execution of Bosnian Muslim prisoners. According to the facts of the case, between 13 and 19 July 1995, 7,000 to 8,000 Bosnian Muslim men were systematically murdered in mass executions, with the remainder of the Bosnian Muslim population approximating 25,000 women, children and the elderly being forcibly transferred out of the enclave.

There were also numerous reports of rapes committed in Potocari, a nearby town which was described as having been taken over by a 'campaign of terror' causing grave civilian suffering, which was said to have been aggravated for the women of the town, who had to witness the forceful removal of their young sons, who had been 'dragged away, never to be seen again'.[101] Moreover, U.N. peacekeepers (UNPROFOR) had observed the rape by two Serb soldiers of a young Bosnian Muslim woman. Other witnesses, including Bosnian refugees, were reported as having witnessed the rape, but had been unable to do anything about it because of Serbian soldiers standing by.[102] Amid the panorama of systematic violence directed against the civilian population of Potocari culminating in the atrocious acts committed at Srebrenica, the Trial Chamber used highly evocative language to illustrate the trajectory of events. The judges created a sense of Muslim Bosnia through the images of conservatism, traditionalism and remote villages, against which the 'moral map' of the Bosnian Muslim woman was subsequently drawn.[103] In one such passage they described 'patriarchal Bosnia' in the following way:

> In a patriarchal society, such as the one in which Bosnian Muslims of Srebrenica lived, the elimination of virtually all that men had made it impossible for the Bosnian Muslim women who survived the takeover Srebrenica to successfully re-establish their lives. Often, as in the case of witness DD, the women had been forced to live in collective and makeshift accommodations for many years, with a dramatically reduced standard of living.[104]

A further passage similarly evokes the strong sensation of patriarchy as inherent in Bosnian Muslim society and therefore a key cultural factor lying at the heart of the sexual violence attacks against women:

> It was common knowledge that the Bosnian Muslims of the Eastern Bosnia constituted a patriarchal society in which men had more education, training and provide material support for the family.[105]

Apart from producing a strong binary between female and male roles in prewar Bosnian society, the two passages highlighted carry strongly 'Orientalist' undertones, which locate the cause of violence in culture. This interpretation is curiously reminiscent of structural feminist interpretations of the conflict and its gendered identities, and speaks to the trend in much of late liberal discourse of depoliticising issues such as inequality, subordination and social conflict as personal and individual on the one hand, and as neutral, religious and cultural on the other.[106] Moreover, as is illustrated in the subsequent passage, the impact of the violence is closely associated with the cultural construction of gendered identities in the tribunal's reasoning suggesting that the impact of the violence might somehow be different because of the ethnic background of the victims:

> Furthermore, Bosnian Serb forces had to be aware of the catastrophic impact that the disappearance of two or three generations of men would have on the survival of the traditionally patriarchal society. . . . Intent by the Bosnian Serb forces to target the Bosnian Muslims of Srebrenica as a group is further evidenced by their destroying homes of Bosnian Muslims in Srebrenica and Potocari and the principal mosque in Srebrenica soon after the attack.[107]

The impression created here is of the intent of the perpetrators being driven entirely by ethnic motivations, which are construed as central to the offence. In this way, the court marginalises any sense of the violence as injurious of individual autonomy. The overdetermination of gender and ethnicity has been strongly criticised by Buss, who has argued that the tribunal has deployed a reductivist understanding of the Bosnian Muslim women of Srebrenica, who were constructed as the 'biological reproducers of the community'.[108] Moreover, in its stereotyping of Bosnian Muslim women, it has come dangerously close to treating women as a 'special needs' category to men, reinforcing the marginalisation of women from international law in a very predictable way. Not only are the women in the passages highlighted variously described as mothers and wives in need of protection, they are inevitably construed as the victims of this conflict, produced by colonial narratives that are as present here as in past discourses on wartime sexual violence jurisprudence.[109]

The intersectional analysis produced by Buss has been useful in highlighting the legal modalities by which gender and ethnicity are made to collide in ICTY wartime sexual violence jurisprudence and thereby occlude the deep-rooted, structural factors of armed conflict. However, as argued in chapter 4, an intersectional framework for understanding the gendered identity in armed conflict might not be sufficient to meet the complexities inherent in such situations.[110] In spite of the significant impact of intersectionality in the human rights arena, there are significant limitations to such a framework.[111] Given its insufficient emphasis on the broader, structural dimensions, intersectionality has been challenged on the basis that it fragments both subjectivity and the forces that produce it. Recent feminist theorising in particular has suggested that intersectionality discourses have run their course, as they lack pertinent political effect. As Joanne Conaghan has put it:

> Even within the context of a focus on subjectivity, current feminist theoretical models do not deliver because they fail to produce an effective agent of political change. Indeed, the absence of sustained historical engagement in much contemporary theorising makes the idea of change conceptually problematic; in a sense there is only the present to be confronted and only what is before us to map and represent.[112]

While intersectional analyses of modern-day wartime sexual violence jurisprudence have been indispensable for purposes of this book and have significantly increased its understanding of the margins and fault lines of inequality regimes, they have not sufficiently interrogated and challenged identity categories and their social positions as effects of power. While Doris Buss has urged a greater inquiry into the structural dimensions underlying gender-based violence and more attention to the way in which social categories, such as ethnicity, are produced by surrounding discourses and the powers that sustain them, this book suggests that feminist investments with the law in the current political and legal moment might not be the best way forward in the pursuit of gender justice and equality. The idea is that law should perhaps not be the starting point on an inequality analysis, and that disciplines outside of the law might provide fresh new insights.

Part X

The value of non-feminist critiques

This book has been informed by the idea that feminism might not have unique epistemic purchase on women's condition. Janet Halley has made a strong case for such a possibility in the context of sexuality.[113] Her underlying argument is that 'no one theory, no one political engagement, is nearly as valuable as the invitation to critique that is issued by the simultaneous incommensurable presence of many theories'. More specifically, she has asked:

> [w]hether "our" engagement with erotic, sexual and gender politics would be better off – whether feminism might be better off – if we left ourselves some room to imagine erotic, sexual, and gendered life under terms that some would think, or even that everyone would think, to "Take a Break from Feminism?".

The feminism Halley advocates taking a break from is 'governance feminism': a feminism that 'rules' and 'wants to rule',[114] even if this is 'power masquerading as servitude'.[115] She has shown this in her discussion of feminist power exercised in global and local governance, which is often pursued through 'informal, opaque, ideologically committed NGOs that strategise hard and sometimes with success to render themselves indispensable when major new fluidities in formal power emerge.'[116] Largely through concerted activism and NGO initiatives, feminist power has infiltrated international criminal legal processes but, as argued previously, without necessarily producing uniformly positive results for women.

By way of reminder, at the heart of governance feminism is its preoccupation with a subordination theory: 'a distinction between something m and something f, a commitment to be a theory, and a practice about the subordination of f to m; and a commitment to work against the subordination of f'.[117] This encompasses a range of liberal, radical, cultural and other feminisms, and is encompassed by Brown's term 'feminist foundationalism'. Although, as noted, Halley's views are distinctly American in outlook, the type of feminism she deplores has, undoubtedly, become the most influential globally, and hence her critique is of wider relevance. Although she admits that not all feminist varieties are resolvable into her formula of 'governance feminism', preoccupied with the subordination of women to men, her argument is nonetheless indispensable to the critique pursued by this book to the extent that it 1) criticises dominant modalities of feminism, and 2) introduces the idea of taking decisions in the split between theories. This is a form of contrapuntal strategy that attunes well to the present analysis. Attention to this type of argument may promote a more complex and insightful feminist analysis, as well as make room for other discourses which may provide refreshingly new insights pertaining to the questions that feminists engage with.

Halley has asked whether the new civilising modes of feminism could be analogous to adult behaviour on the playground running to the rescue of the little girl, who stumbles, falls and scrapes her knee.[118] At first, the girl is still and composed while waiting for the dizziness and surprise of the experience to subside. But up rushes the adult, overindulging in sympathy and urgently concerned about whether her leg might be broken. The adult exclaims: 'Has she broken her leg? Is she bleeding? How did it happen? We must not let it happen again! Poor thing!' For the first time, and prompted by the adult screams, the little girl experiences fear and begins to cry.

The adult behaviour in the playground serves as a rather powerful metaphor speaking to feminism's commitment to identifying itself with female injury. To represent women as 'end points of pain' and to imagine them as lacking the agency to cause harm to others and particularly harm to men (as the invisibility of male sexual injury in wartime sexual violence jurisprudence suggests) is problematic. It is problematic because feminists 'refuse' to see women, even injured ones, as powerful actors. It is therefore feminism itself that objectifies women and erases their agency by unintentionally intensifying their pain.

To be sure, there are pitfalls to 'taking the kind of break' suggested by Halley. There are always 'costs'[119] associated with this endeavour. These include the possibility that the epistemic vigilance needed to resist 'male epistemic hegemony' could be relaxed and that in this way further splits among feminists about their conceptual location would ensue. This in turn could risk new fissures in the intellectual, social political and legal endeavour, which could demobilise and demoralise feminists and lay them open to co-optation by those who oppose women's well-being. As Halley puts it rather powerfully:

> If, for instance, feminism is our best weapon against the constant pressure of male sexual violence, weakening feminism in any of these ways could actually result in some guy's decision to rape a woman he could otherwise leave unmolested, or some prosecutor's willingness to see reasonable doubt in a rape case that would otherwise have seemed a clear prosecutorial priority.[120]

Halley concedes that these anxieties are valid, but nonetheless believes that a 'break from feminism' is a risk worth taking. It is a danger worth confronting because feminist 'paranoid structuralism' and 'convergentism' in their normative or political priority of carrying a brief for f have produced undesirable results, chief amongst them their inability to see around the corner of their own construction. Unless it 'takes a break' from itself, feminism won't be able to see injury to men; it won't be able to see injury inflicted on men by women, and most significantly from the point of view of this book, it won't see other interests, other forms of power, other justice projects.

Part XI

Conclusion

This chapter has provided the second limb in the bridge between the discussion of gender-based violence and wartime sexual violence jurisprudence as subjects of legal analysis overviewed in chapters 2, 3 and 4, and their more critical inquiry pursued in chapters 5 and 6. It has explained and crystallised the constitutive elements of the analytical approach adopted in the book, most important of which has been to reassert the value of critique as a feminist method. It has addressed the problem of the perceived crises of normativity and subjectivity informing much of the debate in current feminist scholarship by arguing that the absence of a unified subject need not block certain feminist pursuits.

A contrapuntal strategy has helped to clarify the narrative of the book by adding perspective to the existing debate, and by arguing that wartime sexual violence jurisprudence of its own cannot deliver the twin normative feminist aims of gender justice and equality, or reflect in full the gendered experience of wartime. The book has argued that Western liberal notions of autonomy and choice interpreted through an ethnic lens have come to firmly frame the views and arguments of both the proponents and opponents of the rape-as-genocide versus the all-women-as-victims debate. In this way, it has exposed the limitations of the autonomy/choice/ethnicity framework, which has been treated as an ideological given, existing prior to the female self.

Two salient trends in ICTY wartime sexual violence jurisprudence have been highlighted: the reading of gender identity through an ethnic lens, and the portrayal of women as victims, wives or mothers. As has been noted in chapters 1 and 2, these two trends form the 'feminist' core of the debate. The chapter then focused on demonstrating the intersection of gender and ethnicity in key ICTY decisions by showing that dominant feminist readings of wartime identities produced a problematic narrative of gendered identity in wartime. To this end, this part of the chapter provided an account of the rhetoric of female victimhood as tied to ethnic identity, as it shone through the judgements and the dominant feminist discourses surrounding it. In part VIII, the chapter then turned to the opponents of these interpretations of female victimhood and of the idea that the Yugoslav conflict was in essence a 'war against women', highlighting how these as well are more often than not articulated within the same conceptual framework. Part IX finally took a step back in order to consider the limitations of the currently prevailing preoccupation with the intersection of gender and ethnicity, as well as notions of autonomy and consent.

The aim of the chapter has been to visibilise women's agency in armed conflict by identifying marginalised female subjectivities that have not formed part of the dominant narrative around the Yugoslav conflict, and that might well tell another story of wartime, or provide an elsewhere to the dominant narratives. At the same time, the chapter has showcased that female agency, however unlikely under conditions of extreme coercion, was a reality in wartime Bosnia-Herzegovina, as the examples of female testimony drawn upon in the case law analysis have demonstrated. In this way, the analysis has gone against the grain of a majority of feminist texts on the Yugoslav war, as those have deployed highly essentialised and ethnicised readings of female identity in wartime, having conceived of Bosnian Muslim women in particular as victims of war. The chapter concluded by following Janet Halley's call for feminism to 'take a break' from itself, not as a way of diminishing its normative value, but in order to consider its own institutional investments with power and reassert its emancipatory purchase. Attention to this type of argument may promote a more complex and insightful feminist analysis, as well as make room for other discourses, which may provide refreshingly new insights into questions that feminists engage with. These insights would hopefully avoid falling into the trap of position-taking and steer clear of reducing war to a neatly delineated struggle between those 'have culture' and 'those whom culture has'.[121] Once it returns from its 'break', feminism will hopefully again contribute to a more imaginative and inclusive debate about female identity and power.

Notes

1 W. Brown, 'Untimeliness and Punctuality: Critical Theory in Dark Times', in W. Brown (ed), *Edgework: Critical Essays on Knowledge and Politics* (Princeton, NJ: Princeton University Press, 2005). See also W. Brown, 'Revaluing Critique: A Response to Kenneth Baynes', 28 *Political Theory* (2000), at 469; and Brown & Halley (2002).

2 4 See Brown (2001) for an in-depth exploration for what this reveals about our current political and intellectual condition.

3 Brown & Halley (2002), at 25.

4 Brown (2005), at 5.

5 Brown & Halley (2002), at 31.

6 Brown (2005), at 16.

7 N. Lacey, 'Theory Into Practice? Pornography and the Public/Private Dichotomy', 20 *Journal of Law and Society* (1993), at 93, reprinted in N. Lacey, *Unspeakable Subjects: Feminist Essays in Legal and Social Theory* (Oxford: Hart Publishing, 1998), at 71, 95.

8 The anti-pornography debate in North America is an example of this paradox. The 1980s mass-scale feminist anti-pornography campaign has led to a change in the law in the United States and Canada, which generally construes pornography as harm to women. But research has shown how this change had remarkably repressive repercussions, see e.g. M. Valverde, 'The Harms of Sex and the Risks of Breasts: Obscenity and Indecency in Canadian Law', 8 *Social & Legal Studies*

(1999), at 181. More recent liberal/feminist debates around issues of trafficking, particularly on whether prostitution should be included in anti-trafficking measures, have arguably further removed women from the ostensible goal of feminist liberation and empowerment. Radical feminists have contested the distinction between forced trafficking and prostitution, arguing in part that like trafficking, prostitution does not represent a choice, but constitutes economic and physical coercion. Radical feminists thus argue that anti-trafficking measures harm women because they are used to prevent the migration of women for purposes of labour, as well as to punish sex workers. For a discussion, see e.g. K. Engle, 'Liberal Internationalism, Feminism, and the Suppression of Critique: Contemporary Approaches to Global Order in the United States', 46 *Harvard International Law Journal* (2005), at 427, 436 citing K. Barry, *Female Sexual Slavery* (1979); C. MacKinnon, 'Prostitution and Civil Rights', 1 *Michigan Journal of Gender and Law* (1993), at 13–31.

9 Lacey (1998), at 97.

10 Ibid. In her other work, Lacey explains that she uses the term critique broadly to identify projects within legal theory which are specifically concerned to go beyond the superficial appearance of legal practices and discourses, and to question, unsettle, expose to careful scrutiny not only current laws and their organisation but also claims to authority and legitimacy which legal officials, law-makers and legal practices and theories implicitly express. (N. Lacey, 'Closure and Critique in Feminist Jurisprudence: Transcending the Dichotomy or a Foot in Both Camps?', in N. Lacey (ed.), *Unspeakable Subjects: Feminist Essays in Legal and Social Theory* (Oxford: Hart Publishing, 1998), at 167, 168). See also N. Lacey, 'Feminist Legal Theory and the Rights of Women', in K. Knop (ed.), *Gender and Human Rights* (Oxford: Oxford University Press, 2004), at 13, 42–47.

11 E.g. D. E. Chunn & D. Lacombe (eds.), *Law as a Gendering Practice* (Oxford: Oxford University Press, 2000).

12 V. E. Munro, 'On Power and Domination: Feminism and the Final Foucault', 2 *European Journal of Political Theory* (2003), at 79, 81, referring to C. Smart, *Feminism and the Power of Law* (London: Routledge, 1989); I. M. Young, *Justice and the Politics of Difference* (Princeton, NJ: Princeton University Press, 1990); J. Butler, *Gender Trouble: Feminism and the Subversion of Identity* (London: Routledge, 1993); and Butler (1993) as a range of disparate theories broadly falling within this Foucauldian category.

13 Brown (2002), at 556, 574. See also J. Butler, 'The Question of Social Transformation', in J. Butler, *Undoing Gender* (New York: Routledge, 2004). Butler argues that theory is itself transformative.

14 W. Brown, *Regulating Aversion: Tolerance in an Age of Identity and Empire* (Princeton, NJ: Princeton University Press, 2006), at 86.

15 Brown (1995), at 30, 39, citing C. Di Stefano, 'Dilemmas of Difference: Feminism, Modernity and Postmodernism', in L. Nicholson (ed.), *Feminism/Postmodernism* (New York: Routledge, 1990).

16 Brown (1995), at 42.

17 Di Stefano (1990), at 76, cited in Brown (1995), at 39. See also S. Benhabib, 'On Contemporary Feminist Theory', 36 *Dissent* (1989), at 369.

18 Mullaly (2006), at 20, citing S. Benhabib, *Situating the Self: Gender, Community and Postmodernism in Contemporary Ethics* (Cambridge: Polity Press, 1992), at 16.

19 Brown (1995), at 40. In her chapter 'Finding the man in the State' in *States of Injury* (1995), at 166, she employs a gendered analysis of liberalism, arguing that capturing the masculine subject as such is not necessary in order to detect masculine traits of the modern liberal state.

20 Ibid.
21 Brown (1995), at 40. 'They cannot be anointed as 'authentic' or 'true' since the experience they announce is linguistically contained, socially constructed, discursively mediated and never just individually "had"' (Original emphasis, Ibid at 40–41).
22 Brown, (2003), at 365, 367.
23 Ibid (emphasis added.) For an expanded version of this argument, see Brown (2002), at 568.
24 Otto (2006), at 318, 321.
25 Ibid at 320.
26 In the one instance in the ICTY, where sexual violence charges were initially put forward against a high-ranking female political leader, as in the case of *The Prosecutor v. Biljana Plavšic*, the charges of sexual violence were subsequently dropped in return for plea bargain. For an overview, see: *The Prosecutor v. Biljana Plavšic* (IT-00–39 & 40/1); (27 September 2003) (Sentencing Judgement).
27 Otto (2006), at 320–321.
28 *Prosecutor v. Kunarac* (IT-96–23-T & IT-96–23/1-T), Judgement, 22 February 2001. (hereinafter referred to as the *Kunarac* Trial Chamber Judgement). 877 For an in-depth discussion of the events leading to the violent overthrow and siege of Foca: see *The Prosecutor v. Gagovic* (IT-96–23-T), Indictment, 1 December 1999 & It-96–23/1-T, 3.
29 *Prosecutor v. Kunarac* (IT-96–23-T), Amended Indictment, 1 December 1999 & (IT-96–23/1-T), at 3 March 2000.
30 *Kunarac* Trial Chamber Judgement, at paras 35–36.
31 Ibid at para 37.
32 Another passage describing the transfer of some of the women from the detention camp to private residences reinforces the sense of female subjugation in the following way: 'Some of the women from Partizan and Kalinovik High School were at some point moved to different houses and apartments where they continued to be raped and mistreated. In particular, at "Karaman's house" in Miljevina, soldiers had easy access to women and girls whom they raped. FWS-75, FWS-87, A.S., FWS-132, FWS-190, D.B. and other women were kept in the house for some time. There, they were raped many times by many different soldiers. On 3 August, FWS-75, FWS-87, D.B. and FWS-190 were taken from Alad'a to Miljevina where they were handed to DP3, the man who appeared to be in charge of "Karaman's house"'. See: Kunarac Trial Chamber Judgement, at para 41.
33 For a more detailed account, see paras 53–60. During her two-month stay at the Karaman's private residence, the witness was continuously raped by Serb soldiers, alongside a number of other girls held inside the house. In addition to having to endure sexual violence on a daily basis, the women were also forced to undertake household chores, such as washing, cooking, laundering and cleaning. The emphasis on the witnesses' obligation to undertake household chores adds to their sense of their passivity for in this rendering they firmly occupy the most traditional of roles associated with female identity both in wartime, as well as in peacetime, the woman-as-mother identity 'protected' in this instance by the combatant, who here acts as the head of the household.
34 Ibid at para 68.
35 Ibid at para 79.
36 For a discussion see Lacey (1998), at 106.
37 Ibid.
38 Ibid at para 85.
39 Another instance, where one of the women witnesses seemingly engaged in consensual sexual relations with Dragoljub Kunarac, concerns a situation inside a private

residence in Ulica Osmana Dikica in the town of Alad'a, where the girls held were invited to take a shower and help themselves to clothes that were in the cupboard. Kunarac, who stayed in one of the adjoining rooms then testifies that one of the girls, D.B., soon joined him, taking the initiative to unbutton his clothes and kiss him leading them to eventually engage in sexual intercourse, which Kunarac testified as having been 'completely unexpected' for him. Ibid at para 133.

40 Kunarac's visit to the house followed his sighting of FWS-87 at a funeral, which prompted him to realise that she had not been returned to the Partizan sports hall, despite an earlier agreement to this effect. Kunarac's return to the town of Miljevina, the location of the Karaman house, followed on from his temporary recall back to central command in Kalinovik. Ibid at paras 135–140.

41 Ibid at para 140.

42 This point has also been made by Miranda Allison, who has argued that there is evidence from the Yugoslav conflict that at least some of the 'soldier-rapists' possessed a sense of guilt. Thus, according to testimonies of internees and rape survivors some Serbian soldiers in the detention camps took sedatives or stimulants to enable themselves, at least in the early days, to commit rape. Many others sought resolve or escape in alcohol, while some wept. See: M. Allison, 'Wartime Sexual Violence: Women's Human Rights and Questions of Masculinity', 33 *Review of International Studies* (2007), at 75–76.

43 The defence for Radomir Kovac first makes explicit reference to their 'romantic' relationship in paragraph 141 by refuting the witness's testimony regarding her stay in his house as marked by brutality and grave violence of a sexual nature, arguing instead that they were 'in love with each other' and that witness 'FWS-87' stayed with him out of her 'own free will'. Moreover the defence also contested the supposed lack of freedom of movement of the other girls held in captivity in the same house, claiming that they were free to move around as they wished, and that in relation to food 'they were no worse off than any other inhabitant of Foca'. What is more, the defence dismissed the claims of forced nude dancing as 'pure fantasy' and the allegation that witnesses FWS-87 and A.S. had been sold as not true, instead claiming, on the latter point, that Kovac had paid for their safe transfer to Montenegro. See *Kunarac* Trial Chamber Judgement, at para 141. The counterarguments of the defence thus significantly complicate the picture of female agency in the scenario presented by the Trial Chamber so far.

44 Witness D, for example, a cousin of the accused's father claimed that Kovac came to visit her with a girl, FWS-87, whom he introduced as his girlfriend at the end of November 1992. According to this witness, that evening FWS-87 behaved 'beautifully, wonderfully, nicely', 'like all of us' and danced. Other than seeing the witness on a number of other occasions with Kovac in the market, in the street and in cafés, she was also told by the accused that he had received a letter from her in which she expressed his gratitude towards him. However, the witness conceded that she had never actually physically seen the letter. Ibid at para 145.

45 Another witness, DI, a saleswoman who knew Kovac from before the war, states that judging from the girl's behaviour on a number of occasions it was obvious that the two were a couple, an impression that was reinforced when she saw witness FWS-87 carrying shopping bags to his apartment a number of times. Ibid at para 146. Another witness, DV, a nurse who worked in Kovac's unit stated that witness FWS-87 had been introduced to her by Kovac as his girlfriend, had seen the girl enter and leave his apartment, and had observed that the two were leading a 'good' relationship. Ibid at para 147.

46 The subsequent discovery of FWS-87's religious identity subsequently prompted embarrassment, as she states that previously she did not know the girl was Muslim. The same witness goes on to say that she saw FWS-87 again on several occasions in the street, at the market or in cafés recalling in particular that she had seen the girl with two other girls in the Café Leonardo, one of the local bars in

which Bosnian-Serb military and paramilitary personnel would congregate. Ibid at para 145.

47 This is corroborated by further testimony from witness DI, a saleswoman who knew Kovac from before the war, and DK, a cousin of the accused who worked as an investigator for the defence team and was also said to have been present during that encounter. According to witness DI, the behaviour of the couple clearly suggested that they were a couple, in fact leaving no doubt in her kind that this was the case. However, it ought to be stated that the witness did not talk to Kovac or the girl on this occasion. Ibid at para 146.

48 She saw FWS-87 on a number of other occasions such as at the Café Leonardo, where she was accompanied by other girls, who were introduced to witness DV. Ibid at para 147.

49 Ibid at para 149.

50 The witness went on to describe that Kovac behaved very 'nicely' to the girls. On another occasion, they finally talked about the girl, prompting the witness to inquire whether it was 'normal' to have that kind of girlfriend, meaning a Muslim girlfriend, to which he answered that it was his 'own business'. Subsequently, the witness saw the girls on another 15–20 occasions, either in the presence of the accused, sometimes on their own, sometimes in his company. In particular, she recalls seeing him with the girl on orthodox New Year's Eve (13 January) 1993, where he was seen dancing with the girl. As the witness remarks, at all times Kovac seemed to have paid particular attention to them so that no one would bother them, suggesting further a relationship of intimacy and affection. From the end of 1992, he continued to see witness FWS-87, but not the other girl, suggesting that this was a more serious relationship. Ibid at para 149.

51 For a typical 'culturalised' feminist account of female identity in wartime Bosnia-Herzegovina, see: L. Boose, 'Crossing the River Drina: Bosnian Rape Camps, Turkish Impalement, and Serb Cultural Memory', 28 *Signs: Journal of Women in Culture and Society* (2002), at 71. See also: A. K. Wing & S. Merchant, 'Rape, Ethnicity, and Culture: Spirit Injury from Bosnia to America', 25 *Columbia Human Rights Law Review* (1993–1994), at 1.

52 Ibid at para 150.

53 See *Kunarac* (IT-96–23-T/1-T), Trial Chamber Judgement, 22 February 2001, at para 188.

54 Ibid at para 206.

55 Ibid at para 210.

56 Ibid at para 214.

57 As Janet Halley has previously pointed out in her critique of feminist advocacy surrounding the establishment of international criminal tribunals and the prosecution of gender-based violence, structuralist feminist ideas have reconceptualised '[w]ar not as an event, but as a situation, as the life of everyday'. In this vein, it made sense for a 'feminist universalism' to look at the eruption of 'ethno-nationalist' conflicts in the Balkans as a 'war against women', and it made 'ever more sense' to talk about the war without any acknowledgment that men died in it. In Halley (2008–2009), at 7.

58 Early on, many in the 'genocidal camp', including MacKinnon, contended rapes by Serbian men of Croatian and Bosnian Muslim women constituted genocide, but later, as Croatia became an aggressor in the war, the focus shifted to the rape of Bosnian Muslims.

59 See e.g. MacKinnon (1983), at 635, 647.

60 See MacKinnon (1994), at 183, 190.

61 Ibid at 189–190.

62 MacKinnon (1994), at 73.

63 See e.g. Diane Conklin, who argued that 'Replicated in the tens of thousands, the act of mass scale rape is genocide . . .'. In D. Conklin, 'Special Note to Breaking

the Wall of Silence: The Voices of Raped Bosnia', 99 *American Journal of International Law* (1996).

64 Askin (1997), at 257–269 (quoting Wing & Merchan (1993), at 1, 5 (emphasis added).

65 Engle (2005), at 778, 792.

66 R. Copelon, 'Gender Crimes as War Crimes: Integrating Crimes against Women into International Law', 46 *McGill Law Journal* (2000), at 239.

67 In R. Copelon, 'Surfacing Gender: Reconceptualizing Crimes against Women in Time of war', in A. Stiglmayer (ed.), *"The Rapes in Bosnia-Herzegovina" in Mass Rape: The War against Women in Bosnia-Herzegovina* (Lincoln, NA: University of Nebraska Press, 1994), at 197–198.

68 Ibid at 198.

69 In 1994, Copelon was particularly disillusioned with '[t]he complete failure of the United Nations and the international community in general to recognize that persecution based on gender must be recognized as its own category of crimes against humanity'. Ibid at 206–208.

70 *The Prosecutor v. Zejnil Delalic*, Zdravko Mucic (The Prosecutor v. Delalic et al.), (IT-96–21-T) (hereafter referred to as *Celebici* case), Trial Chamber Judgement, 16 November 1998, at para 33.

71 It is interesting to note that the Trial Chamber acknowledges in its summary of the demographic proclivities that the mix of ethnicities in Konjic lived together 'harmoniously' and in an 'integrated fashion' until the escalation of tension and outbreak of hostilities in 1992. Ibid at para 121.

72 *Celebici* Indictment at para 2.

73 *Celebici* Trial Chamber Judgement, at para 929.

74 Ibid at para 932.

75 The witness testimony was based on a graphic account of the violence perpetrated against her. The Trial Chamber describes the coercion compounding the violence in the following way: 'Upon her arrival at the prison-camp, she was taken by a driver, Mr. Džajic, to a room where a man with a crutch was waiting, whom she subsequently identified as Hazim Delic. Another man subsequently entered the room. Ms. Cecez was interrogated by Mr. Delic, who asked her about the whereabouts of her husband and slapped her. She was then taken to a second room with three men including Mr. Delic. Hazim Delic who was in uniform and carrying a stick, then ordered her to take her clothes off. He then partially undressed her, put her face down on the bed and penetrated her vagina with his penis. During this time, Mr. Džajic was lying on another bed in the same room and the other man was present standing guard at the door of the room. In *Celebici* Trial Chamber Judgement, at para 937.

76 Ibid at para 938.

77 Ibid.

78 In fact the only reference to the sexual violence being potentially ethnically motivated is made in the Trial Chamber's allusion to the testimony of witness T, who testified that Hazim Delic had boasted to him that he had raped 18 Serb women, and that it was his intention to rape more in the future. See *Celebici* Trial Chamber Judgement, at para 928.

79 Ibid at paras 941.

80 The Trial Chamber stressed the intentionality of the act committed by Hazim Delic, who was the official running the prison camp. Ibid at para 940.

81 See *Celebici* Trial Chamber Judgement, at para 941.

82 MacKinnon (1999), at 184.

83 K. Engle, *Feminism and Its Discontents* (2005), at 778–779.

84 Ibid at 780.

85 Engle describes that in the early investigations of the war in Bosnia-Herzegovina journalists alongside mental health workers and legal advocates sought to find 'raped women' who would speak with them. In a rather ironic reversal of roles, it was often women and girls who denied having been raped that were not believed. This trend stands in stark contrast to the past, where rape victims had long encountered the difficulty of being believed. As Engle puts it, 'At some level, all Bosnian Muslim women were imagined to have been raped.' Ibid at 794.

86 Ibid at 795.

87 Ibid at 798.

88 Ibid at 803.

89 In *Prosecutor v. Kunarac* (IT-96–23&IT-96–23/1), (hereinafter *Kunarac* Appeals Chamber), at paras 129–133 (original emphasis).

90 In fact, as Engle points out, the Appeals Chamber uses the fact that women were detained in 'de facto military headquarters, detention centres and apartments maintained as soldiers' residences' to conclude that they 'amount[ed] to circumstances that were so coercive as to negate any possibility of consent'. This leads Engle to conclude that by presuming coercion, the ICTY's sexual violence jurisprudence makes consensual relationships 'legally impossible' in some sets of circumstances like the one found in Foca. Ibid at 804.

91 Ibid at 806.

92 Ibid at 807.

93 In Engle (2005), at 53.

94 Brown (2006), at 17; see also Brown (1995) and Brown (2001).

95 W. Brown, 'Symptoms: Moralism as Anti-Politics' in Brown (2001), at 40.

96 Buss, (2007), at 6.

97 As she has put it, the increased visibility of wartime sexual violence has occurred against a strict backdrop of 'strictly ethnic' dimensions to the conflict, directly interwoven into the Tribunal's jurisprudence. Yet the intersection of gender and ethnicity in the Tribunal's jurisprudence reveal some of the mechanisms through which sexual violence and gender become visible, but only superficially so. As she reasons, the focus on gender in the context of an overdetermined assessment of ethnic conflict becomes a means for '[o]ccluding rather than opening up the complex dimensions of violence against women'. Ibid at 3.

98 Ibid at 6.

99 As Buss points out, the question engaging feminist scholars at the time of the Yugoslav conflict was whether to advocate '[a] complex picture of wartime rape in which the violence done to women was systemic, structural, but at the same time shaped by the 'peculiar situation of armed conflict'. In D. Buss, 'Sexual Violence, Ethnicity and Intersectionality in International Criminal Law', in E. Grabham et al. (eds.), *Intersectionality and Beyond* (London: Routledge-Cavendish, 2009), at 109.

100 For a summary of the facts see: ICTY Case Information Sheet (IT-98–33) "Srebrenica-Drina Corps". Radislav Krstic. 'Summary'. Available at: www.icty.org/x/cases/krstic/cis/en/cis_krstic_en.pdf (last accessed in March 2011).

101 *The Prosecutor v. Radislav Krstic* (IT-98–33-T), Trial Chamber Judgement, 2 August 2001, at para 517.

102 Much like the pattern in other cases already examined, the rapes would be preceded by a separation of military-aged men from the women, children and the elderly, who were transported to the nearby town of Bratunac. After being detained in Bratunac for between one and three days, the prisoners were transported elsewhere as the buses to transfer the women, children and elderly became available. Subsequently, 'thousands' of Bosnian Muslim prisoners were executed with some being killed individually or in small groups by the soldiers who captured them and some were killed in places where they were temporarily detained. Most,

however, as the Trial Chamber describes it were 'slaughtered' in 'carefully orchestrated mass executions' commencing on 13 July 1995 in the region just north of Srebrenica. Prisoners who had not been killed on 13 July 1995 were subsequently bussed to execution sites further north of Bratunac, within the zone of responsibility of the VRS Zvornik Brigade, with the larger-scale executions taking place between 14 and 17 July 1995. Available at: ICTY Case Information Sheet (IT-98–33) "Srebrenica-Drina Corps", Radislav Krstic. Available at: www.icty.org/x/cases/krstic/cis/en/cis_krstic_en.pdf. See also: *The Prosecutor v. Radislav Krstic* (IT-98–33-T), Trial Chamber Judgement, 2 August 2001, at para 46.

103 For a more extensive discussion of the way in which the Balkans as a region has been reproduced in academic literature, see: Todorova, Imagining the Balkans (2009).

104 *The Prosecutor v. Radislav Krstic* (IT-98–33-T), Trial Chamber Judgement, at para 91.

105 Ibid at para 592.

106 As Wendy Brown has shown, modern liberal discourses produce a dichotomy between culture as saturating and defining non-Western people and moral autonomy as informing the rational subject of liberalism, for whom culture is a mere choice. In liberal ideology the former is uniquely capable of being 'culturally neutral and culturally tolerant', while the latter is entirely subsumed by cultural notions. For liberal individualists in the West, culture is, thus, optional, while for non-Western, non-liberal people (including ethnic and religious minorities within liberal societies), culture is not only fixed and static, but also 'saturating and authoritative'. In Brown (2006), at 151–154.

107 *The Prosecutor v. Radislav Krstic* (IT-98–33-T), Trial Chamber Judgement, at para 595.

108 Buss (2007), at 15.

109 See Zarkov (1995), at 105.

110 Intersectionality has been described as 'signifying the complex, irreducible, varied, and variable effects which ensue when multiple axes of differentiation – economic, political, cultural, psychic, subjective and experiential – intersect in historically specific contexts'. In A. Brah & A. Phoenix, 'Ain't I a Woman? Revisiting Intersectionality', 5 *Journal of International Women's Studies* (2004), at 76.

111 In the current moment, U.N. Human Rights Committees and Special Rapporteurs explicitly use intersectionality as a framework for dealing with gender issues. The concept is particularly prominent in the work of former Special Rapporteur on Violence against Women, Professor Yakin Ertürk. Examples include U.N. Commission on Human Rights, 'Towards an effective implementation of international norms to end violence against women' (2004), Report of Special Rapporteur on violence against women, its causes and consequences', Yakin Ertürk, E/CN.4/2004/66, 26 December 2003; and U.N. Commission on Human Rights, 'Intersections on violence against women and HIV/AIDS' (2005), Report of the Special Rapporteur on violence against women, its causes and consequence, Yakin Ertürk, E/CN.4/2005/72, 17 January 2005.

112 Conaghan (2009), at 40.

113 Halley (2006). See also Halley (2004), at 57; B. Cossman, D. Danielsen, J. Halley & T. Higgins, 'Gender, Sexuality and Power: Is Feminist Theory Enough?', 12 *Columbia Journal of Gender and Law* (2003), at 601.

114 Halley (2006), at 22.

115 Halley (2003), at 608.

116 Ibid at 21.

117 Halley (2006), at 4–5.

118 In Halley (2006), at 346.

119 Halley (2004), at 64.

120 Ibid at 66.

121 Brown (2005), at 20–21.

7 Conclusion

The book is a critical feminist analysis of ICTY wartime sexual violence jurisprudence as it is constructed in contemporary feminist legal scholarship and the surrounding debate. Today, wartime sexual violence is an endemic phenomenon that disproportionately affects women. In the Yugoslav context, sexual violence has firmly come to frame gendered and ethnic identity, with the figure of the raped woman having turned into the metaphor for the conflict. The ubiquity of sexual violence in the conflict has provoked some strong regulatory responses, as well as much controversy about how to interpret the act – as violence directed exclusively against women because they are women, or as a group harm targeting an ethnic identity? The book has explored how the debate around wartime sexual violence is currently conducted and what implications this might have for a critical feminist engagement with the issue. It has asked: what is wartime sexual violence jurisprudence considered to represent for women in the current historical and political moment?

In brief, the answer depends on whether one conceives of wartime sexual violence through a structuralist lens and therefore as an act of male domination or whether violence against women is understood through a socio-economic context, where the manifestation of violence is the result of female poverty and lack of opportunity. For proponents of the culturalised, structuralist view of gender-based violence, the act signifies a blatant lack of autonomy and the near total oppression of women. Opponents of this view, in contrast, consider female agency possible and believe that even in a situation as coercive as wartime, women's emancipation and empowerment are possible. In both cases, there is a characteristically 'feminist' set of frames at play: the preoccupation with women's autonomy and choice and the normative imperative of gender equality and justice. Rather than taking a position for or against either of these positions, the author has made the case for interrogating these frames.

It has done so by using the methodological idea of counterpoint, which is an analytical technique, characterised by an anti-hegemonic sensibility and a deliberate practice of multiplicity and juxtaposition. In this way, the book has presented an elsewhere to the currently prevailing positions. Rather than being objective and/or comprehensive, it has aimed to offer perspective. After giving some preliminary background, it proceeded to an overview of the evolution of gender-based violence as a subject of international human rights law. Chapter 2 charted how the term 'gender' replaced 'the woman' in human rights discourses; it documented the struggle faced by feminist activists in incorporating gender-specific terminology into the Rome Statute and it overviewed the salient human rights provisions and declarations which have helped make gender-based violence visible as a subject of international law. At the same time, it adopted a critical angle in relation to the use of gender mainstreaming policies and illustrated some feminist concerns in this regard. This discussion was intended as a general sense of the debate. Chapter 3 carried forth in this vein by mapping out the trajectory of wartime sexual violence traditionally seen as a historical footnote to its recognition today as a core violation of international criminal law. It also introduced a feminist critique of international humanitarian law, while primarily focusing on the key legal developments in ICTY and ICTR wartime sexual violence jurisprudence that have contributed to the sense of 'success' accomplished by the tribunals in this area. Chapter 4 was a largely 'ground-clearing' exercise as it overviewed various feminist approaches to human rights, gender, ethnicity, culture and armed conflict in order to highlight their advantages and disadvantages from the point of view of engaging with an issue such as wartime sexual violence. The types of approaches overviewed were liberal and universalist feminism, radical and 'governmentality feminism', poststructural and postcolonial feminism and intersectionality feminism. The chapter emphasised the value and contribution of non-feminist discourses, which constituted a vital element of the analysis pursued throughout the book.

Chapters 5 and 6 were the crux of the book, as it was there that the critical feminist analysis of the wartime sexual violence debate was crystallised. Chapter 5 provided an in-depth legal analysis of the landmark cases adjudicated to date in the Yugoslav Tribunal, interjected with a brief historical background to the events and patterns of wartime sexual violence that have defined the Yugoslav conflict in the popular imagination. In this way, it has highlighted the legal modalities through which gender became closely intertwined with notions of ethnicity. The chapter argued that dominant gender stereotypes continue to persist in international law partly because of the strong structuralist feminist tendencies permeating the tribunal's legal reasoning and partly because of the ICTY's failure to interrogate the ontological essence of the Yugoslav conflict. Finally, Chapter 6 crystallised the critical feminist approach adopted in the book. It did so by explaining the constitutive elements of this approach. The first element was the value of critique as a feminist method. Second, the chapter addressed the perceived crisis of feminist subjectivity and normativity by arguing that they are not in crisis. Third, the chapter explained that the book pursued a normative project, contending it was not necessary to have a strong, unified concept of the female subject. The final chapters were both guided by the idea of counterpoint in their structure and substance. In adopting this approach, the book has purported to resist the impulse of taking positions on one or the other side of the debate. Instead, it has been interested in highlighting, engaging with and interrogating the very parameters of the notions underlying gender, ethnicity, autonomy and choice as the characteristically 'feminist' sets of frames at play in the debate. It is believed that these also influence a range of other contemporary debates involving women: sex trafficking, pornography and religious dress. If this is so, the analysis pursued is of wider relevance to other gender-specific issues.

The book has been concerned to outline both the legal victories as well as the questions that surround the criminalisation of wartime sexual violence in the contemporary political and historical moment. It has shown that while these legal developments might have been useful from a feminist perspective, as they allowed feminists a voice at the negotiating table, the institutionalisation of feminist concerns has not necessarily led to a better understanding of wartime identities, their interactions with each other, and their overall experience under the extraordinary circumstances of armed conflict, regardless of the cultural context in which they materialise. The book has, moreover, shown that gender as a fluid and multifaceted social category has not been visibilised in ICTY wartime sexual violence jurisprudence. In spite of the advances achieved in international criminal law to redress sexual violence against women, entrenched gender dichotomies have been resurrected rather than dismantled. In designating 'governance feminists' with a central role in shaping the tribunal statutes and its rule-making processes, international law has authorised Western feminist ideas triggered by notions of 'protecting' or 'saving' other women from their fate. It therefore appears as if structuralist feminists have won the debate within the current human rights and international legal order.

In reverting to a fixed gaze on female subordination as the cause of female injury, 'governance feminism' has been complicit in the reproduction of reified gendered identities in international law, while at the same time abandoning its critical origins based on the questioning of sovereignty, authority, mastery and control. The book has argued that feminism is today transmitting a new tradition for which it may be the sovereign authority itself. It has suggested that if feminism carries forth in this vein, it won't comprehend late modernity or the age in which we live as marked by economic exploitation of women in the 'Global South', or be able to unmask the use of tropes like 'humanitarian intervention' as empty slogans that camouflage the real power dynamics underlying today's global order. In particular, as Anne Orford has suggested, a feminist reading of international law has to avoid seeing the world in terms of a 'battleground of male and female individualism', in which the goal of feminism would be merely to move women from the female domain of sexual reproduction to the male domain of 'social-subject production' via the sacrifice of the 'Other Woman'.[1]

It is therefore more important than ever to pay careful attention to the context of the increasing economic integration and the context of globalisation within which stories of war are narrated and represented to a wider audience. International legal texts produce knowledge about 'other' people and tell stories about the horrors and atrocities that occur in distant lands. They therefore wield immense power in the reproduction of power relations and reinforce the imperialist discourses of the past when they pit the 'uncouth and infantilised' native against the morally sound liberal, who in his invasion of foreign lands acts for entirely altruistic motives seeking to rescue 'the uncivilised' from themselves. In the context of the armed conflict in the former Yugoslavia, which has often been portrayed in strongly ethnicised terms, the imperialist desire to know and to gain access to 'other' people has served as a strong impulse in the creation of the international criminal tribunals, authorising Western 'experts' to speak about those who were constructed as in need of 'our help', while denying those deemed as 'undeserving' the same treatment. The failure to consider the involvement of international organisations or the role of international law in contributing to the kind of crisis, which ultimately manifested itself in the brutality marking the Yugoslav and the Rwandan conflicts, has meant that rather than examining the role played by the international community in contributing to modern-day conflicts, legal texts have continued to understand the causes of such conflicts as rooted in ethnic or nationalist attributes. In this way, they have removed the phenomenon of the violence witnessed from the historical powers that created and sustained it in the first place. The book has argued that the process of 'culturalising' wartime identities in the age of 'ethnic conflict' has been symptomatic of a wider trend in late modernity of depoliticising structural problems such as inequality, subordination and social conflict as personal and individual on the one hand, and as neutral, religious and cultural on the other. In this way, certain subjectivities, such as the Bosnian Muslim rape victim have been visibilised, as this was deemed a personalised war against their group identity, while other subjectivities such as the everyday woman in wartime Bosnia who tried to make a living regardless of her ethnic identity, but rather because of a basic human instinct for survival were occluded from the dominant legal narrative. These powerful stories of everyday individual agency and courage in the face of horror have gone missing from the dominant account of war, yet are so central to an understanding of the dynamics of armed conflict.

The book has highlighted how the framing of issues through certain discursive practices 'presumes the creature it needs to explain',[2] in this way erasing the structural conditions in which subjectivity is formed. It has argued that the framing of wartime sexual violence issues as human rights claims under available legal frameworks has assigned deep political social problems to a rather impoverished analytical spectrum, which evades power and history, understood in a broader, more materialist sense. Rather than ignoring the materialist and structural dimensions the book has brought them to light. Feminism has been complicit in this project in its refusal to see beyond its traditional preoccupation with subordination theory, as well as its refusal to see beyond identity politics as the means by which to explain deeply political and complex situations of power that have often created the conditions of inequality, poverty and injustice. The type of 'break' from feminism advocated is therefore done not against women, or in the interests of destabilising female subjectivity to deny normative feminist ideas their rightful place in the historical struggle for gender equality and justice. Instead, the impulse of this project has been strongly informed by the interests of those women who have been sidelined from dominant narratives and left out of mainstream feminist strategies. The book has sought to create a more imaginative portrayal of women by seeing past injury as constitutive of female subjectivity. In this way, different types of female subjectivity that neither necessarily conform to pre-determined norms and modes of thinking, yet are indispensable for a sustained advocacy based on justice and equality have been reinvigorated to allow for a broader reflection about the place of women in the contemporary legal and political moment.

Notes

1 Orford (2006), at 66.
2 Brown (2006), at 86.

Bibliography

Books and articles

Agamben, G., *Means without End: Notes on Politics* (Minneapolis: University of Minnesota Press, 2000).

Alison, M., 'Wartime Sexual Violence: Women's Human Rights and Questions of Masculinity', *Review of International Studies* (33) (2007), 75.

Allen, B., *Rape, Warfare: The Hidden Genocide in Bosnia-Herzegovina and Croatia* (Minneapolis: University of Minnesota Press, 1996).

Alston, P., 'The Myopia of Handmaidens: International Lawyers and Globalization', 3 *European Journal of International Law* (1997), 43.

Alvarez, J., 'Crimes of State/Crimes of Hate: Lessons from Rwanda', 24 *Yale Journal of International Law* (1999), 365.

Anghie, A. & B. S. Chimni, 'Third World Approaches to International Law and Individual Responsibility in Internal Conflicts', *Chinese Journal of International Law* (2003), 77.

Arbour, L., 'Stefan A. Riesenfeld Award Lecture-Crimes against Women under International Law', 21 *Berkeley Journal of International Law* (2003), 196.

Askin, K. D. & D. Koenig (eds.), *Women and International Human Rights Law* (Ardsley, NY: Transnational Legal Publishers, 1994).

———, 'Sexual Violence in ICTY and ICTR Indictments and Decisions: The Current State of Prosecutions Based on Gender-Based Crimes before the ICTY and ICTR', 93 *American Journal of International Law* (1999), 97.

———, *Women and International Human Rights* (Volume 1) (Ardsley, NY: Transnational Publishers, 1999).

———, 'The ICTY: An Introduction to Its Origins, Rules and Jurisprudence', in R. May, et al. (eds.), *Essays on ICTY Procedure and Evidence in Honour of Gabrielle Kirk McDonald* (The Hague, Boston: Kluwer Law International Law, 2000), 13.

———, *International Criminal Law and the International Criminal Court Statute: Crimes against Women, Women and International Human Rights* (Volume 2) (Ardsley, NY: Transnational Publishers, 2000).

———, 'The ICTY: An Introduction to Its Origins, Rules and Jurisprudence', in *Essays on ICTY Procedure and Evidence* (The Hague, Boston: Kluwer Law International Law, 2001), 16.

———, 'Reflections on Some of the Most Significant Achievements of the ICTY', 37 *New England Law Review* (2002–2003), 903.

———, 'Prosecuting Wartime Rape and Other Gender-Related Crimes under International Law: Extraordinary Advances, Enduring Obstacles', 21 *Berkeley Journal of International Law* (2003), 288.

Bakic-Hayden, M. & R. M. Hayden, 'Orientalist Variations on the Theme "Balkans": Symbolic Geography in Recent Yugoslav Cultural Politics', 51 *Slavic Review* (1) (Spring 1992), 1.

Bantekas, I. & S. Nash, *International Criminal Law* (London: Routledge-Cavendish, 2003).

———, *International Criminal Law* (3rd Edition) (London: Routledge-Cavendish, 2007).

Barkan, J., 'As Old as War Itself: Rape in Foca', *Dissent* (2002), 1.

Barrett, R. P. & L. E. Little, 'Lessons of Yugoslav Rape Trials: A Role for Conspiracy Law in International Tribunals', 88 *Minnesota Law Review* (2003–2004), 30.

Bass, G., *Stay the Hand of Vengeance: The Politics of War Crimes Tribunals* (Princeton and Oxford: Princeton University Press, 2000).

Bassiouni, C. & J. J. Paust (eds.), *International Criminal Law: Cases and Materials* (2nd Edition) (Durham, NC: Carolina Academic Press, 2000).

Batinic, J., 'Feminism, Nationalism and the War: The "Yugoslav Case" in Feminist Texts', 3 *Journal of International Women's Studies* (1) (November 2001), 1.

Baynes, K., 'Rights as Critique and the Critique of Rights: Karl Marx, Wendy Brown and the Social Function of Rights', 28 *Political Theory* (4) (August 2000), 451.

Bedont, B. & K. Hall-Martinez, 'Ending Impunity for Gender Crimes under the International Criminal Court', 5 *Brown Journal of World Affairs* (1999), 65.

Benhabib, S., *Another Cosmopolitanism* (Oxford: Oxford University Press, 2006).

Bennouna, M., 'The Characterisation of the Armed Conflict in the Practice of the ICTY', in R. May, et al. (eds.), *Essays on ICTY Procedure and Evidence in Honour of Gabrielle Kirk McDonald* (The Hague, Boston: Kluwer Law International Law, 2000), 55.

Benson, L., *"The End of Titoism" in Yugoslavia: A Concise History* (Basingstoke, Hampshire and New York, NY: Palgrave Macmillan, 2004), 132.

Binion, G., 'Human Rights: A Feminist Perspective', 17 *Human Rights Quarterly* (1995), 509.

Bjelic, D. I., 'Introduction Blowing Up the "Bridge"', in D. Bjelic & O. Savic (eds.), *Balkan as Metaphor: Between Globalization and Fragmentation* (Boston, MA: MIT Press, 2002), 1.

——— & L. Cole, 'Sexualizing the Serb', in D. Bjelic & O. Savic (eds.), *Balkan as Metaphor: Between Globalization and Fragmentation* (Boston, MA: MIT Press, 2002), 279.

Boas, G. & W. Schabas (eds.), *International Criminal Law Developments in the Case Law of the ICTY* (Leiden: Brill Academic Publishers, 2003).

Bond, J., 'International Intersectionality: A Theoretical and Pragmatic Exploration of Women's International Human Rights Violations', 52 *Emory Journal of International Law* (2003), 71.

Boose, L., 'Crossing the River Drina: Bosnian Rape Camps, Turkish Impalement, and Serb Cultural Memory', 28 *Signs: Journal of Women in Culture and Society* (2002), 71.

Boric, R., 'Against the War: Women Organizing across the National Divide in the Countries of the Former Yugoslavia', in R. Lentin (ed.), *Gender and Catastrophe* (London: Zed Books, 1998), 36.

Bourke, J., *Rape: Sex, Violence and History* (Berkeley, CA: Shoemaker and Hoard, 2007).

Brah, A. L. & A. Phoenix, 'Ain't I a Woman? Revisiting Intersectionality', 5 *Journal of International Women's Studies* (May 2004), 75.

Brems, E., 'Enemies or Allies? Feminism and Cultural Relativism as Dissident Voices in Human Rights Discourse', 19 *Human Rights Quarterly* (1997), 136.

Brown, W., *States of Injury: Power and Freedom in Late Modernity* (Princeton, NY: Princeton University Press, 1995).

———, 'Revealing Critique: A Response to Kenneth Baynes', 28 *Political Theory* (2000), 469.

———, 'Suffering Rights as Paradoxes', 7 *Constellations* (2000), 230.

———, *Politics Out of History* (Princeton, NJ: Princeton University Press, 2001).

———, 'Symptoms: Moralism as Anti-Politics', in *Politics Out of History* (Princeton, NJ: Princeton University Press, 2001), 18.

———, 'At the Edge', 30 *Political Theory* (4) (August 2002), 556.

———, *Left Legalism/Left Critique* (Durham, NC: Duke University Press, 2002).

———, 'Gender in Counterpoint', 4 *Feminist Theory* (2003), 365.

———, *Regulating Aversion: Tolerance in the Age of Identity and Empire* (Princeton, NJ: Princeton University Press, 2006).

Brownmiller, S., *Against Our Will: Men Women and Rape* (New York, NY: Random House, 1975).

Bunch, C., 'Women's Human Rights as Human Rights: Toward a Re-Vision of Human Rights', 12 *Human Rights Quarterly* (1990), 486.

———, 'Transforming Human Rights from a Feminist Perspective', in J. Peters & A. Wolper (eds.), *Women's Rights, Human Rights: International Feminist Perspectives* (New York: Routledge-Cavendish, 1995), 11.

Buss, D., 'Women at the Borders: Rape and Nationalism in International Law', 6 *Feminist Legal Studies* (2) (1998), 171.

———, 'Prosecuting Mass Rape: Prosecutor v. Dragoljub Kunarac, Radomir Kovac and Zoran Vukovic', 10 *Feminist Legal Studies* (2002), 91.

——— & A. Manji (eds.), *International Law: Modern Feminist Approaches* (Oxford and Portland, OR: Hart Publishing, 2005).

———, 'The Curious Visibility of Wartime Rape: Gender and Ethnicity in International Criminal Law', 25 *Windsor Journal of Access to Justice* (2007), 3.

———, 'The Rwanda Tribunal and the Making of Ethnic Rape', presented at Sexual Abuse and Exploitation of Women in Violent Conflict, Emory University and the Netherlands Defence Academy Workshop (17–19 June 2007), Amsterdam, NDL; revised and presented at American Society for Law, Culture and Humanities, Annual Conference (March, 2008), San Francisco.

———, 'Sexual Violence, Ethnicity, and the Limits of Intersectionality in International Criminal Law', in E. Grabham, et al. (eds.), *Intersectionality and Beyond: Law, Power and the Politics of Location* (London: Routledge-Cavendish, 2008), 105.

Butler, J., *Gender Trouble: Feminism and the Subversion of Identity* (New York: Routledge, 1990).

Byers, M. & G. Nolte (eds.), *United States Hegemony and the Foundations of International Law* (Cambridge: Cambridge University Press, 2003).

Cahill, A. J., 'Feminist Theories of Rape: Sex or Violence?', in *Rethinking Rape* (Ithaca, NY: Cornell University Press, 2001), 16.

———, *Rethinking Rape* (Ithaca, NY: Cornell University Press, 2001).

Campanaro, J., 'Women, War and International Law: The Historical Treatment of Gender-Based War Crimes', 89 *Georgetown Law Journal* (2000–2001), 2557.

Campbell, K., 'The Gender of Transitional Justice: Law, Sexual Violence and the International Criminal Tribunal for the Former Yugoslavia', 1 *International Journal of Transitional Justice* (2007), 411.

Canning, V., 'Who's Human? Developing Sociological Understandings of the Rights of Women Raped in Conflict', 14 *International Journal of Human Rights* (November 2010), 849.

Carpenter, R. C., 'Surfacing Children: Limitations of Genocidal Rape Discourse', 22 *Human Rights Quarterly* (2000), 428.

Cassese, A., *International Criminal Law* (Oxford: Oxford University Press, 2003).

Chappell, L., *The Politics of Gender Justice at the International Criminal Court: Legacies and Legitimacy* (Oxford: Oxford University Press, 2016).

Charlesworth, H. & C. Chinkin, 'The Gender of Jus Cogens', 15 *Human Rights Quarterly* (1993), 63.

———, 'What are "Women's International Human Rights?"', in R. J. Cook (ed.), *Human Rights of Women: National and International Perspectives* (Philadelphia: University of Pennsylvania Press, 1994), 54.

———, 'Human Rights as Men's Rights', in W. Peters (eds.), *Women's Rights: Human Rights* (Routledge: London, 1995), 103.

———, 'The Mid-Life Crisis of the Universal Declaration of Human Rights', 55 *Washington and Lee Law Review* (1998), 781.

———, 'Feminist Methods in International Law', 93 *American Journal of International Law* (April 1999), 379.

———, *The Boundaries of International Law* (Manchester: Manchester University Press, 2000).

——— & S. Wright, 'Feminist Approaches to International Law', 85 *American Journal of International Law* (1991), 613.

Charlesworth, H. & M. Wood, '"Mainstreaming Gender" in International Peace and Security: The Case of East Timor', 26 *Yale Journal of International Law* (2001), 313.

Charney, J., 'Universal International Law', 87 *American Journal of International Law* (1993), 529.

Chesterman, S., 'Never Again. . . . and Again: Law, Order and the Gender of War Crimes in Bosnia and Beyond', 22 *Yale Journal of International Law* (1997), 299.

Chinkin, C., 'A Gendered Perspective to the International Use of Force', 12 *Austin Yearbook of International Law* (1988–1989), 279.

———, 'Peace and Force in International Lawin', in D. Dallmeyer (eds.), *Reconceiving Reality: Women and International Law* (Washington, DC: The American Society of International Law, 1993), 212.

———, 'Rape and Sexual Abuse of Women in International Law', 5 *European Journal of International Law* (1994), 326.

———, 'A Critique of the Public/Private Dimension', 10 *European Journal of International Law* (2) (1999), 387.

———, 'Women's International Tribunal on Japanese Military Sexual Slavery', 95 *American Journal of International Law* (2) (2001), 335.

——— & S. Wright, 'The Hunger Trap: Women, Food and Self-Determination', 14 *Michigan Journal of International Law* (1992–1993), 262.

Chomsky, N., 'Humanitarian Imperialism: The New Doctrine of the Imperial Right', *Monthly Review* (September 2008).

Cockburn, C., 'The Gendered Dynamics of Armed Conflict and Political Violence', in C. O. N. Moser & F. C. Clark (eds.), *Victims, Perpetrators or Actors? Gender, Armed Conflict and Political Violence* (London: Zed Books, 2001), 13.

———, 'The Continuum of Violence: A Gender Perspective on War and Peace', in W. Giles & J. Hyndman (eds.), *Sites of Violence: Gender and Conflict Zones* (Berkeley and Los Angeles, CA: University of California Press, 2004), 24.

Conaghan, J., 'Intersectionality and the Feminist Project in Law', in E. Grabham, et al. (eds.), *Intersectionality and Beyond: Law, Power and the Politics of Location* (London: Routledge-Cavendish, 2009), 28.

Cook, R., 'Women's International Human Rights Law: The Way Forward', 15 *Human Rights Quarterly* (1993), 230.

———, *Human Rights of Women* (Philadelphia: University of Pennsylvania Press, 1994).

———, 'International Human Rights and Women's Reproductive Health', in J. Peters & A. Wolper (eds.), *Women's Rights, Human Rights: International Feminist Perspectives* (New York: Routledge, 1995), 256.

Coomaraswamy, R. & L. Kois, 'Women and International Human Rights' Law', in K. Askin & D. Koenig (eds.), *Women and International Human Rights Law* (New York: Transnational Publishers, 1999).

Copelon, R., 'Intimate Terror: Understanding Domestic Violence as Torture', in R. Cook (ed.), *Human Rights of Women* (Philadelphia: University of Pennsylvania Press, 1994), 116.

———, 'Recognising the Egregious in the Everyday: Domestic Violence as Torture', 25 *Columbia Human Rights Law Review* (1994), 291.

———, 'Surfacing Gender: Re-Engraving Crimes against Women in Humanitarian Law', 5 *Hastings Women's Law Journal* (1994), 243.

———, 'Gendered War Crimes: Reconceptualizing Rape in Times of War', in J. Peters & A. Wolper (eds.), *Women's Rights, Human Rights: International Feminist Perspectives* (New York: Routledge, 1995), 206.

———, 'Gender Crimes as War Crimes: Integrating Crimes against Women into International Criminal Law', 46 *McGill Law Journal* (2000), 217.

Cossman, B., D. Danielsen, J. Halley & T. Higgins, 'Gender, Sexuality and Power: Is Feminist Theory Enough?', 12 *Columbia Journal of Gender and Law* (2003), 601.

Crenshaw, K. W., 'Demarginalizing the Intersection of Race and Sex: A Black Feminist Critique of Anti-Discrimination Doctrine, Feminist Theory and Antiracist Politics', 129 *University of Chicago Legal Forum* (1989), 139.

———, 'Mapping the Margins: Intersectionality, Identity, Politics, and Violence against Women of Colour', 43 *Stanford Law Review* (1991), 1241.

———, 'Mapping the Margins: Intersectionality, Identity Politics and Violence against Women of Color', presented at the World Conference against Racism (2001), Durban, South Africa.

Dallmeyer, D. (ed.), *Reconceiving Reality: Women and International Law* (Washington, DC: The American Society of International Law, 1993).

Das, V. & A. Kleinman, *Violence and Subjectivity* (Berkeley, CA: University of California Press, 2000).

De Brouwer, A.-M., *Supranational Criminal Prosecution of Sexual Violence: The ICC and the Practice of the ICTY and ICTR* (London: Intersentia, 2005).

De Londras, F., 'Prosecuting Sexual Violence in the Ad-Hoc Tribunals for Rwanda and the Former Yugoslavia', *UCD Working Papers in Law, Criminology & Socio-Legal Studies* No. 06/2009.

Di Palma, C. & K. Ferguson, 'Clearing Ground and Making Connections: Modernism, Postmodernism, Feminism', in K. Davis, et al. (eds.), *Handbook of Gender and Women's Studies* (London, Thousand Oaks, New Delhi: Sage, 2006), 131.

Dixon, R., 'Rape as a Crime in International Humanitarian Law: Where to from Here?', 13 *European Journal of International Law* (3) (2002), 697.

Dolgopol, U. & J. Gardam (eds.), *The Challenge of Conflict: International Law Responds* (The Hague, Netherlands: Martinus Nijhoff Publishers, 2006).

Douzinas, C., *The End of Human Rights* (Oxford: Oxford University Press, 2000).

———, 'The Many Faces of Humanitarianism', 2 *Parrhesia Journal* (2007), 1.

Dunoff, J., S. Ratner & D. Wippman (eds.), *International Law Norms, Actors, Processes: A Problem Oriented Approach* (New York: Aspen Law & Business, 2002).

Edwards, A., 'The 'Feminizing of Torture under International Human Rights Law', 19 *Leiden Journal of International Law* (2006), 349.

Eisler, R., 'Human Rights: Toward and Integrated Theory for Action', 9 *Human Rights Quarterly* (1987), 287.

Engle, K., 'Female Subjects of Public International Law: Human Rights and the Exotic Other Female', 26 *New England Law Review* (1992), 1509.

———, 'International Human Rights and Feminism: When Discourses Meet', 13 *Michigan Journal of International Law* (1992), 517.

———, 'After the Collapse of the Public/Private Distinction: Strategizing Women's Rights', in D. Dallmeyer (ed.), *Reconceiving Reality: Women and International Law* (Washington, DC: The American Society of International Law, 1993), 143.

———, 'Feminism and Its (Dis) Contents: Criminalizing Wartime Rape in Bosnia and Herzegovina', 99 *American Journal of International Law* (2005), 778.

———, 'International Human Rights and Feminisms: When Discourses Keep Meeting', in D. Buss & A. Manji (eds.), *International Law: Modern Feminist Approaches* (Oxford and Portland, OR: Hart Publishing, 2005), 47.

———, 'Liberal Internationalism, Feminism, and the Suppression of Critique: Contemporary Approaches to Global Order in the United States', 46 *Harvard International Law Journal* (2005), 427.

———, 'Calling in the Troops: The Uneasy Relationship among Women's Rights, Human Rights and Humanitarian Intervention', 20 *Harvard Human Rights Journal* (2007), 189.

———, 'Judging Sex in War', 106 *Michigan Law Review* (April 2008), 941.

Engle Merry, S., *Human Rights & Gender Violence* (Chicago: University of Chicago Press, 2006).

Fabian, K. L., 'Proof and Consequences: An Analysis of the Tadic & Akayesu Trials', 49 *De Paul Law Review* (1999–2000), 981.

Flax, J., 'Postmodernism and Gender Relations', in N. Fraser & L. Nicholson (eds.), *Feminism/Postmodernism* (Minneapolis: University of Minnesota Press, 1989), 39.

Gagnon, V. P., *The Myth of Ethnic War: Serbia and Croatia in the 1990s* (Ithaca, NY: Cornell University Press, 2004).

Gallagher, A., 'Ending the Marginalization: Strategies for Incorporating Women into the Human Rights System', 19 *Human Rights Quarterly* (1997), 283.

Gardam, J., 'Gender and Non-Combatant Immunity', 3 *Transnational Legal & Contemporary Problems* (1993), 347.

———, 'Proportionality and Force in International Law', 87 *American Journal of International Law* (1993), 391.

———, 'Women and Armed Conflict: Why the Silence?', 46 *International & Comparative Law Quarterly* (1997), 55.

———, 'Women, Human Rights and International Humanitarian Law', 324 *International Review of the Red Cross* (1998), 421.

———, 'Origin and Nature of Human Rights and Humanitarian Law', in J. Gardam (ed.), *The Library of Essays in International Law* (Boston, MA: Dartmouth Publishing, UK, 1999), 459.

——— (ed.), *The Library of Essays in International Law* (Boston, MA: Dartmouth Publishing, UK, 1999).

——— & H. Charlesworth, 'Protection of Women in Armed Conflict', 22 *Human Rights Quarterly* (2000), 148.

——— & M. Jarvis, *Women, Armed Conflict and International Law, XV and 290* (The Hague and New York: Kluwer Law International Law, 2001).

Giles, W. & J. Hyndman (eds.), *Sites of Violence: Gender and Conflict Zones* (Berkeley and Los Angeles, CA: University of California Press, 2004).

Gilligan, C., *In a Different Voice: Psychological Theory and Women's Development* (Cambridge, MA: Harvard University Press, 1982).

Goldstone, R. J. & E. A. Dehon, 'Engendering Accountability: Gender Crimes under International Law', 19 *New England Journal of Public Policy* (2003), 121.

Goldsworthy, V., 'Invention and In(ter)vention: The Rhetoric of Balkanization', in D. I. Bjelic, 'Introduction Blowing Up the "Bridge"', in D. Bjelic & O. Savic (eds.), *Balkan as Metaphor: Between Globalization and Fragmentation* (Boston, MA: MIT Press, 2002), 25.

Grabham, E., et al. (eds.), *Intersectionality and Beyond: Law, Power and the Politics of Location* (London: Routledge-Cavendish, 2008).

Graham, R., 'Male Rape and the Careful Construction of the Male Victim', 15 *Social Legal Studies* (2) (2006), 187.

Green, J., et al., 'Affecting the Rules for the Prosecution of Rape', 5 *Hastings Law Journal* (1994), 171.

Green, L., *The Contemporary Law of Armed Conflict* (3rd Edition) (Manchester: Manchester University Press, 2008).

Gunning, I., 'Arrogant Perception, World-Travelling and Multicultural Feminism: The Case of Female Genital Surgeries', 23 *Columbia Human Rights Law Review* (1991–1992), 189.

Hagan, J., *Justice in the Balkans: Prosecuting War Crimes in the Hague Tribunal* (Chicago: University of Chicago Press, 2003).

Halley, J. & W. Brown, 'Suffering the Paradoxes of Rights', in W. Brown & J. Halley (eds.), *Left Legalism/Left Critique* (Durham, NC: Duke University Press, 2002), 420.

———, 'Take a Break from Feminism?', in K. Knop (ed.), *Gender and Human Rights* (Oxford: Oxford University Press, 2004), 57.

———, 'Describing Governance Feminism', 29 *Harvard Journal of Law & Gender* (2006), 340.

———, *Split Decisions: How and Why to Take a Break from Feminism* (Princeton and Oxford: Princeton University Press, 2006).

———, 'Rape in Berlin: Reconsidering the Criminalisation of Rape in the International Law of Armed Conflict', 9 *Melbourne Journal of International Law* (2008), 78.

———, 'Rape at Rome: Feminist Interventions in the Criminalization of Sex-Related Violence in Positive International Criminal Law', 30 *Michigan Journal of International Law* (2008–2009).

Harris, A., 'Race and Essentialism in Feminist Legal Theory', 42 *Stanford Law Review* (1989-1990), 581.

Hartsock, N., 'The Feminist Standpoint: Developing the Ground for a Specifically Feminist Historic Materialism', in S. Harding & M. B. Hintikka (eds.), *Discovering Reality: Feminist Perspectives on Epistemology, Metaphysics, Methodology and Science* (The Hague: Kluwer, 1983), 283; reprinted in Nicholson, L., *The Second Wave: A Reader in Feminist Theory* (London: Routledge, 1997), 216.

Hayden, R. M., 'Imagined Communities and Real Victims: Self-Determination and Ethnic Cleansing in Yugoslavia', 23 *American Ethnologist* (4) (November 1996), 783.

———, 'Biased "Justice": Humanrightsism and the International Criminal Tribunal for the Former Yugoslavia', 47 *Cleveland State Law Review* (1999), 549.

———, 'Rape and Rape Avoidance in Ethno-National Conflicts: Sexual Violence in Liminalized States', 102 *American Anthropologist* (1) (March 2000), 27.

Healey, S., 'Prosecuting Rape under the Statute of the War Crimes Tribunal for the Former Yugoslavia', 21 *Brookings Journal of International Law* (1995), 327.

Heathcote, G., 'Naming and Shaming: Human Rights Accountability in Security Council Resolution 1960 (2010) on Women, Peace and Security', 4 *Journal of Human Rights Practice* (1) (2012).

Herman, E. & D. Peterson, 'The Dismantling of Yugoslavia: A Study in Inhumanitarian Intervention and a Western Liberal-Left Intellectual and Moral Collapse', 59 *Monthly Review* (5) (2007).

Hosken, F., 'Toward a Definition of Women's Human Rights', 3 *Human Rights Quarterly* (1981), 1.

Jarvis, M. 'An Emerging Gender Perspective on International Crimes', in G. Boas & W. Schabas (eds.), *International Criminal Law Developments in the Case Law of the ICTY* (Leiden: Brill Academic Publishers, 2003), 157.

Kalajdzic, J., 'Rape, Representation and Rights: Permeating International Law with the Voices of Women', 21 *Queen's Law Journal* (1996), 457.

Kapur, R., 'Post-Colonial Economies of Desire: Legal Representation of the Subaltern', 78 *Denver University Law Review* (2000–2001), 85.

———, 'The Tragedy of Victimization Rhetoric: Resurrecting the "Native" Subject' in International/Post-Colonial Feminist Legal Politics', 15 *Harvard Human Rights Journal* (2002), 1.

———, 'Unveiling Women's Rights in the War on Terrorism', 9 *Duke Journal of Gender, Law & Policy* (2002), 211.

———, 'The "Other" Side of the Legal Regulation of Globalization Cross-Border Movements', 22 *Canadian Women's Studies* (2003), 6.

———, *Erotic Justice: Law and the New Politics of Postcolonialism* (London: Glasshouse Press, 2005).

Kennedy, D., 'The International Human Rights Movement: Part of the Problem?', 15 *Harvard Human Rights Journal* (2002), 101.

Kesic, O., 'Women and Gender Imagery in Bosnia: Amazons, Sluts, Victims, Witches, and Wombs', in S. P. Ramet (ed.), *Gender Politics in the Western Balkans: Women and Society in Yugoslavia and the Yugoslav Successor States* (Philadelphia: Pennsylvania State University Press, 1999), 186.

Kesic, V., 'A Response to Catherine Mac Kinonn's Article "Turning Rape Into Pornography": Postmodern Genocide', 5 *Hastings Women's Law Journal* (1994), 267.

———, 'Muslim Women, Croatian Women, Serbian Women, Albanian Women . . .', in D. Bjelic & O. Savic (eds.), *Balkan as Metaphor* (Cambridge, MA: MIT Press, 2002), 311.

Knop, K. (ed.), *Gender and Human Rights* (Oxford: Oxford University Press, 2004).

Koskenniemi, M., 'The Politics of International Law', 1 *European Journal of International Law* (1990), 4.

———, 'Between Impunity and Show Trials', 6 *Max Planck Yearbook of United Nations Law* (2002), 1.

———, 'The Lady Doth Protest Too Much, Kosovo and the Turn to Ethics in International Law', 65 *Modern Law Review* (2002), 160.

Kouvo, S., 'The United Nations and Gender Mainstreaming: Limits and Possibilities', in D. Buss & A. Manji (eds.), *International Law: Modern Feminist Approaches* (Oxford and Portland, OR: Hart Publishing, 2005), 237.

Kritsiotis, D., 'The Tremors of Tadic', 43 *Israel Law Review* (2010), 262.

Lacey, N., *Unspeakable Subjects: Feminist Essays in Legal and Social Theory* (Oxford: Hart, 1998).

———, 'Feminist Legal Theories and the Rights of Women', in K. Knop (ed.), *Gender and Human Rights* (Oxford: Oxford University Press, 2004), 13.

Lentin, R., *Gender and Catastrophe* (London: Zed Books, 1998).

Loizidou, E., 'The Trouble with Rape: Gender Matters and Legal "Transformations"', 7 *Feminist Legal Studies* (1999), 275.

Longinovic, T. Z., 'Vampires Like Us: Gothic Imaginary and "the Serbs"', in D. Bjelic & O. Savic (eds.), *Balkan as Metaphor: Between Globalization and Fragmentation* (Boston, MA: MIT Press, 2002), 39.

MacDonald, G. K., 'The International Criminal Tribunals: Crime and Punishment in the International Arena', 7 *International Law Society Association Journal of International and Comparative Law* (2001), 667.

MacKinnon, C., 'Feminism, Marxism, Method and the State: Toward Feminist Jurisprudence', 8 *Signs* (Summer, 1983), 640.

———, 'Pornography, Civil Rights and Speech', 20 *Harvard Civil Rights-Civil Liberties Law Review* (1985), 1.

———, *Feminism Unmodified: Discourses on Life and Law* (Cambridge, MN: Harvard University Press, 1987).

———, 'A Rally against Rape', in *Feminism Unmodified: Discourses on Life and Law* (Cambridge, MN: Harvard University Press, 1987), 81.

———, 'Prostitution and Civil Rights', 1 *Michigan Journal of Gender and Law* (1993), 13.

———, 'Rape, Genocide, and Women's Human Rights', in A. Stiglmayer (ed.), *"Mass Rape: The War against Women" in Bosnia-Herzegovina* (Lincoln, NE: University of Nebraska Press, 1994), 183.

——— & A. Dworkin (eds.), *In Harm's Way: The Pornography Civil Rights Hearing* (Cambridge: MN: Harvard University Press, 1997), 438.

———, *Are Women Human? Reflections on the Universal Declaration of Human Rights* (The Hague: Martinus Nijhoff Publishers, 1999).

———, 'From Ausschwitz to Omarska, Nuremberg to The Hague', in C. MacKinnon (ed.), *Are Women Human? Reflections on the Universal Declaration of Human Rights* (The Hague: Martinus Nijhoff Publishers, 1999), 174.

———, 'Human Rights and Global Violence against Women', in C. MacKinnon (ed.), *Are Women Human? Reflections on the Universal Declaration of Human Rights* (The Hague: Martinus Nijhoff Publishers, 1999), 34.

———, 'Rape as Nationbuilding', in C. MacKinnon (ed.), *Are Women Human? Reflections on the Universal Declaration of Human Rights* (The Hague: Martinus Nijhoff Publishers, 1999), 169.

———, *The Recognition of Rape as an Act of Genocide-Prosecutor v. Akayesu* (Guest Lecture Series of the Office of the Prosecutor, 27) (The Hague, October 2008); reprinted in 14 *New England Journal of International and Comparative Law* (2) (New England School of Law, 2008), 101.

Malcolm, N., *Bosnia: A Short History* (London: Macmillan General Books, 1994).

Malekian, F., 'Philosophy of International Criminal Justice', 38 *Cornell International Law Journal* (3) (Fall, 2005), 674.

Manjoo, R., 'Women, Peace and Security-Negotiating in Women's Best Interests', 7 *Global Policy* (2) (2016).

Marravilla, C. S., 'Rape as a War Crime: The Implications of the International Criminal Tribunal for the Former Yugoslavia's Decision in the Prosecutor v. Kunarac,

Kovac & Vukovic on International Humanitarian Law', 13 *Florida Journal of International Law* (2000–2001), 321.

McCall, L., 'The Complexity of Intersectionality', 30 *Signs* (Spring 2005), 1771.

McDougall, C., 'The Sexual Violence Jurisprudence of the International Criminal Tribunal for the Former Yugoslavia and The International Criminal Tribunal for Rwanda: The Silence Has Been Broken but There's Still a Lot to Shout About', in U. Dolgopal & J. Gardam (eds.), *The Challenge of Conflict: International Law Responds* (International Humanitarian Law Series) (The Hague: Martinus Nijhoff, 2006), 331.

McGoldrick, D., 'Criminal Trials before International Tribunals: Legality and Legitimacy', in D. Mc Goldrick, P. Rowe & E. Donnelly (eds.), *The Permanent International Criminal Court: Legal and Policy Issues* (Portland, OR: Hart Publishing, 2004), 8.

McIntyre, G., 'Defining Human Rights in the Arena of International Humanitarian Law: Human Rights in the Jurisprudence of the ICTY', in G. Boas & W. Schabas (eds.), *International Criminal Law Developments in the Case Law of the ICTY* (Leiden: Brill Academic Publishers, 2003), 219.

Meron, T., *Human Rights and Humanitarian Norms as Customary Law* (Broadbridge, Gloucestershire: Clarendon Press, 1989), 209.

———, 'Rape as Crime under International Law', 87 *American Journal of International* (1993), 424.

———, 'The Normative Impact on International Law of the International Tribunal for the Former Yugoslavia', in Y. Dinstein & M. Tabory (eds.), *War Crimes in International Law* (The Hague, Boston: Martinus Nijhoff, 1996), 211.

———, 'Answering for War Crimes: Lessons from the Balkans', 76 *Foreign Affairs* (1997), 2.

———, 'Is International Law Moving towards Criminalization?', 9 *European Journal of International Law* (1998), 18.

———, 'The Humanization of Humanitarian Law', 94 *American Journal of International Law* (2000), 239.

Mertus, J., 'When Adding Women Matters: Women's Participation in the International Criminal Tribunal for the Former Yugoslavia', 38 *Setton Hall Law Review* (2008), 1297.

Miller, A., 'Sexuality, Violence against Women, and Human Rights: Women Make Demands and Ladies Get Protection', 7 *Health and Human Rights* (2) (2004), 16.

Mohanty, C. T., 'Under Western Eyes: Feminist Scholarship and Colonialist Discourses', in C. T. Mohanty, A. Russo & L. Torres (eds.), *Third World Women and the Politics of Feminism* (Indianapolis, IN: Indiana University Press, 1991).

Moser, C. O. N. & F. C. Clark (eds.), *Victims, Perpetrators or Actors?: Gender, Armed Conflict and Political Violence* (London: Zed Books, 2001), 3.

——— & A. Moser, 'Gender Mainstreaming since Beijing: A Review of Success and Limitations in International Institutions', 13 *Gender and Development* (2) (July 2005), 11.

Mullally, S., Gender, *Culture and Human Rights: Reclaiming Universalism* (Oxford and Portland, ON: Hart Publishing, 2006).

Muller, J. Z., 'Us and Them: The Enduring Power of Ethnic Nationalism', 87 *Foreign Affairs* (20 March/April 2008), 18.

Munro, V. E., 'On Power and Domination: Feminism and the Final Foucault', 2 *European Journal of Political Theory* (1) (2003), 79.

———, 'Feminism(s), Law and Liberalism(s)', in V. E. Munro (eds.), *Law and Politics at the Perimeter: Re-Evaluating Key Debates in Feminist Theory* (Oxford: Hart, 2007).

Murphy, S., 'Sexual Violence in Decisions and Indictments of the Yugoslav and Rwandan Tribunals: Current Status', 93 *American Journal of International Law* (1999), 100.
Murphy, T., 'Feminism Here, Feminism There: Law, Theory and Choice', in D. Buss & A. Manji (eds.), *International Law: Modern Feminist Approaches* (Oxford and Portland, OR: Hart, 2005), 67.
Mutua, M., 'Never Again: Questioning the Yugoslav and Rwanda Tribunals', 11 *Temple International & Comparative Law Journal* (1997), 167.
———, 'What Is TWAIL?', 94 *American Society & International Legal Procedure* (2000), 31.
Nadj, D., 'The Culturalisation of Identity in an Age of "Ethnic Conflict"-Depoliticised Gender in ICTY Wartime Sexual Violence Jurisprudence', 15 *International Journal of Human Rights* (5) (June, 2011), 647.
——— & R. Manjoo, 'Bridging the Divide: An Interview with Professor Rashida Manjoo, UN Special Rapporteur on Violence against Women', 23 *Feminist Legal Studies* (3) (November 2015), 329–347.
Nesiah, V., 'Toward a Feminist Internationality: A Critique of U.S. Feminist Legal Scholarship', 16 *Harvard Women's Law Journal* (1) (1993), 189.
Niarchos, C., 'Women, War, and Rape: Challenges Facing the International Criminal Tribunal for the Former Yugoslavia', 17 *Human Rights Quarterly* (1995), 649.
Nowrojee, B., 'Shattered Lives: Sexual Violence during the Rwandan Genocide and Its Aftermath', 39 *Human Rights Watch/Africa* (1996).
Nussbaum, M., *Sex and Social Justice* (Oxford: Oxford University Press, 1999).
———, *Women and Human Development: The Capabilities Approach* (Cambridge: Cambridge University Press, 2000).
Nyamu, C. I., 'How Should Human Rights and Development Respond to Cultural Legitimization of Gender Hierarchy in Developing Countries?', 41 *Harvard International Law Journal* (2000), 381.
O'Hare, U., 'Rethinking Human Rights for Women', 21 *Human Rights Quarterly* (1999), 366.
Okin, S. M., *Is Multiculturalism Bad for Women* (Princeton, NJ: Princeton University Press, 1999).
Olsen, F., 'Statutory Rape: A Feminist Critique of Rights Analysis', 63 *Texas Law Review* (1984–1985), 387.
———, 'International Law: Feminist Critiques of the Public/Private Distinctions', in D. Dallmeyer (ed.), *Reconceiving Reality: Women and International Law* (1993), 157. *American Society of International Law* 143.
Oosterveldt, V., 'The Definition of "Gender" in the Rome Statute of the International Criminal Court: A Step Forward or Back for International Criminal Justice?', 18 *Harvard Human Rights Journal* (2005), 55–84.
Orford, A., 'The Politics of Collective Security', 17 *Michigan Journal of International Law* (1995–1996), 373.
———, 'Contesting Globalization: A Feminist Perspective on the Future of Human Rights', 8 *Transnational Legal & Contemporary Problems* (1998), 171.
———, 'Muscular Humanitarianism: Reading the Narratives of the New Interventionism', 10 *European Journal of International Law* (4) (1999), 679.
———, 'Feminism, Imperialism and the Mission of International Law', 71 *Nordic Journal of International Law* (2002), 275.

———, *Reading Humanitarian Intervention* (Cambridge: Cambridge University Press, 2003).

——— (ed.), *International Law and Its Others* (Cambridge: Cambridge University Press, 2006).

———, 'A Jurisprudence of the Limit', in A. Orford (ed.), *International Law and Its Others* (Cambridge: Cambridge University Press, 2006), 1.

Otto, D., 'Violence against Women: Something Other Than a Human Rights Violation?', 1 *Australian Feminist Law Journal* (1993), 159.

———, 'Holding Up Half the Sky but for Whose Benefit? A Critical Analysis of the Fourth World Conference on Women', 6 *Australian Feminist Law Journal* (1996), 7.

———, 'Subalternity and International Law: The Problems of Global Community and the Incommensurability of Difference', 5 *Social & Legal Studies* (3) (1996), 337.

———, 'Rethinking Universals: Opening Transformative Possibilities in International Human Rights Law', 18 *Australian Yearbook of International Law* (1997), 1.

———, 'Disconcerting Masculinities': Reinventing the Gendered Subject(s) of International Human Rights Law', in D. Buss & A. Manji (eds.), *International Law: Modern Feminist Approaches* (Oxford and Portland, OR: Hart, 2005), 318.

———,' Lost in Translation: Re-Scripting the Sexed Subjects of International Human Rights Law', in A. Orford (ed.), *International Law and Its Others* (Cambridge: Cambridge University Press, 2006), 318.

Papic, Z., 'Women in Serbia: Post-Communism, War and Nationalist Mutations', in R. Lentin (ed.), *Gender and Catastrophe* (London: Zed Books, 1998), 153.

Paulus, A., 'The Influence of the United States on the Concept of the "International Community"', in M. Byers & G. Nolte (eds.), *United States Hegemony and the Foundations of International Law* (Cambridge: Cambridge University Press, 2003), 60.

——— & B. Simma, 'The Responsibility of Individuals for Human Rights Abuses in Internal Conflicts: A Positivist View', 93 *American Journal of International Law* (2) (April 1999), 302.

Peters, J. & A. Wolper (eds.), *Women's Rights, Human Rights: International Feminist Perspectives* (New York: Routledge, 1995).

Petrovic, D., 'Ethnic Cleansing-An Attempt at Methodology', 5 *European Journal of International Law* (1994), 342.

Phillips, A., 'Feminism and Liberalism Revisited: Has Martha Nussbaum Got It Right?', 8 *Constellations* (2) (2001), 248.

Pillay, N., 'Address-Interdisciplinary Colloquium on Sexual Violence as International Crime: Sexual Violence: Standing by the Victim', 35 *Law & Social Inquiry* (4) (2010), 847.

Provost, R., *International Human Rights and Humanitarian Law* (Cambridge: Cambridge University Press, 2002).

Rajagopal, B., 'Introduction: Encountering Ambivalence', in M. Goodale & S. E. Merry (eds.), *The Practice of Human Rights: Tracking the Law between the Global and the Local* (Cambridge: Cambridge University Press, 2007), 273.

Ramet, S. P. (ed.), *Gender Politics in the Western Balkans: Women and Society in Yugoslavia and the Yugoslav Successor States* (Philadelphia: Pennsylvania State University Press, 1999).

Rhode, D. L., 'Feminist Critical Theories', 42 *Stanford Law Review* (1989–1990), 617.

Roberts, K., 'The Contribution of the ICTY to the Grave Breaches Regime', 7 *Journal of International Criminal Justice* (2009), 743.

Romany, C., 'State Responsibility Goes Private: A Feminist Critique of the Public/Private Distinction in International Human Rights Law', in R. Cook (ed.), *Human Rights of Women* (Philadelphia: University of Pennsylvania Press, 1994), 85.

Russell-Brown, S. L., 'Rape as an Act of Genocide', 21 *Berkeley Journal of International Law* (2003), 350.

Said, E. W., *Orientalism* (New York: Random House, 1979).

Scharf, M. P., 'The Legacy of the Miloševic Trial', 37 *New England Law Review* (2002–2003), 915.

Schomburg, W. & I. Peterson, 'Genuine Consent to Sexual Violence under International Criminal Law', 101 *American Journal of International Law* (2007), 121.

Scott, J. W., 'Gender: A Useful Category of Historical Analysis', 91 *American Historical Review* (December 1986), 1053.

Seifert, R., 'The Second Front: The Logic of Sexual Violence in Wars', 19 *Women's Studies International Forum* (1/2) (1996), 35–43.

Sellers, P. V. & K. Okuizumi, 'International Prosecution of Sexual Assaults', 7 *Transnational Law & Contemporary Problems* (1997), 45.

———, 'Rape under International Law', in B. Cooper (ed.), *War Crimes: The Legacy of Nuremberg* (New York, NY: TV Books, 1999), 159.

———, 'Individual(s') Liability for Collective Sexual Violence', in K. Knop (ed.), *Gender and Human Rights* (Oxford: Oxford University Press, 2004), 154.

Silber, A. & L. Little, *The Death of Yugoslavia* (London: Penguin Book, 1995).

Simpson, G., *Great Powers and Outlaw States: Unequal Sovereigns in the International Legal Order* (Cambridge: Cambridge University Press, 2004).

Sivakumaran, S., 'Sexual Violence against Men in Armed Conflict', 18 *European Journal of International Law* (2) (2007), 253.

Skjelsbaek, I., 'Sexual Violence and War: Mapping Out a Complex Relationship', 7 *European Journal of International Relations* (2) (2001), 211.

Sofos, S., 'Inter-Ethnic Violence and Gendered Constructions of Ethnicity in the Former Yugoslavia', 2 *Social Identities* (1) (1996), 73.

——— & B. Jenkins (eds.), *Nation and Identity in Contemporary Europe* (London and New York, NY: Routledge-Cavendish, 1996), 257.

Spivak, G., 'Can the Subaltern Speak?', in P. Williams & L. Chrisman (eds.), *Colonial Discourse and Postcolonial Theory* (New York, NY: Columbia University Press, 1994), 66.

Stepanova, E., 'Trends in Armed Conflicts: One-Sided Violence against Civilians', *Stockholm Peace Research Institute Yearbook* (2009), 1.

Stiglmayer, A., *"The Rapes in Bosnia-Herzegovina" in Mass Rape: The War against Women in Bosnia-Herzegovina* (Lincoln, NE: University of Nebraska Press, 1994), 82.

Sullivan, D., 'Women's Human Rights and the 1993 World Conference on Human Rights', 88 *American Journal of International Law* (January 1994), 152.

Tallgren, I., 'The Sensibility and Sense of International Criminal Law', 13 *European Journal of International Law* (3), 561.

Teitel, R., 'The Universal and the Particular in International Criminal Justice', 30 *Columbia Human Rights Law Review* (1989–1990), 285.

Temkin, J., *Rape and the Legal Process* (Oxford: Oxford University Press, 2005).

Thomas, D. Q. & R. E. Ralph, 'Rape in War: The Case of Bosnia', in S. P. Ramet (ed.), *Gender Politics in the Western Balkans: Women and Society in Yugoslavia and the Yugoslav Successor States* (Philadelphia: Pennsylvania State University Press, 1999), 203.

Todorova, M., *Imagining the Balkans* (Oxford: Oxford University Press, 2009 updated edition); Van den Hole, L., 'A Case Study of Rape and Sexual Assault in the Judgements of the International Criminal Tribunal for Rwanda (Akayesu and Musema) and the International Criminal Tribunal for the Former Yugoslavia (Celebici, Furundzija, Kunarac, Todorovic, Sikirica and Kvocka)', 1 *Eyes on the ICC* (2004), 54.

Varady, T., 'Minorities, Majorities, Law, and Ethnicity: Reflections of the Yugoslav Case', 19 *Human Rights Quarterly* (1997), 18.

Wald, A., 'What's Rightfully Ours: Toward a Property Theory of Rape', 30 *Columbia Journal of Law & Social Problems* (1997), 459.

Wenger, A. & S. J. A. Mason, 'The Civilianization of Armed Conflict: Trends and Implications', 827 *International Review of the Red Cross* (December 2008), 831.

Williams, P. & L. Chrisman, *Colonial Discourses and Post-Colonial Theory* (New York, NY: Columbia University Press, 1994).

Wing, A. K. & S. Merchan, 'Rape, Ethnicity, and Culture: Spirit Injury from Bosnia to America', 25 *Columbia Human Rights Law Review* (1993–1994), 1.

Wood, E. J., 'Variation in Sexual Violence during War', 34 *Politics & Society* (2006), 307.

———, 'Armed Groups and Sexual Violence: When Is Wartime Rape Rare?', 37 *Politics & Society* (2009), 131.

Woodward, S. L., *Balkan Tragedy: Chaos and Dissolution after the Cold War* (Washington, DC: Brookings Institution, August 1994).

———, 'Violence-Prone Area or International Transition?', in V. Das & A. Kleinman (eds.), *Violence and Subjectivity* (Berkeley, CA: University of California Press, 2000), 24.

Zahar, A. & G. Sluiter, *International Criminal Law* (Oxford: Oxford University Press, 2008).

Zalihic-Kaurin, A., 'The Muslim Woman', in A. Stiglmayer (ed.), *"The Rapes in Bosnia-Herzegovina" in Mass Rape: The War against Women in Bosnia-Herzegovina* (Lincoln, NE: University of Nebraska Press, 1994), 17.

Zarkov, D., 'Gender, Orientalism and the History of Ethnic Hatred in the Former Yugoslavia', in H. Lutz, et al. (eds.), *Nationalism, Racism and Gender-European Crossfires* (London: Pluto Press, 1995), 105.

———, 'The Body of the Other Man: Sexual Violence and the Construction of Masculinity, Sexuality and Ethnicity in Croatian Media', in C. O. N. Moser & F. C. Clark (eds.), *Victims, Perpetrators or Actors?: Gender, Armed Conflict and Political Violence* (London: Zed Books, 2001), 69.

———, 'Towards a New Theorizing of Women, Gender and War', in K. Davis, M. S. Evans & J. Lorber (eds.), *Handbook of Gender and Women's Studies* (London: Sage, 2006), 214.

———, *The Body of War: Media, Ethnicity, Gender in the Break-Up of Yugoslavia* (Durham and London: Duke University Press, 2007).

Index

For Product Safety Concerns and Information please contact our EU representative GPSR@taylorandfrancis.com
Taylor & Francis Verlag GmbH, Kaufingerstraße 24, 80331 München, Germany

www.ingramcontent.com/pod-product-compliance
Ingram Content Group UK Ltd.
Pitfield, Milton Keynes, MK11 3LW, UK
UKHW010959180926
475701UK00004B/461
9780367590413